THE MEDIEVAL SIEGE

To Stephen and Jane

THE MEDIEVAL SIEGE

Jim Bradbury

THE BOYDELL PRESS

First published 1992 by The Boydell Press, Woodbridge
Reprinted in hardback and paperback 1994
Reprinted in hardback 1998

The Boydell Press is an imprint of Boydell & Brewer Ltd
PO Box 9, Woodbridge, Suffolk IP12 3DF, UK
and of Boydell & Brewer Inc.
PO Box 41026, Rochester, NY 14604–4126, USA

ISBN 0 85115 312 7 hardback
ISBN 0 85115 357 7 paperback

British Library Cataloguing in Publication Data
Bradbury, Jim
Medieval Siege
I. Title
940.1
ISBN 0–85115–312–7

Library of Congress Cataloging-in-Publication Data
Bradbury, Jim.
The medieval siege / Jim Bradbury.
p. cm.
Includes bibliographical references and index.
ISBN 0–85115–312–7
1. Siege warfare – History. 2. Sieges – Europe – History.
3. Europe – History, Military. I. Title.
UG444.B83 1992
355.4'4–dc20
92–13727

This publication is printed on acid-free paper

Printed in Great Britain by
St Edmundsbury Press Ltd, Bury St Edmunds, Suffolk

Contents

Illustrations

Photos supplied from Corpus Christi College, Cambridge, are reproduced by courtesy of the Master and Fellows of Corpus Christi College, Cambridge.

Photos supplied from Christ Church, Oxford, are reproduced by courtesy of the Governing Body of Christ Church, Oxford.

Preface

The original intention of this book was to provide a companion volume to *The Medieval Archer*. The theme of sieges seemed to demand a broader definition of 'medieval', in particular it seemed important to notice and incorporate the significant contribution to medieval siege warfare of the later Roman Empire. It also seemed a subject which would benefit from a broader geographical base. At the heart of the archer book was the English longbow, which dictated reasonable bounds to the study. With regard to sieges, it seemed remiss to ignore, for example, crusading sieges, Byzantium, or Spain. The result, of course, was to provide a much stiffer task than was at first envisaged. Siege warfare was so widespread and so common in the middle ages, that there is hardly a primary source which cannot contribute to its study. Unless all hope of ever concluding the work was to be abandoned, some restrictions had to be made. The decision was therefore taken to concentrate on the information provided by narrative sources, particularly those which had been translated; and also to select mainly texts which were most likely to prove rewarding. Some sources in Latin were taken on board where it was clear that important material existed, and one or two other languages have been grappled with for the same reason. In the end, though, it could not for one moment be claimed that this was a comprehensive study of all, or even most, of the relevant material. A certain amount has been stumbled upon in diplomatic sources and in literary works, but there has been no attempt systematically to investigate this material.

One of the other difficulties of the subject, is the lack of recent surveys from which one could borrow, and which would act as guides. Some research on crusading sieges was proceeding parallel with the work on this book, but not wishing to tread on the toes of those working on theses, this study was made independently. However, having completed my manuscript, some years later than intended, I then read the completed thesis by Randy Rogers: 'Latin Siege Warfare in the Twelfth Century'. This is an excellent and detailed work on that aspect of the subject, and should certainly be referred to by anyone pursuing that area of siege warfare. I have not substantially altered my text as a result of reading this work, but have added a number of footnotes. Rogers' thesis is particularly important in its use of German secondary works, and on siege weapons and machines, where the sources often do not allow clear conclusions. We differ occasionally, but I like to think that by and large this book and the thesis are complementary. At present, I believe the work by Bill Zajak is not yet completed, and I have not read it, though I have benefited from a number of conversations. I am sure that this work will add considerably to our knowledge.

It is always pleasant to record one's gratitude to those who often quite selflessly give of their time and expertise to help. Among the many to whom a debt is owed, mostly I hope acknowledged in the footnotes, I must especially, but rather sadly offer my thanks to the late Allen Brown. His great enthusiasm for, and knowledge of, medieval warfare, and especially of castle studies, both inspired me initially, and then guided me in some of the early stages of this work. Even when he knew of the serious illness which brought his death, there seemed no decline in his interest and kindness. Among others who have given help of one kind or another, I would mention Ian Peirce and Julia Walworth, who gave advice on the illustrations, David D'Avray, Paul Fouracre, Cyril Edwards, Susan Kreuse, Jonathan Phillips and Matt Bennett. I have often found papers given to Institute of Historical Research seminars in London on the Early Medieval period and on the Crusades to be useful guides. Of those who organise these seminars, to all of whom I owe some debt, I would particularly mention Jinty Nelson and John Gillingham, who over many years have given help and advice. Discussions after these seminars in such hostelries as the University Tavern and the Birkbeck Bar were possibly even more helpful: if only the beer were as good as the conversation! A considerable debt is also owed to Richard Barber, not least for his understanding and patience, as a manuscript promised in a couple of years took a good deal longer to produce. The time would have been even greater had I not taken early retirement from my teaching post at West London, partly in order to be able to concentrate more on writing, a decision I have had little cause to regret. As to my wife, Ann, anyone who could stay with me through the hours spent on research and writing and still give cheerful encouragement deserves more than a medal.

Selsey, 1991

Abbreviations

AmHR	*American Historical Review*
ANS	*Anglo-Norman Studies*
ANTS	Anglo-Norman Text Society
Ant.J	*Antiquaries Journal*
AJ	*Archaeological Journal*
BN	Bibliothèque National
BL	British Library
BM	British Museum
BIHR	*Bulletin of the Institute of Historical Research*
Cal.	Calendar
CG	*Château-Gaillard, Etudes de Castellologie Medievale*, Caen
CHF	Classiques de l'Histoire de France
EETS	Early English Text Society
EHD	*English Historical Documents*
EHR	*English Historical Review*
EHS	English Historical Society
FSI	Fonti per la Storia d'Italia
HA	Historical Association
HMSO	Her Majesty's Stationery Office
HMC	Historical Manuscripts Commission
HT	*History Today*
Howlett	*Chronicles of the Reigns of Stephen, Henry II and Richard I*, ed. R. Howlett, 4 vols, RS no. 82, 1889
IPMK	*The Ideals and Practice of Medieval Knighthood*, Papers from the Strawberry Hill Conferences
JMH	*Journal of Medieval History*
MGH	Monumenta Germaniae Historica
MGH SRG	MGH Scriptores Rerum Germanicarum
NS	New Series
PP	*Past and Present*
PR	Pipe Roll, published by Pipe Roll Society, 1884 etc.
PRO	Public Record Office
Proc.	*Proceedings*
RAB	Harper-Bill, C., C. Holdsworth and J. Nelson, eds, *Studies in Medieval History Presented to R. Allen Brown*, Woodbridge, 1989
RIS	Rerum Italicarum Scriptores
RHC	Recueil des Historiens des Croisades, 5 vols, Paris, 1844–95

RHC Occ.	RHC Historiens Occidentaux, Paris, 1844–95
RHF	Recueil des Historiens des Gaules et de la France, ed. M. Bouquet and L. Delisle, 24 vols, Paris, 1869–1904
RHS	Royal Historical Society
RS	Rolls Series
Ser.	Series
Setton	Setton, K.M., *A History of the Crusades*, 6 vols, Wisconsin, 1955–89

CHAPTER ONE

Civilisation under Siege, 450–750

The Influence of Rome

The subject of this book is siege warfare from the fall of the western Roman Empire in the fifth century, to the fall of Constantinople in 1453. This emphasis on Roman civilisation is not without significance for medieval siege warfare, and especially with regard to this first chapter. The influence of the Romans on early medieval siege warfare was considerable, both in methods of fighting, and in style of fortification. We shall conclude this book with the fall of Constantinople in 1453 and the expansion of the Ottoman Turks, a reminder that there was direct continuation of the Roman Empire throughout our period. Both strands are important to us: the influence of the ancient Romans; the development of the continuing Eastern Empire and its impact upon the West.

Roman influence on medieval siege warfare was great, but there were also significant changes in methods and fortification arising from medieval invention and initiative. The result was a form of warfare with a nature of its own, which deserves study. The castle is more or less synonomous with the middle ages, and is symbolic of the siege warfare of the period. In ancient times sieges were commonly of towns. In the middle ages one more often finds the object of attack to be a castle than a town.

Our first two chapters cover a period of transition. The Roman Empire in the West had collapsed, at least structurally, in the fifth century. Historians have argued for continuity into the early middle ages of social and economic aspects of the Roman world, but it cannot be denied that the political pattern changed drastically.[1] Instead of one imperial power, there emerged various independent barbarian kingdoms. We can still agree that

1 Pirenne proposed the thesis of continuity from Roman times to the early middle ages in *Mohammed and Charlemagne*, and *Medieval Cities*; for comment on Pirenne, see Havighurst, *The Pirenne Thesis*, and Hodges and Whitehouse, *Mohammed, Charlemagne and the Origins of Europe*.

much survived: the barbarians admired and valued *Romanitas*. Early medieval Europe had retained Roman titles, social divisions, and economic patterns. Men lived in and preserved Roman towns and Roman buildings; they travelled on Roman roads and drank water which was supplied through Roman pipes. Roman forts and walls were still standing, and well fortified Roman structures were used for shelter, often they became the focus of early medieval sieges. Nor were Roman siege techniques forgotten or ignored: they were learned by the enemies of Rome, as well as by the descendants of the Romans. The battering ram and the *balista* were as familiar in medieval Europe as in the late Roman period. The new men of power chose Roman cities as their capitals, their enemies besieged them inside the same Roman walls.

It may be argued that in the early middle ages siege warfare was Roman rather than barbarian. Sieges were still mainly of towns, especially of capital and key cities. In the later medieval period, the memorable sieges were generally of castles, such as those of Château-Gaillard or Rochester. In the early middle ages, as in Roman times, the major sieges were of great towns, such as Constantinople and Paris. The siege of Constantinople in the fifteenth century, which brings this study to its close, is a sign of a new era, in which again castle warfare will have less significance. The reasons for these changes are not simple, but for the time being let us suggest that they resulted chiefly from the social structure of the time, as reflected in its military manifestations. We should not wish to claim that all medieval sieges were of castles, or that we have an invariable rule. Of course one can find examples in ancient times of the siege of smaller places, just as in the central middle ages towns might be besieged. In the latter case, however, one frequently finds that the attackers soon broke into and held the town, and were in fact besieging the citadel, or in a medieval town, its castle.

Roman Fortification

Roman fortifications survived into the early middle ages, and sometimes throughout the middle ages. They also provided a tremendous inspiration to medieval architects. Scholars of the medieval Renaissances have shown the great influence of ancient art and culture upon the medieval West, but few have given much attention to its effect on military architecture.[2] One suggestion of this book is that Renaissance ideas, from the Carolingian, Ottonian, Twelfth Century, as well as the Italian Renaissance, included a return to ancient military writings and models, and that this affected methods of fighting and styles of fortification.

[2] For comment on the two major European Renaissances, see for example Brooke, *The Twelfth-Century Renaissance*, Hollister, *The Twelfth-Century Renaissance*, Hay, *The Italian Renaissance in its Historical Background*, Laven, *Renaissance Italy*, *1464–1534*.

It is possible that the rounded tower of the twelfth and thirteenth centuries was the result of the study of ancient writers. The concept of its validity for defence was not new in the twelfth century. Vitruvius, writing in the time of Augustus, explained the advantages for defence of round towers. He was an architect who assisted in the rebuilding of Rome under Augustus. Vitruvius says of himself that he was short and not good-looking, and that writing was his consolation. He considered that towers should be rounded or polygonal, because this gave more protection against rams and mining. He also saw the benefit of projecting towers, allowing the enemy to be attacked on his exposed flanks, and making approach to the curtain wall difficult. Vitruvius gave detailed advice on siege weapons, including measurements for their manufacture. As he said, 'only those craftsmen can deal with the design who are familiar with the general treatment of numbers and their multiples'.[3]

According to Vitruvius, the Tyrian emperor Rephrasmenos had improved the ram during the Carthaginian siege of Cadiz. He had set up a pole with a cross-beam, like a balance, on which the ram could be drawn back. Vitruvius claimed that Ceras the Carthaginian was the first to provide the ram with a platform, wheels, and a penthouse covered with ox hides. He added that mobile towers were developed by Polydus a Thessalian, together with his pupils Diades and Charias. They prefabricated them for Alexander the Great, so that the army could carry the sections and construct the towers when required. From the towers, weapons could be used, and water thrown against fire. The same engineers developed the bore and what Vitruvius calls a 'climbing machine'. He also describes a ram used on rollers, pulled backwards and forwards by ropes, and a tortoise with wheel axles that allowed it to turn sideways, providing cover for men to fill ditches. To Callias of Rhodes, Vitruvius attributes a crane. When Callias wished to demonstrate its use, he displayed drawings showing a city wall. Vitruvius also described siege operations. He explained how to deal with mines by deepening the defensive ditches, and preparing water to flood them. The work of Vitruvius shows that the ancient world possessed sophisticated fortifications and ideas about siege warfare.

The works of Vitruvius and Vegetius were well known in the middle ages. Copies of both were made during the Carolingian Renaissance, and appear frequently throughout the middle ages. Medieval men read ancient works on warfare, and made use of them. Suger the abbot of St Denis, minister to two kings of France, had read Vegetius. On two occasions we hear of learned men, who knew the work of Vegetius, advising commanders: Brother Guérin the hospitaller bishop advised Philip Augustus at Bouvines; and the unidentified 'Brother G' helped Geofrey V, count of Anjou, at the siege of Montreuil-Bellay. There are no less than twenty

3 *Vitruvius on Architecture*, ed. Granger, p. 51 on round towers; Book IX Chapter X on catapults, Chapter XI on *balistae*, Chapter XIII on sieges.

manuscripts of Vegetius written in the eleventh and twelfth centuries in the Bibliothèque-Nationale in Paris alone. The study of such ancient writings, and the respect shown for ancient ideas, makes it certain that Roman siege war influenced medieval siege war.

Finó, in modern times, has suggested that the keep which Henry III built at St Emilion in 1237, is of pure Roman type.[4] The twelfth and thirteenth century fortifications which are similar to Roman works speak of revival rather than continuity. In the tenth and eleventh centuries towers had been commonly rectangular rather than round. Rectangular towers also had their Roman predecessors, as Vitruvius makes clear in arguing against them, and they may indeed have a continuous history through from the ancient world. The first castle towers we know of in the West, at Doué-la-Fontaine and Langeais, are rectangular stone structures. But whence came the inspiration for rounded keeps?

In the period immediately following the fall of the Western Empire, there seems to have been little new building for fortification, certainly little in stone beyond some repair work. But late Roman fortifications themselves underwent important developments. If early medieval fortifications do not seem to compare closely with classical models, it may be due less to the rise of a barbaric and primitive style, than to the influence of the irregular forms of the late Roman period. In any case, many Roman structures were still in good working order, and needed no more than repairs. For this reason, it is often difficult to separate early medieval from Roman work.[5]

Roman walls were used for defence in many towns which figured in early medieval warfare, for example, at Le Mans, Sens and Senlis. Sometimes non-military Roman buildings were used for protection, as for example, the Trophée of Augustus at Turbie, or the Mausoleum of Hadrian in Rome. Both these were transformed into medieval castles, the latter of course becoming the papal castle of Sant' Angelo.

The third century AD was a key period in western defensive architecture. Until that time, many Roman cities were unwalled. The early earthwork defences in Britain seem to be an exception to the rule. From the mid-third century, Stephen Johnson sees a major change in Roman defences, a new trend in design, which he describes as 'the direct forerunner of medieval castle design'.[6] Whether the change came entirely from fears about external attack, was caused by internal dangers, or was simply to satisfy civic pride, is unclear. It may be significant that Britain was early in urban defence, since it was especially vulnerable to attack from the sea. From the third century onwards, Roman defences employed massive walls,

4 Finó, *Forteresses*, Chapter I on the late Roman Empire, pp. 35–72; and on Suger, p. 23, on Vegetius, p. 24, on Henry III, p. 12.

5 Johnson, *Late Roman Fortifications*.

6 Johnson, p. 10.

high and thick, together with projecting towers and heavily fortified gateways. Not that such defences were novel, even then. Vitruvius had explained the theory, and advised on practical building methods. He emphasised the importance of building on firm foundations, of making the foundations broader than the superstructure, and of using tie-beams. Early medieval Dijon, as described by Gregory of Tours, was a realisation of just such ideals: thirty defended gates, walls that were thirty feet high and fifteen feet thick, with thirty-three projecting towers.[7]

Late Roman fortifications were not always of square or rectangular plan. Towns like Dijon, with its roughly circular outline, were more common. Le Mans was built not to a regular plan, but to fill the high ground overlooking the Sarthe. Angers has been described as a 'city acropolis'. It is no coincidence that these three examples were the nuclei of medieval defences. The extent of defensive work in the West in the third century was considerable. We are told that Probus fortified seventy cities within the space of only seven years.[8] One factor that added to the number of irregular defences in the late Roman period, was the re-use of prehistoric forts, generally on defensible hilltops. A hundred of these re-used forts have been identified in the Rhineland alone. But newly-built fortifications were often irregular too. The series of late Roman coastal fortifications in Britain known as the Saxon Shore forts, provide several examples of irregular design. Some it is true, such as Portchester, were rectangular, but others, like Pevensey, are completely irregular. Pevensey itself is roughly oval. It seems probable that the changes to be witnessed in these British forts reflect development in Roman urban fortification in Gaul.

Comparison between the late Roman crisis, as the barbarian attacks increased in intensity, and Europe in the eighth and ninth centuries, when new barbarian threats emerged, has some interest. At times when stability decreased, and defence might well become a very local matter, fortification could be undertaken for small social units. The protection of family, household, and local community, becomes paramount in emergencies. It was not necessarily the town which offered protection, there was always the possibility of occupying the neighbouring hill fort, constructing hasty earthwork defences, or making use of a building which was strongly made even if not originally intended for defence. The Romans in the late period certainly fortified small sites as well as large. We have an inscription from southern Gaul concerning one Postumus Dardanus, who 'enclosed and fortified space for his family and retainers'.[9] In the early middle ages, local groups sometimes re-occupied abandoned Roman forts. There are examples of bishops who used such sites as protective *castra*.

7 Gregory of Tours, ed. Krusch & Levison, p. 120, on Dijon; Gregory of Tours, ed. Thorpe, p. 182; see also R. Latouche, *Grégoire de Tours*, for a modern French translation.

8 Johnson, p. 115.

9 Johnson, p. 242.

The survival of Roman fortifications into the early medieval period is obvious in many areas. In Britain, Gildas, one of the few writers whose work has come down to us from this period, described 'twenty-eight cities and a number of *castella* and well-equipped fortifications: walls, castellated towers, gates and houses'. Bachrach has epitomised Merovingian strategy in war as the 'acquisition and defence of as many fortified cities and *castra* as possible'. The continued use of Roman fortifications in the West is an easily accepted fact, and of tremendous influence upon early medieval warfare.[10]

Roman Siege Methods

Just as Roman fortifications influenced early medieval fortification, indeed often were used as early medieval fortifications, so were Roman methods of siege warfare influential. The ideas of Vitruvius and Vegetius were not lost. It can be shown that the practical methods of siege in the early middle ages were far from being primitive and barbaric. It seems likely that siege methods developed on the foundation of Roman efforts. Medieval siege warfare was in no way inferior in its methods, nor was it lacking in subtlety. If this argument of building on Roman knowledge is to be sustained, it is important to recognise the nature of late Roman methods, since Roman siege warfare itself did not stand still.

We have seen that in the late Roman period fortifications were modified, and surely improved, with the introduction of more heavily walled towns, more irregularity of shape, and more variety in small fortifications such as private fortresses. Siege methods were bound to adapt to these developments. It has been said that siege warfare developed from the straightforward attack by storm into a more complicated use of tactics and machines. But historians have put too much emphasis on this by underestimating earlier achievements. We have seen in Vitruvius that early Roman knowledge of siege warfare was considerable, and much of that knowledge itself came originally from the Greeks. Military know-how is apparent in early sieges. We find such methods as the making of approach works, and recognition of the need to cut supplies. In Julius Caesar's siege of Alesia the Romans made three kilometres of siege-works in five weeks. The Romans used carefully constructed weapons based on mathematical principles: Ammianus in the fourth century speaks of the development of the use of models for the making of siege engines. Vegetius goes into detail on what might be attempted in mining. Roman siege methods were an important factor in their military successes. Gildas does indeed claim that the Britons

10 Gildas, *Ruin*, p. 16, on cities; Bachrach, p. 127 on Merovingian strategy.

were *not* subdued by engines of war, but in making the claim at least suggests that such weapons were used.[11]

Byzantine Fortification

The continuity of Roman influence is unquestionable in the East. The Byzantine Empire was simply the surviving eastern part of the Roman Empire. It is true that it evolved and became 'Greek' in its outlook, but the Byzantines saw themselves as 'Romans', they saw no break with the Roman past. They derived their military inspiration from that past. The Byzantine general Philippicus was fond of learning, and 'drew his military knowledge from the experts of the past'.[12] Byzantine sources are extremely useful to us, for they are informative about the West as well as the East. They were been contemptuous of all other nations, whether Germanic westerners, Persians, or Arabs – to the Byzantines all were barbarians – but they also give us interesting accounts of these enemies.

Constantinople was itself a focal power point: capital of the Eastern Empire and target of all groups who aspired to dominate the Near East, Asia Minor, and Eastern Europe. It was therefore the target of several major sieges, accounts of which provide us with important evidence from the early medieval period. Byzantium demonstrates both the continuity of Roman ideas, and a good deal about the practice of early medieval siege warfare. The defences of Constantinople are probably the best example of fortification from this age.[13] The strength ofthe city was renowned, and it is interesting to see how these defences were tested and improved during the early middle ages. Constantinople survived only because each great siege exposed certain defensive weaknesses which were then remedied. The city is also a marvellous example of continuity in fortification.

The walls were begun in the fourth century AD, and frequently repaired thereafter, but they remained 'remarkably uniform', and an example of 'remarkable conservation'.[14] For historians there is considerable difficulty in distinguishing the building done in any one period: it is, for example, difficult to tell the Roman from the early medieval work. There were several major additions and repairs. In the early fifth century Theodosius II added the land walls to the original sea walls of Constantine, which suggests amongst other things an increased threat to Constantinople from the western approach. Improvements were then made by the Prefects Anthemius and Cyrus. Repairs were made frequently. There was a recurring

[11] On Ammianus, Julius Caesar, and Roman siege methods, Finó, p. 55. Ammianus, p. 441 on the use of an onager at Adrianople. On the Britons, Gildas, p. 18.

[12] Theophylact, p. 40.

[13] For details on the defences of Constantinople, see Tsangadas.

[14] Tsangadas, pp. 67, 68.

threat from earthquakes, as, for example that in 447, which destroyed fifty-seven towers. But rebuilding was generally prompt, and there were soon five lines of defence with 192 towers. The wall was thirty to forty feet high, and thirteen to sixteen feet thick. It had projecting towers, and a sixty feet wide moat. The first great siege in 626 led to the building of the Heraclian wall, and the enclosure of the Blachernae suburb. This included three hexagonal towers with brickwork at the top. Later Leo V added a new wall and moat in front of the Heraclian wall. The Arab threats in the seventh and eighth centuries showed the weaknesses of the Golden Horn in face of a strong naval enemy. As a result, the Byzantines improved the sea walls, and placed a great chain across the Golden Horn. The siege of Thomas demonstrated that the walls needed to be higher, which was also implemented. A series of thirty inscriptions along the walls of the Golden Horn show the importance of Theophilus in these improvements.

One example of close contact between Byzantium and the West in the early middle ages, was the attempt by the great Justinian to reconquer the lost western provinces. Our knowledge of these events owes much to Procopius of Caesaria, who accompanied Justinian's general Belisarius to the West. In addition to a straightforward historical account, Procopius wrote the waspish, titillating and strange work known to us as the *Secret History*. It puzzles one to know his motives. Why should he choose to destroy the reputation of those he seemingly relied upon: the emperor Justinian, the empress Theodora, and the general Belisarius? He says, for example, that Justinian and Theodora 'destroyed the greatness of Rome', and were 'a pair of blood-thirsty demons'. Procopius tells us that in Italy Belisarius relied greatly on fortifications, refusing even to land unless he had such shelter. Procopius offers this as a criticism, an example of cowardice, though to be frank it makes excellent military sense.[15]

The Byzantines continued for some time to retain and fortify strongholds in the West, such as Ravenna. Constantinople itself was the best known fortified city in the world, and was a model and ideal for other cities. Thus, through the agency of the Eastern Empire, Roman fortifications remained in use, were improved, and played an important rôle in medieval siege warfare.

Byzantine Siege Warfare

One of the major developments in medieval warfare came from a Byzantine invention. The Byzantines had continued to use the familiar Roman engines. In 711, for example, one hears of 'rams, catapults, and all sorts of siege-engines for attacking fortified positions'. At sea, in the seventh

15 Procopius, *Secret History*, p. 68.

century, they developed a devastating new weapon, Greek Fire, which was to become a major weapon in land warfare in later times. One writer described Greek Fire being used through 'a nozzle mounted on the forward part of the prow', which would 'eject against the enemy the material that will burn'.[16]

Greek Fire was said to have been invented by Kallinicos, a Syrian. The western writer, Liutprand, in the tenth century, said the Byzantines used Greek Fire not only from the prow of their ships, but also from the stern and on both sides, and 'hurled their fire all around them'. The *Russian Chronicle* of the eleventh century called it 'lightning from heaven'. Theophanes said that it was dropped through pipes upon Russian ships. The Russians were by no means the first to encounter this dreaded weapon, which could be aimed against enemy ships in days when ships were very vulnerable to fire. The nature of Greek Fire made it very difficult to put out. The rôle of Kallinicos in the invention of Greek Fire is not entirely clear. Some kinds of inflammable weapons were already known. The main distinction of Greek Fire seems to have been that it exploded on impact, causing conflagration, and that it could be aimed. Whether Kallinicos was responsible for both these aspects is not clear. He was an engineer who had fled from the Arabs in Heliopolis to join the Byzantines. According to Theophanes, it was Kallinicos who 'devised a sea fire which ignited the Arab ships and burned them with all hands. Thus it was that the Romans returned with victory, and discovered the sea fire'. During the eighth-century sieges of Constantinople, their enemies saw 'how strong the liquid fire was'. The siphon which shot Greek Fire has been called 'the world's first flame thrower'.[17]

Part of our problem, in seeking to know the truth, is that Greek Fire was a very well kept military secret. It was many years before other nations gained access to it, and even then we are not sure they discovered the original formula. No doubt the Byzantines themselves went on experimenting and improving the mix. Descriptions of Greek Fire in use give some clues to its contents. The fact that it gave rise to black smoke, suggests the inclusion of petroleum and resin. It probably also contained saltpetre, which would have caused it to explode, though there has been some debate over this. Naptha or crude oil seems to have been the base, to which was added ingredients to make it more inflammable, such as pitch or quicklime. The first use of the new weapon, in the battle of Cyzicus, had an immediate and startling impact. Thereafter it featured prominently in Byzantine sea battles. It seemed to be almost impossible to deal with, and played a major rôle in the defence of Byzantium in the early middle ages.

In the siege of Constantinople during the 670s, Constantine IV used

[16] On Greek Fire, see Bradbury, *Greek Fire*, pp. 326–31, and p. 344; also Davidson, *The Secret Weapon*.

[17] Geanokoplos, *Byzantium*.

biremes from which catapults hurled Greek Fire, and built a fleet of dromons specially equipped with siphons from which Greek Fire could be aimed and expelled. The ships carried large cauldrons filled with incendiary material. The Arab ships were 'engulfed in flames'. The siege was broken in large part by the success of the new weapon, and its use led to a retreat by the Arab fleet and final disaster wreaked by a storm. It has been suggested that this victory was 'an event as momentous for the Byzantines as the first use of atomic weapons by man in the present times'.[18]

The Byzantines used traditional Roman siege weapons and methods, and developed some of their own, of which the most sensational was Greek Fire, though apparently in this age they did not use it from a land base but only from on board ships.

The Early Medieval Sieges of Constantinople

In a book of these proportions we cannot cover in detail all the great sieges of the middle ages, but at the same time we do not wish to get too far divorced from the drama and suffering of the real thing. In this earliest medieval period, there are no better examples of sieges than the great attacks on Constantinople itself. They demonstrate the value and strength of Roman and Byzantine defences, together with the novel developments of the age. They also show, even in defeat, the stength, ingenuity, and advanced methods of the 'barbarian' enemies of Byzantium.

There were many attacks on the richest target of the age, including three major attempts against the city. The first occurred in 626, when the Persians and Avars combined to besiege Constantinople. It was a short siege, but dangerous. Theophylact Simocatta, who himself lived under Heraclius in the seventh century, described the frustration of the Avar leader, the kagan. The eastern leader, angered by failure, turned crimson, his eyebrows shot up 'and almost threatened to fly off his forehead'.[19] The Avars had brought a large army to besiege the land walls and blockade the city, and Constantinople was surrounded. The attackers possessed siege engines of the traditional Roman kind, as used by the Byzantines themselves, and built twelve high wooden towers. They also had sufficient knowledge and intelligence to pick out the two main weaknesses in the city's defences: the land walls in the Lycus Valley; and the defences of the Blachernae region.

The Byzantines were equal to the threat. They were fortunate to obtain intelligence of an intended attack, and how it was to occur. They themselves gave an early false signal for the attack, and lured their enemies into a trap. The Avars attacked too soon and were defeated. The kagan, finding

18 Tsangadas, pp. 114, 120.
19 Theophylact, p. 28.

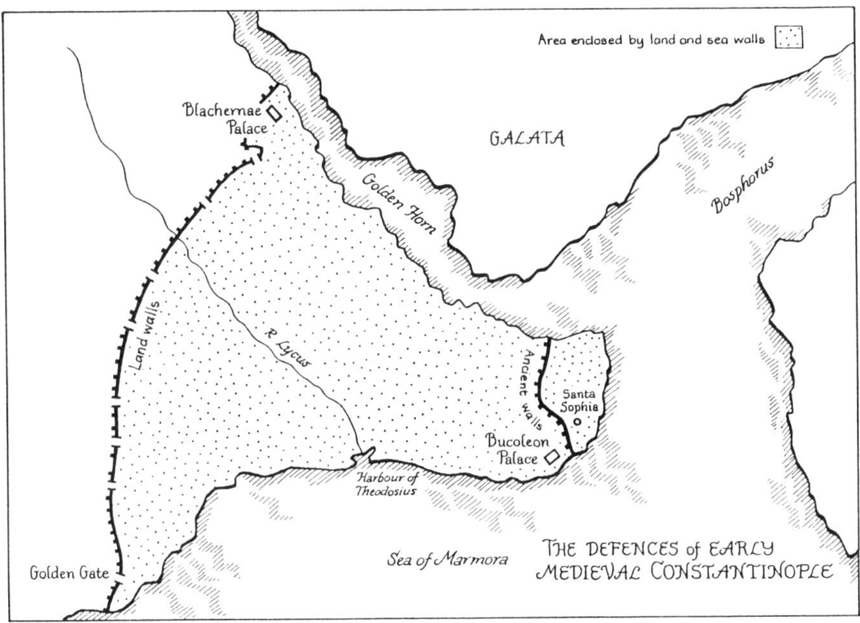

also that supplies were low, decided to abandon the siege. The Byzantines attributed their salvation to divine protection, and in their accounts of the siege, emphasised the rôle of the patriarch of Constantinople, who had organised the painting on all the west-facing city gates of sacred images showing the Virgin Mary holding the infant Christ. The west was the direction from which the Avars were attacking. 'It is against these sacred images, oh alien nations and demonic tribes, that your war is directed', and against which, of course, they failed.[20]

The second of the three major sieges of Constantinople in the early middle ages occurred between 674 and 678. It came about in consequence of the great Islamic expansion. The Arabs had caught the Middle East, and indeed the world, by surprise. From an area not previously noted for its military achievements, ignited by the faith and enthusiasm of a new religion, they burst out of Arabia into an ever widening fan, stetching through North Africa to the Middle East. In their path the Persian Empire, previously seen as Byzantium's greatest rival and threat, crumbled and collapsed. Persian civilisation was swallowed readily by the Arabs, and contributed to their own developing culture. Byzantium also buckled under the strain, but survived in truncated form. The 674 siege was the first time the Arab attack reached as far as Constantinople itself, and the threat was alarming. Already the Byzantines had been beaten at sea in the battle of

20 C. Mango, 'Heraclius', p. 46.

the Masts. In 670 Muawiyah, the caliph, turned his attention to Constantinople.

Fortunately for the Byzantines, since the attack by the Persians and Avars, the defences of the city had been repaired and improved. The weak points had been reinforced. Muawiyah took the Cyzicus Peninsula, and established his base there. The young emperor, Constantine IV, built up his fleet in defence. Now, for the first time, the new weapon of Greek Fire was put to a serious test. The Arabs could find no answer to the devastating weapon, and abandoned their attack.

There was a second great Arab siege between 717 and 718. The Byzantines knew that their first success had done no more than postpone the threat from Islam. As al-Walid prepared for a new assault, the city filled and sealed its granaries with enough food to withstand a three year blockade. The emperor, Leo the Isaurian, who ironically had been assisted to the throne by Arab support, outwitted the besiegers. The Byzantine writers praised his tricks, though they appear to an uncommitted reader as underhand and even dishonourable. In the eyes of medieval Christians promises made to the infidels were not of much account. The Arabs camped before Constantinople in 717, with an army said to number 80,000 men. They protected themselves within a camp around which they built a ditch and a dry-stone wall. Suleiman arrived with a large fleet, only to be badly mauled by the Byzantine ships with their Greek Fire. This attack also depleted Arab supplies. Leo made an agreement with the Arabs, and then broke his promises. The Byzantines were presumably in a strong position, with plenty of provisions and solid defences. They could even supplement their diet with fish caught by lines thrown from the walls. Theophanes says that their Arab attackers were reduced to eating a disgusting concoction made by kneading together in pans human excrement and human corpses![21] It is hardly surprising that they suffered from a plague-like disease. But they were persistent, and the siege continued. Even when the blockade was penetrated they did not at once give up. But at last, in 718, they departed, the defences had held out.

The Siege Techniques of the Barbarians

So far there is likely to be little dispute. It may readily be agreed that the Byzantines would continue to use Roman fortifications and siege methods. There is also likely to be little surprise in the idea that the Persians and the Arabs had sophisticated weapons and methods too, even if they could not manage to take Constantinople. We may, anticipate a little more argument

[21] Theophanes, p. 90.

Fifth century illustration of the siege of Troy

with regard to the West. The picture here is usually of a collapsing Roman world taken over by relatively primitive barbarian peoples. But is this the case?

Roman continuity may be established, at least in some degree. Roman ways, Roman life, endured longer than was once thought, and did not sink without trace in the fifth century. It cannot be denied that some elements of Roman civilisation were absorbed into early medieval barbarian Europe, and it may be added that these elements included military ones. There is nothing new about this suggestion, which has been expressed, for example, by Bachrach in his study of Merovingian warfare. He concluded that in the early medieval centuries, society, and especially military society, reflected '*Romania* more than *Germania*'.[22]

There were, of course, some direct Roman survivals. Studies of Arthurian Britain, though discovering little about Arthur himself, have demonstrated the survival of Romano-Britons into what has usually been seen as Anglo-Saxon England. The Arthurian stories seem to have been built upon a military resistance to the Anglo-Saxon advance which went on for possibly a century after the supposed collapse of Roman Britain in the early fifth century. Archaeology has shown that at South Cadbury there existed a sub-Roman fortress, of earth and timber, irregular in shape but of Roman

22 Bachrach, p. 2.

derivation.[23] Romano-Britons within fortifications played an important part in resisting the invasion. When, at the end of the fifth century, the South Saxons attacked Pevensey, it was still garrisoned, and the inhabitants were all killed after it was stormed. The great victory which, at least temporarily, halted the advance, was called by Gildas not the battle, but the 'siege of Badon Hill'.[24] St Patrick still saw himself as a member of a civilised Roman society under attack in the west from the barbarian Irish.

Bachrach believes that, in Gaul, Roman soldiers were the direct ancestors of military garrisons in the Merovingian period. He suggests, for example, that the *milites* and *laeti* of the Merovingian period were the direct descendants of Roman soldiers and colonists, such as the Suevian colonists in the *Notitia Dignitatum*, and the Roman cavalry regiments at Besançon. Certainly Merovingian sieges were nearly all of places that had been fortified in the Roman period, for example Verdun, Paris, Arles, Carcassonne and Angoulême. Bachrach argues that early medieval Gallic forces were most successful when they contained important elements from the Romanised area, still operating in the Roman style.[25] But there is need for a note of caution with regard to his conclusions. The fact that garrison troops are called *milites*, that commanders are given Roman titles, and that troops are found where previously there had been Roman garrisons, is not conclusive of direct descent. Those writing in Francia in the early middle ages were bound to use Latin terms of this kind even if the people they described were of Germanic descent. That *miles* means something quite different in the thirteenth century to what it meant in the seventh century is quite clear. It may well be that *miles* in the seventh century meant something quite different to what it had meant in the second century. To conclude that whenever the word *milites* appears one has descendants of Roman soldiers, and that whenever the word *laeti* appears one has descendants of Roman colonists, is placing more burden on the words than they will bear. One would not wish to deny Roman influence, quite the reverse, but we should be hesitant about applying direct continuity too broadly. The fact that warfare was centred on the old Roman cities only proves that they were good fortifications and well-sited strategically, not that their defenders were of Roman descent.

The case for the continued use of fortifications and similar siege weapons is stronger than the case for hereditary Roman troops. We frequently find barbarian groups defending ancient walls, and barbarian armies using Roman siege methods and weapons. One feature of medieval warfare, which is demonstrated time and again, is the speed with which groups copy the methods and weapons of their enemy: superiority in either was usually short-lived. From the use of early medieval rams, catapults and other

23 On South Cadbury, see for example Morris, *Arthur*, p. 99, or Wood, *Dark Ages*, p. 49.
24 Gildas, p. 98, *usque ad annum obsessionis Badonici montis*.
25 Bachrach, pp. 24, 45.

weapons we can see that they were just as effective as their Roman predecessors. There is no doubt that a new political structure replaced the imperial West. Power was transferred to barbarian rulers and their aristocracy. They took over towns, villas and hunting lodges.

In England, Aethelweard in his *Chronicle* recorded that the Romans had made 'cities, fortifications, bridges and streets with wonderful skill, which are to be seen to this day'.[26] Gregory the nineteenth bishop of Tours was himself the son of a 'senator'. He was born in 539 at Clermont-Ferrand. He was small and often ill. His health was hardly likely to be improved by his habit of taking potions made up of dust and relics. He may be comtemptuous of the barbarity and savagery of his contemporaries, such as Childeric, whose life was 'one long debauch', or King Ragnacher who 'could not even keep his hands off the women of his own family', or Queen Fredegund who repented of her sins 'rather late in the day, it is true'; yet, at the same time, Gregory shows how Roman fortifications were used and respected. The maintenance of an internal water supply was undertaken and its importance recognised. He describes the use of city gates which could be locked, and the defences of Dijon with its 'mighty walls', fifteen feet thick and washed by the river, with its four gates and thirty-three towers each twenty feet high and made of squared stone.[27]

An examination of the barbarian sieges in the West, and of the enemies of Byzantium in the East, will show us that knowledge of fortification and siege warfare was not confined to Roman Byzantines and pockets of surviving *Romanitas* in the West. As in other instances, the civilised contempt for the barbarians was often exaggerated. In the West, after all, the barbarians proved militarily superior. From the beginning, the barbarian attack on the Romans involved siege warfare. Although unsuccessful, Attila the Hun himself besieged Orléans. The walls 'were already rocking under the shock of the battering-rams', and about to collapse, when Aetius made his last minute appearance to save the city. Of course, as Gregory of Tours reminds us, 'no one has any doubt that the army of the Huns was really routed by the prayers of the bishop'.[28]

In a review of Persian, Avar and Arab opposition to early medieval Byzantium, one meets a variety of sophisticated siege techniques. The Persians recognised the importance of destroying the food crop before a siege, as, for example, did Kosroes in 622 to 623. The Arabs in 648 to 649 had 'all sorts of engines'. In 704 to 705 the Arabs did in fact get into

26 Aethelweard, *Chronicle*, p. 5.

27 Gregory of Tours, ed. Krusch & Levison, p. 120, as son of a senator, ed. Thorpe, p. 7; and ed. Thorpe for the debauched Childeric and the debauched Ragnacher, pp. 128, 156; on Queen Fredegund, p. 296; on Dijon, pp. 182–3, and ed. Krusch & Levison, p. 120, and n. 7 above.

28 Gregory of Tours, on Attila, ed. Krusch & Levison, p. 48, ed. Thorpe, p. 116; on Aetius, ed. Thorpe, p. 118.

Constantinople, by utilising good information, and crawling through a pipe. The Arab attackers of Nicaea in 727 used catapults. There is a story about a certain Constantine, a groom, who threw a stone and broke an icon of the Virgin. He dreamed later that the Virgin appeared and told him that his act would 'rebound on his own head'. Next day on the walls he was hit by a stone from an Arab catapult, which 'smashed his head and face', and killed him. There is an episode in Theophylact about a Byzantine traitor who showed the Avars how to make siege weapons, and there is no reason to believe that such things are untrue. The hero Busas had been captured by the Avars when out hunting. He tried to negotiate his release, but his efforts were foiled through the actions of the man who was having an affair with Busas' wife. Busas, in revenge, then showed the Avars 'how to construct a sort of besieging machine' for long range attack, and gave them 'skilled instruction in the technology of siege-craft'. The Avars used his machine as a prototype for others. Perhaps this is only Byzantine snobbery, wishing to attribute advanced skills in their enemy to their own treachery, but in any case it shows that the barbarian Avars possessed powerful siege engines.[29]

There are many other examples of barbarian and enemy groups using siege engines. At Driyipera, whether aided by the Byzantines or not, the Avar kagan 'constructed siege-engines'. They also employed most of the common methods of siege. For example, against Daras, the Persians maintained a six month siege, constructing mounds and ramparts, and diverting the town's water supply. They built counter-towers, and finally took the stronghold. The Slavs, in a situation where they needed to improvise, also protected themselves when attacking. According to Theophylact on once occasion they fortified themselves behind wagons, like a cowboy wagon-train.[30]

All in all, in the East one feels that the Byzantines misrepresented the abilities of their enemies, and that we should not be fooled because they are called 'barbarians' into believing that they were primitive in their methods of war. Nor indeed should we too easily accept that the Byzantines were more 'civilised' than their enemies. There are many examples of Byzantine savagery. Justinian II trampled on the necks of his enemies during heats of the races and threw men into the sea in sacks. The inhabitants of Byzantine Pergamon, during the siege by Maslama, cut open a pregnant woman, boiled the foetus in a pot, and dipped their sleeves in the sacrifice. It is true, that in this latter case, Theophanes thought it 'disgusting to God', but it still happened. On the other side of the coin, one can

29 The Arabs possessing engines, Theophanes, p. 43; on Constantine the groom, Theophanes, p. 97; on the traitor Busas, Theophylact, pp. 65–6.

30 Use of siege engines by barbarians and other peoples: Theophylact, on Drizipera and the Avars, p. 165; on Daras and the Persians, p. 88; on the wagons of the Slavs, p. 180.

find examples of civilised behaviour by the enemies of Byzantium. During the siege of Tori the kagan sent food to his enemies during a truce.[31]

In the West the barbarians proved no less advanced than their counterparts in the East. Bachrach attributes advanced methods to direct Roman descent, but admits the sophistication. For example, Leudegisel prepared rams with wheels and sheds over them. Bachrach suggests that although the Merovingians undertook sieges, there were limitations to their abilities. In Italy they could take some places, but not the stronger cities like Pavia. He makes the same point about Childebert in Septimania. There is indeed a passage in Gregory of Tours where Clovis agrees to abandon a siege, after Aridius had asked why he should go on with it against 'a stronghold which is too well fortified for you to capture'? Clovis had been preparing his attack in classical manner, by destroying the surrounding food supplies in fields, meadows, vineyards and olive groves.[32] It should, however, be noted that he agreed to withdraw in return for tribute. Negotiation, ransom as at Chastel-Marlhac, and tribute, were a regular part of Frankish siege warfare. But surely this does not demonstrate weakness, only the use of all the methods of siege? The Franks were not always 'honourable'. At Vitry-le-Brulé they ignored a safe-conduct given to Munderic, and he was killed. Trickery and subtlety were a part of the Frankish panoply. Nor should we be too scornful of their stress upon religion. We may find it difficult to agree with Gregory of Tours, or with the Byzantine patriarch that divine intervention and sacred icons saved the day, but we should recognise that for leaders conducting the defence, appeal to religion was an important morale booster. The Byzantine practice of parading with icons is well known, and similar things happened in the West. The inhabitants of Saragossa, when besieged by Lothar and Childebert, put on hair shirts, fasted, and sang psalms while parading around the walls, followed by women in black with ashes on their heads, their hair blowing free as they wept and wailed. The besiegers were nonplussed and withdrew. The Franks also recognised the usefulness of bringing on violence by provocation. When Guntram attacked Gundovald at Comminges, he shouted to the besieged leader that he was no more than a painter who had been used to whitewashing, and a Ballomer (an insult whose specific meaning is lost in time). When Gundovald was finally inveigled into leaving the fortification, he was shut out by his fellow inmates, and left to his fate. He was hit on the head by a rock, killed and dragged through the camp so violently that his hair was pulled out.[33]

31 On the Byzantine uncivilised behaviour; Justinian II, Theophanes, p. 72; Maslama, Theophanes, p. 74; Tori, Theophylact, p. 196.

32 On barbarian limitations see Bachrach, p. 61, and Gregory of Tours, ed. Krusch & Levison, p. 80; ed. Thorpe, p. 147.

33 On Frankish practices, Gregory of Tours: on Munderic, ed. Krusch & Levison, pp. 111–12, ed. Thorpe, pp. 174–5; on Saragossa, ed. Krusch & Levison, p. 125; ed. Thorpe,

In general, it is clear that the barbarian West was familiar with all those aspects of siege warfare that had been known to the Romans. Ammianus Marcellinus had said that the barbarians were stupid when confronted by walls. If it had been true in his time, which is doubtful, it does not seem to be true of the early medieval period. Fredegar described an ordinary siege at Bourges. The city was surrounded by a counter-fortification, 'so that no one would have dared to leave or enter'. They took the town, repaired the defences, and left it under new control. Siege warfare and the significance of good defences seem to be well recognised.[34]

In Britain Gildas testifies to the ability of the invaders, attacking a province well fortified with stone walls. He says: 'all the major towns were laid low by the repeated battering of enemy rams'. They tore down walls and towers from the base. They could also build their own fortifications. According to the *Anglo-Saxon Chronicle*, Ida of Northumbria built Bamburgh 'which was first enclosed with a hedge, and afterwards with a wall'. The invasion proceeded in steps, depending on taking major towns.[35]

The building of fortifications was a regular part of early medieval warfare. Often there was no need to build since there were excellent fortifications built by the Romans, still in existence, and often in the most useful and important strategic positions. Nevertheless new fortification was sometimes required in emergency situations. In Fredegar's account of the rebellion by Radulf duke of Thuringia against Sigebert, the rebel 'put up a wooden stockade round his position on a rise above the banks of the River Unstrut in Thuringia, and when he had assembled every possible man from all parts, fortified himself with his wife and children within this field-work to withstand a siege'. The stronghold had a gate, and was effective enough to protect Radulf until he could make a successful sortie and beat off his enemies.[36]

Gregory of Tours described the Franks defending themselves against the Romans with 'an endless barricade solidly constructed from huge tree-trunks', and the Franks were to be seen 'climbing about on the barricades as if on the ramparts of turrets'. On a later occasion, Lothar I is described as building 'a great circle of barricades among the trees', though in this case it was taken by storm. The Franks in addition to repairing the stone fortifica-

pp. 186–7; on Comminges, ed. Krusch & Levison, p. 357, ed. Thorpe, pp. 417–24: *Tune es ille, quem Ballomerem nomine saepius Galliarum incolae vocitabant*; compare p. 335; n. 4 suggests taken from a priest who had earned contempt.

34 On barbarian stupidity, see Johnson, p. 246; on Bourges, Fredegar, *Chronicle*, p. 112. But Ammianus, p. 420, also shows barbarian success against cities.

35 Anglo-Saxons, on rams, see Gildas, p. 98; on Bamburgh, *Anglo-Saxon Chronicle*, p. 12, the E version for 547.

36 Fredegar, p. 73.

tions left to them by the Romans, built their own strongholds made of earth and timber.[37]

This is not to imply that the barbarians were ignorant of walls and their uses. The frequency with which Roman walls were used for protection demonstrates this, and those walls would have been useless if not repaired and rebuilt after attack. They were also aware that successful siege warfare could not rely on walls alone. A broader strategy was always required. When Sigebert was besieged in Arles, the bishop of the city encouraged him to make a sortie: 'if you remain penned up inside the city walls you will have no chance of defending either us or the territory'. The point was well made and was a constant factor in medieval siege warfare. Besiegers needed contact with outside relief, reinforcements, allies. In this instance, however, the bishop though making a good enough case to persuade Sigebert, was only trying to get rid of an unwanted guest. When Sigebert and his men went out, only to be beaten by Guntram, the bishop broke his word and locked the gates against his former guests who therefore found themselves trapped.[38]

The Franks, like the Romans, the Byzantines, the Avars, the Arabs, and indeed all the militarily important groups of this age, possessed their own range of siege engines. Those who attacked Leudegisel, prepared new machines against him, including wagons fitted with rams. In sieges, Gregory of Tours describes the Franks using rocks, flaming barrels of pitch, and boxes filled with stones. They could fill a moat in order to use engines. Lothar I, attacking towns along the Seine, was able to cut holes in the stone walls. They possessed hurling machines, towers, climbing ladders, and inflammable materials. In fact, after this age, we shall find very little that is novel. The foundation of every area of our study of medieval siege warfare is laid in this first period.[39]

37 On barricades, Gregory of Tours, ed. Krusch & Levison, p. 53: *velut e fastigiis turrium sagittas turmentorum ritu effudere*; p. 120: *castrum firmissimis muris in media planitiae*; ed. Thorpe, pp. 120–1, 185.

38 Gregory of Tours, ed. Krusch & Levison, p.162: *Egredimini foris et inite certamen, quia non poteritis sub murorum conclusione degentes neque nos neque urbis istius subiecta defendere*; ed. Thorpe, pp. 223–4.

39 For Leudegisel, Gregory of Tours, ed. Krusch & Levison, p. 359: *novas ad distruendam urbem machinas praeparabat, plaustra enim cum arietibus, cletellis et axebus tecta, sub qua exercitus properaret ad distrundos muros*; ed. Thorpe, p. 420; for Lothar I and the holes, Bachrach, p. 76.

CHAPTER TWO

The Second Onslaught, 750–950

In the Carolingian era, siege warfare followed the lines laid down in the time of the Merovingians. Major sieges were still of towns. The barbarian destroyers of the western Roman Empire had by now established their own civilisation, but that itself was to be under threat from a second wave of attacks on land and sea by the Saracens, the Magyars, and the vikings. Civilisation has always in the last resort been established and defended by success in war. As Kenneth Clark has said of this age, European civilisation survived only by the skin of its teeth.[1] It is worth stressing the magnitude of the danger, since the means of overcoming it was largely through fortification tested by sieges, not least by the defence of Paris, dramatically besieged by the vikings in the ninth century. Just as the saving of Constantinople had marked the survival of eastern Christendom, so the saving of Paris marked the survival of western Christendom. They are major landmarks in the history of Europe.

There is a move in this period towards a new kind of siege warfare. Increasingly through the Carolingian period there is emphasis on fortification to defend campaigning armies, requiring smaller strongholds. This is the age that sees the beginnings of the castle. It is possible that the conflict between Carolingian civilisation and infidel or pagan attackers was responsible for the development of the new type of fortification which was to transform siege warfare into its medieval form.

The Vikings

The most dramatic attacks on Carolingian civilisation were those made by the vikings. In the eighth century the Saracen threat had probably seemed greater, but the victory of Charles Martel at Poitiers marked the limit of

1 Clark, *Civilisation*, p. 1.

Islamic advance in western Europe. Although the Carolingians had still to fight a prolonged battle against the Saracens, especially in Spain, the major problem now came rather unexpectedly from the unregarded and seemingly primitive north. Raids from the north had occurred two centuries before, but it was the eighth century that saw the serious beginnings of a viking onslaught which came near to breaking western Christendom. Beginning with raids, the vikings came in ever greater numbers, won victories in battle, and finally settled in various parts of Europe: Iceland, Ireland, England, Scotland, Normandy, and for a time on every river in western Francia including the Somme, the Seine and the Loire.

This aggression may in the first place have been provoked by Charles Martel's attack on Frisia. At any rate there was a series of raids by Scandinavians in the early ninth century against the coast from Frisia to Aquitaine. Under Louis the Pious, the son of Charlemagne, the raids became more numerous and more serious. By the mid-ninth century Rorik is said to have had six hundred ships on the Elbe. From 841 to the end of the century there were almost annual raids against Francia. It is surely right to stress the perilous nature of these attacks for Francia, and to counter Wallace-Hadrill's amusing under-estimate of the situation as simply tourists roughing up the natives. It is probably also right to question the low numbers for viking bands. The evidence is too uncertain to allow categoric statements, and what records there are suggest at least fair-sized groups.[2]

Attacks were made on many of the great towns of Francia, and not only those on the coast. Thus in the mid-ninth century there were raids, for example, upon Rouen, Quentovic, Nantes, Tours and Poitiers. In 873, according to Regino of Prüm, they descended like locusts on the city of Angers from which the citizens had fled in panic. The vikings took over the city and used women and children to repair the ditches and ramparts. Angers then became a base from which they devastated the surrounding region. In 882 the royal palace at Aachen was burned down. Two years later a chronicler described the destruction they had caused: 'on every street lay the corpses of clergy and laity, noblemen and commoners, women, youths and babies'.[3]

The viking threat was not confined to western Europe. Scandinavians travelled the rivers eastwards as far as Constantinople. They played a rôle in the development of principalities in Russia: as warlords, princes, merchants and traders. They were engaged in the renewed attacks made by the Rus against the scarred walls of Constantinople. In 860 when the Byzantine fleet was occupied in the Mediterranean, while the emperor with the army was heading towards Asia Minor, the Rus came to attack the great

2 The quote on tourists is from Wallace-Hadrill, *Vikings*, p. 5. On size of viking bands, see also Sawyer, *Age of the Vikings*, pp. 123–6; McKitterick, pp. 231–3.

3 Regino of Prüm, *Chronicon*, p. 105, on locusts 873; and on corpses, 884, *Annales Vedastini*, p. 54

city, which had been left in the hands of its prefect, Nicetas Ooryphas. 200 ships entered the Bosphorus and began to devastate the outskirts, and the Rus entered the Sea of Marmora to overrun the Islands of the Princes. On the island of Plati they forced their way into the church and broke the communion table, smashing it on the ground. They seized twenty-two servants of the patriach and cut them to pieces with axes against the stern of a ship. The chronicler asked: 'Why has this dreadful bolt fallen on us out of the farthest north? . . . I see a fierce and savage tribe fearlessly poured round the city, ravaging the suburbs, destroying everything, ruining everything, fields, houses, herds, beasts of burden, women, children, old men, youths, thrusting their swords through everything'.[4] This seems to have been a sudden raid and was quickly repelled when the emperor returned, though the Byzantines attributed their survival to the procession with the Virgin Mary's robe, which they carried round the walls and then dipped in the sea. The weather was said to have been absolutely calm, but once the garment was dipped in the water a great storm arose and caused the besieging ships to go.

Three times in the early tenth century the Rus headed against Constantinople. In 907 Oleg arrived with a considerable fleet. He avoided the chains across the entrance to the Golden Horn by using wheels to carry the boats overland, which was sufficient to persuade the Byzantines to come to terms. Could the Turks have known of this in 1453? The treaty of 911 gave the Rus trading privileges, the right to join the emperor's army, and allowed them to have as many baths as they wanted! There was to be one more major effort against the city by the Rus, in 941, when their fleet was destroyed by the great weapon of the Byzantines, Greek Fire.

In the West the vikings were able to demand enormous amounts in tribute. It was a sure sign of the reality of their threat that often these sums were paid, in spite of the protests of chroniclers. They received great quantities not only of gold and silver, but also of corn, wine and livestock. Thus in 860 Weland received silver, food and wine. In 845 the vikings received seven thousand pounds in silver to leave Paris. Between 845 and 926 they were paid no less than forty thousand pounds of silver. The vikings who made agreements generally kept them, but of course they could not bind other viking groups, so you might pay off one group only to find yourself attacked by another. Before the development of strong monarchies in Scandinavia, no one could be held responsible for the bands of pirates, raiders and invaders.

As in the East, so in the West, the Christians were forced into making agreements and treaties with the vikings. They would also at times ally with them. Berno, a Seine viking, gave fealty to the emperor Charles the Bald in 858. In 888 the citizens of Meaux in their own defence made an

[4] Vasiliev, p. 188.

agreement with their attackers, and opened the gates to them. The Irish often made allies of vikings, and one even finds conflicts between Irish allied to the Danes on one side, against Irish allied to the Norse on the other. A native chronicler said: 'the Irish suffer evils not only from the Norwegians, they also suffer many evils from themselves'.[5] In England the Britons of Devon and Cornwall allied with vikings against the Saxons. In 862 Salomon of Brittany hired twelve Danish ships to aid him in his fight against Robert the Strong on the Loire, and Robert in his turn allied with the vikings on the Seine. At times the vikings became subjects of the Frankish emperors, and of local princes and lords. In England vikings from Ireland were accepted into the service of Aethelred's queen. In Ireland itself we are told that Aed Findhaith had power over the Norse, though it did not endure, and they killed him. He was hacked with spears, axes, and swords, so that they 'made little pieces of him'. They cut off his head, stuck it on a pole and used it for target practice with bows. When they had done, they threw the head into the sea.[6]

The raids reached a peak in the mid-ninth century with larger forces perhaps better seen as invaders than raiders. They came to stay, wintering in the area under attack. The first occasion when this is known to have happened was in 843 when they remained on Noirmoutier. In 855 they wintered in Sheppey off the English coast, and in 856 Sidroc and Berno spent the winter on the island of Oiselle in the Seine. It became common to find the vikings spending years, perhaps their lives, in the West. They might make agreements in which hostages were exchanged, they might even seek grants of land. In 882 Godfried went to the emperor, and according to the *Annals of Fulda*, the latter 'like Ahab' received the viking leader as a friend and made terms, exchanging hostages. The vikings, as a sign of peace, hoisted a shield on high and threw open the gates of their fortress. The Franks were allowed in, and went to look round. Once they were inside, the vikings took down the shield, closed the gates, and made their visitors captive in order to seek a ransom. This certainly sounds like a tale told by the enemy. Normally the vikings were punctilious about keeping their word. Whatever had happened within the camp, the emperor still baptised Godfried. The story illustrates the fact that with longer stays the vikings inevitably constructed their own fortifications, as they did at Courtrai and Louvain.[7]

The vikings were gradually absorbed into the political life of Christendom. On several occasions vikings were turned against other Scandinavians. In the end emperors granted extensive lands to a number of viking

5 *Fragmentary Annals of Ireland*, p. 145.
6 *Fragmentary Annals*, pp. 137–9.
7 *Annales Fuldenses*, First Continuation, 882, p. 98. I am grateful for the use of a translation by Tim Reuter, which will shortly be published by Manchester UP.

leaders, with the intention not only of making peace and gaining allies, but also of giving coastal regions into the hands of viking allies who would promise to defend the lands that were now theirs against other attackers.

In the ninth century Rorik was given lands as well as tribute paid with church treasure. Lothar received him into allegiance and granted him Dorestad and other lands. It was agreed that anyone who killed a viking ally should be executed or blinded. According to the annalist the Christian army was 'greatly saddened' at this.[8] It does however demonstrate the attempt to bring the vikings within the ambit of Carolingian law. Possibly the first land gift to a viking was that to Hunald in 826 in Frisia, which passed on to his son Godfried who held it until 856. The vikings were to gain something close to a permanent grip on the western Loire and Seine regions, not only receiving but even expecting tribute as a right. Christianity was virtually eliminated, there were no bishops in Avranches, Bayeux, Evreux, Lisieux, Coutances, Bordeaux or Nantes.

In the end, the only part of Francia which remained in viking hands was Normandy, the land given to the Northmen. In or about 911 the West Frankish king, Charles the Simple, made a grant to the leader of the vikings on the Seine, the details of which are found in the rather unreliable chronicle of Dudo of St Quentin. He described the incident at St Clair-sur-Epte where a ceremony took place, which Dudo claims humiliated the emperor. Rollo would not stoop to kiss his foot, saying 'I shall not bend my knee to anyone, nor shall I kiss anyone's foot'. He ordered one of his soldiers to do it, and the man 'taking hold of the king's foot, lifted it to his mouth, and as he was standing when he gave the kiss, he made the king fall over. There was much laughter then, and some disturbance'.[9]

It is doubtful if these details can be accepted as an entirely accurate version. Historians have argued, and reasonably now established, that the grant to Rollo was not as extensive as Dudo says. He was probably given only the area immediately around the Seine. It is also unlikely that the relationship between king and viking leader was as Dudo described, no doubt to the delight of his Norman audience. Charles the Simple was presumably establishing a feudal relationship with Rollo as his vassal, which Dudo's account seems to imply. He was also using the vikings as a buffer against further Scandinavian invasion. This is made clear by the fortunate survival of a charter, which shows that Dudo's account is not entirely fictional. The diploma was issued by Charles the Simple in 918 for the abbey of St-Germain-des-Prés, and refers to land granted to Rollo 'for the safety of the kingdom'. Other lands granted to the vikings soon reverted to Frankish control, but in Normandy Rollo established a viking dynasty which endured. They won control over the wider area of the duchy

8 *Annales Fuldenses*, First Continuation, 882, p. 99.
9 Dudo of St Quentin, pp. 167–9.

of Normandy, which became one of the major French principalities. William the Conqueror was a direct descendant of Rollo.[10]

Viking Fortifications

The vikings contributed to the history of siege warfare not only by besieging the fortifications of Christendom, but also by constructing strongholds of their own. They were already beginning to fortify the towns developing in Scandinavia, such as Hedeby. In Francia and elsewhere they needed to protect their campaigning armies. These viking fortifications are one element in the development of a new style of fortress in the West, designed not to protect a whole population permanently but for immediate military protection. They preferred sites that were isolated by nature, such as islands, peninsulas, desolate places in marshes and forests.

Thus they fortified the island of Oiselle in the Seine, not far from Rouen, and the peninsula of *Fossa Givaldi* near Bougivae protected by a marsh. In England their earliest winter camps were on the islands of Thanet and Sheppey. In 871 they chose a site near Reading protected on either side by the Rivers Thames and Kennet. Islands were much favoured: Noirmoutier in the Loire, La Camargue in the Rhone, Walcheren in the Scheldt, and an island near Neuss in the Rhine. Louvain was a fortification in a loop of the River Dyle, surrounded by marsh. In Ireland the *Annals* describe a Danish camp made in a dense, tangled wood thick with brambles; and a Norse camp which was 'a small place with a strong fortification around it'. It was here that Hona, an Irish chief and a druid who was allied to the Norse, fought upon the ramparts, and was hit on the jaw with a large stone wielded by a man from Munster, so that all his teeth were knocked out. He said: 'I shall die of this', and did.[11]

There are frequent chronicle references to viking fortifications, built for winter, to protect the campaigning army, or to shelter it while besieging an enemy. Yet, oddly, little is known about the nature of viking fortifications. Some headway has been made in the study of towns and fortresses in Scandinavia, but in the West surprisingly few viking strongholds have been identified, and even fewer have been excavated satisfactorily.[12]

Written accounts give some assistance. We have already noted, for example, the mention of favoured types of site, and sometimes of the smallness of forts. They were obviously reasonably good fortifications, since the vikings generally proved capable of defending them against enemy

10 For discussion on 911, see, for example, D. Bates, *Normandy Before 1066*, pp. 8–9; for 918, *Receuil des Actes de Charles III Le Simple*, i, no. 92, pp. 209–11.

11 *Fragmentary Annals*, pp. 109–11.

12 See, for example, E. Roesdahl, *Viking Age Denmark*, For general advice on the Vikings and archaeology, I am indebted to Dr Susan Kreuse.

attack. In 895 the Danish fort by the River Lea, some twenty miles from London, was able to withstand an attack by the citizens of London in which four king's thegns were killed. At Nymegen the vikings built a fort, and 'put a strong rampart and wall around it'. The *Annals of Fulda* mentioned that their strongholds were kept well-stocked. The annalist commented that they did this because they did not dare to fight, one feels inclined to add that they did not need to. The writer says that Lent was wasted and the Franks were only able to kill a few vikings they caught outside the defences: a good Christian concept of the purpose of Lent! Einhard makes a similar point, writing that the vikings did not dare to resist 'except when they were safe behind the earthwork of some fortified place'. Through the early stages of the viking attacks, they could rarely have possessed forces large enough to consider fighting pitched battles.[13]

Perhaps the most exciting find in recent times has been made in England at Repton, though the conclusions to be drawn are far from clear, and the full excavation results have yet to be published.[14] On what is now the site of Repton School have been unearthed some remarkable discoveries. Whatever the truth about them, their significance can not be questioned. Repton was the major Mercian monastery, the house of St Guthlac, it had already been used for royal Mercian burials. In 873–4 the viking army used it as a winter base. It was never entirely to recover from this episode, but later the site was revived for an Augustinian priory. The excavations began in 1972, and in the third season was found a large defensive ditch. The ditch enclosed a site of some three and a half acres. The church tower had been incorporated into the defences. In the vicinity are several mounds, which had unfortunately attracted diggers in the seventeenth century, when some damage was done to the site. Some finds were published in 1727, in a very unsatisfactory manner from a modern point of view, including reference to the body of a nine foot giant in a coffin. Altogether about 250 bodies have been found, and some coins dating to 873–4. It remains open to doubt who had been buried. Eighty per cent of the bodies were male, seemingly not showing signs of severe wounding. It has been variously suggested that they might have been Mercians beaten in the battle with the vikings; monks and nuns from the double monastery killed by the vikings; vikings killed in the battle; vikings who had died of disease during the winter. It still seems possible that the burial ground might be a Mercian

13 On the Lea, 895, *Anglo-Saxon Chronicle*, ed. D. Whitelock, p. 57; and *Two of the Saxon Chronicles Parallel*, i, p. 89, *ge weorc be Lygan xx mila bufan Lunden byrig*. On Nymegen, *Annales Fuldenses*, 880, p. 96; on being well stocked, *Annales Fuldenses* 886, p. 104; the Einhard quotation is from *The Life of Charlemagne*, ed. Thorpe, L., London, 1970, p. 39; from Einhard, *Vita Karoli Magni*, p. 21: *qua hostis exire potuisset, tali munitione prohibuit.*

14 For early reports on Repton, see *Medieval Archaeology*, xxvii, 1983, pp. 172–4, and xxix, 1985, pp. 168–9; and *Current Archaeology*, c, 1986, pp. 140–1.

cemetery, and that the bodies do not belong to the year of the viking winter at all.

In some ways even more remarkable is the channel that has been found, cut through the twenty foot high cliff and running from the centre of the enclosure to the River Trent. It is some ten metres wide, thirty metres long, and five metres deep, and had been filled in during the twelfth century. It appears to be a 'vast boat-slip' with a 'u-boat pen'.[15] In other words it is thought to have been made by the vikings in order to bring their ships up from the river into the safety of the enclosure they themselves had made round Repton. Until the archaeological finds are more fully explained, one must hold on to the possibility that both the defences and the slipway were Mercian, but early hints from those concerned have very much suggested that what we have here at last is evidence for the nature of a viking fortification made during a single campaign. One may also note some similarities between the defences of Repton, and those of early towns in Scandinavia.

Scandinavian Fortifications

We now know something about fortification in the homeland of the vikings. Several Scandinavian towns developed at about this time, and were provided with earthwork defences: ditches, and ramparts with wooden stockades. The Danevirke is a remarkable earthwork, described as 'one of the largest of western Europe's ancient defensive works'. It probably had its origins in the ninth century. The *Carolingian Chronicle* says that Godfried built a 'rampart so that a protective bulwark would stretch from the eastern bay called Ostarsalt, as far as the western sea'. A second phase was added in the tenth century, possibly the work of Harold Bluetooth.[16]

There are also the great circular fortresses of Scandinavia including Trelleborg. There has been much discussion over the dating and function of these important earthworks. They are enormous in size, and carefully shaped and constructed, with a regular plan of streets of boat-shaped houses. They are thought to belong to the late tenth century. The best explanation of their function is that, like royal Frankish fortifications, they stood at the heart of great estates, and contained garrisons and those concerned with supply and services. Trelleborg, Fyrkat, Aggersborg, and Nonnebakken can be compared with the fort on Walcheren, which also had a circular rampart. They probably were placed to have regional control rather than to muster armies for foreign invasions. It is suggested that

15 *Current Archaeology*, c, p. 141.

16 On Scandinavian fortifications, see Roesdahl, *Viking Age Denmark*; and p. 141 for the Danevirke; for the Godfried rampart, see *Carolingian Chronicles*, p. 89.

Harold Bluetooth may have been responsible for them, with subsequent political developments explaining their early abandonment.[17]

The significance of viking influence on siege warfare is considerable. They were themselves capable of building sophisticated defences, albeit in earth and timber. It is not clear to what extent they influenced Carolingian defences, or alternatively based their own fortifications on Carolingian and perhaps also Slav models. Certainly they provoked the Franks into improving their own fortifications and system of defence, and it may be that the new Frankish structures in turn owed a debt to viking models, particularly those which were constructed hastily to protect campaigning armies. Is it purely coincidental that we know nothing of Frankish earthwork fortifications before the viking onslaught, that the vikings were expert in building earthwork fortifications already, and that in the subsequent age one finds the appearance of earthwork motte and bailey castles? It may be so, but it seems more likely that the Carolingians owed at least some debt to the viking example. We shall return to this problem in our next chapter on the origins of castles.

It has been claimed that the viking menace 'grew with telling', but we may be sure that this was a major menace to the new Carolingian form of European civilisation. Those who suffered the viking threat, and wrote about it, viewed the scandinavians as a frightening pagan threat to Christendom. They saw them in much the same way as the Romans had seen the Huns: hostile, terrifying and completely alien to their own way of life. The Irish annalist was much surprised to find that the Danes, for the sake of piety, would abstain from meat and women, if only for a while.[18]

Carolingian Francia

In the centuries immediately after the fall of the western Roman Empire, once the barbarians had established themselves, the art of fortification seems to have been relatively neglected. Kenneth Clark claimed that from the three centuries after the fall of the Western Empire, almost the only stone building to survive is a church.[19] Our chapter on the Merovingian period may have shown that the situation has been exaggerated. Clearly there was a certain amount of building in stone, including considerable repair work. We have also shown that a good deal of fortification in earth and wood was undertaken. In the period before Charlemagne, many rural

17 See Roesdahl, p. 147, on the fortresses, and for a view which credits Harold Bluetooth.
18 Sawyer, *Kings and Vikings*, p. 95, believes it grew with telling; and for the quotation on meat and women, see *Fragmentary Annals*, p. 93.
19 For a good general review of Carolingian France, see McKitterick, *The Frankish Kingdom*; the quotation from Kenneth Clark, is *Civilisation*, p. 17, and refers to the Baptistery at Poitiers.

strongholds were built, 'the remains of many of which are still to be seen'. No doubt by the ninth century Francia felt more secure, so that town walls and new fortresses seemed less necessary. There is evidence that some old fortifications were dismantled and the stone re-used. Ebbo, archbishop of Rheims, was given permission by Louis the Pious to destroy the walls of his city in order to rebuild the cathedral. In 859 Wenilo, archbishop of Sens, was allowed to use stone from the walls of Melun to build a church. The survival of so many Roman fortifications suggests that many not only continued in use, but were also kept in repair. It is worth noting that we only know about the few examples of destruction because permission had to be sought to tamper with defences.

Attitudes changed again with the viking threat. In 883, for example, Fulk the archbishop of Reims rebuilt the walls of his city using materials from the church which the vikings had damaged. If the Carolingian monarchs had been complacent in the preceding period, they now reversed their view with a vengeance. Walls were rebuilt in many places, for example at Metz in 883 and Langres 885. In 898 Charles the Simple gave permission to the bishop of Noyon to rebuild the defences of both Tournai and Noyon. The abbot of St Vaast fortified both his abbey and the town of Arras.

The new infidel and pagan attacks were a stimulus to renewed fortification. The Carolingian Empire sought to protect its population within walls. In the end the best permanent answer proved to be a restored system of fortification, with new methods of providing permanent garrison forces to man the walls. The course of the struggle saw important development in siege warfare: the Carolingians defending their own strongholds, and also having to attack those built by their enemies .

The viking raids were a nuisance under Charlemagne, but became a greater threat under Louis the Pious and his successors. Richer described the Frankish king building strongholds 'against viking pirates, at the points which seemed exposed to pirate attack'. Charlemagne had already discovered the value of fortification in his Saxon wars. According to Einhard, he 'left garrisons at strategic points along the frontier'.[20] Here are signs of the new use of smaller fortifications for specifically military purposes. Charlemagne was well aware of the problems when an enemy used fortifications, as the Lombards at Pavia, and the Avars with earthwork defences and their 'nine rings'. The neglect of fortifications before the viking raids began has certainly been exaggerated. It is clear from the internal warfare in the Carolingian Empire that fortifications were already playing a large part. It is true that enemy fortifications once taken, were destroyed or neglected, this may well have been because there were inadequate forces to garrison them, and for fear that they would be re-used by opponents. In Francia

[20] On viking pirates, see Richer, *Histoire de France*, i, p. 19; on the frontier garrisons, see Einhard, ed. Thorpe, p. 40.

itself there seem to have been many defended sites in the eighth century. The chronicles frequently refer to strongholds which should probably not yet be called castles, but which seem not always to have been towns, as for example at Loches, Thouars, Argentan, Clermont and Fronsac.

Oman believes that one of Charlemagne's greatest innovations was the introduction of a system of 'fortified posts'.[21] Few of them were ever captured, though Eresburg fell through treachery in 776, and Karlstadt was stormed by the Saxons in 778. From 800 the coastal zone was on the alert, and Charlemagne himself went to inspect the northern region. Soon afterwards ships were placed at the mouths of northern rivers to guard them. By 814 there were fleets on the Garonne, the Loire, and at Ghent and Boulogne. Charlemagne also ordered his son Louis to make similar arrangements for Aquitaine. The capitularies show that garrisons were provided to complete the defensive system. The viking attack on Dorestad in 835 provoked Louis the Pious to improve the defences of Francia. The circular fortifications on Schoewen and elsewhere are probably the result of this action. One of Louis' strongholds at Walcheren fell to the Danes, but on the whole they were a sound investment.

In the later ninth century the Franks took a renewed interest in defence. The capitularies between 862 and 864 show work on defences on the Seine and the Spanish March, as well as efforts made to provision and man them.[22] The *Annals of St Bertin* record that young men were called upon to finish the building of the fort at Pîtres and then to garrison it. The capitulary of 813 envisages the necessity for making defensive camps, and among the supplies that must be brought are pickaxes, hatchets and iron-tipped stakes. There survives a summons to abbot Fulrad in 806 with instructions that the troops he sends must bring spades, axes, picks and stakes, and he was told: 'see that there is no neglect, as you prize our favour'. In 884 'guardians of the frontier' were expected to meet the viking threat.[23]

The major fortification against the vikings was the work of Charles the Bald, the youngest son of Louis the Pious. From 862 he built fortified bridges to block the rivers against viking inroads into central Francia. It is not always clear to what extent his orders were obeyed, and sometimes there was neglect and delay. At the assembly at Pîtres in 864, Charles the Bald produced a plan of defensive fortifications, and through the following years it was gradually implemented. In 869 orders were given to fortify Le

21 Oman, *A History of the Art of War in the Middle Ages*, i, p. 83. Oman's work has become dated in many respects, but was an important starting point for many ideas on military history, and still remains useful.

22 *Capitularia Regum Francorum*, ed. A. Boretius and V. Krause, e.g., ii, pp. 159, 302, 310, 332. and see McKitterick, p. 192.

23 *Annales Bertiniani*, 869, p. 98; I am grateful for the use of a translation by Dr Jinty Nelson, shortly to be published by Manchester UP. On the 806 and 813 capitularies, see Oman, i, pp. 81–2; on the guardians of the frontier, *Annales Fuldenses*, 884, p. 101.

Mans and Tours in order to protect the local populations. A number of cities had ditches and walls built or improved. In 883, for example, the defences of Cologne were improved, and the walls were provided with gates, bars and locks. The idea of fortifying bridges to block the way of the vikings up the rivers seems to have originated with Charles the Bald. In 789 he had two bridges built on the Elbe, one at least of which had wood and earthwork fortifications at each end. He also had a bridge built at Pont de l'Arche near Pîtres, upstream from the viking base at Oiselle, which had fortified bridgeheads. When the Seine defences had been organised, Charles the Bald turned to the Loire: Le Mans, Tours and Orléans were fortified, and a bridge built at Les-Ponts-de-Cé near Angers. At Trilbardou the return route of the raiders was blocked on the Marne by building a bridge with bridgeheads. The vikings had to abandon their plunder and agree terms in order to get back. Other bridges on the Oise and Marne were constructed, by 885 the new bridge at Pontoise had been finished by Aletramnus, and by 869 stone fortifications had been completed at Pîtres. Paris itself benefited, and under bishop Gozlin the island in the Seine was joined to either bank by a fortified bridge, which was to play such an important rôle in the great siege, though in 887 the vikings managed to break through the bridge of Paris and ravage the heart of Francia. It was said of Charles the Fat that he opposed the vikings 'not in battle, but by building fortifications, so that their passage by ship could be prevented'. In addition to improving town defences and constructing fortified bridges, numerous unlicensed strongholds rose during the period of crisis.[24]

Carolingian Siege Methods

In order to gain some idea of siege techniques during the Carolingian age, it is best to view a few of the operations. They are selected for us, since although sieges were numerous, detailed descriptions of them are few. Nevertheless, by examining the warfare of the Carolingians both within Francia and against external enemies, we can obtain enough information to form some concept of defensive and offensive siege tactics at the time.

The emperor Charlemagne was engaged in many sieges. There survives an interesting description of his attack of Pavia in 773, seen from the viewpoint of the besieged, told by Notker, the monk of St Gall. The monk says of himself that he was 'a toothless person with a stammer' who has done his humble best to describe the events. For us, Notker has the

24 For a number of helpful hints for reading on this period, I am indebted to Dr Jinty Nelson, whose forthcoming book on Charles the Bald will be widely welcomed. I am also grateful to her for letting me see the translations of the chronicles of St Bertin, by herself, of St Vaast by Simon Coupland, of Fulda by Tim Reuter, and of Regino of Prüm by Peggy Brown.

Carolingian Sieges

advantage of possessing some military knowledge, and he is also describing happenings from his own lifetime. He had been brought up by an old soldier, Adalbert, who had fought against the Saxons and the Avars. He gives us a description of the mysterious nine rings of the Avars, seemingly an elaborate hedged earthwork. Notker's account may however owe something to his literary pretensions, and to Virgil's nine circles of Styx. His account of the siege of Pavia is also coloured by flowery language and a touch of imagination, but it remains of interest.[25]

Desiderius, the king of the Lombards, was angered by Charlemagne's repudiation of his daughter. The emperor had married the girl, and then after only a year, possibly at the prompting of his mother, had cast her off. Desiderius defied the emperor, and shut himself up in the walled city of Pavia. He was joined by Otker, a Carolingian noble in revolt against Charlemagne. The two of them went up into a high tower to watch Charlemagne's army approach. Desiderius was astounded as wave after wave arrived, in each of which he expected to see the emperor, each time to be told by Otker that still the great man had not appeared. The baggage train came, troops from many nations, Charles' personal escort, his clerics. In the end Desiderius, according to Notker, sobbed and stammered: 'let us go and hide'. Charlemagne finally arrived, the light gleaming from his weapons, like the dawn of a new day, in iron armour and on an iron-grey horse. Otker himself fainted at the sight. It was, says Notker, 'a battle-line of iron'. The attack made the walls of Pavia shake. The citizens in their 'madness' thought they could resist the emperor's might. Charlemagne surrounded the city, and ordered the building of a church, secure in his strength and his trust in God. The *Carolingian Chronicle*, more laconically than Notker, tells us that Charles besieged the city with much effort, spending Christmas and the entire winter there, before taking it.[26]

Charles was also engaged in siege warfare against the Saxons. As in the Merovingian age, we can see that the 'barbarian' enemies of the Frankish state were generally well equipped with knowledge in this type of war. In 776 the Saxons managed to get into Lubbecke by a trick, mixing with the foragers who came out from the town, and entering it with them when they returned, though this trick seems to have been used with suspicious frequency and might just be a good tale. They attacked the town when the citizens were asleep, but were resisted to the extent that terms had to be agreed.

At Syburg the Saxons besieged the Franks, and set up siege engines, though the chronicler sneers that they did more damage with their engines to themselves than to the Franks – another suspiciously frequent comment

25 *Einhard and Notker the Stammerer*, pp. 162–5; Notker Babulus,*Gesta Karoli*, 773, p. 84: *ego balbus et edentulus*; p. 49: *Terra inquiens Hunorum VIIII circulis cingebatur*; Pavia, pp. 82–5.

26 *Carolingian Chronicles*, p. 50; *Annales Regni Francorum*, on Pavia, p. 36. For line of iron, Notker, p. 84: *acie ferri*.

to belittle one's foe.[27] The Saxon engines did not do the trick, so they prepared faggots to fire the town, but God intervened and sent two shields red with flame over the church so that the Saxons fled. It is difficult to know what a modern reader should make of these pious accounts, beyond a recognition that monkish chroniclers thought safety lay in the hands of God. Accounts of sieges in the Frankish period, when the enemy was often pagan, are particularly prone to this kind of description. All the same, it still tells us that the Saxons could fire a town, and possessed siege engines. Since the vikings also used engines, it is clear that barbarian Europe in the viking age had at least some sophistication in military equipment.

The siege of Barcelona also took place during the reign of Charlemagne, though it was conducted by his son, the future emperor Louis the Pious. It lasted through the winter of 800 to 801. Louis was supported largely by men from Aquitaine and Septimania, that is from southern Francia. We have a detailed description, and again a rather literary one, by the monk Ermold the Black who seems himself to have come from the Midi, and is probably to be identified as Hermoldus the chancellor. His poem which describes the siege was written in honour of Louis the Pious.[28]

Barcelona was held by the Moslems, and had long been a threat to Christians. Ermold describes the holding of the Frankish assembly at which the decision was made to mount a major attack. The king declared 'The Almighty has given us the mission to protect the people. It is the time of year when nation clashes with nation in arms. Where shall we go?' In response to this somewhat casual approach to making war, William count of Toulouse kissed the king's feet, and then described the ravages made by the Saracens. Of all their strongholds, he suggested, Barcelona was the key, the one town which was 'the cause of all our ills'. The king was moved, clasped Count William in his arms and exchanged kisses with him. The decision to attack Barcelona was made.

Ermold then takes us to Barcelona, and recounts an anecdote or two to show what kind of enemy the Franks had to meet. He described the devastation around the city for which the Moors were responsible. They had taken Christian captives, including the mother of a certain Datus. Datus therefore approached Barcelona, in hope of recovering her. He was offered a deal: his horse in exchange for his mother, otherwise his mother would be put to death. His reply is a little surprising to us: 'Kill my mother, I cannot stop you. I shall never hand over the horse you demand, wretch. It is not for you to handle its bridle'. The Moor then brought the unfortunate mother on to the walls and killed her before her son's eyes. The poet intends that we see this as a Moorish atrocity, with possibly a touch of irony in regard to the Frankish love of horses. At any rate, Datus boiled

27 On Lubbecke, 776 and Syburg, 776, *Carolingian Chronicles*, pp. 51–3; *Annales Regni Francorum*, p. 43: *pugnas et machinas praeparare . . . petrarias et clidas*.

28 Ermold Le Noir, *In Honorem Hludowici*, pp. 21–48.

with rage, and went off to become a monk, perhaps to contemplate the relative value of mothers and horses.

The Franks came to Barcelona and surrounded it with their tents, amidst the noise of trumpets. They attacked using the *testudo*, ladders and stones. They made engines and moved them up, making the walls shake, as well as the Moors on them. The Moorish commander, Zado, demanded: 'What is that noise?', presumably blissfully unaware of developments to date! He decided he needed help from Cordoba, a good example of the importance of defending garrisons keeping touch with outside support. According to Ermold, Zado was full of fear of the Franks, who were never beaten in war, who lived their whole lives in arms, and were used to battle from their youth: 'the very name of "Frank" makes me tremble'. This at least shows us how the Franks liked to see themselves. All the same, Zado ordered the walls to be strengthened, increased the guard, and improved the defences at the gates. Young Frankish warriors with a ram battered the rampart with great blows. One Moor called down to them: 'Why do you try to destroy a city which Roman effort took a thousand years to build?' It did not stop them. One of the Franks seized a bow and shot at the man, hitting him in the head so that he fell from the wall with a cry, his blood spattering the Franks below.

The engines could not break the gates. Louis was determined not to go until the place fell, and Count William declared that he would rather eat the horse he was riding than abandon the siege. The walls were mined. The defenders were reminded that no help had come, and that they were suffering from hunger and thirst. The Moors made a sortie. Zado himself was captured, and taken to Louis' tent. He pretended that he would order his men to open the gates to the Franks, but in his own language shouted to them to continue their resistance, a ploy which won him the admiration of his captors. For another month the siege went on. The Franks rained arrows on the walls so that the Moors no longer dared to show themselves or to cross the town. The king himself hurled a javelin which stuck in the rampart. Finally the Moors opened the gates and surrendered. On the following day Louis made a triumphal entry. He left a Frankish garrison inside, and went home with shields, armour, clothes, valuables, horses and Zado himself.

Under Charles and his successors siege warfare played an important part in the wars to the east. Whatever the nine rings were, the Avars and Slavs employed earthwork fortifications a good deal. At Rastig Charles the Bald entered an enormous fortification which, according to the *Annals of Fulda*, was 'quite unlike any built before it'. The same chronicle also mentions the Slavs encircling a site 'with a very strong wall' and having a very narrow entrance to trap attackers.[29]

29 On the nine rings, see *Einhard and Notker*, pp. 135–6, and n. 25 above, though Halphen suggests the idea may be taken from the circles of Styx in Virgil's *Aeneid*. On Rastig and the Slavs, see *Annales Fuldenses*, 869 and 870, pp. 69, 75.

Engines are a commonplace of Carolingian siege warfare. At Brissarthe, a viking force under Hasting took shelter within a basilica-style villa made of stone. The Franks surrounded this *castrum* with their tents, and next day built mounds for their engines. It is interesting to note that the Franks made mounds for military purposes, presumably, in this case, for engines to shoot from a distance. The vikings attempted a sortie, but were forced back inside. One of the Frankish leaders, Robert, unwisely pursued them while not wearing helmet or hauberk, and was killed. The other Frankish leader, Ranulf, was wounded by an arrow shot from a window, and the siege was abandoned.[30]

Riché, among others, has suggested that the trebuchet originated in this period. We shall examine the development of siege weapons in more detail in a later chapter. Suffice it to say for now that the evidence is inadequate: the trebuchet, the great siege engine operated by a counter-weight, is generally thought to have appeared in about the twelfth century. Riché's only evidence for an early date is the remark by Regino of Prüm that 'new and unusual kind of engines' were used, with no further hint as to what they were.[31]

The battle of the Dyle in 891 was also part of the conflict with the vikings, and a vital Frankish victory. It arose, like so many medieval battles, from a siege. The vikings had pitched camp by the River Dyle at Louvain, and there 'after their fashion, they surrounded it with a fortified ditch'. Arnulf, King of the East Franks, came with an army to face them. He crossed the river but, having lost the Alemannic contingent, was hesitant to fight. The position was perilous for an army in the open, with marsh on one side, the river on the other, and no room for the cavalry to attack. Arnulf ordered his men to dismount: 'When I get down from my horse and signal with my hand, follow me'. He encouraged them with the thought that they were attacking in the name of God. His men wisely appealed to him to leave a cavalry force to provide protection for the rear. And so 'the armies clashed like iron on stone'. The chronicler said that the Danes had never been known to be beaten inside a fortification, but the Franks won the battle, and the vikings fled, many drowning in the river, 'grasping each other in heaps by hand, neck and limbs, they sank in hundreds and thousands, so that their corpses blocked the river bed'. Two viking leaders, Sigfried and Gotfried were killed and sixteen of their standards were captured. The infrequency of Frankish successes against viking fortifications suggests that they were well-made, and that Frankish

30 Regino, p. 92.

31 Riché, *Daily Life in the World of Charlemagne*, believes the trebuchet was used at Angers in 873; Regino, p. 105 on new engines. R. Rogers, *Latin Siege Warfare* has useful discussion on the historiography of siege weapons, including the views of Schneider, who supported a view of trebuchets developed by the vikings, see Rogers, p. 20 (microfiche).

techniques may not have been much more advanced than those of their enemies.[32]

The siege of Bergamo occurred in 894. It was a Frankish attack, showing some classic techniques. In advance of the siege, the layout of the stronghold was surveyed from the surrounding hills. There was an attempted storm on the first day of attack, but it failed. At dawn on the next day, after hearing mass, stones were shot. The king's bodyguard formed a *testudo* to approach the walls, 'holding their shields above their heads like a roof'. They also mined the wall, with the defenders emptying on to their heads containers full of stones, even in desperation pulling stones from their own walls to drop. The mined wall collapsed to great shouting, and the army entered 'like a whirlwind'. The leader of the defence, Count Ambrosius, took refuge in a tower, but was captured. The angry Franks at once hanged the count from a gallows.[33]

Advance intelligence about a situation was often vital. At Mouzon in 947 the kings sent a force against the deposed archbishop Hugh. They attacked at dusk and from all sides, making an all-out assault because they knew the garrison was weak. Fresh men took over in shifts from those who were tired to keep the attack going, and indeed the place surrendered within one day. It was equally important to appreciate the strength of the defences. Montaigu near Laon was besieged in 948. The attackers noted the poorly fortified enclosure, which seems also to have been small. The inhabitants were cowed by a strong attack, and surrendered. A third important factor was timing. The siege of Laon in 948 was badly planned since it began with winter approaching, and Lothar had not time to make the necessary machines 'without which a hill of such height could not be stormed'. He had to tell the army to disperse and come back to start again in the spring![34]

The renewed siege in the following year is of considerable interest because of the detailed description given by Richer. The chronicler says it was his own father who advised the king on how to take the place. The whole story is somewhat dubious, it seems unlikely the king would have required such mundane advice, or that he would have been particularly delighted to receive it. The ploy that Richer says was used is also a trick that was often recounted. One wonders if it could have been used in fact as often as it is described. Surely somebody would have got the message! There is still value in the account for what it tells us about siege methods, and because the chronicler clearly had at least some first hand knowledge of events.

According to Richer, his father Raoul was a *miles* of the king, whose

32 I am grateful to Dr Jinty Nelson for pointing out the significance of the battle of the Dyle; *Annales Fuldenses*, Second Continuation, 891, pp. 119–20.

33 On Bergamo, *Annales Fuldenses*, Second Continuation, 894, pp. 123–4.

34 Richer, i, pp. 229, 271–2, on Mouzon 947, Montaigu 948, and Laon 948.

advice was always valued. Raoul advised his master first to examine the layout of the site with great care, and to see how well it was guarded. Richer's father was given the task of organising a spying expedition, and then armed with information went to the king with a plan. He was given the go-ahead, and authority to put the scheme into effect. Troops were placed in hiding near the town. Then Raoul and his chosen party, dressed in disguises, watched in the evening as the citizens came out on their daily foraging trip. Raoul's group wore the same clothes, and a similar number, with faces hidden in their hoods against the sun, approached the gate as if they were the foragers returning. Once allowed into the city, they dropped their bundles and drew their swords. The attackers were protected by a tower on the left, houses on the right, and the town wall to the rear. They held the gate so that the hidden force could now come in, then massacred the citizens without pity. However they do not seem to have had complete success. Some defenders continued to resist from the tower, and the account peters out inconclusively.[35]

A similar trick is reported by Richer, also organised by his father, against Mons in 956, and there is an earlier account about Montreuil-sur-Mer in the 930s, when Arnulf of Flanders dressed men in dirty old clothes so they would not be noticed, in order to enter the town and contact a traitor. The latter was offered a choice of a gold or an iron ring for his reward: gold if he helped, chains if he did not. He chose to help, appearing at night on the walls with a torch to show which entrance had been left open for them.[36] Another reference in Richer implies that the idea of rendability might date from the tenth century, and is suggestive of the development of castle warfare. The duke of Paris showed his intended loyalty to King Lothar by offering to open all his *oppida* for a royal visit. Our Carolingian sieges show a full range of methods and weapons being used. In addition to engines, the account of Senlis in 949 suggests that the defending citizens were using crossbows.[37] Sieges are still of towns for the most part, but the importance of camps and towers points towards strongholds which are becoming more like castles.

Alfred's England

Alfred has long been treated as a miracle-worker in bringing about the survival of England from the brink of collapse. There is a degree of truth in this view: Alfred and his successors did halt the viking advance, and even put it into reverse. What has not been acknowledged so often, is the debt

35 Richer, i, pp. 275–82.

36 On Mons and Montreuil-sur-Mer, Richer, ii, p. 17, and i, p. 143.

37 On Senlis 949, Richer, i, p. 283.

he owed to continental example. Just as Charles the Bald and the Franks built fortifications and organised defences, so did Alfred and his successors. That is not to say there are no distinct features about the English system, but it clearly used the continental developments as a model. The system in England depended on three major factors: the building of fortified settlements; opposition to the viking control of seas and rivers; organisation of the manning of the defences. Sawyer has rightly suggested that Alfred: 'learned the lesson of the campaigns in Francia'.[38]

Like the Franks, Alfred was provoked by the Scandinavian menace. The vikings in England, as on the continent, raided, wintered, and then settled. They built fortifications off the coast, and then inland, and used them as bases. Necessarily the early viking bases were quickly constructed defences for an army on campaign. Such defences may have been partly based on the plan of Scandinavian earthworks, and possibly on Frankish fortification. The English burhs were themselves a cross between military enclosures and fortified settlements, and seem to have begun in response to the viking menace. They were not, of course, the first fortifications to be built in England, where for example Roman defences had been repaired and used. We find evidence for a few sieges in the pre-viking period, though rarely in detail. In 755 there was a kind of siege at Merton, when the king was staying in what the *Anglo-Saxon Chronicle* calls a stronghold. He was besieged by Prince Cyneheard who had heard his father was there 'with a certain loose woman' and with only a few men to protect him. The building was surrounded, and when the king emerged he was killed with his men. Supporters of the king came to Merton to seek revenge, and Cyneheard shut himself within. The gate was broken down, and Cyneheard and his companions killed.[39]

In the viking wars the English had fortifications ready for use. There is mention of an *arx* in London, with reference in 899 to those '*in Lundonia arce*', which one is tempted to translate as 'in the Tower of London'. It could mean simply the city defences, but *arx* is most commonly used to describe a citadel within a city. It may be of interest to note that a contemporary chronicler described the tower defending the bridge at Paris as an *arx*. At any rate, the English had a number of walled cities, and new fortifications. King's thegns seem normally to have resided within fortifications and in 893, we are told, they were 'at home in their fortresses'.[40]

The war against the vikings in England involved several sieges. Both sides sought shelter behind fortifications, as for example did the English in London. The Danes were besieged at Buttington on the Severn for several

38 Sawyer, *Kings and Vikings*, p. 92.

39 On Merton, *Anglo-Saxon Chronicle*, pp. 30–1.

40 Aethelweard, p. 52, for 899: *in Lundonia arce*; on being at home in their fortresses, *Anglo-Saxon Chronicle*, 893, p. 56; Thietmar of Meuseburg, *Chronicle*, in *EHD*, ii, pp. 347–50.

Defence of a burh

weeks, and suffered hardships as supplies dwindled. They were reduced to eating their horses, and according to the *Anglo-Saxon Chronicle* died of starvation. The English garrison at Bedford was besieged, but made a sortie and defeated the enemy. At Reading it was the vikings who sortied, bursting out 'like wolves' to win a victory. Many of the king's thegns shut themselves up for safety inside the stronghold of Chippenham. The vikings saw it was unprepared, and 'unfortified except for ramparts thrown up in our fashion'. They besieged the place believing that victory would come from 'hunger, thirst and the siege', since there was no water in the vicinity. However, an English sortie at dawn took them by surprise, and they fled to their ships. Alfred's famous last ditch refuge at Athelney was also fortified with 'elegant workmanship' by the king himself. In 885 the vikings besieged Rochester, and built a counter-fort in the process, but Alfred was able to relieve the place. In England, as in Francia, the viking use of defences could be frustrating. At Nottingham 'protected by the defences of the stronghold they refused to give battle'.[41]

Under Alfred and his successors were constructed a series of fortified places or burhs, sometimes refortifying earlier sites, sometimes building anew. Many of the burhs would develop into towns, and may have had some economic as well as military function from the beginning. They may well have owed a debt in design and function to Frankish estate strongholds. Certainly they had a regional significance, as demonstrated by the way garrisons were drawn from the territory around the burh. Thus, for example, in 914 Edward the Elder went to Buckingham and stayed there four weeks while burhs were built on the two sides of the river. In 917 the burh of Towcester was constructed, and immediately attacked by the

41 *Anglo-Saxon Chronicle*, on Buttington, 893, p. 56; and on Bedford, 917, p. 65. Asser, in *Alfred*, ed. Keynes & Lapidge, p. 78, on Cippenham 876, p. 83, and Athelney 876, pp. 84, 103; on Rochester 885, p. 86; and on Nottingham 868, p. 77.

Danes, only to be saved by the arrival of reinforcements. According to the *Anglo-Saxon Chronicle*, Towcester was 'provided with a stone wall', and in other cases existing towns, such as Colchester, had their defences repaired. Asser described Alfred's building activities, but showed that the king suffered the same delays in execution which the Frankish rulers had endured. Alfred had to cajole and punish where there was delay, and where fortifications were not finished by the time they were needed. The chronicler says: 'I am speaking here of fortifications commanded by the king which have not been begun, or else, having been begun late in the day, have not been brought to completion'. Famously, Alfred also built a fleet to complete the defensive system. It may have had mixed fortunes, but it shows his appreciation of the need to deal with the viking menace on its own terms.[42]

The English also followed the Franks in using bridge defences against the vikings. In 920 at Nottingham was constructed: 'the bridge over the Trent between the two burhs'. We have already noted the placing of opposing fortifications on the river at Buckingham. As in Francia, there could be no plans for fortification of burhs and bridges without a parallel organisation of their garrisons. In England there was developed a taxation system based on the burhs incorporating assessment by hides. The *Burghal Hidage* and other related documents indicate an association between the assessment and the burhs. Probably each district around its burh was expected to provide enough cash to support a garrison for its local fortification. Both the system and the tax were to be modified, but the original connection is hardly to be doubted.[43]

There is a detailed description of the siege of Chester in 918, unexpectedly preserved in the *Irish Annals*. Ingimund left Ireland for Britain with a band of Norsemen. The British under Cadell defeated him, and since Aethelred I was ill at the time, Ingimund appealed to his wife Queen Aethelflaed for lands 'on which he could build barns and dwellings, for he was tired of war'. She gave him land near Chester, but his eyes were soon drawn to the wealth of the city. He proposed to his viking friends that they seize the city. When they tried to do so, they were resisted by the 'many freemen' within, who themselves appealed to the queen for aid. The royal reply advised them to fight outside the city, keeping a group of cavalry hidden within the open gates. In the battle the vikings were beaten, but still did not withdraw. They mined the wall, using hurdles on props to cover their activities at the foot of the wall. The king and queen appealed to the Irish to desert the 'common enemy', which they did, but still the Norse continued the siege. The defenders, now including the Irish, hurled down boulders and crushed the hurdles, but the vikings then supported the

[42] *Anglo-Saxon Chronicle*, on Buckingham 914 and Towcester 917, p. 64. On fortifications commanded by the king, *Alfred*, ed. Keynes & Lapidge, p. 102.

[43] On Nottingham 920, *Anglo-Saxon Chronicle*, p. 67. The Burghal Hidage is Robertson, *Anglo-Saxon Charters*, p. 246.

A siege from the Utrecht Psalter

hurdles more strongly on 'great columns'. The next effort of the defenders was to put ale and water in great cauldrons, boil it, and drop it on the miners so that 'their skin peeled off'. The vikings responded by adding hides over the hurdles. Finally the English scattered beehives collected in the town 'which prevented them from moving their feet and hands because of the number of bees stinging them'.[44]

Already in this period we have indications of a code of conduct respecting sieges. Maurice Keen has examined the laws of war in a later period, but clearly such conventions and agreements between combatants has a long history. The laws of Alfred the Great show an attempt to control private warfare. If men are besieged, the attackers are to hold off for seven days so long as the enemy does not emerge to fight. If the besieged surrender, then they should be kept unharmed for thirty days while kin and friends are informed. A man with a just cause but without the force to deal with it himself should go to the ealdorman, or failing that to the king.[45]

The Siege of Paris

To conclude this chapter let us examine the greatest set piece siege of the age. It caught contemporary as well as later notice because of its importance. Fulk, the archbishop of Rheims, wrote to Louis the Fat that if Paris fell, the realm would also collapse. In addition to being the most significant siege of the period, it also merited a lengthy and detailed account in a poem describing what its author Abbo called the 'battles' of Paris.[46]

44 *Fragmentary Annals*, pp. 169–75.
45 The excellent and pioneering work on the laws of war is Keen, *The Laws of War*; on Alfred, see Asser, in *Alfred*, ed. Keynes & Lapidge, pp. 163–70.
46 Abbo, p. v on the letter, and p. 2 on battles: *bellorum Parisiace polis*.

It had seemed, when Louis III won his great victory at Saucourt, that the Frankish position against the vikings was greatly improved. But the situation was suddenly altered by the unexpected death of the monarch. It seems that the young king spotted a girl he fancied, chased her in fun on horseback, and had an accident which killed him. It was in the period of political turmoil following his death that the threat to Paris was posed. The vikings on the Seine in 885 advanced once more towards central Francia. Despite Frankish attempts to block their route, they reached Paris. There the new fortifications worked sufficiently well to hold up the advance. The vikings attempted to destroy this last major obstacle, and sat down to besiege not only the bridge fortifications on the Seine, but also the city itself. In an age when military responsibilty was devolving from bishops to lay counts, the transition was nicely marked in Paris by a joint defence led by the city's bishop, Gozlin, and the count of the region, Odo.

The author of the poem about the siege was Abbo, a monk at St-Germain-des-Prés. He came from Neustria, from the region between the Seine and the Loire, and was in Paris during the siege. He could only have been a young man at the time, since ten years later he was still only a deacon. His own abbot, Aimoin, to whom it was dedicated did not think much of the poem, according to the modest, young author. And in more recent times, Oman has described it as being 'couched in the vilest Latin . . . in excruciating false quantities'.[47] The work is addressed to Bishop Gozlin, and is full of praise for the efforts of the city's two chief defenders: Gozlin and Odo, count of Paris. The poet tells us that his work is about actual events, as he is not made in the mould of the great ancient writers, who were able to invent, though one suspects that invention is not altogether beyond his capabilities. He was clearly in love with Paris, 'shimmering like a queen over all other towns', protected by the Seine with 'its arms caressing your walls'. He also mentioned the new defences, with the bridges and their towers which linked the island in the river to both the north and south banks.[48]

The vikings arrived in seven hundred ships under Siegfried. They tried to bargain their way through, but without success. Bishop Gozlin insisted that he had been entrusted by the king to defend the city, and would do so to the best of his ability. Siegfried blustered with threats, and gave them a day's grace to make up their minds.

Next day the siege began in earnest. The vikings attempted to destroy the tower guarding the bridge to the right bank. They leaped from their ships to the attack. The defence was led by Count Odo and his brother Robert the Strong. The vikings selected this target because, though begun in about 870, it was still incomplete – yet another example of the unsatisfactory response to royal plans for defence. It also shows us the vikings'

47 Oman, i, p. 140.
48 Abbo, pp. 8, 12, 14.

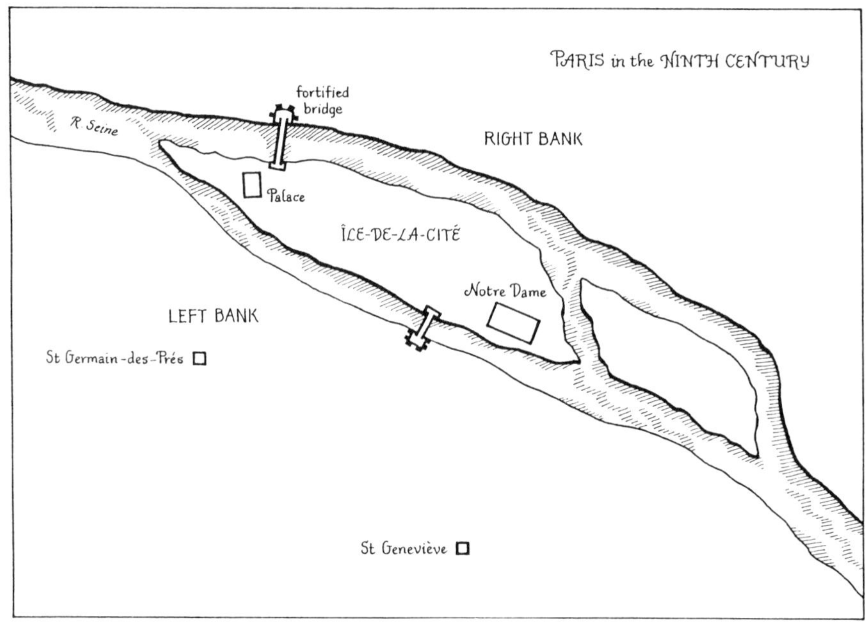

sharp eye for a weak point on which to concentrate attack. However, the unfinished tower held out, and over-night the defenders hastily erected an upper stage in wood. Paris became proud of its courageous defence, but if the city had been taken, the citizens might well have shouldered the blame for their dilatory efforts in building fortifications.

Next day the vikings were faced by a heightened tower, of which 'night was the mother'. In the morning, according to the poet, both the sun and the Danes returned: there was a fierce fight, and *balistae* were used against the tower, presumably siege engines rather than crossbows, though the Latin word may mean either. The vikings tried to mine the wall with iron picks, but the defenders poured on their heads a liquefied mixture of wax and pitch which had been heated in a fierce furnace. The citizens also had their engines, and one bolt from a *balista* transfixed seven Danes, the human kebab then being ordered off to the kitchen by a humorist among the defenders.[49]

Abbo says there were 40,000 Danes attacking 200 defenders of the tower.[50] We may wonder about his figures, but can reasonably assume that it was a large viking army. Noise filled the air, stones landed on painted shields, arrows pierced helmets. Danes returned from raiding on horseback to join the attack on the tower, but still the defence held. The vikings returning to their camp tore their hair and wept, and their women asked

49 Abbo, p. 22, l. 90: *Nox fuit ejus genitrix*; and the kebab, l. 87: *Conmiscentur eis funde lacereque baliste*.
50 Abbo, p. 24.

them why they were coming back before they had succeeded. Finally a breach was made, but a group of Franks stood in the gap while their comrades desperately gave them cover from the top of the tower. The vikings used fire against the gate, and smoke enveloped the men and the building, and hid the view of those watching anxiously from the city walls. Citizens sallied from the town behind two bearers with saffron banners. The vikings were driven back from the tower, but Robert the Strong was wounded in the fighting. At night once more hasty repairs were made to the battered tower.

After three desperate days of fighting, the vikings drew off. The initial attempt to storm the tower had failed, so now they moved to the right bank and built a new camp, apparently using stone in its construction. They raided around, committing various atrocities according to Abbo: killing children, young, old, infants before the eyes of their parents; enslaving freemen, and freeing serfs – which the poet obviously saw as a crime. They prepared for a more sustained assault, building siege engines, another indication that the 'barbarians' of early medieval history knew not only how to use siege engines, but also how to make them.

So the attack was renewed. A thousand grenades of lead were shot on to the town. The vikings attacked in three groups on land, while at the same time a painted ship headed for the bridge. On land they formed a *testudo* of shields, a 'ceiling' to protect themselves.[51] One viking was hit in his open mouth by a javelin, and another was killed by an arrow shot from the tower, and fell into the ditch he was helping to fill. They brought up one of the belfries, shooting arrows from its openings, occupied the ditches and made mounds of earth ready for the final assault.

The tower was surrounded, but not the whole city, which suggests that the viking force was not enormous, and that they lacked the resources to blockade the city. This seems a more likely conclusion than the view that the vikings lacked the military sense to do the job properly. In Abbo's account which, if we disregard its literary flights and probable exaggerations, is still our best source, the siege seems to have been mainly of the bridgehead tower. Possibly the vikings' aim was simply to break the obstacle on the river. Nevertheless attacks were made on the city: the three engines were dragged into position, one against the tower, one against the gates, and one on the heights of Montmartre. The defenders made 'pieces of wood with iron teeth' to use against the engines, as well as mangonels.[52] The vikings were still not able to get a belfry close enough to the tower, and tried instead to set fire to the bridge. The sky turned dark with smoke.

[51] Abbo, on catapult p. 28, l. 7: *Centeno catapulta nimis de corpore pernix*; on wheeled machine pp. 30–2, on p. 30, l. 205: *Ergo bis octonis faciunt . . . monstra rotis*; on *balista* p. 22, on *testudo* p. 36, l. 266: *Et tanta miraretur testudine picta.*

[52] Abbo, p. 42, ll. 360–1: *Magno cum pondere nostri/Tigna parant, quorum calibis dens summa peragrat.*

In the city the streets were empty, mothers beat their naked breasts (according to Abbo the eye-witness), and men cried out. The vikings mocked their enemy, beating with hands on shields. The defenders came out and captured two of the belfries, but the vikings still managed to force their way into the city: one broke a church window with a branch; one fell from a high tower on to the roof of a church. Count Odo himself fought on the ramparts at the time of crisis, and again the city was saved.

The worst of the menace was past, but there were still some anxious moments. One night the bridge between the city and the left bank broke in the middle, and this encouraged the Danes to renew their attack on the relevant tower, so that the earth trembled, but again they failed. They tried lighting a wagon against the gate, filling the air with smoke, they shot catapults and fired the tower, but they could not take it.

The king approached to relieve Paris, sending on ahead Henry duke of Saxony. The duke surveyed the viking position: to 'see for himself how the army could attack their camp, or where they should pitch their own camp'.[53] Judging by Abbo's response the city was not especially welcoming. The siege was not over yet, which suggests that the viking force was at least large enough to risk combat with the relief force, and Siegfried made renewed efforts, digging ditches to defend himself. Nor was the city in good heart: Bishop Gozlin died, and there was plague in the town from the unburied corpses. On one occasion the vikings reached the island at that part where the walls were at their lowest. Duke Henry himself died, when his horse fell into the viking ditches. They caught and killed him, though his own men were able to rescue the body. It seems that the vikings also received reinforcements. There was yet another furious exchange of bolts, lead and great stones. The city responded by appealing to God, and in the style usually associated with Constantinople, but clearly favoured in the West too, the citizens carried the Virgin in procession to the eastern end of the city.

Abbo gives little credit to Charles the Fat, but the arrival of the king led to a victory in battle outside the walls, and brought the siege to an end. The *Chronicle of St Vaast* is critical of the agreement the king made with the vikings: 'a truly most lamentable decision', paying ransom for the city and giving the vikings permission to go on to Burgundy, leaving the land reduced to a desert.[54] Probably the Frankish victory was not as overwhelming as they claimed, but Paris had been saved, and the occasion was a landmark in the history of the viking threat and in the history of Europe.

In the ninth century siege warfare was still focused on repelling external invasions, with Carolingian civilisation sheltering behind town walls. In the early medieval period, the sieges of Constantinople and Paris are

53 *St Vaast*, 886, p. 43. I am indebted to Simon Coupland for the use of his translation of this chronicle, which is shortly to be published by Manchester UP.
54 *St Vaast*, 886, p. 62.

symbolic of the warfare of the age, but change was on the way. The fortification of camps, bridges, smaller sites, especially during the course of the viking wars, led to a new style of fortification in the West, which saw the beginnings of European castles. Allied to social and military changes, the castle would take the West into a new age of siege warfare.

CHAPTER THREE

The Beginnings of Castle Warfare, 950–1060

Early Castles

The beginning of castle warfare is of enormous importance to our study, since it signifies the beginning of a new kind of siege warfare, essentially the start of that kind of siege war which is special to the medieval period. Yet one cannot easily grasp the vital moment, the development was not as dramatic and sudden as some have suggested. Neither the knight on horseback, nor the castle, nor the feudal society of which they are representatives, emerged overnight in 950 or any other date. They are all gradual developments which slowly merged into the new medieval world.

Some features, thought to be typically medieval, were in evidence during the very early post-Roman period, and sophisticated siege methods were already widely known and used. There were not many elements in fortification which were new to the tenth century, and those which were novel were not earth-shaking advances on what had gone before. One development which does appear to be new was the motte and bailey castle, but its chief merits were cheapness and speed of building, otherwise it had no particular advantage over stone towers with enclosures which had long been in existence, continued to co-exist with motte and bailey castles, and in the long run outlasted them.

It has been said that the castle is distinct from other fortifications because it is both a fortification and a residence. There is some truth in this, but simple definition and distinction is not always possible. Archaeologists have shown that structures which fulfil these requirements existed where they were not expected, for example, at Goltho in Lincolnshire during the Anglo-Saxon period.[1] Nor is it easy to distinguish the citadel in an early medieval town from the castle in a later medieval town. Even the same word, *arx*, was used for both, and this is true of all the Latin words. If castles were new, they did not require the invention of new words, except

1 Beresford, 'Goltho', pp. 13–36.

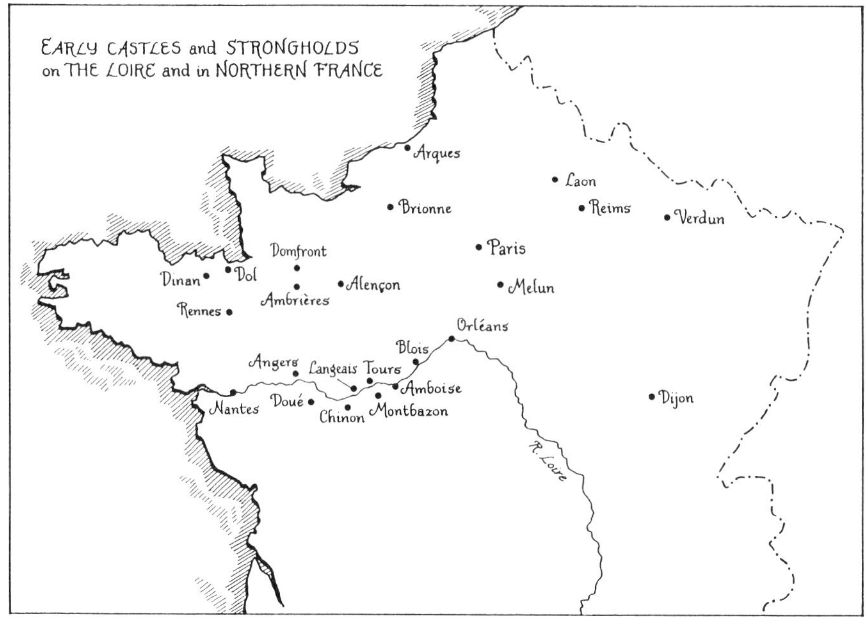

in remoter areas, and this was partly because in both appearance and function they resembled things that were already known.

Which are the earliest known castles? The accepted examples for this claim are two fortifications in the same region, Doué-la-Fontaine, and Langeais in the Loire Valley. Doué has only fairly recently achieved the distinction of being labelled the earliest European castle, since its antiquity was only appreciated as a result of the excavation between 1967 and 1970. Doué was a comital palace which changed hands between the counts of Blois and Anjou. The hall seems to have been built in about 900 AD by the count of Blois, suffered a serious fire, and was then restored in the mid-tenth century with an extra storey. At the same time, the ground floor entrance was blocked so that entry had to be by the first floor, and a forebuilding was constructed over the entrance. In other words it was rebuilt to resemble a stone tower keep, for which it is a model. In about 1000 AD a motte was added round the tower. It was captured from Blois by Fulk Nerra, count of Anjou, in about 1025.[2]

These are interesting changes, but do they deserve to be interpreted, as they usually are, by suggesting that in the mid-tenth century Doué was transformed into a castle? If so, all we are saying is that a castle requires a certain standard of fortification, since Doué was already a residence, and as a stone hall, already possessed some defensive strength. In other words, all that hap-

2 R.A. Brown, *English Castles*, p. 24; J. Bradbury, 'French Castles', in *Castles: A History and Guide*, p. 149.

pened in the tenth century was an improvement of the defences, presumably because of the need for better defence in the period of great hostility between the two counts who fought over it. To some extent, that is indeed all that we wish to suggest: that the emergence of 'castles' was in most cases simply the improvement of the defences of existing defended residences. Purpose built castles would emerge, but many of our best known early castles were existing residences, usually already defended. There was a considerable amount of such improvements made in the tenth century, which has therefore been seen as the time when castles first appeared, but it becomes a less dramatic development when viewed in this way.

Motte and Bailey Castles

During the tenth and eleventh centuries kings and counts possessed stone built palaces which were continually strengthened defensively. By the eleventh century there were also innumerable earthwork fortifications, whose structure varied considerably. An earth bank and ditch was probably the most common defence for early fortifications. Many of the eleventh-century earthwork fortifications were simply enclosures with timber buildings within, others enclosed a raised mound, often artificially built up of earth. The motte and bailey castle typically consisted of the motte or mound, with a timber keep on or in it, and a palisade round the summit; and the bailey, an earthwork enclosure usually consisting of a bank and ditch with a palisade.

The origin of motte and bailey castles is obscure, indeed unknown. We are familiar with this type of castle in England, because it was far and away the most common kind of castle built by the Norman conquerors. About half a dozen had been built in England by continental supporters of Edward the Confessor, but in the fifty years or so after 1066 hundreds were built, and the face of the countryside was altered for ever. It has been suggested that the Norman Conquest itself saw the development of this kind of castle. Well authenticated motte and bailey castles are difficult to locate on the continent before 1066, but probably because archaeology has not yet made much headway on this subject, rather than because such castles did not exist. There are many grounds for believing that they are earlier than 1066. There are large numbers of motte and bailey sites which are potentially earlier but have yet to be excavated. There are such castles depicted on the Bayeux Tapestry, which admittedly was probably not made until ten years after the Conquest, but is portraying events before 1066, and shows three such castles in Brittany: at Dol, Rennes and Dinan; as well as those at Bayeux and Beaurain, and one in England built by the invaders at Hast-

[3] Wilson, *Bayeux Tapestry*: for Rouen, pl. 13; for Dol, pl. 21; for Rennes, pl. 22; for Dinan, pl. 23; for Bayeux, pl. 25; for Hastings, pl. 49–50.

ings.[3] Motte and bailey castles also appeared in Italy, built by the Norman conquerors, making it very likely that they knew of them in Normandy, and then built them in both England and Sicily. There are also motte and bailey castles in other regions, notably in the Low Countries and on the Loire.

One possible cause of the motte and bailey development was the need to heighten settlement sites because of flooding in the low-lying northern coastal regions. There is no doubt that mounds were made for this purpose, and could well have simply become fashionable in other areas where their defensive merit remained, if the original cause did not. It is also significant that motte and bailey castles first seem to have appeared in areas attacked by the vikings, and might represent Scandinavian fortification, or a new and quick style of fortification suitable against raiders. It is also possible that they were developed by Scandinavians who settled in these regions. We know that vikings stayed for a time on the Loire and along the northern coasts, and even more permanently on the Seine, where Normandy was founded as a duchy under the viking dynasty of Rollo. There is no doubt that some of the lords who built themselves castles were of Scandinavian extraction, some even boasted of it. Scandinavians knew about earthwork defences, and earth mounds, their town development of the period shows the use of earth banks and ditches, for example at Hedeby.[4] Scandinavian burial mounds, among a people still pagan, look remarkably like mottes. They had encountered Frankish fortifications, and seen their worth. On the whole motte and bailey castles, where built defensively, were put up by lesser men, by local lords with fewer resources than kings, dukes and counts: a motte offered some of the advantages of a stone tower, without the same expense. The suggestion is, then, that Scandinavian settlers in the west, emulating Frankish defences, were responsible for adapting their knowledge of earthwork structures in order to create new fortified residences.

A well known excavated site, at the Husterknupp, shows the story of the emergence of at least one motte and bailey castle.[5] It began as a fortified residence, a farmstead with an enclosure. Gradually a mound built up as the strong point and focus of the settlement, and by the twelfth century it had become a fully developed motte and bailey castle: the stronghold on the motte, the original enclosure as the bailey. What we have here, from a lesser man than the counts of Blois and Anjou, is a very similar process, a residence already fortified to some degree, having its defences strengthened between the tenth and twelfth centuries.

4 On motte and bailey castles and viking fortification, see Roesdahl, *Viking Age Denmark*, and Davison, 'Early earthwork castles'.

5 For Husterknupp, see R.A. Brown, *English Castles*, p. 37; W. Anderson, *Castles*, p. 41; A. Herrnbrodt, 'Der Husterknupp'.

Counts and Castellans

It is thought that castles developed with feudalism, and again there is some truth in the idea. This is not the place to go into a lengthy discussion of the nature and definition of feudalism, which is a modern concept, and has been interpreted in many different ways, to the point where an accepted definition is perhaps impossible. One could almost wish to dispense with the term altogether, but it is too late in the day.[6] A typical definition, and one which will suffice us for now, is that feudalism was a form of society, existing when the fief was significant as the basis of an exchange between lord and vassal of military service for land. There seems now to be a consensus among historians that the symptoms of feudalism, mounted knights and castles, appeared on the scene rather later in the day than was once thought. We may therefore, perhaps, take it that feudalism itself is not to be sought until a later period, perhaps the eleventh rather than the eighth century.[7]

It has been said that castles emerged for defence against invaders: Saracens, vikings, and Magyars; but more significant development appears to be occurring in the period after these threats had passed their peak. It was in the succeeding period, in the later tenth and the eleventh centuries, during which Europe was recovering from the onslaught, and when the great western principalities were becoming established, that castles emerged. Perhaps they simply signify the increased social importance of their possessors. Royal fortification takes up little space in this present discussion, because what we are really looking at is a matter of social mobility. We are not discussing the appearance of a new class, since most of the aristocracy of the period were descended from the old Carolingian nobility, but rather a change in the balance of power between different social groups.[8] In particular, it is the age of rising comital power, and of the struggle of princes not only with royalty, but with the menacingly emergent group of castellans. Castles are the sign of the rise of these two groups: counts and castellans. Castles have more to do with internal social struggle in the west than with defence against external invasion. Hence they fail to conform in distribution to frontier patterns. Of course they were used to

6 E.A.R. Brown, 'The Tyranny of a construct'.

7 Duby, *The Chivalrous Society*', *and La Société au XIe et XIIe siècles*; Poly and Bournazel, *La Mutation Féodale* Fourquin, *Lordship and Feudalism*; M. Chibnall, 'Military Service in Normandy before 1066'; Le Patourel, *Norman Empire*, p. 253; R.A. Brown, *Normans and the Norman Conquest*, p. 81 and n. 154; Dunbabin, *Making of France*, pp. 232–7; Bates, *Normandy Before 1066*, pp. 106, 113–14. There is hardly consensus about the origins of feudalism, or even over what feudalism was; and for a move in the other direction, i.e. to seeing signs in an earlier period, see J. Nelson, 'Ninth Century Knighthood'.

8 On continuation of nobility, see e.g. Dunbabin, pp. 101–8, Bates, *Normandy Before 1066*, p. 111.

defend frontiers, but their scatter across the land shows that this is not a complete explanation of their function. They represent much more the rise and fall of individuals and families.

Castles could certainly be used for offensive purposes, for example, by the Normans in the conquests of England and Sicily, and by the Franks moving eastwards, and on crusade, but they were employed rather as the Romans used forts when invading Britain than as fortified residences. In other words, if we are to treat such structures as castles, we must see that castles were not always fortified residences, even though in time that it what they became. Many castles were built initially for military purposes alone.

What emerges is to some extent a blurring of our definitions and distinctions. We see that the castle is not altogether a novelty, that citadels, stone and earth fortifications, residential fortifications all have a long pedigree. However, just as the massive appearance of stone walls around Roman towns in the period of the later Roman Empire must have significance, so does the appearance in large numbers of smaller fortifications in the tenth and eleventh centuries. That significance seems to be not defence against invasion, but the appearance of a more aggressive society, vying among its families for power as it began to expand outwards. It represents in some sense the economic emergence of Europe with its rising population. It is a world in which more political power and more economic resources are in the hands of those who had previously been of less significance, the counts and castellans.

Threats to the West

We should not, therefore, expect startling new siege techniques in an age when the development in fortification is less dramatically new than we might have been led to anticipate. What we do find, however, are some excellent detailed narrative descriptions of the siege methods employed. We should also note the change of emphasis from siege in defence against invaders from outside Christendom who have different methods of warfare, to in-fighting between Christian lords using very similar techniques to each other.

Perhaps because the struggle was often between Christians, or perhaps because it was frequently between rivals of more or less equal strength, negotiation seems to play a greater rôle. It also speaks for the strength of the fortifications in this period: had they been easy to take, negotiation would rarely have been necessary. When it was necessary to make a longer siege, we find all the classic techniques employed: mining, ramming, escalade, throwing engines, as well as trickery, efforts to affect morale and so on. When sieges were fought to the finish, the penalties exacted could be ferocious, as when, at Alençon, William the Conqueror cut off the hands and feet of the offending garrison. An even more unpleasant fate befell nearly all the garrison captured by Theobald I in Italy, when he castrated them. One captive, more fortunate than others, had a loving wife, who came to beg for mercy as he was about to suffer his fate: she ran out distraught, fired by love for her husband, with hair flying, tearing at her cheeks with her nails. She begged for 'that member on which the warmth of our body depends', and on which 'the hopes of children in the future are centred'. She said if her husband offended again the victor could take any part of him, hands or feet, but should still 'leave what is mine': fortunately for both, Theobald was in merciful mood.[9]

The mid-tenth century saw the last major threat of external invasion of the early medieval period. The nomad Magyars had been raiding into eastern Europe for about half a century, a threat which undoubtedly helped to precipitate military reform within the recently developed kingdom of the East Franks, where Henry the Fowler 'accomplished something like a military revolution'. He reorganised the army and the defences, owing some debt to the ideas of Charles the Bald's activities against the vikings. Henry I introduced a system which required a proportion of the landed classes to fortify and garrison strongholds: one in every nine was to live in a stronghold and build shelter there for his eight fellows. They should continue to see to the land, and would supply a proportion of their product to supply the stronghold. Henry also gave greater emphasis to the training of his army, and the increased use of mounted warriors.[10]

The nature of the respective fortifications of the Germans and the Magyars remains a matter of some debate. Once again we find that the so-called civilised power has no monopoly. Henry the Fowler did develop Werlar, another site which gradually evolved from a palace with some fortification, to a site which in plan has interesting similarities to motte and bailey castles, having two small enclosures and two large ones, almost like a double motte and bailey castle.[11] The extent this fortification had reached under Henry is, however, uncertain. The Hungarians also possessed interesting fortifications in earthwork and timber: they had a policy of scorching the earth around their strongholds, making 'defensive wastes' which included traps and obstacles, and thus making sieges against them difficult. They developed unusual ramparts, some with earth boxed between timber, others where the clay was fired into a ceramic state. This latter technique seems to have been deliberate, and may have been

9 Bates, *William the Conqueror*, p. 34; William of Jumièges, p. 126, on Alençon. For a discussion on the date, see Douglas, *William the Conqueror*, pp. 384–85, and Bates, *William the Conqueror*, pp. 255–6. On Tedbald I, Marquis of Spoleto, see Liudprand of Cremona, p. 148

10 For Henry the Fowler see Leyser, *Medieval Germany*, p. 14.

11 On Werlar, Anderson, *Castles*, p. 40; and Stearns, *Greater Medieval Historians*, p. 206, for Adam of Bremen.

achieved by building vertical air shafts through the rampart then firing timber so that the clay was turned to a shiny, tough consistency which made assault difficult.[12]

When the Hungarians attacked Pavia in Italy, in 924, they surrounded the town with earthworks, and pitched their tents in a circle around their target. They threw torches over the wall, so that an inhabitant could claim 'our fair Pavia in fire has passed away'.[13] During the course of their raids, they had killed the Bavarian leader Liutpold in 907, and taken tribute. It was Henry the Fowler who stopped the payment of this tribute, and so provoked a new clash. At last the Hungarians were defeated in the battle of Riade on the River Unstrut. Now the tables were turned.

There was one last major clash, but significantly it arose out of internal dispute within the German kingdom. There was rebellion against Otto I led by his own son, Liudolf. In 954 the latter called in the Magyars to his aid, and thus lost the sympathy and support of most of his countrymen. The rebellion melted away, but the Magyars continued to threaten: they besieged Augsburg, a city surrounded by rather sub-standard walls, lacking towers, and by 955 seen as old and in poor condition. Udalrich, bishop of Augsburg, collected a force for its defence. The Magyars tried to storm the East Gate, but the bishop's men made a sortie and held on. At night the garrison patched the ramparts and built new block-houses. The female citizens made procession, praying for delivery. The next day the Magyars brought up engines, their men driven forward with whips, but still failed to take the city. Now Otto I arrived with an army, and the Magyars abandoned the siege to fight him. The bishop of Augsburg himself mounted and encouraged the Christians, though wearing a stole and not armour, and carrying no weapons. Stones fell around him but he was unhurt. Otto's army included men from all over Germany. The Magyars assembled their force by using smoke signals. Otto advanced with the Angelus, the standard of St Michael, carried before him, and won a famous victory. The Magyars were pursued past the city walls, some drowning in the Lech in their efforts to escape. The battle of the Lechfeld in 955 was a genuine turning point in European history: the Magyar invasions were halted, and they now chose to settle in Hungary. Otto I had won a great reputation as the defender of Christendom, and this assisted greatly in his obtaining from the papacy the title of Holy Roman Emperor. After the battle, the Hungarians settled: they became Christian and established a new kingdom. They also developed castles in an interesting way: founding a political organisation based around castles at the

12 On Hungarian fortification, see Fügedi, p. 37 on defensive wastes, and p. 28 on ceramic ramparts.

13 For Pavia, see Liudprand, pp. 110–11; the quotation is on p. 111.

centre of counties. By the time of King Stephen of Hungary, there were some 45 of these castle-counties.[14]

The siege of Augsburg is more in the pattern of early medieval siege warfare, both in its style, and in its cause. In the mid-tenth century the focus in the West moved to warfare within the Christian lands, where the possession of castles by counts and castellans was vital in determining the nature of the conflicts. However the depth of this development was greater in the Frankish heartlands than elsewhere in Europe. Castles appeared more slowly outside Francia, and so in these fringe areas warfare also retained a more old-fashioned appearance.

England also retained a pre-castle form of warfare. Here the Scandinavian invasions had a further success in the eleventh century when Sweyn and his family eventually won control, and Cnut and his sons became kings of England. The central event of their triumph, at least in the eyes of the author of the *Encomium Emmae*, was the siege of London in 1016.

Cnut decided to concentrate on London because 'the chief men and the army were within'.[15] Aethelred II, the Unready, died in London before the siege got under way, but the citizens still resisted, encouraged by his son Edmund Ironside who left the city in order to rally support. The Danes blockaded London, building ditches and ramparts, and bringing up ships. The citizens surrendered, but the garrison held out, which proves the existence of a citadel in London before the Tower of London was built. Cnut held the city, but did not feel safe there, fearing the attitude of the Londoners, and needing to be somewhere more secure in order to repair his ships, so he withdrew to Sheppey for the winter. Edmund re-entered London, and stayed there through the winter months. He challenged Cnut to single combat, a frequent ploy of the underdog, and was refused, remarking: 'you who want to fight in winter, beware lest you fail to appear even when the time is more appropriate'.[16] In the spring Cnut won the battle of Ashingdon, partly through the failure of Eadric Streona to fight for Edmund. Cnut's victory was reinforced by the death of Edmund in the same year.

Cities rather than castles also continue to figure in sieges in other parts of Europe. In Italy, before the arrival of the Normans, the Greeks and Lombards 'tried to defend their ancient rights and liberties behind the walls of their great cities and towns'.[17] We have already seen cities involved in early tenth-century sieges in Italy, as that of Pavia by the Magyars.

14 On Augsburg and the Lechfeld, see B.H. Hill, *Rise of the First Reich*, pp. 15–18; Leyser, *Medieval Germany*, pp. 43–66; Gerhard, pp. 401–2.

15 On London, see *Encomium Emmae*, pp. 23–5, the quotation is on p. 23; *Anglo-Saxon Chronicle*, ed. Whitelock, p. 95; Thietmar of Meuseburg, *Chronicle*, in *EHD*, ii, pp. 348–9.

16 *Encomium Emmae*, p. 25.

17 Orderic Vitalis, ii, p. 100.

Eleventh-century illustration of a siege

Sieges in Francia

In Francia, however, now diverging into the separate kingdoms of France and Germany, one can see the beginnings of castle warfare. Structurally the difference is the growing number of small fortifications, representing the growth in power of the counts and castellans. Instead of a national system of fortifications built for public defence, such as the burh system in England, where Worcester, for example, was built 'to shelter all the folk', one finds smaller, private fortifications built by lords for their own protection.[18]

It might be thought that smaller fortifications would be easier to surround and to take, but they were also easier to defend in depth. It would normally be possible to find a vulnerable point in a long stretch of town walls, easier to find one traitor among a mass of citizens, easier to implant spies among the hundreds of ordinary folk, than to get into a highly fortified castle, well sited and with a committed garrison.

The early tenth-century sources record a good deal of building activity, repairing and strenthening existing fortifications, with concentration upon smaller strongholds, citadels and castles. One of the best sources for the tenth century is Richer's *History of France*. His own father was involved in the warfare, and though the author borrowed some of his material from classical sources, he is informative on details of siege warfare. Richer mentions the building of an *arx* at Guisnes in 931; and at Laon in 938 he refers

[18] *Cartularium Saxonicum*, ii, p. 222.

to the 'recently built' citadel occupied by the count's garrison. In the mid-tenth century one hears of *castella* at Dijon, La Fere, Montfelix, and Roucy.[19]

Richer's account of the siege of Verdun by King Lothar in 985 reinforces the idea of changing defensive organisation. The stronghold was on a steep cliff over the Meuse. There was no approach from the rear which was a rocky precipice. Lothar prepared engines, but when no help came after eight days, the citizens surrendered. Lothar left his queen in command, but the story was not finished. In the king's absence, Count Thierry of Lorraine managed to break in by employing a ruse, and took control of the Enclosure of the Merchants, which appears to have been virtually a castle. It was a walled enclosure separated from the town by the Meuse, and only linked to it by two bridges.

Lothar returned and found himself having to prepare a siege for the second time, when success proved less easy. He had to settle down to blockade, fortifying his camp with earthworks, and building siege engines, which the enemy also possessed. Lothar himself was wounded on the mouth by a missile. The royal army attached hooks to the enemy engine, and nearly pulled it over: the men inside fell out and were attacked and killed. Finally the garrison surrendered.[20]

On the death of Lothar in 986 there was a struggle for control in West Francia, which resulted in the triumph of Hugh Capet and the establishment of a new dynasty. Hugh's rival was Charles duke of Lower Lorraine, who, according to Richer, damaged his chances by marriage to a woman of the military class. One of the keys to success in this conflict was control of Laon. Charles made his bid for control, and arrived at Laon at sunset, with his men hidden around. They made a great noise at the town gate, and although some of the inhabitants threw stones from the walls, Charles had made arrangements whereby the gates were opened to him. The army entered amidst blasts from trumpets, cries, and the clash of arms. Citizens took to their houses or, if in real despair, threw themselves down from the walls. The bishop of Laon was himself captured hiding among the vines. So Charles took the city and put 500 guards in the high tower around which he built new defensive ditches. Charles also made new engines, bringing in the wood for them and employing smiths to make the projectiles. Richer says that his arbalasters were so skilled they could hit birds in flight without fail.[21]

Now Hugh Capet arrived to try and wrest Laon from his rival, or at least to prevent his force within Laon growing any greater. He built a new

19 Richer, i, p. 141, on Guisnes 931 and Laon 938.

20 On Verdun, Richer, ii, pp. 129–39.

21 On the duke of Lorraine's marriage, Richer, ii, p. 161; a reference which clearly implies marriage to someone of lower social standing described as *uxorem de militari ordine*. On Laon, Richer, ii, pp. 169–81. Latouche suggests this is one siege made into two by Richer.

besieging camp with ditches and ramparts, but found Laon hard to approach because of the steep slope before it. Also autumn had arrived, the days were growing short, and the sentries were tired by the long night watches. He decided that it was too late in the year for operations, and disbanded his army with the intention of returning in the spring.

Charles inspected the defences and decided to strengthen them by blocking the gates, making repairs, and filling in spaces between the city wall and nearby houses. He also strengthened the tower within and without. The captive bishop managed to slide down a rope at night, and escaped to join Hugh Capet. In the spring, according to Richer, Hugh returned. He employed a skilled engineer to make a new engine, but the effort of producing it was wasted since they could not manage to pull it up the steep slope. The siege was brought to its conclusion not by engines but by wine: on a certain day both besiegers and besieged seem to have over-indulged. In the case of the besiegers it had made them drowsy and they slept it off, whereas the garrison had been made excited into attempting a sortie: they attacked the besieging camp and fired it, making noxious fumes. For Hugh it was the last straw and he decided to leave Laon to Charles.

Duke Charles also managed to gain Reims by arranging to have the gates opened at night by his ally, the priest Augier.[22] His army then entered the town and pillaged it. According to Richer, its castellan, Arnoul, was in the conspiracy against Hugh, but pretended to be surprised at the entry of Charles. The latter found Arnoul in the tower, and locked him in until he surrendered, when he was taken off to imprisonment at Laon. Richer's version sounds unlikely, the treatment of Arnoul hardly being that given to an ally, though Arnoul did later take an oath of fidelity to Charles and was released, thus no doubt earning Richer's hostility.

Despite these setbacks Hugh Capet had the greater success in the conflict. It was during Hugh's kingship that the siege of Melun occurred in 991. Odo, count of Chartres, believed that Melun should be a family possession, and tried to reclaim it from the king. It was an important strategic stronghold, guarding a crossing of the Seine. It was also a good site, on an island in the middle of the river. Odo sent a spy to gain the trust of the castellan, and then offered the man other towns in return for betraying the king and handing over the castle. Troops were hidden around Melun, and when the attackers were allowed in, the castellan was arrested and imprisoned for show. He was released on giving an oath of fidelity to Odo.

The king came to relieve Melun, building a camp on the south bank of the river. He had made an alliance with the Normans, who appeared on the north bank, and also came up the river in ships. The garrison resisted,

[22] On Reims, Richer, ii, pp. 195–9.

but the Normans broke through the gate and took many captives whom they handed over to the king. He kept some as hostages but released the others, declaring that they had only fought for their own lord. The traitorous castellan and his wife, however, were hanged near the gate, the wife suffering 'unheard of outrage', stripped naked and hanged by her feet alongside her husband. Odo, when informed of the execution of his helpers, expressed no regret over the fate of the man he had suborned, saying that he felt more sorry for the garrison than for a traitor.[23]

Anjou and Blois

The earliest known castles, Doué-la-Fontaine and Langeais, are both found in the borderland between the counties of Anjou and Blois, and represent the new fortifications appearing in the course of the conflict between these increasingly powerful principalities of Francia. And where we have the earliest known castles, we have the earliest known castle warfare, the type of siege warfare which will dominate the West through the rest of the middle ages. The warfare of the period now under discussion is dominated by the conflicts between principalities, and between the counts and dukes and their vassals: a fact which demonstrates that in this period power depended not only on a struggle between kings and aristrocracies, but also on the tensions between magnates, and between magnates and their vassals.

One of the greatest of the counts of the age was Fulk Nerra, count of Anjou from 987 to 1040.[24] His career is an excellent example of the growing importance of castles. He was an aggressive and rumbustious man. He had his first wife burned to death seemingly for her adultery. According to one story his second wife, Hildegard, feared that she was about to suffer the same fate when Fulk sent her a cup with the message that it was from the man she loved best. To escape punishment she leaped out of the window: only later was it made clear that Fulk had meant himself by 'the man she loved best'. Fortunately Hildegard had fallen into the river and not to her death, though one cannot help but wonder about Fulk's response to her action. Fulk also had problems with his son, Geoffrey Martel, himself to become a famous and successful count. At one point Geoffrey rebelled against his father but was defeated: Fulk then beat and kicked his prostrate son before allowing a reconciliation. Perhaps these incidents from

23 On the Melun outrage, Richer, ii, pp. 267–75; the quotation, *inusitato ludibrii* is on p. 274. There is a problem over dating the siege. Here it is 991, but William of Jumièges, p. 93, gives 999. I have preferred Richer's date.

24 For the career of Fulk Nerra, see e.g. Norgate, *Angevin Kings*, i, ch. 3, pp. 143–88; Guillot, *Le Comte d'Anjou*, pp. 15–55; Hallam, *Plantagenet Chronicles*, pp. 22–9; Bachrach, 'Fulk Nerra', pp. 331–42. But for a full biography one still needs the rather dated de Salies.

his private life explain the need he felt to go on pilgrimage to Jerusalem on at least two occasions. Under Fulk Nerra, we see Anjou emerging from the damage done during the viking period, when the Loire like the Seine had been an area for Scandinavian attack and settlement. Fulk's grandson was later to write that his ancestor had 'built many castles in his lands, which had remained deserted and full of undergrowth because of the ferocity of the vikings'.[25]

Fulk Nerra's chief rival was the neighbouring count of Blois. Many of the castles in this region were first built either for defence against each other, or as an act of aggression. The castles were to play a major rôle in their struggle for dominance, several would change hands during it: thus Montboyau had a motte probably built by Fulk Nerra, and a new 'timber tower of marvellous height' built upon the motte after its capture by Odo II of Blois.[26] Montboyau had been erected by Fulk as one of a number of castles intended to threaten Tours, then in the possession of Blois. During Odo I's siege of Montboyau, he had built a great wooden belfry, but one night it had collapsed, crushing the men inside it, and had then been burned by the citizens.

On the occasion of Odo I's siege, Fulk had saved Montboyau by making a diversionary attack on Saumur, where he had taken the town and come to terms with the garrison. The strength of castles in this period, and we may treat citadels within towns as castles, is well demonstrated by the large number of sieges that could not be brought to a conclusion by storming or even blockading, and had to be settled by agreement. The garrison of Saumur agreed to enter the service of Fulk, though he preferred to leave some of his own men in control of the place before going on to besiege and take Montbazon. This was sufficient to lure Odo away from Montboyau, though in the settlement finally reached between the two counts, Fulk agreed to destroy the offending new castle – but he kept Saumur.

The second oldest known castle, Langeais, also figured in this struggle. It too was built, in 994, as part of the attempt by Anjou to pressurise Tours, and was besieged by Odo I in 996. Fulk sought aid from Hugh Capet, but when the latter did not turn up, had to consider Odo's demands, which included one hundred pounds in silver, the placing of Fulk's son in Odo's service, the demolition of Langeais, and the evacuation of Nantes. When the king finally did arrive, Anjou soon lost interest in such an agreement, and Langeais eventually came to Fulk in the settlement. Chinon was another great fortress won from Blois, as was Amboise, which Fulk took by

25 On Hildegard, see Norgate, *Angevin Kings*, i, pp. 165–66, n. 3; Anderson, *Castles*, p. 46. The Fragment by Fulk IV is in Halphen and Poupardin, *Chroniques*, pp. 232–37; the quotation is on p. 233; see also J. Bradbury, *Fulk le Réchin*.

26 On Montboyau, see R.A. Brown, *English Castles*, p. 32; Salies, pp. 169, 224; Halphen, *Comté*, p. 43. It is described as *turrim ligneam mire altitudinis*, from *Chronique Vendôme*, i, pp. 286–7.

siege. Amboise was one of several places which became the centre of new lordships held by vassals of the count, going to the treasurer, Sulpice, who added a great tower to his new possession.

The warfare between Anjou and Blois often extended into Brittany. Fulk attacked Nantes, where the citizens threw down missiles at the Angevins, but surrendered the town after three weeks. The castle, however, held out and only yielded after Fulk's victory in the battle of Conquereuil. Before this battle the Bretons prepared a position by digging trenches in front of their line, which were covered over with branches. The Angevins fell into the trap, literally, and were forced into retreat, but the Breton leader, Conan, was killed, and the victory went to Fulk. It is one of the numerous occasions when the siege of a castle, in this case the citadel at Nantes, depended on the outcome of a battle, or, to put it in another way, when a battle developed from the challenge of a siege. Fulk Nerra was 'the great builder', and a great early exponent of castle warfare. He built a chain of castles in the east and the south of Anjou, along the Loire and its tributaries. He created what has been called 'the first Angevin empire', and had turned Anjou from a lesser county into a great principality.[27]

Anjou and Normandy

The eleventh century witnessed another great conflict of principalities, between Anjou under Fulk Nerra's son, Geoffrey II, known as Martel or the Hammer, and Normandy under William the Conqueror. This clash became the focus of events in France for two decades, and was not resolved even by the time of the death of the two principal contenders. The new King of France, Henry I, was drawn into their quarrels: his support for one side then the other was an important factor, as the power of the monarchy gradually evolved, but the impression is still one of great power remaining in the hands of territorial princes in the mid eleventh century.[28]

William became duke of Normandy somewhat unexpectedly when his father abandoned the duchy, at a time when his position was far from secure, in order to go on pilgrimage to the Holy Land. He was never to return. William would in time prove to be a great duke, but in 1035 he was only a young boy whose illegitimacy made his position even weaker. The frailty of Normandy at this time encouraged the count of Anjou to try and take advantage of it. Geoffrey Martel made full use of the power which his

27 For Fulk see n. 24 above; as the great builder, see Halphen, *Comté*, p. 153; and for the first Angevin Empire, Bachrach, 'Fulk Nerra', p. 331.

28 On Anjou and Normandy, the works cited in n. 24 are of course useful, to which might be added Bates, *Normandy Before 1066*; Bates, *William the Conqueror*; Le Patourel, *Norman Empire*; Douglas, *The Norman Achievement*; Douglas, *William the Conqueror*.

father had brought to the county. He sought to advance Anjou's influence in all directions, at the expense of Blois, Poitou, Brittany, and of course Normandy. Geoffrey finally wrested Tours and the whole of the Touraine from Blois, after a great victory in the battle of Nouy in 1044. In the course of this he had besieged Tours itself for a year. The garrison had brought out the bones of St Martin in their defence, but in this instance without success. Count Theobald of Blois had been captured at Nouy, and had to agree to the surrender of Tours and its territory in order to obtain his release. The count of Anjou played politics not only with the king of France, but also with the Holy Roman Emperor: William the Conqueror's rival was himself a titan among the counts. Geoffrey pressed his chances against Normandy by advancing through the fragile county of Maine which lay between their territories.

During most of the struggle between the Conqueror and Martel, Normandy was on the defensive. This may not be the impression one gets from most English and even French historians, perhaps because they make more use of the Norman than the Angevin sources. It is emphasised that William won the battles of Val-ès-Dunes, Mortemer and Varaville, and that before 1066 he never failed in taking a castle. William did win key battles, but as Guillot has properly pointed out, they were 'defensive victories': battles fought within Normandy as a result of internal rebellion or invasion by the king and the count of Anjou.[29] Most of his sieges in this period were settled not by storming, but by agreement: William was successful, but the degree of his success was considerably limited by the activities of the count of Anjou.

In the early part of William the Conqueror's rule in Normandy, his main concern was to overcome internal opposition, and Brionne played a vital rôle in the struggle. Guy of Burgundy, who held this castle as well as Vernon, had been brought up with William, but he became involved in a conspiracy against the young duke. The rebels were crushed at Val-ès-Dunes in 1047, which William of Poitiers saw as a great day since it led to the dismantling of all the unlicensed castles that had sprung up during the Conqueror's minority. Guy of Burgundy, however, escaped to the castle of Brionne, which was thought to be impregnable, its stone enclosure and stone hall overlooking the Risle: sadly nothing of this remains, since William demolished it. He had to build counter fortifications on the banks of the river to blockade Guy. William of Poitiers actually calls these *castella*, so we have a genuine example of what will become a common feature of siege warfare, the making of counter-castles to protect besiegers against relieving armies or sorties.[30] The defenders showed much spirit and made daily sorties, but gradually the blockade began to bite, and they felt

[29] Guillot, i, p. 81.

[30] William of Poitiers, on Val-ès-Dunes and the *castella*, p. 19; and for the sieges of Domfront, Alençon, Arques, Ambrières, pp. 37–79.

the pinch of famine. Guy sent envoys to William. The siege had lasted three years, but the duke chose to be merciful: Guy remained at court, later returning to Burgundy because his crime tormented him. Reading between the lines, however, the Conqueror had been forced to recognise that taking the castle was too demanding in time and resources. It is a good demonstration of the effect of castle fortification upon warfare, and how it could threaten even a great territorial prince.

By the late 1040s Geoffrey Martel had overrun Maine. When William attacked Alençon and Domfront, the Norman chronicler declared that he was attacking Angevin territory, though the castles stood on Normandy's southern border. Throughout this period William had benefited from the aid of the King of France, Henry I. He had helped save Willliam at Val-ès-Dunes, and now encouraged him to go against the Angevins. William therefore besieged Domfront, even though it was winter. One night he made a surprise move, taking troops against nearby Alençon, which he captured by storm, no doubt provoked to greater efforts by the insolence of the defenders who had dared to wave skins over the walls to remind William that his mother had been a humble tanner's daughter and that he himself was illegitimate. Their confidence in Martel's strength was not well founded: Alençon was stormed and no mercy was shown the offending citizens, who had their hands and feet chopped off.

So William returned to the siege of Domfront. Even today, in ruins, it is an impressive sight, a stone tower standing upon a massive rock over the River Varenne, visible as one approaches through the narrow streets of the quaint town below. Again the ruins are not of the castle of this period; the keep was to be built by Henry I of England, but even without a structure upon it the strength of the site would be clear. William built no less than four counter-castles; he knew that he faced a hard task. Domfront had great natural strength. There was only one direction from which it could be approached, and that was blocked by a ditch cut right across the way. The garrison was determined, reinforced with men placed there by Geoffrey Martel. William himself took the lead in attack, on his horse at all hours, either fighting or on occasions finding time to go hawking. The blockade was maintained; perhaps the defences were too good, supplies could not be smuggled in, and William attacked supply convoys. The garrison's chief hope was in relief from Geoffrey Martel, but when he did come, William left the siege to go against him, and Martel retreated, probably because of news of the king of France's activities in the Touraine. That fact, together with the news of the fate of Alençon, broke the resolve of the garrison at Domfront, but it was a surrender on terms.

William was still not safe from opposition within Normandy, and faced a dangerous rebellion by his uncle, William, count of Arques, son of Duke Richard II, and therefore able to pose as a candidate for the dukedom. His castle of Arques stood on the far side of Normandy from Domfront, on the northern coast. The count had quarreled with his nephew, and decamped from the siege of Domfront. The south now secure, the Conqueror turned his attention northwards. The castle of Arques was built upon its promontory in 1038, with strong ramparts. Again the original castle has been buried under later additions, including the massive keep of Henry I of England. William of Arques himself improved the fortifications before his nephew arrived. The Conqueror attempted storm, and failed, settling down once more to blockade. Again the task proved difficult, and he was forced into accepting terms, though the chronicler makes much of the plight of the garrison. They came out with heads bowed, some on starving beasts, most carrying their saddles. There could be no sight more pitiable than troops in such a wretched condition. According to the chaplain's chronicle, the duke was merciful, and the count deserved pity. But the fact that defeat was not complete is shown by the fact that the duke confirmed his possessions, though the chronicler says it was better to treat him as an uncle than to pursue him as an enemy.[31]

William the Conqueror's efforts to the south provoked a reaction of hostility from some of the lords in Maine, who saw his advances as a threat. When the Normans built the new castle of Ambrières, Geoffrey of Mayenne felt himself endangered and turned to Martel, who formed an alliance to attack the new castle. The besiegers tried to break through the enclosing wall, but were resisted, the garrison hurling weapons and stones, lances and javelins, from on high so that many of the attackers were killed. Then they tried a ram against the wall, but the Conqueror arrived like the US Cavalry, in the nick of time, and Martel and his allies abandoned the siege and retreated.

But the Conqueror was still on the defensive. In 1052 Henry I of France, till then an important prop for the duke, changed sides, possibly now fearing the growing power of Normandy more than that of Anjou. He participated in two invasions of Normandy, in 1054 and 1058, both of which ultimately failed thanks to William's famous victories at Mortemer and Varaville. Both invasions had led to sieges in Norman territory. After Varaville a Norman rebel who had allied with the invaders, Robert FitzGiroie, took refuge in Saint-Céneri, which the Conqueror besieged. Robert, however, died after eating poisoned apples given to him by his wife, though she protested she was innocent of any crime. Even then William did not walk into Saint-Céneri, since Arnoul FitzGiroie took over from his dead brother. Again William made a settlement, recognising Arnoul's possession of the family lands. Robert's body was buried at the monastery of Saint-Evroult. According to Orderic Vitalis, who was a monk there, even though Robert had been dead for three weeks, there was no stench from the corpse.[32]

By 1060 William the Conqueror had established himself in Normandy,

31 William of Poitiers, p. 63.

32 Orderic Vitalis, ii, p. 80.

and fought off serious threats from rebels within his duchy, and invasions by the king of France and the count of Anjou. But in 1060, it was the death of his two great rivals, Henry I of France and Geoffrey Martel of Anjou, which gave William the advantage at last; the king of France had actually been besieging Thimert when he succumbed to his last illness.

CHAPTER FOUR

Kings, Counts and Castellans, 1050–1200

Castles

The techniques of siege warfare did not change tremendously in the eleventh and twelfth centuries, but changes were forced by the emergence of the castle as the main form of fortified stronghold. Before this period fortresses were generally the possessions of the greatest, though certainly at times provided for the protection of the populace. By the eleventh century, society had feudalised and localised: if power had not exactly transferred into the hands of local lords, it had at least been redistributed in such a way that the rôle of such lords had increased considerably. The social and economic growth of local lordship was marked by the rise of local fortifications.

In England there were perhaps a few dozen fortifications before the Norman Conquest, including the half dozen castles built under Edward the Confessor. After the Conquest so many motte and bailey castles were built, that by 1200 there were several hundred fortifications. The special circumstances of invasion called for rapid fortification, and a castle at York was erected in eight days. The growth of castle building in England may have particular reasons, but is not entirely unique. In Normandy it is now accepted that very few castles can be securely dated to the period before 1050.[1] In Maine there seem to have been no castles at all before the tenth century, yet by 1100 there were sixty-two. The growth in castle building in the eleventh century was common to Western Europe. By 1200, in the words of a great French military historian, France had become 'a country of castles', and much the same has been said of Spain. A similar development has been noted in Germany and Hungary. In the eleventh and twelfth centuries castles not only became a common feature of the landscape, but were also made stronger over the years by improved fortification, for

1 For the best review of early castle development in Normandy, and elsewhere, see Brown, *English Castles*.

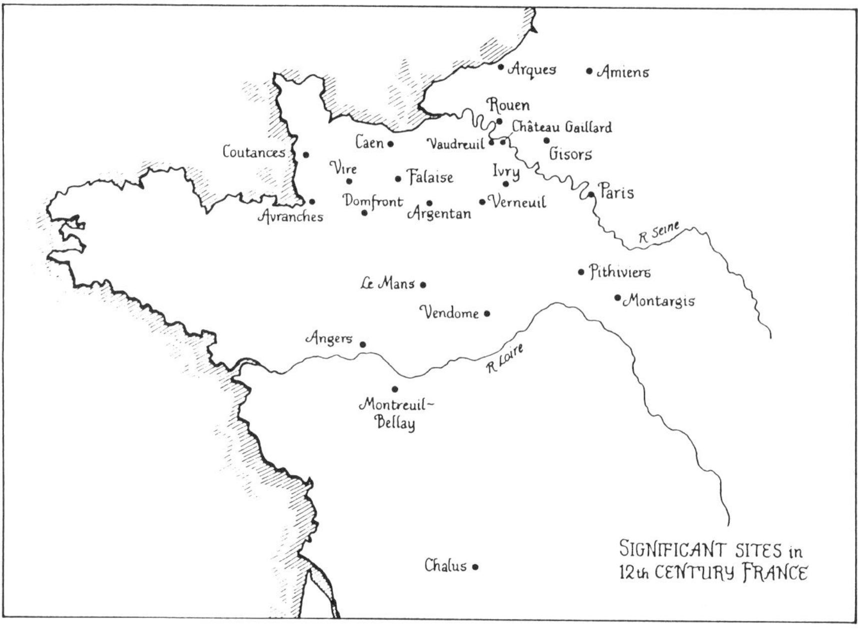

example, by replacing initial wooden defences by stone, by strengthening gatehouses and enlarging ditches.[2]

The skill of the architects who built castles came to be much valued. Orderic Vitalis tells a story about the noted architect Lanfred. In the late tenth century he built a great tower at Pithiviers, as a result of which he was invited to design the castle at Ivry. Having completed the commission he was put to death so that the secrets of Ivry would not be revealed. The Bayeux Tapestry portrays castles in Normandy, England and Brittany, all of the motte and bailey type, with ditches, palisades and timber towers. The motte excavated at Abinger in Surrey shows just such a castle, having an earth mound, with post holes for a rectangular timber tower upon it. The tower on the motte at Durham was described in a twelfth-century source as having four posts on which it rested, one at each corner, and each of the four walls having a gallery fixed to it. Lambert wrote of the tower at Ardres, built by Arnold the seneschal of the count of Boulogne. It had a high mound with a timber house upon it, constructed by Louis, a carpenter from Bourbourg. Stores were kept at ground level, and there were chambers, cellars, and a chapel built high on the east side. It possessed three storeys: the first for stores; the second for residence including a kitchen; and on the third was the family accomodation, the chapel, and a lounge. The castle built at Montargis in 1056 sounds similar: it had a wooden tower contain-

2 For the sixty-two castles in Maine, and a 'country of castles', see Contamine, pp. 44, 45; on Spain as a 'land of castles', see MacKay, *Spain*, p. 15.

The motte and bailey castle at Dol,
from the Bayeux Tapestry

ing a great hall in the upper storey, where the lord, Seguin, and his family lived. We are told that in Flanders it was the fashion for nobles to build earth mottes, and surround them by as large and deep a ditch as possible, adding palisades and towers.[3]

Many lords could afford earth and timber fortifications, and hence the dominance of this type in the age when local lords built castles. It should, however, be noted that throughout this period, and indeed before it, castles were also made in stone. The beginning of this age is marked by the construction of such castles as those at Rouen, London and Colchester, the end of it by the massive structure of Château-Gaillard. Even stone castles could be built quickly if the resources were sufficient. Château-Gaillard was the most advanced castle of its time, very nearly concentric in design, yet it was raised during the two years 1197 to 1198 at a cost of £11,500. For the most part it is true that the greater the lord, the greater the castle he could finance.[4]

Henry I of England was a great castle builder, and also strengthened many existing fortifications. At Rouen he built a new turreted wall round

[3] See Brown, *English Castles*, pp. 30, 32, 34; and for Lanfred, Orderic Vitalis, iv, p. 290; for Abinger, Hope Taylor, pp. 15–43. For Ardres, see also Finó, *Forteresses*, p. 85, and p. 111 for Montargis.

[4] On Château-Gaillard, see Gillingham, *Richard*, pp. 264–5, Brown, *English Castles*, pp. 161–3; and *Magni Rotuli Scaccarii Normanniae*, ii, p. 309.

the tower, and within the wall, buildings fit for royal residence. At Caen he raised a high tower, and heightened the walls to match. Among others he stengthened the tower and walls of Arques, and built at Gisors, Falaise, Argentan, Domfront and Vire. Castles had become vital, but they were not always welcomed by the people. *The Anglo-Saxon Chronicle* notes the amount of castle building that went on during the civil war of Stephen's reign, but also speaks of the builders oppressing the people:

> They filled the country full of castles. They oppressed the wretched people of the country severely with castle-building. When the castles were built, they filled them with devils and wicked men. Then, both by night and day they took those people that they thought had any goods – men and women – and put them in prison and tortured them.[5]

Kings and great princes led the way in castle-building, but they were followed by those aspiring to greater power, and in the end by all lords of any standing. Robert of Bellême became head of a great family with pretensions to ruling a principality. He was reviled by some chroniclers for his cruelty and deviousness, but was also respected as a builder of castles. He fortified Bridgnorth with a high and wide wall, and worked on castles at Shrewsbury, Arundel and Tickhill. Orderic Vitalis says that Robert was the 'resourceful engineer' who designed Gisors. His improvements included the digging of deeper ditches.[6] The enlarging of ditches is as important a feature as rebuilding in stone. Henry I improved the moat at Argentan, and one notes that Stephen's castle at Burwell, although only constructed for a particular campaign, featured a wide rectangular moat. The use of stone certainly became more common, in particular the use of well-cut ashlar. William of Malmesbury credits Bishop Roger of Salisbury as a great builder who used ashlar, laying the stones so closely that the whole looked like a single block. England was not exceptional in castle development, despite the Norman Conquest. As elsewhere castles multiplied, and during the eleventh and twelfth centuries underwent a series of improvements including the use of stone and more massive fortification.[7]

5 The quotation is in *Anglo-Saxon Chronicle*, E, p. 199. On Henry I, see Green, *Henry I*, p. 124, n. 33, 34, 35; Gebelin, *Chateaux of France*, pp. 309–10; and the chronicles of Orderic Vitalis, and Robert of Torigni.

6 On Robert of Bellême, see Florence of Worcester, ed. Thorpe; Florence of Worcester, ed. Stevenson, pp. 323–4; and Orderic Vitalis, iv, pp. 228–30; p. 158 as the ingenious engineer, *ingeniosus artifex*; p. 158 as 'treacherous and devious'; p. 296 on his 'madness' as a 'tyrant', *tirannus*.

7 On Burwell, see Lethbridge, 'Excavations'. On Roger of Salisbury, see William of Malmesbury, *Historia Novella*, p. 25; and *Chronicle*, ed. Giles, p. 442.

The Importance of Siege Warfare in the Age of Castles

The rapid spread of castles as the main form of fortification inevitably affected warfare. From the eleventh century siege warfare was dominated by castles, and this central medieval period was an age of war: the Norman Conquest of England, the civil war of Stephen's reign, wars between France and England, the German expeditions to Italy, the surge against Islam into Spain and the Mediterranean. It was an age of war, yet marked by only a handful of pitched battles. Battle remained a military ideal: if the warrior must die then let it be in battle. A character in the poem about Barbastro says: 'No one should die in a castle or a city, but in hard battle against the infidel. This is how I want it to be for all time.'[8]

The reality was that warfare consisted of perhaps one per cent battles and ninety-nine per cent sieges. One does not wish to suggest that battles were unimportant, it was partly because their consequences were so drastic that they were avoided when possible, but in terms of sheer numbers sieges dominated.[9] In England in this period there were only four major battles. Even those battles which did occur usually developed out of sieges. Battle was the last phase of a complicated wargame of challenge and withdrawal. To challenge an opponent the most obvious ploy was to besiege one of his castles. It was a challenge to lordship. If your opponent wished to retain power, he must demonstrate his ability to protect the castle and the area. Orderic Vitalis described the challenge from Le Mans to Robert Curthose: 'If you wish to retain this castle, come with a strong relieving force'. If the challenge were accepted, a relief force would indeed be sent. When Louis VII besieged Verneuil, Henry II, coming to save it, demanded: 'either raise the siege or shrink not from fighting a decisive battle'. Louis shrank and retreated. It was only at this point, when all the challenges were accepted, and provided the challenger did not now back down, that there would be battle. Siege was almost the invariable preliminary to battle. When Stephen wished to provoke Geoffrey of Anjou to battle in 1137, he planned to besiege Argentan: 'or some other fortress where he might find Geoffrey, whom he hoped to engage in close conflict'. This was one of the many cases where the intention was not fulfilled.[10]

There were many points at which one or other might back down. You could let the castle go; if a relief force appeared, you might abandon the siege. Throughout operations the church was usually doing its best to prevent battle between Christian forces: the idea of just war was gaining

[8] Verbruggen, *Art of Warfare*, p. 67.

[9] For a discussion of the significance of battles in this period, see Bradbury, 'Battles in England and Normandy', pp. 1–4.

[10] On Le Mans see Orderic Vitalis, v, p. 304, and iv, p. 150; and on Argentan, vi, p. 484. For Verneuil, see William of Newburgh, in *EHD*, ii, p. 373.

acceptance, war should only be fought for a good cause, and the church could hardly accept that both parties in a conflict between Christians had right on their side. Clerics generally played the part of mediators, sometimes with success, as between Stephen and Henry of Anjou in 1153. The modern emphasis upon pitched battles, no doubt because of their drama, is not exactly the medieval viewpoint. Chroniclers might describe the feats of battle in glowing colours, but they also saw the importance of the siege. It is interesting that what we call the battle of Lincoln in 1141 was seen by one chronicler as the 'siege of Lincoln', it was one of the many battles which developed from a siege.[11]

Sieges could themselves be decisive without battle. On the First Crusade the taking of Antioch and Jerusalem were the main achievement of the Franks. When Stephen captured Faringdon in 1145 it virtually marked the end of the civil war with Matilda. The fall of Rouen to Geoffrey V of Anjou was the key to his ten year conquest of Normandy, achieved without fighting a single pitched battle. When Normandy fell to the French at the beginning of the thirteenth century, it was the taking of Château-Gaillard and Rouen that denoted success.

Sieges could be equally decisive if unsuccessful or lengthy. Delay gave the defender opportunities to recover, and wasted the enemy's resources. Louis VI had to besiege Amiens for two years; Geoffrey V of Anjou took three years gaining Montreuil-Bellay. Even delay of a matter of weeks could be vital. Falaise held out against Geoffrey for eighteen days during his early invasion of Normandy, and it was enough to cause him to abandon the campaign. David of Scots' invasion of England was severely delayed by the defence of Wark under Jordan de Bussy in 1135. Failure to take a stronghold slowed the pace of attack and weakened morale. To advance leaving behind an intact hostile garrison was dangerous practice.

Thus the existence of well fortified and provisioned castles became the basis of warfare. They were not easy to take if resolutely held. To capture them meant facing the combined threats of disease and vulnerability, and many an attacker was killed during a siege, from Geoffrey de Mandeville at Burwell to Richard the Lionheart at Châlus. An even more exceptional incident accounted for a king in 1088, leading an attack against the gates, and a woman on the tower, 'female in sex but not in spirit', threw down a millstone on his head, and killed him.[12]

The factor of delay caused by a resisting stronghold was well appreciated. The strong castle became a worry: even in the hands of a lesser man, the great could be defied. Verbruggen has pointed out that even the Holy Roman Emperor often failed against supposedly inferior and barbaric oppo-

11 On the 'siege of Lincoln', see the Worcester Chronicle in Stevenson, ii, part I, p. 368. Weaver's edition follows a manuscript ending in 1140.

12 The lady 'female in sex', appears in Mommsen and Morrison, *Imperial Lives and Letters*, p. 112.

sition, for example Henry IV against Nimptsch in 1071, or Henry V against Glogau in 1109.[13] Virtually all military campaigns in this age came to be dominated by the necessity to capture strong points. Frederick Barbarossa's expeditions to Italy were focused around great sieges.

In short, sieges were the common matter of warfare in this age. Geoffrey V of Anjou, as we have said, conquered Normandy without a battle. The whole progress of the conquest from 1135 to 1145 was shaped by sieges, failed and successful: from the early disasters at Le Sap in 1136 and Falaise in 1138, to the series of triumphs that included Fontanei in 1140, Avranches and Coutances in 1141, Verneuil and Vaudreuil in 1143, to the concluding triumphs at Rouen in 1144 and Arques in 1145. Similarly the great rebellion against Henry II between 1173 and 1174 spread over much of England and France. There were a number of fights but no large-scale battle, and again numerous sieges. Henry II's first move at signs of danger was to secure all his castles and strengthen as many as possible either in person or through trusted lieutenants: provisions playing as important a part as fortification. He himself inspected Normandy, and gave orders for others to do the same in England and Aquitaine.

We should not forget the consequences of the great importance of siege warfare, for these were more than political and military. The whole of society may not have been involved in the fighting, but it was caught up in the effects. Destruction around focal points was essential, to deny provisions to either defenders or foraging attackers. First destroy the land then the castles was a maxim of war in this age.[14] The effects on a peasantry and a society so dependent upon the annual harvest could be catastrophic. Starvation and illness often followed in the wake of war. Europe then had similarities to the third world now: disaster was always imminent. On a lighter note, it was said that after the 1173 to 1174 rebellion matters were so bad that the English had to drink water, whereas previously they had drunk beer seven days a week, and they had always been better at drinking than fighting.[15]

Garrisons

The evidence for the eleventh and twelfth centuries is more detailed than that for the previous periods, and allows us to view more closely the methods and effects of siege war. Warfare affected large numbers of people

13 On Nimptsch and Glogau, see Verbruggen, *Art of Warfare*, p. 290.

14 The maxim is from Jordan Fantosme, p. 35, no. 42, l. 450: *Primes guaster la terre e puis ses enemis*.

15 Jordan Fantosme, p. 53, no. 76, ll. 697–8: 'There is nothing to drink but spring water where there was wont to be beer every day of the week'; *N'i ad beivre fors ewe de funteine/U sout aveir cerveise en la semeine*.

through its destruction, but at the same time those actively involved were often surprisingly few. Whole towns and armies might be concerned, but in general the sieges of this age were of castles. Even where the castle was within a town it was common for the attackers to break into the town fairly quickly, and for defence and fighting to be concentrated around the castle or citadel which could often resist long after the town had fallen.

We cannot, even in the twelfth century, be absolutely certain of the size of garrisons. It is well known that chroniclers were given to exaggerating numbers, and other documents do not yet give very clear evidence in this respect. Nevertheless some appreciation of the size, nature and attitude of garrisons is important to our understanding of siege warfare. Gradually monarchs were developing the resources which would eventually give them an unassailable lead in siege war. Garrisons like fortifications needed wealth to support them. In this period it was often landed wealth which was used to obtain military service, but cash and stipendiaries were important too. Richard FitzNigel says in the *Dialogue of the Exchequer*: 'in war money is poured out in fortifying castles, in soldiers' wages, and in numerous other ways'. In the Pipe Rolls for the twelfth century, about twenty per cent of royal income was spent on defence; between 1172 and 1173, with crisis looming, over £2,000 was spent on castles; and during the years of rebellion garrisons cost a further £2,000.[16]

Garrisons in normal times were often formed from men executing their feudal duties, performing castle-guard. Like most aspects of feudalism this seems to have been flexible and open to arrangement, rather than following an invariable system. Commonly service from surrounding estates was tied to the local castle. An interesting document survives relating to Burchard the Bald, Count of Vendôme and his own castle.[17] The count himself was responsible for providing defence for five months, including two months from the treasury and three months from tax. The remaining seven months were to be covered by his vassals for one month each. Their duty was to maintain five watches a night, consisting of two for the gates, one for the walls, and two for general patrols. Equally commonly, stipendiary troops were paid to perform garrison duty, but one should not assume that these were inferior forces. When the King of Scots tried to win over the garrison at Carlisle by offering them silver, their leader replied: 'we are loyal men and safe'.[18] The attitude of the garrison could indeed be vital. At Le Mans they desired to be loyal, but to whom? Neither Robert Curthose nor Henry I, though invited, showed much interest in coming to relieve the place, so the garrison itself chose to surrender to a claimant to the

16 On money in war, Richard FitzNigel, *Dialogus*, p. 2; on the Pipe Rolls see Beeler, *Warfare in England*, pp. 178–9, 183; and Brown, *English Castles*, p. 116.
17 On Burchard the Bald, see Contamine, *War in the Middle Ages*, p. 47; Métais, *Cartulaire*, ii, p. 6, *De Consuetudinibus Bucardi Comitis in Vindicino*, dated about 1025 to 1030.
18 Jordan Fantosme, p. 106, no. 145, l. 1411: *Nus eimes in dedenz bone gent asseure.*

County of Maine, Helias, since they 'had no natural lord'. Their move was instrumental in Helias' success.[19]

The size of garrisons was not always large, sometimes indeed they were surprisingly small. It is true that usually we are given only the number of knights, and that the total garrison was probably rather larger, but, for example, when Brough became involved in the war in 1174 it held only six knights. There are hints that such small numbers were not exceptional: at Hereford 'a few knights' shut themselves in the castle, and at Pont-Echanfry one hears of a garrison of eight stipendiary knights.[20] On occasion there seems to have been virtually no garrison at all, as when Hugh Bigod entered Norwich, or on two occasions under Stephen at Lincoln, as when Ranulf of Chester was able to walk in and take over. Here it is true the garrison seems to have spent much of the time in the town, and when the king came he captured seventeen knights in the town. Stephen was also able to capture Wareham because it was inadequately garrisoned. Small numbers could encourage attack, as when the English came to Llanstephan, saw 'how very small was the force defending within the castle', and decided to scale the walls.[21] Troops often had to be spread thinly to defend many castles, so it is not surprising that some were left with little more than token forces, and it is clear that field armies were often raised by drawing on garrison troops, so that again a castle might be left with but few men. The overall impression is that a resident garrison was relatively small, and that only in time of imminent threat might a larger force be assembled for defence. Even then more stomachs demanded more supplies, and a place could last only as long as its provisions, so a careful equation had to be worked out for the ideal size of a garrison. On the whole it is probable that very large defending forces were the exception rather than the rule.

In contrast to the small numbers quoted so far are figures for larger and more important strongholds under attack. When Philip Augustus attacked Le Mans, it had a garrison of thirty knights and sixty men-at-arms at the time of surrender. The garrison at Tours when it was captured held eighty knights and a hundred men-at-arms. When Robert of Bellême left Bridgnorth to defend itself for him against Henry I, he provided three of his own men and eighty stipendiary knights. Other figures given during the period include two hundred knights at Stafford; one hundred knights under William FitzThierry for Henry I at Noyon-sur-Andelle; a hundred at Caen against Geoffrey of Anjou; thirty knights at Le Sap; thirty knights at Orbec

19 On the surrender to Helias, Orderic Vitalis, v, p. 306.

20 On the few knights in Hereford, William of Malmesbury, *Historia Novella*, p. 36; and compare John of Worcester, ed. Weaver, pp. 48–9. On Brough, Jordan Fantosme, p. 110, no. 153, l. 1478, says there were at least six: *chevaliers plus de sis*. On Pont-Echanfry, Orderic Vitalis, vi, p. 534, says there were *octo gregariis militibus*, probably suggesting sub-standard knights.

21 On Llanstephan, see *Brut Y Tywysogion*, pp. 120–2.

under two castellans; 140 men at Pont-Audemer for Waleran of Meulan; five hundred men-at-arms at Rosate against Barbarossa, and at Tortona a hundred knights and two hundred archers. These figures cannot be taken as absolutely accurate or as completely representative, but they do give some impression of normal garrisons, often at times when they might well have been reinforced for a crisis.[22]

Castellans and Feudalism

The localised political structure of this age encouraged both the development of castles, and of castle warfare. There is a thin line between a castellan employed by the prince, and an hereditary lord: the one could easily become the other. Allen Brown has called the castle 'the perfect architectural expression of feudal lordship', but power which might be royal, comital, seigneurial or castellan, in other words the castle did not represent any one of the layers of social and political power in this age but all of them. As the *Historia Novella* put it; 'there were many castles all over England, each defending its own district', and adds 'defending their own districts, or rather plundering them': the castle could represent illicit as well as legitimate power.[23]

Princes sought control over castles within their territories with varying results. It would be difficult to show that any prince had complete power over all castles in his area, though the dukes of Normandy, for example, did try to establish rights of entry and rendability over all castles in the duchy. The 1080 Council of Lillebonne tried to establish limits on castle-building in Normandy, stipulating measurements beyond which ducal permission would be required with regard to the depth of ditches, flanking palisades, wall walks, crenellation, and hoarding. The kings of France towards the end of this period were making similar claims in the kingdom.[24] It is probable that King Stephen's somewhat surprising tactics of arresting great lords for slight or possibly fabricated opposition to him, was an attempt to enforce rights over castles. For example when the bishops were arrested in 1139, and Geoffrey de Mandeville a few years later, the king demanded

22 On the larger numbers: Le Mans and Philip Augustus, *EHD*, ii, p. 407, and on Tours, ii, p. 408. For Bridgnorth, Stafford, Noyon, Caen, Le Sap, and Orbec, see Orderic Vitalis, vi, pp. 24, 218, 516, 470, 220. For Pont-Audemer, see Symeon of Durham, ii, p. 274, and ed. Stevenson, p. 612. On Rosate and Tortona, see Otto of Freising, ed. Mierow, pp. 18, 134; on Rosate, 1154, Otto of Freising, ed. Waitz & Simson, p. 2: *quingentos milites armatos*; on Tortona, pp. 122–32.

23 Brown, *Castles: A History and Guide*, p. 14, on lordship. On defending own district, see William of Malmesbury, *Historia Novella*, p. 40: *Castella erant crebra per totam Angliam, queque suas partes defendentia, immo ut verius dicam, depopulantia.*

24 For a good discussion on rendability, especially with regard to Philip Augustus, see Coulson, 'Fortress-Policy'.

they hand over their main castles. One chronicle says that Bishop Roger had built his castles 'to steal the royal majesty'. The archbishop of Rouen claimed that men should hand their castles to Stephen since the king 'fought for the peace of all'. Such claims could never be entirely substantiated, even by stronger princes than Stephen.[25]

The destruction of unlicensed castles is part and parcel of the same struggle for control over castle building. Adulterine castles tended to appear in times of disorder. It was a sign of the restoration of order and of the new man's power that these structures should be demolished. After his victory at Tinchebrai in 1106, which made him master of Normandy, Henry I demolished unlicensed castles as part of his policy of keeping down counts and castellans.[26] And it is well known that Henry II taking over in the wake of the Anarchy ordered the demolition of adulterine castles. Some that were useful were kept, and a veil is drawn over which ones were truly unlicensed in a period when his mother had been in opposition to a legally appointed king. The point was the demonstration of power rather than of inflexible destruction. Henry did, for example, order Stephen's brother Henry, bishop of Winchester, to destroy three castles built near his cathedral city.

Destruction was also a possibility for any castle or even city which opposed the prince. Frederick Barbarossa, after victory, ordered that Piacenza should remove its fortifications, fill the trench outside the walls, and destroy all the towers. Geoffrey of Anjou had the castle of Montreuil-Bellay rased to the ground after its three-year defiance. Plunder and penal measures were common. After involvement in rebellion, Wigmore had an additional tax imposed upon it.

The position of a castellan could be perilous. Where loyalty was not firmly placed, and when the political situation was fluid, a false step could be fatal. Orderic Vitalis describes the dilemma for those in England and Normandy torn between support for Robert Curthose and William Rufus: 'no man, as Christ says, can serve two masters', but choose the wrong one and much could be forfeit.[27] The attitude of the overlord could be capricious. There were times when Henry I acted ruthlessly, but he pardoned Burchard and Henry of Gisors on the grounds that they were vassals both of himself and of the king of France. Princes needed loyal men in key positions, including those who held major castles. For royal castles, and for

[25] On stealing the royal majesty, 1139, *Gesta Stephani*, p. 74: *sed ut regias ab eo dignitatem subriperent*. On fighting for the peace of all, William of Malmesbury, *Historia Novella*, p. 28, the quote is p. 33: all men should hand the keys of their castles to the king, *qui pro omnium pace debet militare*.

[26] Orderic Vitalis, vi, p. 98.

[27] Orderic Vitalis, iv, p. 270, from Matthew vi, 24, and Luke xvi, 13: Malcolm of Scots making his peace with Robert Curthose, but the latter does go on to say that things have changed now.

those of nobles this was vital; hence the significance of keeping both a loyal nobility, and of employing trusted captains. Henry I was accused of handing castles to 'new flatterers', but his reasons are clear.[28]

On the other hand comital or royal power could be threatened by the rise of those below. In the end Robert of Bellême was crushed by Henry I, but he had threatened to become an independent count with his accumulation of castles and wealth, and under Curthose it was said that 'no ducal censure could touch him'. He had thirty-four castles and thousands of men, and, if Orderic Vitalis can be believed, he abused his power by putting out men's eyes, hacking off hands and feet, and carrying out unheard of tortures to obtain ransoms.[29] Curthose was a weak prince, and it was said he 'feared the vassals in his own duchy more than they feared him'.[30] Waleran of Meulan seems in general less of a villain than Robert of Bellême, but in rebellion against Henry I he captured peasants in the forest and cut off their feet. There can be no doubt that, at times, powerful local castellans became uncontrolled local tyrants, their castles the bases for all sorts of crime: plunder, rapine, enslavement, theft. One such castellan was brought to book by William count of Nevers in 1115. This excommunicated thief took refuge in his castle which the count had to besiege. Similarly Louis VI of France was asked by his bishops to destroy a castle which had become 'the enemy of pilgrims and all humble folk', and King Stephen destroyed Guitry in the Vexin, 'a den of thieves'. From Saint-Pois Wiliam de Chaumont had carried out destructive raids before he was captured and his corpse thrown before the gate to persuade the men in his castle to surrender. There was some truth in the claim by princes that they needed to control castles in order to keep the peace. As Henry I suggested, his men were in castles 'to protect the country people'.[31]

Siege Tactics

With the growth in the number of castles it was inevitable that castle warfare should become the focus of the history of sieges. At the same time there is an increase in the volume of surviving evidence that allows a closer

28 Orderic Vitalis, vi, p. 392: *modernos adulatores*.

29 On no ducal censure touching Robert of Bellême, and his abuses, see Orderic Vitalis, iv, p. 298. On the latter, compare Orderic, iv, p. 160. On the thirty-four castles, see Orderic, vi, p. 32, and iv, p. 300.

30 On Curthose not being feared, see Orderic Vitalis, v, p. 26.

31 These comments on the functions of castles are all from Orderic Vitalis. On Waleran and the peasant, vi, p. 348; on the count of Nevers, 1115, and Louis VI and Thomas of Marle, vi, p. 258; on Guitry and Saint-Pois, vi, pp. 490–2; on protecting the country people, vi, p. 346.

examination of siege warfare. It is now possible to let the records take us through the process of siege with examples from each stage.

As we have suggested, the siege was a form of challenge: a castle or stronghold represented lordship and local power, whether in the hands of a local lord a prince or a king. The *Gesta Stephani* says that castles allowed the ruler to keep the inhabitants of the area 'more sternly in check, and at the same time to possess more securely the surrounding district'.[32] A siege meant a challenge to control in that particular region, which could be either resisted or allowed. If the existing authority had any strength then it was likely that the garrison would be loyal, the defences in good order, the fortification well provisioned, and the challenge resisted in the hope that an overlord, an ally or a relieving force could appear.

Weakness was likely to be revealed quickly under pressure. William FitzAlan's uncertainty about his garrison at Shrewsbury was shown by the fact that he insisted on an oath that they would not surrender to Stephen when he himself left. In the event they fled. If the walls and gates did not seem in good order, sturdy resistance was discouraged. At Dol the defenders felt thus about their defences, but did not lack courage. They could not envisage a lengthy resistance from within so they chose instead to make a sortie, saying: 'this castle is far from secure, let us not trust it for defence but go out and attack them'.[33] Lack of food or water also discouraged defenders. Baldwin de Redvers rebelled against King Stephen, and must be one of the unluckiest men in history; it is not often that we have a hot summer in England, but 1138 was a scorcher. Baldwin first rebelled at Exeter, but the water supply dried up and he was forced to accept terms. He then went on to the Isle of Wight and defied the king again from behind the walls of Carisbrooke Castle, but once more the well dried up and he had to flee, leaving the castle to surrender to the king.

A siege then was a challenge to authority, and soon showed if the defender was well prepared. Assuming this to be the case, the next step for the attacker was to prepare either for immediate attack or for blockade. The latter involved the destruction of any sources of supply; attackers would seize what they could for themselves and destroy anything else. 'First destroy the land and then your foe'.[34] This was itself a challenge to the lord: he could sit inside his castle, but could he protect the local people?

If there was to be resistance, the best hope for the attacker was a quick surge in which the place was stormed. As in all warfare, surprise could be a vital element, and speed of movement could provide it. Richard the Lionheart, like his father, was noted for such speedy attacks. Against the French he was said to be 'more swift than the discharge of a Balearic sling', and to cover three days marches in one. His father in order to save Dol had gone

32 *Gesta Stephani*, p. 82.

33 On Dol, Jordan Fantosme, p. 14, no. 17, l. 186: *Cest chastel n'est mie fort.*

34 See above, n. 15; Jordan Fantosme, p. 53.

Twelfth-century version of the attack on Troy

without food and sleep and used relays of horses, arriving 'so quickly he seemed to have flown.' Given the chance, capture by storm was always a hope: thus Dangeul was taken, the opportunity arising because the garrison was scattered when the attackers arrived at a surprise time 'out of season'.[35]

But if the attempt by storm failed, or seemed not likely to work, the usual initial step was to make a thorough assessment of the situation. There are still historians who sneer at medieval commanders as if they were fools and idiots, but in all areas of war commanders, then as since, were quite capable of carefully weighing up the position and coming to sensible and practical decisions. Descriptions of commanders making reconnaissance were frequent, for example Frederick Barbarossa did so before Milan, looking for the weak points, as he would also do at Tortona. Reconnaissance of course had its dangers: defenders were only too keen to take a shot at a commander wandering round the walls. Richard the Lionheart was studying the castle of Châlus 'on all sides, examining in which spot it would be most advisable to make the assault', when a defender shot at him

35 For the balearic sling, Roger of Howden, *Chronica*, iii, p. 252: *torto Balearis . . . fundae.* compare iii, p. 305, on the way to Issoudun he 'made three days march into one'. On Henry II and Dol, William of Newburgh, *EHD*, ii, p. 374; on Dangeul out of season, Orderic Vitalis, v, p. 232: *intempestiuus*, a suggestion by Robert of Bellême for attack in January, actually made in February.

with a crossbow from the walls. He was badly wounded by the bolt, and then finished off by the ministrations of the doctor.[36]

Assuming that initial storm had failed or was not feasible, the attackers were likely to settle for longer term success through a blockade. There were still hopes of a quicker victory if they could provoke the garrison to come and fight and then beat them, or if they could negotiate a settlement, or by trickery or luck. No one wanted a siege to go on for months or years, so every avenue was explored. It was common to test the defenders as severely as possible in the early stages, battering them with men, engines and propaganda, but if all the various forms of pressure proved unavailing, then they might have to settle down to cutting off supplies and starving out the garrison.

The pressure applied could be crude and brutal, along the lines of surrender or else, perhaps executing captured defenders in sight of the walls. At Carlisle the besiegers threatened Robert de Vaux that if he did not surrender they would throw him off the keep when they caught him. At Dunwich the attackers set up a gallows to show the defenders what would happen to them if they did not surrender: 'to terrify them', though it did not work.[37] There could be threats to loved ones of the garrison, threats to execute an individual who was important to them. Bishop Roger of Salisbury's mistress, Matilda of Ramsbury, was persuaded to surrender Devizes castle when their son, Roger the Chancellor, was paraded before the gates in a noose. In another incident at the same castle during the civil war, the unfortunate mercenary captain Robert FitzHubert was captured, but his men would still not surrender, even when the captors threatened to hang Robert: so hang him they did. At Crema the besiegers cut off the heads of captured enemies and played ball with them before the eyes of their friends, tossing them from hand to hand. In this case the defenders responded with similar tactics, killing some captured attackers by tearing them limb from limb on top of the walls. Similarly captured defenders of Tortona were hanged, at which the citizens pushed some of their prisoners off the wall. At Crema Barbarossa tied some young hostages to his siege engines, so that if they were attacked the hostages would be killed, but even this did not divert the citizens, whom Rahewin roundly condemns for their inhumanity, the cleric apparently seeing nothing wrong with the emperor's actions. Like most aspects of siege, pressure and propaganda was a two-edged sword, which could be used by either side, the defenders sometimes making much of their comfort and stocks of food to taunt those uncomfortably camped outside. At Limburg the defenders used a different sort of pressure to prolong their resistance as they began to run short of

36 On Châlus, Roger of Howden, *Chronica*, iv, p. 81; *Guillaume le Marechal*, p. 158, and Coggeshall, pp. 94–6.

37 On Dunwich, Jordan Fantosme, p. 65, no. 92, l. 862: *E fait drescier les furches pur els espoenter.*

supplies: they declared that they would eat the fat monks in the city rather than give in, at which the monks handed over their hidden supplies so that the garrison was able to last out until it was relieved.[38]

Pressure could in certain circumstances be applied against captured lords, to get them to order the surrender of a castle. Thus King Stephen threatened to starve Roger of Salisbury in order to get his relations to surrender. Or again, when William of Breteuil was captured, he and his associates were tortured; they were kept in a dungeon for three months, and then exposed in wet shirts on a high place and in a cold wind till they agreed to hand over Ivry.[39]

If storm and threat failed, the last hopes of a quick settlement were bribery and dirty tricks. At Carlisle when the threats against Robert de Vaux proved unavailing, bribery was attempted; he was offered silver, but that also failed. He replied that his men were loyal and that they had plenty of wheat and wine.[40] The dirty tricks used in siege warfare were legion, even the greatest rulers were not averse to trying things that we might consider not quite cricket. Louis VII was accused of making a deal with the count of Aumâle which led to the latter surrendering his castle with no more than token resistance. On other occasions Louis VII attempted a capture by storm during an agreed truce on a holy day, and again, at Rouen, made a sudden attack while an agreed tournament between the two sides was taking place. He was said to have been persuaded to this with some reluctance, but in any case some priests, watching the fun from the walls, saw the enemy preparations, and were able to give warning in time. Equally unprofitable was a broken agreement by the enemies of Barbarossa, who having sought a truce so that the siege was raised, then came out and attacked the withdrawing forces only to be beaten by them in the fight which ensued.[41]

If all else failed then the besiegers had to settle down to a prolonged blockade, interspersed with further attempts at storm. Once more the maxim 'first destroy the land and then one's foe' applied. It was a help if you could time your attack to leave the enemy ill provisioned. A chronicler mentions the usefulness of being able to spring the attack at the moment when the old harvest had been used up, and the new one not yet gathered in. At Dunster King Stephen left nothing at all 'that could serve his enemies for food or any purpose'. As always this could be a two-way

38 On Matilda of Ramsbury, Orderic Vitalis, vi, p. 532; on Robert Fitz Hubert, William of Malmesbury, *Historia Novella*, pp. 43–4; on Tortona, Crema and Limburg, see Otto of Freising, ed. Mierow, pp. 135, 284–5, 47; ed. Waitz & Simson, on Tortona, pp. 122–32; on Crema, pp. 287–9, 291–5; on Limburg, p. 30.

39 On the wheat and wine, Jordan Fantosme, p. 109, no. 149, l. 1445: *I ad enz le chastel asez vin e furment.*

40 On the torture in cold shirts, Orderic Vitalis, iv, p. 286.

41 On Louis VII see William of Newburgh, in *EHD*, ii, pp. 372, 382; on Barbarossa, Otto of Freising ed. Mierow, p. 46.

process, and at Le Mans, for example, Helias made things difficult for the attackers by himself taking in to the castle what could be gathered, and then destroying the rest, 'so that the cruel raiders could find nothing'.[42] One raiding army of Scots was advised not to leave behind even meal for the next day, not so much as an ox for the plough; and at Belford they fired the farms, took clothes, oxen, horses, cows, ewes and lambs, as well as money and valuables. Rahewin describes in detail the destruction done around Milan, where vineyards were flattened, figs and olive groves destroyed, so that famine and disease followed.[43]

Camp conditions were certainly a cause of many failed sieges, usually from illness and death, with the attendant loss of manpower and morale. At Cologne the chronicler describes the 'stench of the camp', which as he remarks 'is usually the case'. Illness was indeed a common fear for both besiegers and besieged, brought on by poor food and difficult conditions. Le Sap was one of many places where destruction led to shortages as flocks and herds were killed. The Angevin attackers had meat, but not fires or salt, and were clearly so ravenous that they set upon the meat raw, without salt or bread. It seems they were short of bakers and cooks. As a result of this, says the chronicler: 'by God's judgement almost all suffered from dysentery; plagued by diarrhoea, they left a trail of filth behind and many were barely capable of dragging themselves back home'. The general intention is plain enough: besiegers should 'destroy far and wide, since when the supplies of the countryside were used up, they would begin to hunger'.[44]

The successful cutting of lines of supply could bring success; it was important to capture provisions being sent for the relief of the garrison. Orderic describes the taking of vital supplies: horses, wagons with bread, wine and gear. We obtain a picture of the provisions in an attacking camp when Geoffrey of Anjou abandoned Falaise, leaving behind clothes, weapons, wagons, bread and wine.[45] Wark became desperate under siege when there was nothing left to eat except one live horse and one preserved in salt. Appleby surrendered quickly because it lacked provisions. Rouen yielded to Geoffrey of Anjou in 1144, because supplies ran out, and the lack of provisions at Dol when besieged by Henry II was a significant factor in its surrender. Jordan Fantosme mentions how important it was to con-

42 On denying provisions, the maxim again see n. 14 above from Jordan Fantosme; compare Mompesson and Morrison, *Imperial Lives and Letters*, p. 135: 'devastate far and wide since, when the supplies of the countryside were used up, they would begin to hunger'; and Otto of Freising, p. 45, devastate round and then besiege, as Rahewin says, 'famine will fight for them'. On attacking with harvest used up, Orderic Vitalis, v, p. 242; on Dunster, Willliam of Malmesbury, *Historia Novella*, p. 37; on Helias and Le Mans, Orderic, v, p. 258.

43 Otto of Freising, ed. Mierow, p. 218.

44 On the stench at Cologne, and destruction leading to hunger, see Mompesson and Morrison, *Imperial Lives and Letters*, p. 135; on the diarrhoea, Orderic Vitalis, vi, p. 472.

45 Orderic Vitalis, vi, p. 526.

trol the surrounding roads, in order to stop supplies, as, for example, at Rouen when Henry II made use of his Welsh troops to cut the French supply routes.[46] Supply by water also had to be blocked: as at Cologne when supplies sent down the river were intercepted by the besiegers.

Blockade entailed cutting off entry and exit, preventing reinforcement and provisioning, and if possible destroying existing supplies, not least of water. Sometimes a fortification had a well-defended internal supply of water, though at times even this could be diverted or contaminated. In other cases water supply was vulnerable, and a natural object of attack; fetching and carrying water could become the most vital and most dangerous operation during a siege. At Exeter, as we have seen, the two wells dried up, and the garrison survived for a time on wine before making an agreed surrender. At Alençon the besiegers tunnelled underground and cut the pipes which supplied the castle with water, thus causing the place to surrender. At Tortona Barbarossa polluted the water supply, putting rotted and putrid corpses of men and animals in the spring, followed by torches of sulphur and pitch which made the water bitter and undrinkable.

If a castle was well fortified, well supplied, neither easily reduced nor open to bribery, in the end the besiegers had to settle down to the potentially long process of blockade: the scene was set for the siege as it is generally pictured. The countryside around was wasted, negotiation, threat and trickery had failed. Careful reconnaissance was made of the site, to see where routes had to be blocked, and where were the possible weak spots for attack. Routes of entry by land and water were guarded, and special watch was kept over the gates.

It would be tedious, even if it were possible, to examine in any detail every siege and every method employed. Perhaps first we can obtain a general view taken from various sources, and then look in more depth at a few of the actual sieges that occurred. The common siege in this period is of a castle or of a citadel. Once the blockade was in place, attack usually followed through stages: taking the outer defences or the town, then the bailey, and finally pressing the keep. Storm would generally be tried early on, and later again when it was felt the moment had come for an all-out effort. In the meantime there would be continual harassment from archers and engines, so that the defenders could never relax. Larger engines and belfries would usually be constructed on the site and then moved into position: the engines would batter at walls and gates; the belfries would cover various actions, and allow the attackers to overlook the walls, either to give cover for the action below, or to allow direct access on to the walls. Guard had always to be kept against counter-attack, so there must be a force ready to deal with a sortie: an armed clash could be decisive, particularly if the attackers suffered defeat. Defenders would also build their

46 Roger of Howden, *Chronica*, i, p. 282.

engines, and aim at the besieging camp, at the engines and belfries, and at the attackers themselves. An attempt at storm later in the siege would generally be the time when the belfries were pushed into position in an attempt to gain the walls. Mining, scaling, battering and missiles would often be employed together: tunneling was used, for example at Cenarth Bychan near Pembroke, mining and ladders at Dol, picks to pierce the wall at Carlisle, battering rams against Rome, ladders and rams at Cologne. All methods of attack had their perils: ladders, for example, could be pushed from the wall, as happened at Llanstephan so that the climbers fell into the ditch.

Engines and belfries were now a commonplace in sieges, demonstrating amongst other things the wealth and strength of the attackers. King Stephen at Shrewsbury made an engine from a large amount of timber brought there. The moat was filled at the king's orders; fires were lit to cover activity, and the engine was pulled forward so that the gate could be forced, causing the defenders to creep out and flee.[47]

There was always a search for the novel weapon which could spring a surprise. Occasionally one hears of an odd weapon called the crow, which consisted of a pole on a pivot, with a hook at one end. It could be dangled over the walls like a giant fishing rod to try and catch men below. Henry, the son of the king of Scots, was dragged from his horse by a crow at Ludlow in 1139, but managed to escape. Orderic Vitalis describes a similar idea used at Vatteville, where Walter FitzWilliam was captured as he stood on the ramparts in his hauberk defending the castle. He was caught by an 'artifical hand' with iron hooks, dragged out and taken prisoner.[48]

At Montreuil-Bellay, after three frustrating years, Geoffrey V of Anjou used a weapon previously only heard of in the East, Greek Fire. It was 1151, and Geoffrey was in the last stages of dealing with a rebellion, and in particular with the rebel lord Gerard Berlai. Gerard's castle with its double walls and a great keep 'rising to the stars', was thought to be impregnable: protected by a deep natural chasm known as the Valley of the Jews. The château now on the site is not Gerard's castle, which was rased after the siege, but the site remains impressive. Count Geoffrey had surrounded the castle with his own camps and towers. To get his belfries across the chasm he brought the people from the nearby fair of Saumur, and encouraged them to drop rocks and rubbish into it; breaches were made in the wall only to be restored at night.[49]

47 On Shrewsbury, 1138, see John of Worcester, ed. Weaver, pp. 50–1; and Howlett, iv, p. 137.

48 On the crow at Ludlow, 1139, see Robert of Torigny, ed. Stevenson, p. 712; on Vatteville, Orderic Vitalis, vi, p. 346: *ingeniosa manus uncis ferreis implicuit, irremissibiliter extravit*.

49 On Geoffrey V and Greek Fire, see Bradbury, 'Greek Fire'; the translation is from John of Marmoutier's *Historia Gaufredi Ducis*, which I am preparing for publication.

Geoffrey V was an educated count, and it seems found time, even at the height of the siege, to read the *De Re Militari* of the Roman writer Vegetius. In deference to a group of monks who approached him, the count put down the book, and an aged monk picked it up and began to read:

> It so happened that he had come upon that section in which Vegetius Renatus explains in more detail how a tower which has been restored with joined timbers can be captured quickly. The pensive count, taking note of the old man deep and preoccupied in his reading, said: Stay with me tomorrow, dear brother, and what you find in your reading, you shall see put into practice.[50]

On the following day Geoffrey decided to use one of his engines to hurl Greek Fire at the offending keep:

> So he ordered an iron jar, tied with iron bands and hanging from a strong chain, to be filled with the oil of nuts and the seeds of cannabis and flax. The opening of the jar was to be sealed with an appropriate iron strip and firmly locked. Then he ordered the jar to be replaced in the heated furnace for a long time until the whole thing glowed with overpowering heat, so that the oil bubbling inside was boiling. The chain was cooled by throwing water over it, then the jar was taken out and fixed to the pole of a mangonel. With careful aim and great force, while still glowing, it was thrown by the engineers at the strong beams placed in the breaches. The contents were expelled by the impact, and the discharged matter caused a fire. Then the outflowing oil merged with the balls of fire, supplying food for the flames. The licking flames, vomiting in sudden increase, burned three houses, and hardly allowed men to escape.[51]

At last Geoffrey was able to break in: Montreuil-Bellay was taken, and the rebellion was crushed. Geoffrey was shortly to die, leaving his more famous son Henry II to follow him as ruler of Anjou and Normandy.

A common feature of the castle warfare of this age, as indeed used by Geoffrey at Montreuil-Bellay, was the building of counter-castles to protect the besiegers. They could also be placed so as to block exits, entrances and important routes. They were almost an essential part of any long-term siege, and were built, for example, by William Rufus at Bamburgh, and by Henry I at Arundel in 1102. Stephen built one at Bristol against the earl of Gloucester on the east, to prevent the traffic in both directions and to guard the bridges. He built another at Dunster 'so that he might keep them more firmly in check, and at the same time possess more securely the surrounding district'. Two were built at Wallingford 'to maintain the siege', one of which the chronicler Robert of Torigny thought 'impregnable'. The counter-castle built at Faringdon in 1145 had a rampart and a stockade 'so

50 *Historia Gaufredi Ducis*, ed. Halphen and Poupardin, p. 218.
51 *Historia Gaufredi Ducis*, pp. 218–19.

that a sudden attack of the enemy might not break in', and which would also give a safe refuge to the besiegers.[52] At Burwell, Stephen built a campaign castle against the rebel Geoffrey de Mandeville. It was abandoned as soon as Geoffrey died of a wound received at Burwell, yet it was carefully designed with a large rectangular moat which was never in the event filled, and the beginnings of a stone wall and gatehouse. The more ordinary counter-castle at Bentley in Hampshire has been excavated to give some idea of the form of these fortifications, and is comparable to a motte and bailey construction, which is probably what one would expect. It must however be said that although we know that many of these counter-castles were built, very few have been identified and examined. Obviously they were usually built quickly, under pressure for temporary purposes, and were probably rushed versions of ordinary earthwork fortifications. The enemy seeing the counter-castles built against them by Henry I at St Ouen ridiculed them as being in the one case 'ill-positioned', and in the other as looking like a 'hare's form'.[53]

Breaking into the outer defences was commonly achieved by the use of large throwing engines. William the Lion, King of Scots, at Wark ordered up a stone-thrower saying that if his engineer spoke the truth it would demolish the gate and 'we shall take the bailey in no time at all'. In fact the first stone from this engine 'barely tumbled out of its sling' and hit one of his own knights, saved from death by armour and shield, which King William apparently found highly amusing though one doubts that his knight did. As we shall discuss at a later point, this reference to the use of a sling on an engine is one of the earliest clear mentions of a trebuchet. A second engine was ordered up to hurl fire, but the wind changed direction and blew back on the Scots themselves, at which point the king decided fate was against him, and ordered that they fold up their tents and go. However, on the whole engines were becoming more important, and mostly they proved more effective than William the Lion's. Orderic speaks of Robert of Bellême at Bréval bringing up 'a most ingenious invention to the siege'. He built engines which were wheeled against the enemy's castle 'hurling great stones at the castle and its garrison'. Stones could of course kill as well as make breaches: William Rufus on one occasion narrowly escaped death when a stone hit the knight standing beside him, smashing bone into brain. From the tower they shouted: 'See now the king has fresh meat', an example of medieval wit. Another instance of the use of stone occurred in Rome, when there was an attempt on the life of the emperor, Henry IV. The idea was to drop a stone on his head in the place where he

52 On Dunster, keeping in check, and Faringdon, 1145, see *Gesta Stephani*, pp. 82, 182; on Wallingford, Robert of Torigny, p. 151.

53 On Burwell, see Lethbridge, 'Burwell'; on Bentley, see Stamper, 'Excavations'; for the siege castles ill-place and like a hare's form, see Orderic Vitalis, vi, p. 186: *Vnus enim Malassis et aliud nuncupatur Trulla Leporis*.

regularly prayed by placing the stone on a beam in the ceiling, but the emperor obviously prayed too well: he moved at the vital moment, the stone missed, and the man responsible for dropping it fell through the hole to his death, to be pulled limb from limb by the crowd.[54]

It was common to place a battery of engines at a good vantage point and then hammer away at the chosen section of wall. At Rouen in 1174 they operated a system of eight-hour shifts to keep the attack going day and night.[55]

Barbarossa in Italy

Frederick Barbarossa's sieges during his Italian campaigns will make excellent examples of siege methods employed during this period. They are described in detail in the work begun by the emperor's uncle, Otto bishop of Freising, and continued by the cleric, Rahewin. We shall examine three of these sieges, at Milan, Crema and Tortona, to see how operations were carried out in the twelfth century.[56]

The siege of Tortona appears in the first part of *The Deeds of Frederick*, and is therefore in the part of the work begun by Bishop Otto. Tortona stood on its rock like a watchtower over the plain, protected by walls and fortifications, including an ancient brick tower known as the Rubea, said to have been built by Tarquin the Proud.[57] The siege occurred in 1155, when Tortona had earned the emperor's hostility by siding with Milan against him. He ordered the city to abandon Milan, which it refused, so he prepared to attack. Men were sent to make reconnaissance, which was accomplished after some delays caused by a rise in the level of the waters of the river. Barbarossa attempted straight away to storm the town, and the imperial forces managed to enter the suburbs, breaking through the wall, and taking a number of towers. The citizens rushed to try and find refuge in the citadel, which became the focus of the siege. It was garrisoned by

54 On engines, William the Lion at Wark, Jordan Fantosme, pp. 92–4, where the sling is called *funde*; on Robert of Bellême at Bréval, Orderic Vitalis, iv, p. 288: *ingeniosissimum artificem*: the engine threw large stones and was wheeled. On the fresh meat, Orderic, v, pp. 258–60: which continues in the same vein: 'take it to the kitchen to be served for him at dinner'. On Henry IV, 1088, Mompesson and Morrison, *Imperial Lives and Letters*, p. 112.

55 On the shifts at Rouen, William of Newburgh in *EHD*, ii, p. 382.

56 On Barbarossa in general, see the biographies by Jordan, Pacaut, and Munz, and Jordan, *Henry the Lion*. Rogers, *Latin Siege Warfare*, reviews the sources for these sieges in Lombardy in detail in ch. 4. Here Otto of Freising and Rahewin are used chiefly. The latter's borrowings from classical sources do not generally invalidate his usefulness. See Otto of Freising, *Deeds of Frederick Barbarossa*, ed. Mierow; and for the Latin, *Gesta Friderici Primi Imperatoris*, ed. Waitz & Simson.

57 Otto of Freising, ed. Mierow, on Tortona, 1155, pp. 18–20, 132–42; and see n. 38 above.

Knights storming a gate, a twelfth-century view of the death of Hector

Milanese allies of Tortona, as well as by local men: a hundred knights and two hundred archers sent from Milan.

The siege began in February, rather early for such action. Siege works were dug all round, so there was no way out. Frederick Barbarossa, took up his position to the west, with Henry the Lion, duke of Saxony, to the south in the suburbs, and with Pavian allies to the east and the north. Archers, crossbowmen and sling-men were used to pin the enemy down while larger engines were constructed. Propaganda and pressure was also used. The garrison was publicly accused of treachery against their own prince, and were told that if they did not surrender they would be hanged on the gallows which was set up before their eyes.

The garrison made sorties, and some of the attackers were captured and hanged from the gallows before the walls. Engines aimed rocks against the walls, and one mangonel scored a great hit on the upper fortifications, which broke into three parts and collapsed, killing three knights in armour who happened to be standing in the cathedral taking part in a council of war. There was fighting to control the water supply to the city: the Pavians, for Frederick, guarded the spring from which the defenders had to draw their water, and there was hard fighting around it. The mass of fallen rubble had diverted the river which ran through the suburbs and made the water filthy, but the defenders held on.

Barbarossa was frustrated by the delay, and decided on a new all-out attack. Engines were prepared, including 'a quite unusual device',[58] which bored a tunnel towards the Rubea; but the citizens realised what was happening, and dug a counter-tunnel, which brought down that made by the besiegers, trapping and suffocating some.[59] Mining failed, and the emperor's next move was to pollute the water supply, with corpses of men and animals, and with sulphur and pitch. Pressure was increased by an imperial success against nearby Sazanico, which was taken by storm at night while the garrison was sleeping. But still Tortona held out.

Various feats by the attackers were recorded: one imperial sergeant scaled the citadel using a small axe to make footholds while still carrying a sword, despite stones and missiles raining down on him. He killed a man and then returned safely. Barbarossa wanted to knight him, but the hero said he was a plain man of low birth who would rather stay as he was, so the emperor gave him money instead.

At Easter the attack was halted for four days. A number of ecclesiastics came out from the city and claimed that they were trapped by the situation, having no wish to oppose the emperor: 'we are punished for the sins of others'.[60] Hostilities resumed, and the defenders had one last success when a missile damaged one of Barbarossa's engines so that it had to be repaired, but at last Tortona surrendered. The garrison came out as from a prison into the spring air, deathly pale, like corpses rising from their tombs.

Milan itself was the focus of Frederick Barbarossa's attention in Italy, and at the heart of the resistance to him. Otto of Freising's continuator, Rahewin, described the siege, when the emperor decided to approach the city directly. At first the citizens panicked. The great emperor moved on relentlessly: he besieged and took Trezzo, a Milanese castle on the River Adda, and left a garrison there. For Milan itself he made deliberate and impressive preparations, levelling the ground for attack. His army arrived in procession, including men with engines at the rear.[61]

He chose to begin operations against the east gate. The Milanese, having recovered from their initial shock, decided they were safe enough inside their walls, and made a sortie. The emperor tried to fire the gate and its bridge using engines placed on a hill, but failed. Frederick's ally, Henry Jasomirgott, attacked at another gate, but was hindered by a sortie: it was not going to be a quick success. Frederick tried to lure the Milanese out for a decisive battle, but that failed. He surveyed the defences, looking for weak points in the walls. The countryside around was devastated: vines,

58 On the unusual device, Otto of Freising, ed. Mierow, p. 135; ed. Waitz & Simson, p. 125: *no solum turres machinis quati, sed etiam inusitato satis utens artificio cuniculos . . . Aliud itidem invenitur ingenium.*

59 On the hero of low birth, Otto of Freising, ed. Mierow, p. 137; ed. Waitz & Simson, pp. 126–7: *de cuiusdam preruptae audatiae stratoris virtute.*

60 On the ecclesiastics, Otto of Freising, ed. Mierow, p. 141; ed. Waitz & Simson, p. 127.

61 On Milan, Otto of Freising, ed. Mierow, pp. 208–17; ed. Waitz & Simson, pp. 209–26.

figs and olives destroyed. A triple line of warriors shot a hail of missiles against the defenders, killing anyone who appeared on the battlements. The citizens were asked what would become of their families if they continued. Negotiations were set in train, and peace made.

The peace did not last, and a new episode in the war developed from a feud between Crema and Cremona.[62] Barbarosa allied with Cremona and besieged the rival city, Crema. It was sited on a swampy plain, defended by moats and a high double wall, from which the citizens resisted the emperor. A blockade was set up, and siege works built all around the city, while engines were constructed ready for the assault. Barbarossa himself arrived in 1159, to find the conflict under way, both sides using engines. One sortie led to a battle in which so many were killed that the brooks filled with blood. It was at this siege that the imperial forces cut off the heads of captive enemies and played ball with them; the citizens in reply tore their captives limb from limb on the walls. Barbarossa had others hanged in public view, the citizens responded by hanging imperialists in chains. A herald announced for Frederick that no one would be spared, and forty more were hanged, including five Milanese nobles. When the city's bombardment against the imperial engines did some damage, he ordered that hostages be tied to the surviving engines, but the enemy bombardment of them continued. The city had nine mangonels operating, a rare example of what sounds like a precise figure. Some of the hostages who were tied to the engines and suffered death as a result, were children. To Rahewin the citizens were the barbarians in killing their own offspring, and not the emperor, who was engaged in a 'just war'. Even though it was 'unheard of among barbarians', they continued to hurl stones and kill their own children 'hanging there and expecting a most cruel death'.[63]

Milan attempted a diversion to save Crema by attacking Manerbe near Lake Como, but Barbarossa organised a successful relief, and was ready for another all-out attack on Crema. The latter was becoming a serious worry to him, having survived all manner of threats, and seemingly well enough provisioned to endure for some time yet. He had employed a whole variety of devices, from hidden ditches to mantraps 'like mousetraps only stronger', and yet had failed to break his enemy's determination.[64] His own men were becoming disheartened from the continuing failure of their efforts, and from the length of time that had passed and the cold, rainy weather. Therefore he ordered a new attempt at storm.

Belfries were prepared, protected with iron, carrying slingers and archers

[62] Otto of Freising, ed. Mierow, p. 280; and see n. 38 above.

[63] The war is claimed as just in Otto of Freising, ed. Mierow, p. 206, and similar claims are made regarding 'the rights of war', and fighting 'according to the laws of war', pp. 284–5; on killing their own children, p. 285.

[64] On the mousetrap, Otto of Freising ed. Mierow, p. 302; ed. Waitz & Simson, p. 312: *musciplis quidem simillima, sed pro qualitate humani corporis fortiora.*

who were enabled to see over the walls into the city. Red hot, barbed iron weights were thrown against the imperial engines, intended to grip the timbers and set them on fire. Poles to pull the weights off, and water to put out the flames, preserved them. Gradually the belfries were pushed forward, and bridges were lowered so that men could cross to the walls while others gave them cover. 'The entire line set foot on the wall'. Bertolf of Gerach was one who succeeded in leaping on to the wall; He killed many opponents before being himself felled from behind with an axe. He was scalped and the scalp fixed to his helmet as a trophy. One imperial soldier who was captured, had his hands and feet cut off, so that he was forced to crawl along the street: 'a wanton jest', comments Rahewin.[65]

The citizens were finally driven from the outer wall and took refuge in the inner fortifications. Barbarossa intensified the attack until the citizens of Crema were ready to agree terms: the besieged would be allowed to leave with whatever they could carry on their backs, though members of the garrison who had come from elsewhere would have to go empty-handed. This was agreed and done and the city was then looted and burned.

For all his efforts in these sieges, in the long term Barbarossa's Italian war was not a successful one. Later in the reign he suffered serious defeat in the battle of Legnano and was forced to make peace with the Lombard League. In the even longer run, the empire's involvement in Italy looks like wasted effort, a drain on the resources of the German empire, and a factor in diminishing the European rôle of imperial power in the medieval period.

65 On the entire line, is Rahewin in Otto of Freising, ed. Mierow, p. 304, borrowed from Josephus; the wanton jest is also p. 304; ed. Waitz & Simson, p. 314: *iam tota acies in muro pedem ponebat*; p. 315: *grave ludibrium*.

CHAPTER FIVE

The Early Crusades, 1050–1200

The study of siege warfare between Christians and Moslems in the middle ages leads to some unexpected discoveries. One would anticipate more hostile and extreme attitudes between adherents to rival religions than in warfare between Christians, that the enemy would be less leniently treated, that the excuse for immoderate behaviour would be greater. Certainly hatred could be engendered by the conflict, and religious fervour could be a spur to excesses. This chapter is stained with stories of atrocities, massacres, tortures and examples of inhuman behaviour; it is easy enough to find terms of hatred used against opponents of a different race and religion, on both sides. But there are positive attitudes as well: men were prepared, for belief, to endure the greatest deprivation and hardship, to endanger life and limb, to demonstrate the highest courage. In a sense crusading sieges took medieval warfare to its limits.[1]

It is this extremity which makes this part of our story so absorbing. In the twentieth century we sometimes find it hard to relate closely to men in siege circumstances: they appear to have little in common with our present life, we are not experienced in the conditions they met, and which therefore seem remote to us. The history is interesting in an anecdotal sense, but bizarre and amusing rather than close to anything which would affect our own emotions. Perhaps here, in the extremes of hardship, endurance, and courage, we are brought face to face with purely human reactions. For the besieged in such circumstances, defeat might more surely mean death, and resistance would therefore be the more desperate and prolonged. It brings us up against human deprivation: lack of food and water, fears for oneself, one's family, and one's home, and all against a background of daily, grinding threat of assault by a strange host from another land, with other beliefs

1 For general books on the crusades: the standard account in English is S. Runciman, *A History of the Crusades*. For some time the best single volume work available has been H.E. Mayer, *The Crusades*, but this has now been superseded by J. Riley-Smith, *The Crusades, A Short History*. Also worth noting are the well illustrated M. Billings, *The Cross and the Crescent*; and the outstanding work on warfare, R.C. Smail, *Crusading Warfare*.

and ideas, whose engines battered at the walls of your own town, whose great rocks fell upon your streets, your rooftops, even on your friends and your family. Behind this was the knowledge that after defeat without terms would follow rape, torture, bloodshed, death or enslavement for oneself and for all those near and dear. Everything could be lost, your family could be killed, your home taken over or destroyed: life, if even that remained, would never be the same again.

For a besieging army there were other fears, of displacement, of painful death in a foreign and alien land, which could be true for Turks as well as Franks. Crusading was a brave venture: it was costly, demanding and dangerous; many who went did not return. In order to go many had to sell or mortgage their land. The hopes of great gain, often emphasised as a major cause of the crusades, were probably not especially common, and profit was less likely to occur than financial loss. Godfrey of Bouillon, who became the first ruler of the new Latin Kingdom, himself had to mortgage property to the bishop of Liège for 7,000 marks. There was a crusaders' hymn to the effect that fiefs had to be sold in order to gain the Temple of God.[2] As the Lisbon chronicler pointed out, it was a great wrench to leave behind one's family for such a venture, particularly one's growing children. Conditions for the besiegers might well be even harsher than those for the besieged, with the difficulties of maintaining supplies in what was often a difficult land with extremes of weather, of sun and of rain. Such conditions could be harder to cope with in a camp than in a town, in tents and rough huts, with inadequate water and sanitation: conditions that would leave modern sensibilities aghast. The perils of death from disease, as well as from attack by engines or missiles, were as great for the besiegers as for the besieged.

In viewing human activity in such conditions, twentieth-century man may experience occasional insight and sympathy: from knowledge of extreme conditions in our own age, from say London during the blitz and the daily fears of death and destruction for ordinary civilians, or from the horrors of the concentration camps.

Christian and Moslem Attitudes

It will be instructive to examine the respective attitudes of members of the opposing religions in the period of the early crusades. We find virulent hatred, but also sometimes a surprising sympathy. On both sides participants believed themselves to be involved in religious war; both sides believed their cause had the approval of God. Certainly the papacy gave its support and encouragement to the crusading movement, and should prob-

2 Godfrey's mortgage is in Orderic Vitalis, v, p. 208, and n. 2; others give different amounts. The hymn is mentioned in J. Riley-Smith, *First Crusade*, p. 45.

Christians and Saracens in conflict, from a William of Tyre manuscript

ably be seen as inspiring its very existence. The crusades developed from the growing desire of Christians to make pilgrimage to Jerusalem, and in early days those who went were known as pilgrims rather than crusaders. In warfare the Christians found inspiration from God's support: *Deus le vult*, God wills it, was their cry.[3]

The motives of crusaders were mixed, but usually involved some element of religious drive: from Tancred, who was anxious about squaring a warrior's life with a Christian conscience, and found the crusade a welcome solution, to those benighted souls on the People's Crusade who set out in the train of a goose which they believed had been inspired by God.[4] Religious symbols and acts of worship were commonly used to lift morale: hence the practice of making processions with banners led by barefoot priests, or calling for periods of fasting and praying. Thus there were processions at Antioch and Jerusalem, and a three day fast at Antioch.

The finding of the holy lance at Antioch, however dubious the circumstances and however spurious the object, fired enormous enthusiasm and galvanised the struggling crusaders to their greatest triumph. The chronicler, Raymond of Aguilers, claimed to have witnessed the discovery by Peter Bartholomew: Peter located the spot and they dug all day until there

3 Attitudes on crusade have recently interested many historians. Useful translations of Arabic works can be found in F. Gabrieli, *Arab Historians*; and an account of the crusades from the Arab viewpoint in A. Maalouf, *The Crusades through Arab Eyes*. Sources which show a revealing interest in the other side are William of Tyre, and Usamah.

4 For Tancred, see J. Riley-Smith, *First Crusade*, p. 36; from Ralph of Caen, *Gesta Tancredi*, pp. 604–5: *quod militiae suae certamina praecepto videbat obviare domino*: 'the warfare he engaged in as a knight seemed contrary to the Lord's commands'. For the goose, see Runciman, *Crusades*, i, p. 137.

was a large pit. Finally, clad in his shirt, Peter leaped into the pit and found the lance. 'I, Raymond, author of this book, kissed the point of the lance as it barely protruded from the ground'.[5] If some of the crusading leaders had doubts about the lance being genuine, as well they might have done, knowing that an object claiming to be the self-same lance reposed in Constantinople, they were forced to forget their objections in the wave of eager belief that here was a sign of Christ's support. Belief in the find did not disappear even with the subsequent test. Another writer, Fulcher of Chartres, was more doubtful, and spoke of the lance 'deceitfully found by that foolish man'.[6] Peter underwent an ordeal by fire, clutching the lance. He said Christ spoke to him in the flames and promised that although he would be hurt, he would not go to hell. Peter emerged badly burned, and died twelve days later.

Christians could glory in killing for the cause: in the poem about the Cid, one is often presented with the picture of Alvar Fanez as a hero for killing Moors, their blood dripping from his elbow. When Jerusalem was taken, the Christians waded ankle deep in the blood of the slain, and mounds of corpses were piled up, together with heaps of heads, hands and feet. People were beheaded in the Temple of Solomon itself, women and children among those slaughtered. Bellies were ripped open; even those who begged for mercy were killed like 'rotten fruit'.[7] This seems in no way to have diminished the crusaders' pleasure in touring the holy places, and they followed the massacre by a service in church.

Sometimes the actions in the name of Christ were even more horrific, and deserve the label of atrocities. At Nicaea in 1097 Turkish heads were cut off and hurled into the city by the engines. Godfrey of Bouillon ordered that heads be set on poles, and at Antioch the Christians even dug up the corpses of their Turkish enemies, recently killed and buried, and decapitated them. At Ma'arrat there is talk of torturing captives, and eating them, and when Richard I killed 2,700 prisoners at Acre, Ambroise comments: 'for this be the Creator blessed'; and this is our own greatest crusading hero. At Jaffa, when the Lionheart entered, he found that the Moslems had slaughtered the pigs: neither wishing to eat them because of their religion, nor leave them as food for the crusaders. He then proceeded to kill the defeated Moslems and throw their bodies in with those of the pigs.[8]

5 On the Holy Lance, see Raymond of Aguilers, *Historia Francorum*, ed. Hill, English, p. 57; ed. Hill, Latin, p. 75.

6 On the lance being found deceitfully, Fulcher of Chartres, *Chronicle*, ed. McGinty, p. 48; the chronicler viewed it more favourably by pp. 56–7; ed. Hagenmeyer, pp. 237–8, 263.

7 *Cantar de Mio Cid*, ed. R.M. Pidal; the modern translation, used here, is *The Poem of the Cid*, ed. L.B. Simpson.

8 On atrocities; Godfrey and the heads, Raymond of Aguilers, ed. Hill, English, p. 40; on the decapitation of corpses, *Gesta Francorum*, p. 42; on Ma'arrat, Orderic Vitalis, v, p. 141; on Richard I at Acre and Jaffa, Ambroise, pp. 228, 413–14.

It is the practice today to gloss over these horrors, to see them as part of another age, but perhaps as with the more recent holocaust, it is wise to remind ourselves of the inhumanity of man; perhaps the comparison is not such a distant one. The crusading movement, had the unpleasant side-effect of turning Christians upon Jews; many crusades to the East were preceded by attacks in the West upon Christ's 'worst foes the Jews'.[9]

The Roman church approved the crusades at a time when it was developing views to restrict warfare between Christians, with the concepts of the Truce and Peace of God, and the argument that warfare could only be justified if it were just. A just war was more easily acknowledged when it was a war against God's enemies, who could be attacked and killed with impunity, against whom indeed aggression might bring reward from God.[10] In the sermon at Clermont which preached the First Crusade, Urban II encouraged knights to fight the infidel rather than each other. The crusade was for the papacy as for Christian knights, the happy synthesis of a just war and a holy war.

We have already referred to the southern Norman, Tancred, who was torn between what he found in the Bible, and the warfare practised in Italy. For him the crusade was a new opportunity to engage in war without damage to his conscience. As Urban II put it: 'swinging the sword against Saracens is less wicked'. Indulgence was probably intended to be the remission of penance for sins rather than forgiveness of sins, but in crusaders' popular interpretation it was seen as the latter. The sewing-on of crosses, and the taking of vows are further evidence of religious emphasis. Matthew of Edessa saw the mission of the crusade as being 'to free the Holy City of Jerusalem from the yoke of the infidel'.[11]

Something of the puritanical and self-denying elements to be found in medieval monasticism, was also to be seen in the make-up of crusaders: deprivation on behalf of God became a virtue. It helps to explain how on the First Crusade men were able to survive the most diabolical of conditions. The urge to punish the body for the sake of the soul is to be found, for example, in the practice of voluntary branding with crosses. Of course there were crusaders who ignored this; there were some who wallowed in sin, and were as un-Christian in their conduct as it is possible to imagine, but we find time and again an encouragement on crusade to good moral conduct, and a condemnation and punishment of misconduct. Costly clothes were forbidden to the crusaders at Lisbon on the Second Crusade, and women were not permitted to appear in public; each ship had its own

9 On the jews, Norman Cohn, *Pursuit of the Millenium*, in Brundage, *Problems*, p. 41. and Runciman, *Crusades*, ii, p. 254.

10 For a discussion in depth on the just war, see F.H. Russell, *Just War*; and Riley-Smith, *What Were the Crusades*, chs. 2 and 3.

11 On Urban II swinging the sword, see Erdmann, *Origin*, p. 339, from Baudri of Dol; on Matthew of Edessa, see Boase, *Kingdoms*, p. 31.

priest, and the author of a letter describing the siege quotes a long sermon which encouraged righteousness as well as courage. They were fighting 'a just war with the zeal of righteousness. For when a war has been entered upon by God's will, it is not permitted to doubt that it has been rightly undertaken'. The Moslems in Lisbon, on the other hand, were viewed as: 'the most depraved elements from all parts of the world who had come together as it were in a cesspool'.[12]

Such attitudes were reinforced by the open mocking of the Christian religion, as also happened at Lisbon when the Moors waved crosses from the walls, spat and pissed upon them, and used the crosses to wipe their bottoms. Priests without embarrassment could approve warfare and even atrocities: the writer of the account at Lisbon saw nothing wrong with Christians setting eighty Moslem heads on spears, and may himself have delivered the sermon given by a priest holding aloft a piece of the true cross while on board one of the siege towers. The priest promised to remain with the soldiers in the tower, whereupon they all fell on their faces with groans and tears, and called on God to aid them.[13]

Similar attitudes are expressed about the East, where one rarely finds criticism of acts of decapitation and worse, though the western chronicler, Orderic Vitalis, does suggest that at Ma'arrat, when Christian troops proceeded to cook and eat Turkish buttocks, some of the leaders were horrified; but even on this occasion they took no steps to stop it, or to punish those concerned, and the chronicler condones the act by suggesting that 'necessity forced them to break the law'.[14]

At Antioch the crusaders 'cast out the women from the army, married and unmarried, lest perchance, befouled by the mire of riotous living, they might displease God'. There were prohibitions against cheating, theft, drunkenness and fornication, with punishments ranging from head-shaving to beating, branding and death. During the Third Crusade, too, there were regulations in 1190 against gambling, except by knights and clerks, and even in their case not for more than twenty shillings during a period of twenty-four hours; and servants could only gamble with their masters' permission. At the siege of Acre the bishop of Salisbury, Hubert Walter, heard confessions from hungry crusaders who had eaten meat in Lent, and ordered three strokes of the cane on the back for each offence, but lightly! Just as fasting and praying were thought to win God's help, so immoral conduct was thought to turn God away. William of Tyre explained

12 See *De Expugnatione*, ed. David, p. 57, for Lisbon and clothes; on just war with the zeal of righteousness, p. 80: *zelo iusticie, non felle ire, iustum bellum committite*; on the cesspool, p. 95.

13 *De Expugnatione*, on mocking the cross, p. 132; on over eighty heads on poles, p. 140; for the sermon on the belfry, p. 146.

14 For the buttocks, see Fulcher of Chartres, ed. McGinty, pp. 10, 59, for the event; and Orderic Vitalis, v, p. 140 for the comment.

the Christian defeat at Harim in this way, blaming it upon gambling, frivolity and evil pleasures. The crusaders were forever leaving the siege to make their way to Antioch and its easy life, for baths, banquets and debauchery: 'forsaking the work of the siege for the delights of idleness'. Such activities deserved defeat.[15]

This puritanical attitude can be found expressed against groups of fellow crusaders, indeed was probably most readily uttered in such cases. The Anglo-Norman *Itinerarium* thus criticised the French for their wanton conduct, resorting to banquets, women and song, and even 'applauding bands of dancing women'. Ambroise similarly condemned the crusader excesses after the victory at Acre, when he noted they took to wine, women, lust and sin, of which, he says, decent folk were ashamed.[16]

It was believed that godly conduct would be rewarded with military victory, and there were frequent fasts and processions. Clerks prayed behind the belfry at Ma'arrat, and prayers were said to have actually effected the moving of a belfry at Jerusalem when it was stuck fast. It was at Jerusalem that the crusaders placed a gold image of Christ on top of one of the siege towers; and at Acre where one of the throwing engines was named by the Christians 'the Stone Thrower of God'.[17]

Priestly involvement in the crusades was considerable, and thought to be important. On the First Crusade were several bishops and priests, and Adhemar the bishop of Le Puy, while he lived, was probably the guiding hand. The intervention of visionaries was also significant, and it was no coincidence that increasingly visionaries were sought to give encouragement to decisions made by the leaders. On the First Crusade there were no less than six visionaries from the south of France alone, and Peter Bartholomew, the discoverer of the lance had thirteen visions altogether; the lance obviously giving his visions precedence over those of his fellow seers. Among the finds were two fingers of St Andrew, and the latter subsequently appeared in a vision, when he tried to persuade the Christians to place the reliquary more suitably by raising his hand, with two fingers missing! He was the busiest saint, making ten appearances altogether. Among others who materialised was Bishop Adhemar, after his death, showing the crusaders the way to scale the walls of Jerusalem. At Antioch St George had appeared, along with a band of ghostly knights bringing their aid to the Christians.

15 On Christian regulations: casting out women at Antioch, Fulcher of Chartres, ed. McGinty, pp. 43–4, and Brundage, *Problems*; on the 1190 regulations, see Archer, *Crusade of Richard I*, p. 37, and Roger of Howden, ed. Stubbs, iii, p. 58; on the bishop of Salisbury, Ambroise, ed. Hubert & La Monte, p. 191; on Harim and Antioch, William of Tyre, ii, p. 434.

16 On the dancing women, see Archer, *Richard I*, p. 219; and for the decent folk at Acre, Ambroise, ed. Hubert & La Monte, p. 233.

17 Riley-Smith, *First Crusade*: for the Ma'arrat belfry and the tower moved by prayer, p. 83; for the gold Christ, p. 97. For the Stone Thrower of God, Ambroise, p. 202.

Moslem attitudes were oddly similar, like two sides of the same coin. They too felt hatred, committed atrocities, believed they were acting for their faith, and could show courage and sympathy for the enemy. The Christians had come from a distant and alien part of the world, and had beliefs and practices which seemed strange. Moslems also acted at times more viciously than was their wont against these enemies of their religion, and there are examples of Christians being used as target practice for archers, and having their teeth pulled out as torture. Waleran of Le Puiset had his eye put out and his right arm cut so that he would never again be able to use a lance, a mutilation from which he died. On one occasion the Franks captured a Moslem ship full of Christian heads. There are also stories of Christians being crucified and eaten.[18]

The Moslems also viewed this as a holy war, as *jihad*, a military obligation which could have its reward in paradise. The Moslems, like the Christians, believed that God was on their side. There is a delightful story about Roger II, king of Norman Sicily, standing at his window overlooking the sea and watching the arrival of a ship which brought news of the Christian success at Tripoli. Roger asked his court, which included some Sicilian Moslems, what use is Mohamed now to his land and people? A Moslem adviser retorted: 'He was not there, He was at Edessa, which the Moslems have just taken!' The Christian visions of St George and the saints giving aid in battle, had Moslem counterparts; at Acre the Saracens saw ghostly cavalry clad in green coming to their assistance.[19]

Attacks on the enemy's religion were part of the warfare. On the Second Crusade, a Christian priest with a long beard rode an ass while carrying a cross, presumably to inspire the Christians with reminders of Christ. The priest was captured and beheaded, and his ass killed. It was common to mock Christian symbols: at Lisbon the Moors taunted the crusaders that their wives were making the most of their absence and were producing bastards. During the Third Crusade, a Moslem who abused the cross to taunt the Christians was hit by a shot from a crossbow, and 'fell down dead with his legs upraised'. Ibn al-Qalanisi refers to the placing of scalps on a standard after the Franks had been defeated at Banyas. But local, Armenian Christians could be treated even more harshly than the Franks, possibly because they were seen as traitors. After the capture of Baldwin II, his Armenian allies were tortured, flayed alive, sawn in half, burned alive and used as archery targets. Even Saladin, who has a reputation for fairness and mercy, himself beheaded Rainald of Chatillon after Hattin for his previous misdeeds, and ordered that all the captive Templars and

[18] Moslem atrocities: see Orderic Vitalis for the target practice, vi, p. 112; for Waleran le Puiset, vi, p. 124; for the ship full of heads, vi, p. 416. For crucifying and eating, see Fulcher of Chartres, ed. McGinty, p. 10.

[19] The Roger of Sicily story is from Ibn al-Athir, in Gabrieli, p. 52; and see Curtis, *Roger of Sicily*, p. 310. The green clad cavalry is Baha ad-Din, in Gabrieli, p. 221.

Hospitallers should be executed. In 1187, when the Christian defenders of Jerusalem sued for mercy, Saladin refused on the grounds that he wanted revenge for 1099: 'we shall deal with you, just as you dealt with the people of Jerusalem when you took it', though in the end he did agree terms. At Jaffa Saladin was said to have revenged himself for Richard's actions at Acre by collecting ransoms from prisoners, and then beheading them.[20]

The Moslems also had a puritanical streak to their religious attitudes: they also believed in the efficacy of virtuous conduct, and condemned the reverse. They could be scandalised by the ungodly behaviour of the Franks, whom they accused of bringing in shiploads of harlots, for the benefit not only of the troops but even of the priests.[21]

One of the most interesting points about respective attitudes is the growth of some understanding and sympathy, as well as respect for valiant opponents. As the Latin Kingdom developed, the residents came to understand something of each other's religions, and it was the newcomers on either side who tended to be most hostile. For example, local groups made alliances and agreements which newcomers found it hard to accept.

Links between the two groups were established from the start. A rather unlikely example occurred during the siege of Nicaea, where a nun was captured by the Turks and raped; she was later rescued, and pardoned by her own people for having had sex, since it had been forced upon her. Once released, however, she chose to run off with her Turkish lover: 'she found the forbidden fruit, once tasted, sweeter than the hope of heaven'.[22]

The bravery of the enemy was often noted. The *Itinerarium* said none could match the Turks in their warlike excellence. The author of the same work noted that some Moslems converted to Christianity, but he doubted the merit of this, believing it a consequence of terror rather than divine grace. He seemed to find the Turks were fine fellows, apart from their beliefs: 'it was only their superstitious rites and their shameful idolatry that had robbed such warriors of their strength'. The mutual respect of Richard the Lionheart and Saladin is well known. Baha ad-Din retorted of Richard: 'God damn him!', yet at the same time found him 'valorous and shrewd in warfare'. Similarly ambivalent feelings may be seen in Saladin's behaviour after his great victory at Hattin, when Rainald of Chatillon and King Guy were both brought as prisoners into his presence. Rainald had broken the existing truce and attacked a peaceful Moslem caravan. Saladin in person

20 On the ass, see Sibt ibn al-Janzi, in Gabrieli, pp. 62–3; on cuckolding, see *De Expugnatione*, p. 131; on the Hollywood style of dying, see Ambroise, p. 165; for the scalps at Banyas, Ibn al-Qalanisi, in Gabrieli, p. 67; for Baldwin and torture, William of Tyre, i, p. 543; Reynard of Chatillon is from Baha ad-Din, Gabrieli, p. 112; and Jerusalem 1187 and Saladin's revenge, Imad ad-Din, Gabrieli, p. 141.

21 For the harlots, see Imad ad-Din, in Gabrieli, p. 204.

22 For the nun, see W. Porges, *Speculum*, in Brundage, *Problems*, p. 53.

beheaded Rainald, and then turned to the trembling King Guy and asked after his health![23]

Usamah was a tolerant Moslem whose writings give an invaluable insight into respective attitudes in the Holy Land. He had no reason to like the Christians, since Christian pirates had once captured the ship he was travelling in, and destroyed his library of 4,000 volumes which was on board; any modern reader would sympathise with the hatred that might rouse. Nor, as one knowledgeable in medicine, had he much reason to respect Frankish doctors, who ignored his friendly advice; he tells of one Frank with a leg wound for which he advised poultices, only to be overruled in favour of amputation by two blows from an axe, which caused the marrow to spurt out and the unfortunate victim to die. He relates a similar story about a woman with consumption whom the Franks allowed an unwise diet, and then cut a cross on her skull. They removed the brain and rubbed in salt so that she died at once: 'I asked whether they had any further use for me'. To him the Franks lacked honour, and allowed a scandalous freedom to their women, but he also shows that the two groups could live side by side; and he himself befriended a Frank. He has a charming story about a Christian who made Usamah himself face east to pray. Afterwards a Templar, who had witnessed the incident, came up to Usamah and apologised for the behaviour of his fellow Christian, explaining that the man was a newcomer who did not understand the East.[24]

William of Tyre is the Christian counterpart of Usamah, broadly tolerant and knowing something of the ways of the other religion. He gives us a unique view of the Latin Kingdom through the eyes of one born in the Holy Land in about 1130. He was highly educated, knowing French, Arabic, Greek, Hebrew, Persian and Latin, and was well qualified to be tutor to the heir to the throne, Baldwin the Leper. William saw the rise of Saladin, but not the disaster of Hattin. He was passionately fond of his country, love of which, he insisted, urged him on to write.[25]

He found some Turkish actions horrific, such as their treatment of holy pictures after the taking of Antioch: eyes were gouged out, noses mutilated, and the surfaces were smeared with filth. He accused the Saracens of torturing one Christian leader at Jerusalem, so that 'the joints of both his hands and feet were wrenched apart and his limbs became useless'. William had little time for the Moslem religion, and referred to Mohamed himself as 'the seducer'. But he was also critical of crusading excesses, as over the

[23] On the excellence of the Turks in war, and the shameful idolatry, see Archer, *Richard I*, pp. 97, 102–3. On God damn Richard, and Guy's health, see Baha ad-Din, in Gabrieli, pp. 108, 112.

[24] Usamah, in Gabrieli, on his books and the amputation, p. 76; on the skull, pp. 76–7, on facing East, p. 80.

[25] On the career of William of Tyre, see the introduction to William of Tyre by Babcock and Krey.

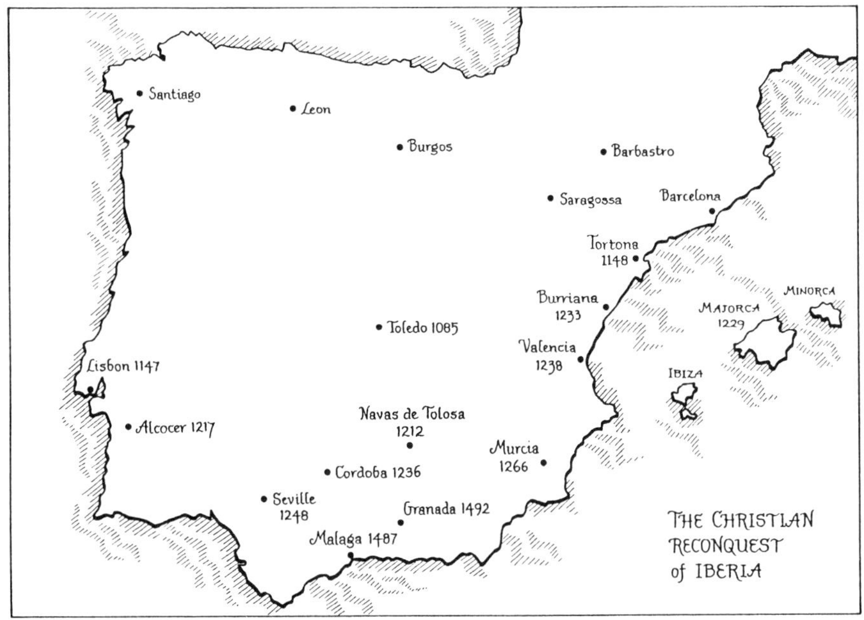

massacre that followed the taking of Jerusalem, of which he says: 'even the virtuous experienced feelings of horror'. He refers to the baptism of some Moslems, for example, the valet 'Baldwin', who later became involved in a plot against his master the king and was hanged. If in the early days Armenian Christians made a useful fifth column for the Franks, so, in William's time, Moslems living in the Christian territories provided a danger: 'there is no more deadly and effective pest than an enemy within one's own doors'. But William, like Usamah, gives evidence of some exchange and understanding. After the conclusion of the siege of Tyre in 1124, the Moslems came out to view the Christian engines, and the Christians were allowed in to admire the fortifications. By this period we even find Moslems and Christians in alliance; the Moslems of Damascus allied with the Franks against Zangi who was a threat to them both. Moslems and Christians were, at least on this occasion, 'united in courage and in purpose'.[26]

Spain and The Cid

Modern historians of the crusades generally deny that developments in Spain merit the label of a crusade. There are some technical arguments for this, such as the absence of a vow; Professor Riley-Smith has written that

26 William of Tyre, on the holy pictures, i, p. 296; on the joints, i, p. 335; on 'the seducer', i, p. 438; on the Jerusalem massacre, i, p. 371; on Baldwin the valet, i, pp. 487–8; on the

the Spanish expedition 'cannot be called a true crusade'. However, since the word crusade itself did not exist in the eleventh century, this decision is one made by modern historians, and little more than a matter of opinion, depending on modern definitions of the concept of a crusade.[27] The main difference seems to be the absence in Spain of the emotive significance attached to Jerusalem. Spain, like the East, saw a clash between Islam and Christendom, with the Christian efforts encouraged by papal support, and by the recruitment of Christians from other areas to assist in the struggle. Indeed often the very same areas which sent men on the First Crusade had provided men for the Spanish venture.

If Spain lacked some of the theoretical foundation made for the First Crusade, and some of the arrangements which accompanied that crusade, this may easily be explained by the fact that the Spanish Crusade came some thirty years or so earlier. The similarities between Spain and the First Crusade seem at least as significant as any differences. It seems mistaken to believe that the knights going on the First Crusade were motivated by religion, whereas those going to Spain went only for greed; the motivation of individuals was surely mixed in both ventures. In 1063 Alexander II offered an indulgence for those fighting for Christ in Spain, and this alone justifies the inclusion of Spain in a chapter devoted to the early crusades. An indulgence was also promulgated in 1089 with regard to Tarragona. To suggest that because Spain saw alliances between Christians and groups of Moslems proves it to be no crusade, is patently ridiculous, since exactly the same thing would happen in the Holy Land. Urban II tried to encourage some knights to stay in Spain rather than go to the East, and in 1099 sent the archbishop of Toledo back to Spain, which suggests that then at least he was not even giving priority to activities in the Holy Land.[28]

Iberia had been invaded by the Moslems in the eighth century, and taken over by them. An Islamic state had been established, which had grown into the independent emirate of Cordoba, making that town the largest in western Europe in the tenth century. In 929 was set up the independent Umayyad caliphate, and this survived until 1031. It was the collapse of the caliphate which offered Christendom its opportunity. Iberia disintegrated into small and relatively weak local units, the twenty-three taifa kingdoms. The small Christian kingdoms in the north were now able to hold their own and attempt expansion.[29]

In 1063 the duke of Aquitaine led an expedition into Spain, in alliance with the Catalans and Aragonese. They besieged Barbastro in the kingdom

enemy within doors, i, p. 495; on viewing the engines, ii, pp. 20–1; on Franks united with Moslems, ii, pp. 73, 105, 108.

27 On Spain as a crusade, Riley-Smith, *What Were the Crusades*, p. 75.

28 Urban II and the archbishop of Toledo, Erdmann, *Origin*, p. 318.

29 For a good, brief account of Spain in this period, see A. MacKay, *Spain in the Middle Ages*.

of Saragossa, cut its water supply, and after forty days took the place, massacring the men and enslaving the women and children.[30] Barbastro itself was recaptured soon afterwards, but it was the first major step in the Reconquest. Alfonso VI of Leon and Castile played an important rôle in this, winning control of surrounding territories, and capturing Toledo in 1085.

The most famous figure in this early stage of the Reconquest was Rodrigo Diaz de Vivar, better known to us as the Cid, the name deriving from an Arabic word for lord. He was born in Bergos in about 1040, and served Alfonso VI. 'God what a worthy vassal, had he but a worthy lord', comments the poem on the Cid. He was sent into exile by the king in 1081 and experienced a series of adventures that saw him move from the service of Moslem masters to making himself king of Valencia from 1094 to 1099, returning to the allegiance of his former master.[31]

Most of the detail about the Cid's life comes from a poem about his adventures written soon after his death. Such information is notoriously difficult for historians to deal with, containing the basis of a factual account, but undoubtedly embroidered for dramatic effect. The poem incidentally includes some interesting remarks on siege warfare in eleventh-century Spain. The Cid went into exile with sixty knights, and soon showed his ability to survive through military activity in a politically divided land. Early on he attacked Castejon at dawn, when most of the inhabitants were out in the fields, bursting unexpectedly through the gates, the Cid himself killing fifteen Moors. The surrounding district now belonged to him, and he took sheep, cattle and clothes to distribute to his men, who included Alvar Fanez, of the elbow constantly dripping with Moorish blood. The Cid made a camp for himself at Alcocer, with a trench round it 'so that neither by day nor by night could they be surprised'.[32] He gained the stronghold of Alcocer by a trick, striking all the tents except for one. The citizens came out in curiosity to examine the remaining tent, and then the Cid's force returned into view and burst in through the open gates, killing three hundred Moors. The Cid fixed his standard to the highest tower.

The people of Alcocer sent for aid to the king of Valencia, who came to try and recover the town, cutting off its water supply. The Christians made an early morning sortie, again for surprise, and won the battle. The Cid went on to besiege Valencia itself, which was given nine months to surrender, and did. The Cid took one fifth of the spoils as his own reward, some 30,000 marks. He now faced some determined efforts to recover Valencia, first by the king of Seville, who was defeated in battle. The poem then introduces the diverting tale of the marriage of the Cid's daughters to two

30 For Barbastro, see A. Ferreiro, 'The Siege of Barbastro'.

31 *The Poem of the Cid*, ed. Simpson, p. 7.

32 *Cid*, ed. Simpson, p. 25.

unworthy princes. The princes were revealed as cowards when a lion escaped. One of them hid under a bench, the other shit himself behind a wine press, while the Cid, of course, grabbed the lion by its mane and threw it back into its cage. The princes, his sons-in-law, took their revenge upon his daughters. When journeying through a wood, they stripped them of most of their clothes and flogged them with whips to which were attached spurs, leaving them for dead: 'much too low in rank were they for our marriage bed'. The daughters, however, were found and saved, and the princes disgraced in combat against the Cid's men. The daughters then found new and high-ranking husbands, their father being finally reconciled to King Alfonso.[33]

The Christian advance was threatened by the intervention of new Moslem invaders from Africa, first the Almoravids, and later the Almohads. Christian success was confirmed in the end by the great victory at Las Navas de Tolosa in 1212, and the Reconquest was completed by 1492 with the taking of Granada.

The First Crusade

The crusades present one of the great dramatic episodes of history. The First Crusade had results probably beyond the expectations of those who initiated it. Yet in the end what was achieved? The movement petered out in strange directions. Students asked to write on the effects of the crusades are hard-put to find any positive consequences. In the period to 1200 there were three major crusades, and several other expeditions which probably ought to be counted, but have been omitted in the traditional numbering scheme; whoever first counted the crusades had his eyes shut before he got to one, and blinked every now and then between the digits. Nevertheless, the crusades we know as the First, Second and Third, were major expeditions by any reckoning, and in this chapter we shall focus on the sieges that occurred during them.[34]

It is odd that more attention has not been given to the siege warfare of the crusades. Even the great work by Smail on crusading warfare somewhat neglects this aspect in favour of battle tactics, yet, as in the West, sieges were far more common than battles, and in many ways more significant. In the East it was a question of controlling the territory step by step, the boundaries depended upon the cities and castles held at any one time.

The First Crusade saw three great sieges, and they determined the

[33] *Cid*, ed. Simpson, for Valencia's surrender, p. 51; the marriage and the lion, pp. 73, 89–90; for too low in rank, p. 106.

[34] For general reading on the crusades, see n. 1 above; for the First Crusade, see Riley-Smith, *First Crusade*. Major sources on the First Crusade include Raymond of Aguilers, the *Gesta Francorum*, Fulcher of Chartres, and Anna Comnena, Peter Tudebod. The new work by C. Marshall helps to fill the gap on crusading sieges.

CILICIA
COUNTY of EDESSA
Edessa
PRINCIPALITY of ANTIOCH
Antioch
Aleppo
Ma'arrat
CYPRUS
Tortosa
Krak
Homs
COUNTY of TRIPOLI
Tripoli
Beirut
Sidon
Damascus
Tyre
Banyas
Acre
Tiberias
Caesarea
Arsuf
Jaffa
Ibelin
Ramleh
Jerusalem
Ascalon
Blanche-garde
Gibelin
KINGDOM of JERUSALEM
Monreal
THE CRUSADER PRINCIPALITIES

progress and outcome of the expedition. After Urban II's preaching, Byzantium viewed the appearance of thousands of pilgrims with mixed feelings. Aid was desperately needed after the disaster at Manzikert, but the Greeks expected mercenary aid for their own exploits, not a mass migration from the West. It seemed wiser, in the event, to direct and assist, rather than to command and lead. Despite Frankish criticism of the part played by the Greeks, the crusade did indeed receive much important and vital aid. Byzantium hoped for, and obtained promises with regard to, the recovery of territories in Asia Minor lost to the Turks. In the early stages this was the crusading target.

The first great siege was that of Nicaea, which the crusaders reached in 1097. They soon found themselves short of supplies, and were already dependent upon provisions from the emperor. Here for the first time on the crusade they built siege engines and brought them up to the walls, they used a *testudo*, and then mined. The engines here were either made by the emperor, Manuel Butumites, or with Byzantine aid, and, as with the fortifications, it remains a moot point how much the Franks learned from the methods of the Byzantines. Byzantium certainly had considerable resources, some of which had been expended upon improving the route to Nicaea.

The city of Nicaea had four miles of walls, and 240 towers. According to William of Tyre, it stood on a plain with mountains around, and woods nearby. The waves of the lake which stretched to the west, touched against the walls, and a wet moat ran round the 'thick walls and lofty towers'. Raymond of Aguilers found them 'clever defences'. The city owed allegiance to the Seljuk leader, Kilij Arslan. For two days the crusaders tried to storm Nicaea. The blockade was only half-hearted, and the Turks were still able to get in by the South Gate, and across the lake. Count Raymond had to come round the city to block one relief attempt to force an entrance. Gradually the Franks settled to a longer effort: the Italian Sicilians, Bohemond and Tancred, took the north; Godfrey of Bouillon the east, and Count Raymond with Bishop Adhemar the south.[35]

When the relief attempt failed, the heads of Turks who had been captured and killed, were hurled into the city 'to cause terror to the garrison'.[36] A further thousand heads were sent to the emperor, which apparently won his whole-hearted approval. Count Raymond attacked the sector where Kilij Arslan's wife resided with two engines, but after several days not one stone had been moved, and the enemy backed up the wall with rubble, so that even if it fell, the entrance would still be blocked. One enemy hurled insults at the Christians till Duke Godfrey himself shot the man with a bow. A knight, in trying to break through a repaired section, was killed and

35 On defences at Nicaea, William of Tyre, i, p. 153; on the clever defences, Raymond of Aguilers, p. 25.

36 On terror to the garrison, *Gesta Francorum*, p. 15.

pulled inside the city by hooks. His armour was removed, and the naked body hurled back to the Franks. After five weeks mining was attempted under the protection of a *testudo*. William of Tyre says that *scrophae*, or sows, were used; though a strong belfry to cover the mining, which had twenty knights inside, was wrecked by rocks thrown from the wall, the joints giving way so that all those inside were crushed to death.[37] Nevertheless the mining continued, under cover of an engine built by a Lombard with special expertise; it proved safe from rocks because it had a steeply sloping roof. Beams were inserted in the tunnel under the tower, and in the evening the beams were fired. During the night the tower collapsed, but the timing was unfortunate for the crusaders, since immediate attack was out of the question, and the defenders were able to mend the breach.

Crusader success only seemed likely when the blockade was properly completed, with further Greek aid. The emperor sent boats, which the crusaders dragged overland from the sea to the lake. Fulcher of Chartres said he saw this done, with knights riding on oxen pulling the boats by ropes. William of Tyre explained that some of the boats were dismantled and then reassembled, and that it took three or four wagons to carry a medium-sized boat. The dragging was done at night over the seven miles to the lake. There were also some larger boats which held fifty or a hundred men.[38] When this new fleet was floated on the lake, the sight of it was enough to bring the people of Nicaea to negotiate, seven weeks and three days after the start of the siege. Kilij Arslan's wife tried to escape over the lake, but was captured and sent to Constantinople.

The capture of Nicaea was an important step, suggesting that the crusade might indeed be able to achieve something of value, after the debacle of the People's Crusade. The Byzantine Empire had gained some recompense for its expenses, and could hope for more as the crusaders moved on to Antioch. If the crusade were to make gains of permanent value, there was urgent need for a good base, and Antioch could provide just that; it had been a great city of the Roman Empire, with long Christian traditions, and had only been captured by the Moslems in 1085. The long drawn-out siege which now ensued is probably the key conflict in the First Crusade, upon which eventual success or failure of the whole expedition depended.

William of Tyre gives us valuable descriptions of many of the places which figure in crusading history. He pictured Antioch as having an iron bridge over the River Orontes, the perimeter of the town defended by four hundred towers.[39] There were two miles of walls around the city embattled in the midst of a plain, with the river to the east and marshy land all

37 On *scrophae* and engines, William of Tyre, i, pp. 157–9.

38 On boats and oxen, Fulcher of Chartres, ed. McGinty, p. 33; on reassembling boats, William of Tyre, i, p. 160.

39 On Antioch, William of Tyre, pp. 199–206.

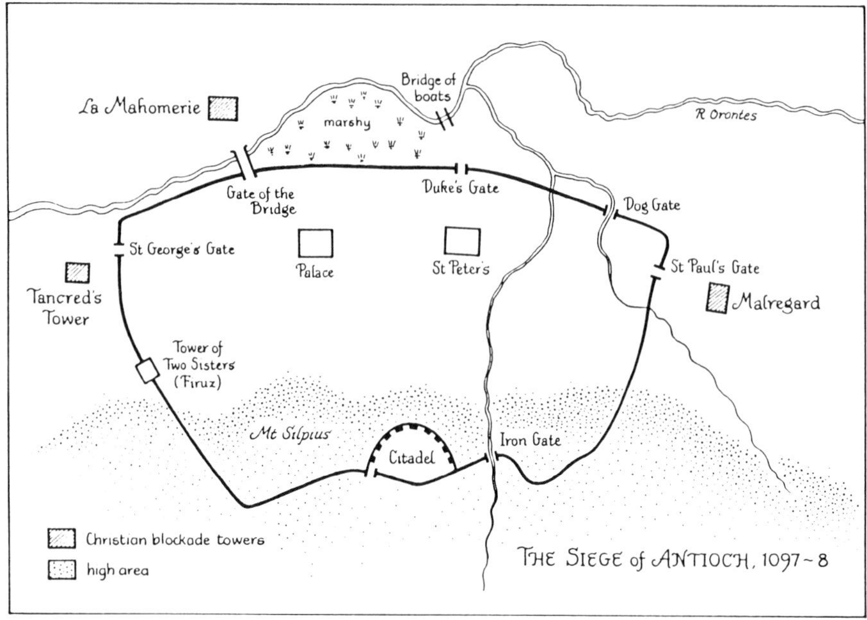

around. William knew it as a beautiful place in a fertile valley between the mountains, with a lake lying in the higher levels. The city was on the nearer and steeper slopes to the south, between the mountain and the river, with a wall running right down to the river. Two peaks stood within the walls, on the highest of which, a thousand feet over the town, perched the citadel. A ravine holding a stream ran between the peaks and through the city, so there was a good water supply. The mountain and the river lay to the west, and the sea was about twelve miles off. Antioch came under the control of Aleppo, and was ruled by Yaghi-Sian, who had providently stored up supplies in anticipation of a siege.

The Christians approached Antioch in 1097. They debated whether to begin the blockade at once, or to wait until winter was over. It was argued that if they did not start now, the town would only be better supplied and stronger by the spring, so the siege was commenced with winter coming on. At first the crusaders, fat with the takings from Nicaea, were able to indulge themselves on the best cuts of meat and good living, but it was not to last.

Antioch posed a testing military problem. It was impossible to surround the town completely, the country around it was too difficult. There were five gates on to the plain, and a bridge over the marsh. The Christians cut down the orchards in order to clear the approach to the city, and also to provide themselves with material for making their own defences. They needed a means of crossing the river, so built a bridge of boats over the Orontes. Three gates were blocked: a tower called 'Malregard' was built

Moslems defending Antioch against the crusaders

outside St Paul's Gate, one by the bridge, and another by St George's Gate. The enemy made life difficult by occasionally opening the Dog Gate and shooting out a hail of arrows, as well as making sorties. The Franks built belfries and engines, but in the end had to depend upon blockade.

After three months, conditions in the Christian camp were deteriorating: prices had risen to seven or eight shillings for grain for a horse for one night; the tents were rotting, and many crusaders were ill. Their Byzantine adviser, Tatikios, suggested that they should abandon the siege, but they chose to persevere.[40] A Turkish relief attempt failed, and the besieged also found themselves in difficulties. Two hundred Turkish heads were hurled into the city by the engines, and others were displayed on poles. After five months the crusaders received welcome aid when Genoese ships brough provisions by sea. There were many notable incidents, including the killing of a Turk by Godfrey of Bouillon, who sliced his opponent in half 'like a young leek', the upper part of the body above the waist fell to the ground, while the lower half continued on its horse into the city.[41] A Christian captive, Rainald Poubert, was made by his captors to stand on the wall and beg for a ransom, but instead he passed on the information that the Turks were in a poor state, and encouraged his friends to continue their attack. He was beheaded for his efforts.

Antioch finally fell through treachery, one of the many occasions when local aid proved invaluable. Antioch was a city whose Christian tradition stretched back to early days. The Tower of the Two Sisters was held by the

40 For the rôle of Tatikios, see J. France, 'The Departure of Tatikios'.
41 On the 'leek', Orderic Vitalis, v, p. 84.

family of Beni-Zarra, whose head was Firuz, a cuirass maker. The latter made contact with Bohemond, and offered to help the Franks to get in. Apparently Firuz' son had discovered his mother in a compromising situation with one of the Turkish rulers of the city, and Firuz having learned of this now sought his revenge. The Turks suspected Firuz' intentions, but he persuaded them of his continued loyalty by himself suggesting that the city's defences be strengthened and the guard increased. Bohemond tried to use the offer, which he kept to himself, to get an agreement from the other leaders that if he could get them into the city, he would be allowed to keep it. Raymond of Toulouse was the chief obstacle to Bohemond's ambitions, but with a large Turkish relief army rumoured to be on the way, pressure increased, and Bohemond clinched the deal after nine months of siege.

On the very night when Firuz intended to let in the Franks, the Turks planned to massacre untrustworthy Christians within the city. Firuz killed his own brother with a sword to prevent the betrayal of his schemes. Every night the guard was checked several times. Firuz waited until all was clear, then signalled to Bohemond, and let down a rope from the tower. Bohemond tied a ladder to the rope, and Firuz pulled it in so that the ladder was in place. Bohemond himself led the way up, and Firuz pulled him inside. The tower was soon seized, the guards killed, and a postern gate into the city was opened. The Christians had finally entered Antioch. They soon opened the Gate of the Bridge, and panic followed, amid the killing and noise, but the Turks were slow to realise that the sounds were not those of Christian traitors being killed as they had planned, and when they did realise, it was too late. Yaghi-Sian fled, but was captured by local Armenian Christians, who cut off his head and sent it back to Antioch. The Christians slaughtered their enemies, so that it was only possible to walk through the streets over piled corpses.[42]

But the siege of Antioch was not over: Kerbogha with his army of relief now arrived outside Antioch, while within the city the Turks still held the citadel on the heights. The Christians besieged the citadel from inside the town, but found themselves besieged by Kerbogha. They improved their position by building defences between themselves and the citadel, but spirits fell once the elation of breaking in had worn off. The Turks nearly managed to enter the city, but the alarm was given in time, and those who had scrambled on to the walls were thrown down again. Bohemond found it difficult to get the Franks to perform guard duty conscientiously, and in the end had to set fire to part of the city in order to smoke some of his fellow crusaders out of the comfortable nests they had made for themselves in the town houses. Again there were shortages, and desperate measures had to be taken: they were forced to eat carrion and leaves, thistles which

42 For Firuz see *Gesta Francorum*, pp. 44–7.

pricked the tongue, dried horse-skin, and seeds of grain found in manure. Prices were high: wine cost too much even to mention, a tongueless horse's head was two or three shillings, and a goat's intestines five shillings; a hen cost fifteen shillings, an egg two shillings, and a walnut a penny.[43]

There had also been desertions, though some of the deserters, like Peter the Hermit were brought back. Stephen-Henry, the count of Blois, has been blamed through the ages for deserting Antioch, but probably his fault has been exaggerated, and few have sought his reasons.[44] He cannot have been entirely without merit, since the crusading leaders had only recently elected him as their commander-in-chief. He had also been ill, and, given the large numbers of crusaders who suffered, plus the awful conditions at Antioch, there seems little reason to believe the sniping suggestion that he was simply pretending. He was condemned by hostile chroniclers attached to other crusading leaders, and by Anna Comnena, who was concerned to protect her father's reputation over the business. Reading between the lines it seems most likely that Count Stephen's mission was to go to the emperor and seek aid for the crusaders at Antioch. If he described the situation as desperate, that was hardly an exaggeration. The count seems to have left before Kerbogha closed in, and once that had occurred, it would have been nearly impossible for anyone outside to know the true position. It seems very likely that the emperor's refusal to continue his march on Antioch had less to do with Stephen-Henry's pessimism, than with the information that Kerbogha and a very large army was now outside the town. The emperor's decision to turn back left Stephen-Henry in an impossible situation; without the emperor and his army the count was in no position to relieve Antioch, or even to get back in. His decision to return to the West was not an heroic one, but is not difficult to understand. The way in which the count died deserves some praise, albeit rather late in the day, after centuries when chroniclers' calumnies have been accepted without question. The story is, of course, that he only went back to the Holy Land, because his wife, the daughter of William the Conqueror, was horrified by his cowardice, and hen-pecked him into going. Could the chronicler really know this? Should we accept this malicious tittle-tattle without

43 For thistles and prices, *Gesta Francorum*, p. 62.

44 Count Stephen-Henry has been ridiculed by chroniclers, such as Orderic Vitalis, v, pp. 106, 324: 'an object of contempt'; and modern historians e.g. R.H.C. Davis: *King Stephen*, p. 3. See *Gesta Francorum*, p. 63; Anna Comnena, pp. 348–9; Raymond of Aguilers, English, p. 49, Latin, p. 77; For Stephen's letters to his wife, see *Die Kreuzzugsbriefe*, ed. Hagenmeyer, pp. 138–40, 149–52; Both Raymond and the *Gesta* have deserters escaping by rope, but not Stephen. Fulcher of Chartres, ed. McGinty, p. 45, says 'all of us grieved, since he was a very noble man and valiant in arms'; ed. Hagenmeyer, p. 228: *quia virerat nobilissimus et armis validus*. The story clearly grew in the telling. One certainly doubts Orderic's pretensions to knowledge about the words and motives of Adela. He has Adela chiding Stephen 'between conjugal caresses'. Even Orderic was not likely to have been on the spot for that information!

question? What we really know is that Count Stephen-Henry chose to raise new forces in the West and return to the Holy Land to die bravely fighting in battle against the Turks. Other 'deserters' were William of Grandmesnil and his brother Aubrey, but, given the awful situation, and the hostile relations between some of the crusading groups, it is not at all surprising that some should choose to return home: cowardice may have been the least of their reasons.

It was at the time when crusading fortunes seemed to be at their lowest ebb, with food short, prices high, no aid from the emperor, that the holy lance was discovered. It is impossible for us now to know the truth of this incident; we shall either be inclined to accept the story of the miracle at face value, or treat it with scepticism. Both these reactions occurred at the time. The announcement of its existence was made by Peter Bartholomew, after receiving the information in a vision. He led others to the spot, and after men had dug all day, Peter wearing only a shirt, leaped into the pit and discovered the lance which had pierced the side of Christ on the cross. Some were sceptical: how could the holy lance be both in this pit, and on display in a church in Constantinople? Fulcher of Chartres considered the object to have been deceitfully found by a foolish man. The existence of doubt is made clear by the fact that shortly afterwards Peter was made to undergo the ordeal, walking through flames with the lance. He claimed to have received another vision in the flames, when he was informed that he would be harmed, but would not go to hell. The flames proved too much, he lived on for a few days and then expired. Even this did not undermine the belief of those who thought the lance to be genuine, and its impact on the crusaders was such that even the most sceptical leader must have soon realised that its value in building morale had been so great that scepticism was best suppressed. 'The despondent spirits of the people rose'.[45] A five day fast was declared, at the end of which it is not surprising that the Christians had halucinations, and saw St George and an army of saints on white horses coming to their aid. Bohemond assembled the Franks before the Gate of the Bridge for a sortie, one might suggest a last desperate hope. Battle was fought and the Turkish army broke and scattered. Kerbogha was defeated, and now the garrison in the citadel finally surrendered. A second major siege triumph had been achieved, and the road to Jerusalem was open.

Militarily, the siege of Jerusalem was less significant than that at Antioch: the victories at the latter had made the fall of Jerusalem almost inevitable; but the taking of Jerusalem was the dramatic climax, the fitting conclusion. The goal of taking Jerusalem had always influenced the

[45] For the Holy Lance, see Fulcher of Chartres, ed. McGinty, pp. 48–9, and n. 6 above; for it deceitfully found: 'thinking it was not the Lord's lance, but another one deceitfully found by that foolish man; see also *Gesta Francorum*, p. 59; and Raymond of Aguilers, English, p. 57.

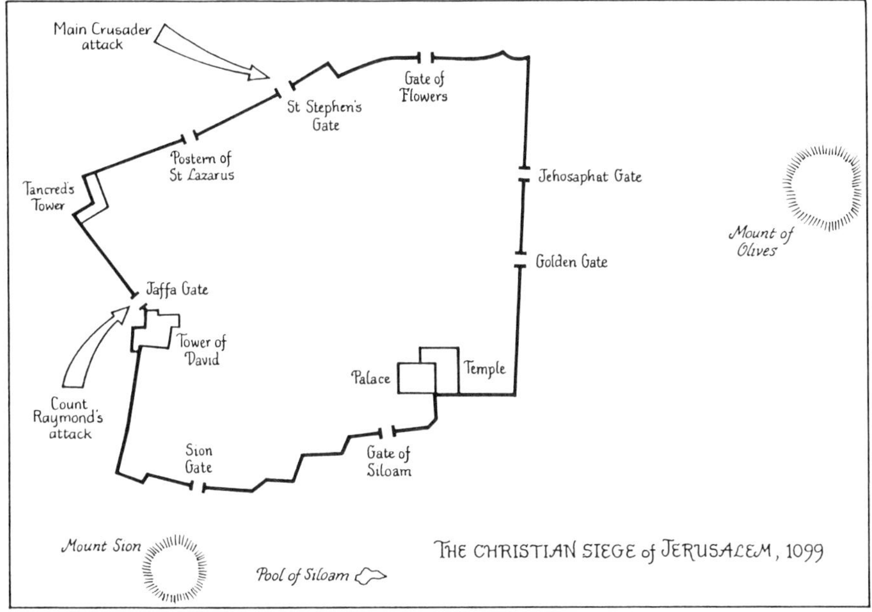

THE CHRISTIAN SIEGE of JERUSALEM, 1099

direction of the crusade, even at the planning stage. Jerusalem was 'the city of our quest'.[46] So the First Crusade moved towards its last great triumph.

William of Tyre, who was born of crusading parents and probably in Jerusalem itself, described his city on its lofty hills, some twenty-four miles from the sea, with the River Jordan fourteen miles to the east.[47] It was, he thought, not a very large city, but dramatically set with ravines around three sides. The valley between two hills divided Jerusalem in two, with Mount Sion to the west, and Mount Moriah to the east. On the west wall stood the citadel, the Tower of David. Water supply was a problem 'in an arid land entirely without water', and therefore rain water was collected in cisterns, and kept for a year.[48] The northern approach was the easiest, and it was on this side that the crusaders camped. They had not enough men to surround the whole city, nor enough ladders and engines for the task of storming. The crusaders, outside the city, had no easy access to water, the few sources that there were had either been polluted, or had become places of ambush. Local people showed them a supply five miles away, but bringing any back proved dangerous and difficult. At one point they went ten days without bread, and such water as they could get, stank.

Collecting materials for making belfries and engines was equally

46 Jerusalem city of our quest, is Raymond of Aguilers, English, p. 83.
47 Description of Jerusalem, from William of Tyre, i, pp. 339–43.
48 On aridity and cisterns, see William of Tyre, i, pp. 346, 352; and compare Fulcher of Chartres, p. 64.

difficult, timber had to be brought from some distance, and was not of good quality. But at last engines were made, and ladders tied together. They decided to alter their plans, and attack at a point where the walls were lower. A procession was made past the walls to build morale. Three belfries were built, and pushed towards the walls, but the town ditch halted progress. They filled in the ditch with stones, earth and rubbish, taking three days and nights. Some Turkish women appeared on the walls, chanting, until they were hit by a stone and killed. Sacks and cushions were set on fire and hurled in to make a smoke-screen. Godfrey of Bouillon and his brother led the storm from the top of one of the belfries, and were among the first to enter Jerusalem by means of the bridge from their tower. They broke in and opened St Stephen's Gate. Count Raymond made a separate assault from the south, and he too was able to get in from his tower over a bridge, opening the South Gate. There followed a dreadful massacre, which Saladin would recall many years later. There may have been some exaggeration over the numbers killed, since it was said that, apart from the garrison, the city was nearly empty at the time of the attack, but there can be little question of the ferocity of the crusader onslaught. The Christians waded through blood up to their ankles. On the fifteenth of July, 1099, the crusaders took Jerusalem. Captives were made to clear the corpses from the Temple, but there too many so that a great stench arose, and the poor had to be paid to give a hand.[49]

The Second Crusade

The taking of Jerusalem marked the establishment of a Frankish state in the East. The Franks already held a number of major centres: Baldwin had established himself at Edessa through marriage and force, and Bohemond had retained his prize of Antioch. Now Godfrey of Bouillon was chosen as the ruler of Jerusalem with the title of advocate. When Godfrey died, his brother Baldwin succeeded him, and used the title of king, the recognised ruler of the new Latin Kingdom.

In the period before the Second Crusade, the territories belonging to the Christians were linked and rounded out. Neighbouring cities of significance were besieged and taken: Arsuf, Caesarea, Acre, Jaffa, Beirut, Tripoli and Sidon among them. A number of new castle strongholds were constructed, including Gibelin, Ibelin and Blanchegarde. Acre, on the coast, was a major site for communications; the first siege had to be abandoned, but was renewed in 1104 with success. This time the crusaders had the assistance of a Genoese fleet and were thus able to complete the blockade. They attacked using 'ingenious machines', and in twenty days the place

49 On Saladin recalling the Christian siege, see n. 20 above; on the poor paid to help, William of Tyre, i, p. 377.

surrendered. William of Tyre emphasised the importance of this gain: 'for the first time a safe and convenient approach was opened to those arriving by sea'.[50]

Tyre itself was finally taken in 1124: 'the metropolis of all Phoenicia', claims William, who became its archbishop. He described it as rich, large, beautiful and fertile, 'entirely surrounded by the waves like an island'.[51] The only possible approach by land was from the east, and that only of the breadth of an arrow shot. Approach for attackers by sea was also difficult because there were hidden rocks under the waters. Tyre had a triple wall, with towers so close together that they nearly touched. The Christians when they besieged Tyre, built a ditch round their camp for protection. The Venetians shipped in materials for their engines; workmen and carpenters were collected, and a tower built which loomed over the city. It was fired by the defenders, but one young man climbed up to the top to put it out with water. It was blockade rather than storm that succeeded, and eventually Tyre surrendered.

Already in the period before the Second Crusade there were signs of the precarious nature of the Latin Kingdom. The Saracens were soon attempting to regain what had been lost, and to take the new Frankish strongholds. In 1144 Zangi besieged Edessa, and so heavy was the bombardment that 'even the birds dared not fly near'.[52] The Moslems brought their own specialist miners from Khurasan and Aleppo to Edessa, and when the wall was brought down, the city was taken by storm. Relations between crusading leaders had always been touchy, and at Haran in 1104, arguments between Baldwin and Bohemond over entry lost them their chance, a 'disgraceful disaster' in the view of William of Tyre. Such squabbles weakened the kingdom. King Fulk, previously count of Anjou, who gained the kingdom through marriage to the heiress Melisende, had to besiege Christian opponents at Jaffa. The Latin Kingdom was a kingdom under siege, its defence a matter which allowed no respite, with inadequate Christian manpower, and constantly hostile neighbours. One could perhaps compare its dilemma with that of the more recent creation in the region, Israel. Life in the kingdom must always have been under threat. William of Tyre said: 'no place was safe outside the encircling walls of the cities'.[53]

The Franks' best hope was probably to become accepted as one of a number of minor political units. At times this seemed likely to occur, as

50 The Second Crusade, no doubt because it failed, is less well covered both by chroniclers and modern historians; but see Runciman, *Crusades*, ii; Odo of Deuil, *De Profectione*; G. Constable, 'The Second Crusade'. For Lisbon, the *De Expugnatione*. On ingenious machines at Acre, and the taking of Tyre, see William of Tyre, i, pp. 455–6.

51 On the metropolis, and the island, William of Tyre, ii, pp. 4–5.

52 On Edessa 1144 and the birds, see Ibn al-Qalanisi, in Gabrieli, pp. 49–50.

53 For the disgraceful disaster, and no safe place outside the walls, William of Tyre, ii, p. 472.

when one or other of the Moslem neighbours sought a Frankish alliance against their own enemies. One such occasion, was the alliance between Moslem Damascus and the Franks against Zangi. Together they besieged and took Banyas in 1140. The residents of the Latin Kingdom came to see such alliances as a part of life, but the constant arrival of Christians from the West who could not believe any accomodation was possible with the enemies of their religion, constantly hampered such developments.

By the 1140s the Latin Kingdom was under strong pressure, and perhaps the seeds of final decay had already been planted. The Moslem neighbours were never to be so weak and divided as they had been in the late eleventh century. The best hope for survival seemed to be a new influx of manpower from the West, and a new crusade was preached by St Bernard on behalf of Pope Eugenius III. The result looked impressive, with figures of far greater European significance than those involved in the First Crusade expressing their interest. The leaders of the new venture were probably the two most powerful rulers in the West at the time: Conrad III, the German king, and Louis VII of France.

However the Second Crusade was a disaster. Louis VII had problems with his wife, Eleanor of Aquitaine; there were scandalous rumours of her affair with her own uncle, Count Raymond. William of Tyre, writing without the constraint of the French chroniclers, makes no bones about it: 'she disregarded her marriage vows, and was unfaithful to her husband'.[54] Odo of Deuil, Louis VII's own chaplain and a monk at Suger's St Denis, tells us much about the journey, but does not trouble to describe what happened in the Holy Land. The army was already badly depleted before the crusade's one major attempt, on Damascus, was made.

Damascus, which William of Tyre saw as 'a city of great menace to us', was a worthwhile objective.[55] It stood on a plain, dry but for a number of ancient canals which irrigated its orchards. These were held in small estates, and surrounded by a maze of mud walls which provided an irritating obstacle to the crusaders. There was also plenty of cover for the Saracens to hamper Christian efforts by ambushes; they also used holes in the defences to poke out weapons suddenly against unwary attackers. There were desertions, some it was said were bribed to leave. The orchards made approach too difficult, and so they decided to move camp and try from another direction, but this proved even more disastrous. They now found themselves in arid country, without a good supply of food and water, and the Saracens recaptured the orchards. There was a major clash after a Saracen sortie, when so many Franks were killed that the corpses created a stench which was enough 'to make the birds fall out of the sky'. The

[54] On Eleanor of Aquitaine, whom he saw as 'a foolish woman', William of Tyre, ii, pp. 180–1.

[55] On Damascus, William of Tyre, ii, p. 186.

English writer, John of Salisbury, said Louis and Conrad barely escaped alive after the annihilation of their armies.[56]

There was an attempt to retrieve losses by taking Ascalon, but the first effort here had to be abandoned, and a second attempt made. Ascalon was another site where the attackers had difficulties in finding water, the defenders relying on cisterns. Ascalon could also reckon on assistance from Egypt, and had strong defences. Blockade had to be by sea as well as by land. The citizens defended in relays, using oil lamps under glass covers to make night as bright as day.

A high tower was built using ships' masts for the timbers, and a cover of wicker and hide. They also constructed rams and covered sheds. With shouts they pushed the belfry forward and attempted to storm the walls. In the meantime, Nureddin tried to divert attention by besieging Banyas, but the crusaders persisted. A gap was made in the wall, but the Templars selfishly refused to let anyone else make use of it, which allowed the enemy time to repair the breach. Dead Christians were hanged from the walls by ropes. One great stone from an engine landed on forty Moslems who were dragging a beam along for the defences, and they were all killed.[57] In the end Ascalon surrendered, the one major success of the Second Crusade in the Holy Land.

There was, however, another and rather unexpected success for the crusade, in the West, with the Christian siege of Moorish Lisbon by a group setting out by sea. One chronicler suggested that the triumph was achieved by 'lesser folk', and they included an important Norman and English contingent.[58] A number of the English sailors were clearly not men of wealth, and only ready to stay on if paid. A detailed account of this siege is found in the writing of an anonymous Anglo-Norman priest, in the form of a letter addressed to Osbern of Bawdsey, but it is of such length as to suggest that the form is a literary device. From comments in the work, it seems that the author was attached to Hervey Glanvill, and was probably a clerk.[59]

Our author accompanied the crusaders, and witnessed the events which he described so graphically. He viewed Lisbon on its hill, with walls descending to the River Tagus, a city surrounded by fruit trees, vines, olives, figs and herds of animals. Inside were narrow streets and 'the most depraved elements from all parts of the world'.[60] The Christians arrived at midday, and disembarked on the shore. They captured the suburb, but were trapped against the walls by a counter attack. After two weeks they set-to

56 For birds from the sky, Ibn al-Qalanisi in Gabrieli, p. 59; on the kings barely escaping, John of Salisbury, *Historia Pontificalis*, p. 11.

57 William of Tyre, ii, p. 230.

58 *De Expugnatione*, p. vii.

59 See introduction to *De Expugnatione*.

60 *De Expugnatione*, p. 95.

and constructed a sow, a ram, and mobile towers. The Anglo-Norman belfry was ninety-five feet high, but when they moved their engines up towards the walls, the enemy attack proved too fierce, and all except the ram were burned. The Anglo-Norman belfry stuck in the sand, and became the target for three enemy mangonels. On the third day it was fired, with subsequent loss of morale.

After six weeks the crusaders were heartened to hear that the enemy had their own problems over food, of which the Christians had plenty. They now decided to stay for the winter, and the ships were pulled ashore, their masts lowered and cordage stored. The Germans mined, but the enemy countered with success. A group of Moors tried to break out by boat, but it was overturned, and one body was found with a message tied to the arm. The Christians continued to press with their stone-throwers, operated by groups of a hundred men at a time. One trick the Franks used was to tempt the hungry Moslems with food in traps, which were sprung to catch the enemy 'like birds . . . causing enormous merriment amongst us'.[61] Mining finally brought down some two hundred feet of wall, but the enemy managed to repair it. A priest carrying part of the True Cross preached a sermon from a belfry as it moved forward, it may have been the author of the letter himself. Crossbowmen and archers from the belfry cleared the opposing section of wall, but the tower got cut off by the tide, and the Moors made a sortie against it. The tower was defended successfully, but in the morning the same thing happened. The belfry got to within eight feet of the wall, when the engineer was wounded by an enemy stone. After two days dogged fighting, the engine was within four feet of the wall, and at last they were able to use a bridge of two cubits in length to cross over to the wall and get in. After seventeen weeks Lisbon fell, an important stage in the Reconquest. But all in all, the Second Crusade had brought little profit for much effort.

The Third Crusade

The Second Crusade had done little to relieve the pressure of Islam upon the new Latin Kingdom. In addition to the threats of attack, the Kingdom of Jerusalem continued to be its own worst enemy, provoking potential Moslem allies into opposition, and antagonising powerful Moslem leaders. King Amaury I was a moderate, reserved man, according to William of Tyre who knew him, though prone to seducing women, for which William asked God's forgiveness. The king was a little odd physically, with breasts like a woman. By attacking Shawar, the king united the Moslems against himself, and was partly responsible for Shirkuh taking over Egypt. William

61 *De Expugnatione*, p. 145.

of Tyre thought that all things had changed for the worse, and 'we ourselves were cause'.[62] Nurredin extended his authority to Damascus, once an ally of the Christians, and then to Egypt, where his general Shirkuh became viceroy. On Shirkuh's death in 1174, his nephew Saladin succeeded him, and became in due course ruler of both Egypt and Syria.

Matters were brought to a head by the actions of Rainald of Chatillon, who had an evil enough reputation among Christians, but to the Moslems was a veritable devil. He is said, after an argument with the patriarch of Jerusalem, to have forced the latter to sit all day in the open under a blazing summer sun, his head smeared with honey to attract insects.[63] Rainald broke the truce with the Moslems by attacking a peaceful caravan, and provoked Saladin to reopen hostilities.

The accession of the young Baldwin IV did not strengthen the Christian situation. He was the pupil of William of Tyre, well-read and intelligent, but he also suffered from leprosy, and was partially paralysed, which did not make him the best military leader the Christians could wish for. He also faced, in Saladin, the rising star of Islam, a ruler of great determination and ability. The tables were now turned with a vengeance. The Christians had to abandon the siege of Haran. Saladin became a familiar and feared figure, leading the attack at many points, surrounded by a bodyguard distinguished by yellow silk over their breastplates. With a series of sieges Saladin began to move in on the Latin Kingdom, taking Beirut, Edessa and Aleppo. As William of Tyre saw it, the whole kingdom seemed to be 'as it were in a state of siege'.[64] The Templars ignored Raymond of Tripoli's order to refrain from attacking Saladin, and as a result Saladin destroyed a Templar force, and besieged Tiberias. The new king, Guy, only gained the throne through marriage, and was not respected by all his own magnates. Perhaps in an attempt to improve his reputation, he misguidedly set out to relieve Tiberias, and only succeeded in getting the Christian army trapped at Hattin in 1187, where they suffered one of the greatest defeats in crusading history and Guy himself was taken prisoner. Saladin's victory at Hattin destroyed the Latin field army, and without it, the isolated strongholds proved vulnerable. One after the other fell to him, including Jerusalem, and the kingdom was in danger of complete annihilation.

The Third Crusade, called in the aftermath of Saladin's victories, is well known in England because of the involvement of Richard the Lionheart, once seen as 'a bad son, a bad husband, a selfish ruler, and a vicious man', but nowadays viewed by practically all as a great hero, soldier and king.[65]

62 William of Tyre, ii, p. 235.

63 On Amaury, and the quote, William of Tyre, ii, pp. 296–300, 358.

64 William of Tyre, ii, p. 490.

65 For a good account of the Third Crusade, see Gillingham, *Richard the Lionheart*; also Runciman, iii, and P.H. Newby, *Saladin*. For the Stubbs quote, see Gillingham, *Richard the Lionheart*, p. 6; and Stubbs' introduction to the *Itinerarium*.

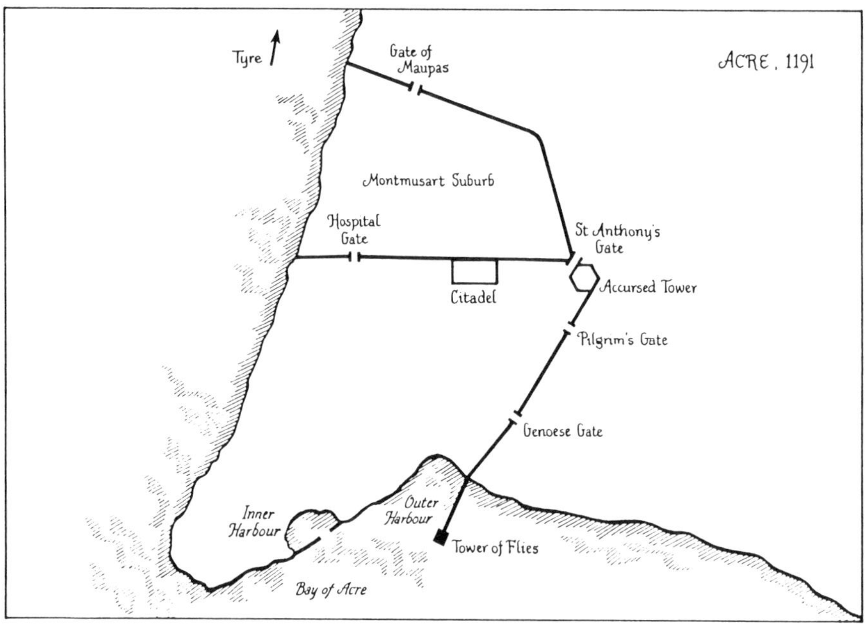

He was one of the three kings who set out for the East, the others being Frederick Barbarossa, arguably the greatest medieval Holy Roman Emperor, and Philip Augustus of France, possibly the greatest king of the Capetian dynasty.

King Guy was released by the all-conquering Saladin, now master of almost all the former Latin Kingdom. Guy surprised many in trying to recover his honour by regaining the city of Acre, which was so important for communications with the West. Despite the urgency of the Latin Kingdom's needs, western aid was slow in coming. Frederick Barbarossa never arrived, dying after a swim while en route. Philip and Richard started their journey together, but then went their separate ways, Richard's journey in particular being eventful and slow.

Acre became the centrepiece of the Third Crusade, so that yet another crusade found its focus in a long and dramatic siege. Acre stood on a triangle of land between the mountains and the sea, with a double harbour inside and outside the walls. The River Belus ran by the city, and around the walls were orchards and a countryside able to support flocks and herds. Blockade would have to be by both land and sea, and when King Guy, with what forces he could muster, started the siege, he had not the men to surround it, or the fleet to assist, nevertheless he persisted.

An excellent account of the siege is found in the poem by Ambroise, probably the name of the original poet who was an eye-witness to the events, possibly a Norman jongleur. The poem that survives is a later version, worked on by others, but retains important information. Ambroise was a supporter of Richard the Lionheart; he depicted a delightful scene of the crusaders setting out 'when roses were with fragrance filled', the pilgrims attended by youths, maids and wives bringing them water as they went.[66]

Ambroise followed Richard's route via Sicily, Rhodes and Cyprus. In Sicily Richard besieged Messina, after an unfortunate incident, which the poet claims was started by Sicilians flogging a girl called Emma who was selling bread. Richard organised a combined land and sea attack on the city, which was stormed, taken, and sacked. So on to Rhodes, where 'the wind was strong, the waves were high', but the walls and towers in ruins.[67] Richard stopped for ten days, one of the many occasions during the crusade when he was laid low by illness. At last he moved on the Cyprus, where he married Berengaria of Navarre. While there he besieged three castles, two of which he took, and was ill again. He came into conflict with the recently established and self-styled 'emperor' in Cyprus, Isaac Dukas Comnenus. Cyprus had been Byzantine, but had been taken over by Isaac, who had actually allied himself with Saladin. Isaac surrendered at Kyrenia, on condition that he was not put in irons. Richard made the promise, and then had him bound in specially prepared silver chains.[68] Richard's actions were useful on two counts: he had defeated an ally of Saladin and an enemy of the Byzantine emperor; and he had gained a valuable base for the ailing Latin Kingdom. The island's position in the eastern Mediterranean made it an excellent supply depot, of which Richard himself was soon making use.

Guy had begun the siege of Acre with 400 knights and 7,000 infantry, but gradually reinforcements arrived as Acre became the focus of Latin survival. Their efforts were threatened by the appearance of Saladin's relief army, and had to improve their own camp with a ditch. Through the winter, towers and engines were constructed. The crusaders tried to keep up the pressure, and their determination was displayed by the efforts of Christian women going up to the walls to shoot bows. Belfries containing 500 men each were advanced to the walls, but burned down. Guy's forces had little success in their attacks, but even though the blockade was not complete, conditions inside were worsening; food was getting short, and the generally discarded parts of animals, such as entrails, heads and feet had to be eaten. Captives were expelled to reduce the mouths which required feeding, or were hanged from the walls, except for some strong young men who were used to work the engines.[69]

66 Ambroise, ed. Hubert & La Monte, p. 41; ed. Paris, col. 8, l. 277: *Quant la rose suef oleit.*

67 For the incident in Sicily, and for Rhodes, see Ambroise, ed. Hubert & La Monte, pp. 53, 78; the Rhodes quote, ed. Paris, col. 35, l. 1271: *Granz fu li vent e haute l'onde.*

68 Ambroise, ed. Hubert & La Monte, p. 106.

69 For the female Christian archers, and eating entrails, see Ambroise, ed. Hubert & La Monte, pp. 152, 156.

One Christian sergeant was hit by a crossbow bolt on his breast, but though it pierced his coif, doublet and hauberk, he was saved by a brief or charm hung round his neck, from which the bolt rebounded. The Turks made one attack upon a knight squatting down to relieve himself; how base, commented Ambroise, 'to take a knight thus unawares'. Others saw his danger and shouted warnings, and he managed to jump aside and avoid the lance aimed at him; he grabbed a stone lying on the ground beside him, knocked the Turk on the head with it, killing him and capturing his horse. According to a Moslem source, the Franks used propaganda to inspire their efforts, including an invented picture of an Arab striking Christ.[70]

King Guy concentrated his attack on the Tower of Flies, which stood at the end of the breakwater. It was said that the name came from the fact that sacrifices had once been carried out there, and had attracted swarms of flies. Two ladders were raised, but they were knocked down by throwing beams at them. When the Christians approached from land with their siege tower, the enemy used Greek Fire against it, and it was destroyed. The ladders and the ships carrying them were also set on fire. New engines were made, including a ram with an iron head, and these were also advanced to the wall, only to face a barrage of beams, jars, fire-brands and Greek Fire, so that they had to abandon the ram. The situation did not look hopeful, the attempts to break in had failed, and the blockade was not complete, the Saracens were still able to get through to the city. On one occasion some of them dressed as Franks, with shaved beards, and approached in a boat with pigs on board, carrying crosses to enhance the disguise. In an attempt to deliver a message, a Moslem dived under the boom across the harbour. He did not make it, and his body was found by his own side, washed up on the shore, but with his message on gold and wax paper still decipherable: 'the only man who has faithfully carried out his duties even after death'. According to the Moslems, a shipload of beauties arrived to solace the crusaders, having fleshy thighs and painted faces, offering themselves for sin, even to the priests. It was during this siege that Saladin suffered from a painful outburst of boils from the waist to the knee, so that he could hardly sit, yet enduring on horseback from afternoon to sunset when he had to.[71]

Saladin was not able to relieve Acre, but he was able to make life uncomfortable for the besieging army. Their situation got worse when the rains came; prices rose to sixpence for an egg, and even the nobles ate grass. Some had to beg for food, and some stole, a number suffered from

70 On the sergeant saved by a charm, the knight caught short, see Ambroise, ed. Hubert & La Monte, p. 161; and the propaganda picture, Ibn al-Athir, in Gabrieli, p. 182.

71 Incidents at Acre: pigs on the boat, the Moslem doing duty after death, and Saladin's boils Baha ad-Din, in Gabrieli, pp. 201, 202, 102; for the beauties, Ibn al-Athir, in Gabrieli, p. 182.

what was probably scurvy, with swellings on limbs and faces, and teeth falling out.

At last aid for Guy arrived in the form of the Third Crusade, with the forces of first Philip II and then of Richard I. Now the city could be properly blockaded. Something of the feeling of the long periods between action in prolonged sieges is conveyed by the story of Philip hawking with a favourite white falcon, which one day flew into the city and was captured. The king promised a thousand dinar to recover it, but rather meanly his offer was refused. Although both kings fell ill, preparations for attack went ahead, and new engines were constructed, paid for by the wealth of the two great kings. Richard was also able to reassemble some of those made in Cyprus and transported to Acre, including the great tower there known as *Malvoisin* or 'Bad Neighbour', and now renamed *Malcousin* or 'Bad Relation'. A Moslem source says they made three towers of sixty cubits in height, against which, at first, the defenders combustible weapons did not work. A man from Damascus promised that he could provide a special recipe of Greek Fire which would do the trick. When fire efforts failed, the Franks danced up and down on top of the towers, jeering at the Saracens, but the new recipe worked, and all three of the towers went up in flames, giving the Franks, in the words of the Moslem author: 'a taste of hell'. The man from Damascus was offered a cash reward, but refused it, saying he had acted for the love of God.[72]

Philip now attempted to mine the wall, and eventually a great section fell, twisting as it went, and almost killing the miners, but still they could not break in. Efforts were redoubled, both kings tried their hand at shooting crossbows, Richard still ill and wearing silk was carried to a forward position. Aubrey Clement vowed to enter Acre or die; he managed to get on to the wall, but was killed. When ladders were used, the weight of the men attempting the climb broke one, and the crusaders fell into the moat. Efforts were concentrated on the Maudite Tower; it was mined and battered. Richard offered two besants for every stone prised from it, increasing his reward to three and then four besants. At last the tower fell, and the air was filled with smoke, but it had happened when most of the nobles were at dinner, and so even this opportunity was wasted. Nevertheless it was the last straw for the defenders, despite the attempts of Saladin from outside to strengthen their resolve. Every time the Christians had mounted a main attack, the citizens had beat drums to warn Saladin to make an effort to attack, but it must by now have become clear that he did

72 For the white falcon, Baha ad-Din, in Gabrieli, p. 213; for *Malcousin* and the towers, Ambroise, ed. Hubert & La Monte, p. 201; ed. Paris, col. 127, ll. 4745–6: *Li reis aveit Male Veisine,/Maisen Acre ert Male Cosine.* For the taste of hell, Ibn al-Athir, in Gabrieli, p. 200.

not have the power to enter Acre, and the citizens came to terms, though some preferred death by throwing themselves from the walls.[73]

The Christians entered the war-torn city with a great shout, placing their standards on the towers. Much damage had been done by the crusaders themselves, but they also found that the church buildings had been ruined by the Moslems. Philip Augustus, ill again, decided to return to France. It was now that Richard committed one of the most famous of crusading atrocities. Saladin was slow to pay the agreed ransom for the citizens who had surrendered against his wishes, and Richard massacred 2,700 captives with blows and bolts. Possibly Richard wished to move on and dared not take so many captives, but Baha ad-din says 'God alone knows what the reason was'.[74]

There were further sieges during the Third Crusade, Richard won the battle of Arsuf, and saved Jaffa from Saladin's siege, the king himself leaping into the water when the crusaders arrived. But he had to abandon the advance upon Jerusalem, and was content to accept reasonably attractive terms, which preserved a remnant of the Latin Kingdom, and allowed access to Jerusalem. Ironically, Saladin died in the following year, but by then the Lionheart had gone, and the crusade had passed into history.

In conclusion it may be said that the early crusading sieges presented great feats of endurance and heroism, as well as horrific scenes of massacre and torture. At Xerigordo, besieged by Turks, the Christians drank the blood of their enemies, let belts and clothes into a sewer to squeeze out the liquid, or urinated into each other's hands, in their desperate search for drink. They dug into the earth or piled it over themselves in search of an escape from the heat and in hope of dampness. The search for food could be equally hard. At Antioch the Christians ate camels, and mules, and even dug up the buried bodies of diseased animals in their great hunger. In bad weather there was cold and wet to contend with: at Damietta the rain came through the tents, and they had to dig ditches around them to carry off the floods. As someone who has had to do the same thing when camped on a hillside with my family during a Welsh summer at Fishguard, I have at least some sympathy for this plight. At Harim the crusaders suffered ten continuous days of cold rain. Conditions for both sides could be harsh; as William of Tyre puts it: 'a wise man might well ask, which condition was the better and which the worse to be dreaded: that of the besieging army, or that of those who were under siege?'[75]

73 For Richard and the crossbow; Aubrey Clement; the besants; the drum roll; the surrender: see Ambroise, ed. Hubert & La Monte, pp. 207–8, 206, 208, 216, 218; and for the surrender see also Ambroise, ed. Hubert & La Monte, p. 222.

74 On Richard's atrocity, see Gillingham, *Richard*, pp. 182–4; Ambroise, ed. Hubert & La Monte, p. 228; ed. Paris, col. 148, l. 5538: *set cenz e deus mile*. Archer, *Richard*, p. 131. Baha ad-Din, in Gabrieli, p. 224, says there were 3,000 killed in cold blood.

75 For Xerigordo, see *Gesta Francorum*, pp. 3–4. For eating camels and buried animals; the

The effect of the Holy War on besieged towns was often very harsh, everything was at issue, sharpening all the usual perils and fears of this kind of warfare. William of Tyre saw the Christians at Jaffa as fighting for wives and children, for liberty and for country, 'for everything in fact of which man deems it noble to die'. The same was true on many occasions for those on both sides.[76]

rain at Damietta; the rain at Harim; and the quote on which was worst, see William of Tyre, i, pp. 271, ii, pp. 366, 432, i, p. 213.

76 On Jaffa, William of Tyre, i, p. 502.

CHAPTER SIX

An Age of Great Kings, 1200–1350

What seems to be emerging from our survey of sieges, is a remarkable continuity in methods and even in weaponry. There are changes of course, and the thirteenth century, for example, sees an increased use of the trebuchet. This improved throwing engine could inflict greater damage on walls and buildings, and therefore necessitated further improvements in fortification. But such changes are not fundamental: we are still dealing with throwing engines, and much the same style of fortification. Trebuchets made little difference to the tactics of siege warfare. What distinguishes each succeeding age is less the change in weaponry and fortification, than the changes in political structure, and therefore of the kind of forces in conflict with each other. There is, for instance, a great difference in siege warfare between invaders and civilisations under threat, such as we met in our early chapters, and in the warfare between princes and their vassals we have found in feudal Europe. What marks out the thirteenth century in western Europe is the increased power of the monarchies relative to their subjects. It gave the great kings an increasing advantage over their subjects in sieges, as it did in warfare in general.

The nature of society and therefore of feudalism was altering, and with it the way in which kings assembled their armed forces. More and more the need was to have control over taxation and resources. In the long run, although others could reap benefits as well, the great rulers gained most from the changes; they gained a monopoly in really large armies, and in the most expensive items of equipment. Only great princes could afford to produce the largest siege engines and large numbers of them, or to raise the supplies needed for provisioning large armies for lengthy periods. Such wealth and strength discouraged baronial opposition, except in the most desperate circumstances. There would be opposition and rebellions, especially when princes abused their powers or proved unequal to their tasks, but on the whole peace and order improved within the domains of the great kings, private warfare diminished, and much of the opposition and warfare, including siege warfare, tended to come less from conflicts

Transport of armour

between kings and their internal vassals, than from external powers with equivalent resources.

Of course there always would be circumstances in which an individual or a group of barons was pushed to extremes, and there are examples of such men risking royal ire and provoking against themselves the employment of those great royal resources just described, as for example in Rochester against King John, or the Bréautés at Bedford against Henry III. But more often opposition to the kings within their kingdoms was likely to take other and more hopeful forms, as through the pressure of national assemblies.

Many of the sieges of this period occurred on the geographical fringes of the great realms, in conflicts of king against king, in attempts by the great to enlarge their realms by conquest, or from a conflict involving religion. The clash of religions in Spain we shall leave till a later chapter, as part of the late medieval clash between Christianity and Islam, but the war against the Cathar heretics in southern France, will be dealt with here. Although it was a religious war, it involved only Christians, and was perhaps even more a war of expansion waged by the kings of France. In such circumstances the power of the monarchy was opposed because so much was at stake: the defence of a homeland by some, as well as the holding to a belief of others. In the end the result was the transformation of the political structure of southern France.

The period saw other struggles for independence from the great powers, where again resistance was undertaken despite the odds. Such fights, though not always successful, were beginning to take on the colour of national interest. Examples are to be found in the battle against the might of France by Flanders, of the Scots against England, or the Italian cities against the German emperors.

But, in the end, what dominates the siege warfare of this period is the control developed by the great monarchs: by Saint Louis, Philip the Fair, Edward I, Frederick II. They could raise enormous siege trains, raise large armies, construct large and numerous siege engines; Edward I had thirteen engines at Stirling.[1] The old struggle over the rendability of fortresses became pretty well obsolete; a great king now expected to have the use and support of castles within his realm. A charming instance of this kind of expectation is met in Edward III's visit to Wark castle in Northumberland. He was campaigning against the Scots, and although there were formalities to be followed, there was no question that when the king arrived he would be able to enter the castle, and would be able to use it as he chose in his efforts against the Scots. It happened at that moment to be in the charge of the beautiful countess of Salisbury, and one cannot but wonder if Edward's choice as a base was entirely on strategic military grounds. He inspected the castle for damage caused in the recent Scottish raid, and ordered certain improvements to be made to the fortifications. The countess had the gates opened for the king, and came out to welcome him, leading him into the castle by the hand, going somewhat beyond the usual ceremonies. Within the castle, the king could not keep his eyes off the countess, to the point where she became embarrassed at his interest. Finally in private, the king leaning against a window deep in thought, the countess pressed him for the cause of his worries. What troubled him, he confessed, was his love for her, but she remarked that she was sure he would not dishonour either her or her husband, so Edward left to take it out on the Scots; there were limits even to the increased monarchical rights.[2]

France

The period 1200 to 1350 is a significant one in the development of France. We have called this an age of great kings, although inevitably not every monarch of the time deserved this epithet. In regard to siege warfare the significance is rather of overwhelming power and resources than of magnificent individuals. To some extent the development benefited all kings, and gave them a considerable advantage in siege warfare within their own realms. There were very few individual magnates who could hope to compete with the financial and other resources of the great monarchs.

1 Peter Langtoft, in *EHD*, iii, p. 257. Langtoft, ed. Wright, ii, p. 356, and n. 2: *trez graunz engines*; and *un engine orrible, et Ludgar apeler*.

2. For Edward at Wark, Froissart, ed. Jolliffe, pp. 118–20; ed. Luce, iii, pp. 131–3.

This period was to some extent an exception to the previous history of medieval France, when kings had been almost invariably long-lived. There were no less than nine kings in this century and a half, and ironically, more insignificant kings than in the preceding age. But there were also some truly great rulers in Philip Augustus, Saint Louis, and Philip the Fair, as well as the founder of the new Valois line, Philip VI. In these kings we see monarchical power spreading throughout the realm, the prestige of the monarchy reaching a peak with Louis IX, which would rarely be surpassed.

It is notable how few sieges occurred within France, for example during the whole of the long reign of Louis IX. This illustrates the theme of this chapter: kings had so much more strength than in previous times, that only rash or desperate men would stand against them in normal circumstances within their own lands. A natural consequence was a considerable improvement in the keeping of law and order.

Philip Augustus

Philip II was the first of the great French kings of this age; under him France approached something like its modern form, since he brought about the collapse of the Angevin Empire which had dominated western France, as well as playing a part in winning domination in Flanders and in the South.[3] As a result of his efforts, there was an enormous increase in the resources of the French monarchy. His long struggle against the Angevin kings of England, endured beyond the death of Henry II at Chinon, the unexpected death of Richard the Lionheart, even beyond the death of John in 1216. This long reign saw its climax with the triumphs against his enemies of the early thirteenth century, against the Angevin Empire and the Holy Roman Empire. The clinching moment of his conquests against John, was the siege and capture of the great Norman castle of Château-Gaillard.[4]

Richard I had built his 'cheeky castle' right over the Seine, pointing a threatening finger towards the territories of the French king. The Norman accounts reveal the tremendous expenditure he had made on the new fortifications, enabling its construction within a year or two during 1196–98. Despite the speed of its building, it was a magnificent architectural achievement, using the contours of the rock on which it stood, and integrating a series of barriers into a coherent defence system, such as

3 On Philip Augustus, the major work is Cartellieri, *Philipp II. August*; the main work in English is J.W. Baldwin, *The Government of Philip Augustus*. The best work on the conflict between Philip and the Angevins, is J. Gillingham, *Angevin Empire*.

4 For Château-Gaillard, see Bradbury, 'French Castles', in Brown, *Castles: A History and Guide*; Coutil; Deville; Gillingham, *Richard the Lionheart*, pp. 262–5; Norgate, *Angevin Kings*, ii, pp. 375–81.

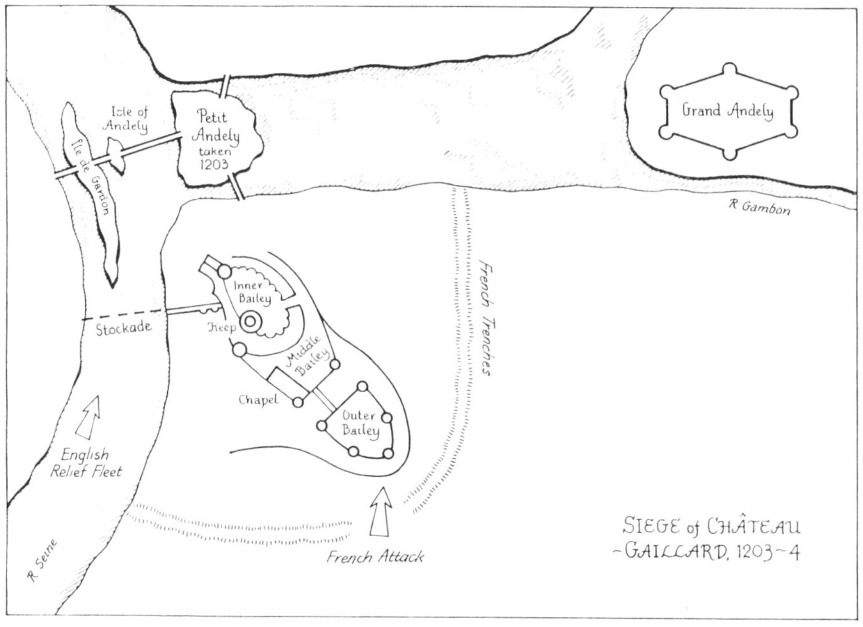

concentric castles would later possess, having triangular outer defences, an inner bailey, and an original style of keep. It is also an aesthetic triumph, the soaring bulk of the castle fashioned by man standing above the steep cliffs, which in turn descend to the beautiful bend of the river. It completed a fortified complex with the settlements of Greater and Lesser Andely on the bank and on an island in the Seine.

In 1203, after the death of Richard the Lionheart, Philip Augustus invaded Normandy against King John; he concentrated on the new castle of Château-Gaillard, in a siege which lasted nearly six months. The garrison for John was commanded well by Roger de Lacy. Richard had believed his 'beautiful daughter' was impregnable, but had provoked Philip's anger against the castle by using it as the place to execute French prisoners, three of whom were thrown to their deaths from the rock, and a further fifteen of whom were blinded and sent back to the king guided by a one-eyed man. Now Philip sought his revenge against Richard's brother. John did attempt what might have looked a brilliant relief had it succeeded, by trying to co-ordinate an attack from the land and one from the river, but the scheme went disastrously wrong. He had been given incorrect information on the tides, and the river force arrived at the wrong time. The relief failed, and John abandoned the castle, leaving its defenders to do their best. Roger de Lacy held on, but inevitably a garrison could not survive for ever without external assistance.[5]

[5] On the beautiful daughter, Norgate, *Angevin Kings*, ii, pp. 416–23, 380 n. 1: *pulchra filia*

Philip had fortified his own position strongly with trenches, had built siege towers, and carefully rationed the provisions to take his army through the winter. In February 1204 the outer curtain was taken after battering by trebuchet and then mining. It was difficult to bring engines close to the middle bailey because of the ground, but a way in was discovered through a garderobe on the west and an unfastened chapel window. One of the besiegers crawled resolutely up the chute of the lavatory and finally got into the chapel, bringing others up after him. The noise of the attackers caused a retreat to the inner enclosure. Again, against the keep, engines and mining were employed. It was possible to mine under the protection of a bridge which was cut from the rock and could not be destroyed. At the last some of the besieged tried to break out through a postern, but without success. On 6th March 1204 the remaining twenty knights and 120 men-at-arms surrendered. After this hard-fought siege, the Angevin Empire collapsed like a pack of cards, though in the end John was able to salvage a few remnants.

The Albigensian Crusade

The Albigensian Crusade began in the last years of the reign of Philip Augustus. It was a situation where belief and local loyalties combined to outweigh fear of the monarchy's power, though initially the enemies of the crusaders did not take the initiative, and did not wish, at first, to oppose the monarchy. It was only late in the crusade that the French crown intervened directly, to determine the outcome. Before that, the crown and the papacy had given only intermittent support to the crusade against the Cathars and their sympathisers in the south of France. The heretics were often protected by the local princes for their own purposes, and the crusaders led by Simon de Montfort achieved a great deal with inadequate forces.[6]

The crusade was proclaimed in 1208, and recruiting began in the following year. Northerners moved into southern France, determined to exterminate the heresy which was seen by the papacy as an abomination, and at the same time to gain lands for themselves. It proved to be a long and difficult struggle. Simon de Montfort fought with great courage and intelligence, and often ruthlessly, welcoming crusading reinforcements which usually arrived only for the season and disappeared again when the term of

unius anni; *Magni Rotuli Scaccarii Normanniae*, ii, p. 309; William the Breton, ii, pp. 181–92. Descriptions of the siege in Cartellieri, iv, pp. 153–79; Powicke, *Loss*, pp. 164–5, 253–6; Warren, *King John*, pp. 86–7, 93–5.

6 For general advice on the Albigensian Crusade, I am grateful to Claire Dutton. A modern account in English is J. Sumption, *Albigensian Crusade*. Ladurie, *Montaillou* is a fascinating account of Cathar life; see also Lambert, *Medieval Heresy*.

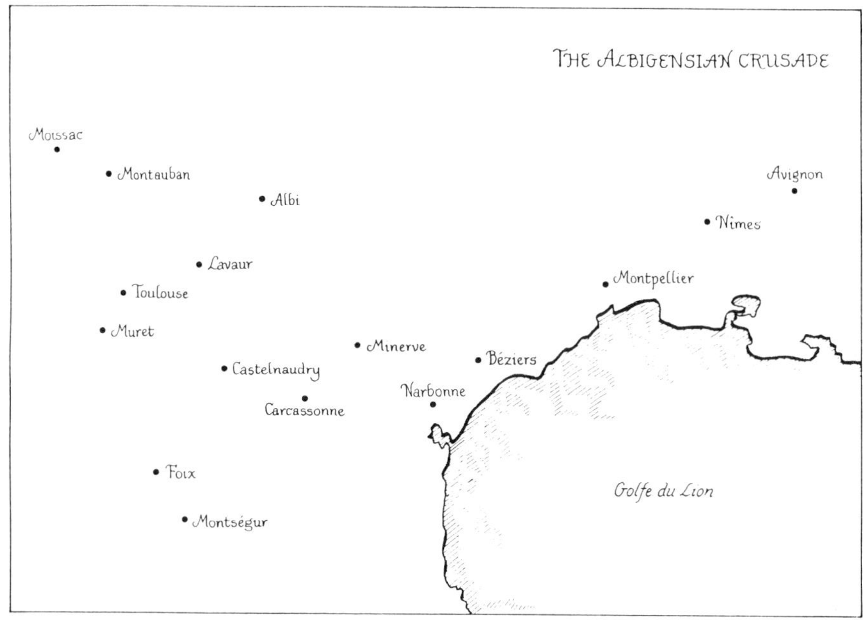

service was completed, leaving him to a difficult winter. Time and again this allowed the southern lords to recover from setbacks, but when the monarchy intervened more directly in the person of Louis VIII, Cathar and southern hopes were crushed.

But even then, the limitations of feudal service made problems for the monarchy. Count Theobald of Champagne joined the siege of Bourges in 1226, but abandoned it after serving his forty days. Only gradually did the southern lords back down from the contest and abandon the heretics, whose support had at times served the political purposes of the lords. Raymond-Roger Trencavel was one such lord, who found himself besieged by the crusaders in the great fortress-town of Carcassonne by the marshes of the Aude. The walls had twenty-six towers and contained the Trencavel palace. The citizens in preparation for a siege had collected provisions from all around, and then burned what remained to deny any help to the crusaders, including a number of floating water mills.[7]

The crusaders attacked Carcassonne at a weak point in the suburbs where the wall was lower than elsewhere. They broke in and occupied the ground between the river and the town, but their attack on the better fortified suburb of Castellare was repelled. A mining belfry was destroyed by fire, but they still managed to breach the wall, only for a sortie to regain all that had been taken and burn the engine. The crusaders' hopes grew with the arrival in their camp of Peter II of Aragon. The latter had once

[7] On Carcassonne, Sumption, pp. 94–100; *Chanson de la Croisade Albigeoise*, i, pp. 62–82.

been on good terms with the Trencavels, and now sought a settlement rather than a fight to the death. The garrison seemed in the last throes: illness was rife, the rotting animal corpses were attracting flies, but the crusaders would only allow harsh terms, which Raymond-Roger refused. In the end, after Peter II had left, terms were agreed, but the crusaders broke all the conventions by ignoring a safe-conduct and capturing Raymond-Roger.

Many interesting sieges marked the development of the Albigensian Crusade, fired by the desperation of the local populace. Another reason for the importance of sieges here was the nature of the country over which the crusade was fought, dominated by fortresses on the peaks of forbidding heights. One such fortress was Minerve, protected by natural ravines, but water, as so often with such sites, was a major problem, the main supply being a well which was within the view of the attackers. A sortie caught the crusaders unaware, in particular their engineer, who at that moment had retired to relieve himself. He was surrounded and killed, and his engine fired, but this gave the alarm, the sortie was beaten off, and the fire put out. Minerve surrendered after this effort had failed to dislodge the crusaders, and clergy led in the victors, singing the *Te Deum* as they went.[8]

The determination of the southerners was demonstrated at the siege of Lavaur, whose castellan was a woman, Giraude de Laurac. Simon de Montfort pressed the siege, filling the moat with earth, but the garrison kept coming out at night to clear it again. In the end however the place was mined and taken. The difficulties for the crusaders came from the determination of the locals, and also from the local power of some of their opponents. Raymond VI, count of Toulouse, was no Cathar, but he had allowed the heresy to flourish. His power in the region was predominant when the crusade began, but he feared a clash with the papacy, and perhaps even more with the monarchy, and often negotiated himself out of awkward situations, willing to abandon the heretics to their fate if need be. But whenever papal and monarchical support for Simon de Montfort waned, Raymond VI proved a very hard opponent to match. Simon himself had no power base in the south, and was dependent on support from outside. There were times when he was frustrated by the southern lords, as for example when he besieged Raymond VI in the latter's capital at Toulouse. On this occasion de Montfort had bitten off more than he could chew. The city had no less than three miles of surrounding walls, and Simon simply did not have enough men to cover them. The garrison hindered his efforts with sorties, and in the end he had to accept the humiliation of retreat.[9]

The crusaders faced similar problems at Moissac, where the defenders were reinforced by 300 mercenaries. Everything points to the crusade being

8 On Minerve, Sumption, pp. 116–18. An interesting paper by M. Barber, 'Catharism and the Occitan Nobility', demonstrates the inaccessibility of these sites.

9 Lavaur and Toulouse, 1211, Sumption, pp. 129–32, 136; *Chanson*, i, pp. 162–6, 190–8.

more than a clash between Catholics and Cathars. Once again Simon lacked the manpower to surround the place, and blockade it properly. He himself was wounded in the fighting that followed. His position became even worse when his lukewarm ally, Peter of Aragon, changed sides and besieged Muret. Against the odds, Simon's great military qualities enabled him to win a battle outside the fortress. It was said that Peter had diminished his chances by exhausting himself during the previous night, which he had spent with his mistress, to the point where in the morning he could not stand upright; he was felled and killed in the battle.[10]

The crusade was far from an entire success for Simon. He had many setbacks, not only from lack of resources, but also from military defeats. At Beaucaire crusaders were captured and hanged from olive trees. A second attempt against Toulouse also failed, and Simon himself was hit by a trebuchet, apparently operated by women. The stone cracked his head and killed him.[11] His son Amaury carried on the crusade, but it was at this point that the monarchy intervened more directly in the person of Louis VIII, son of Philip Augustus, though even he failed in a further attempt against Toulouse, once more hindered by crusaders departing after the completion of their forty days' service. But Louis had far more resources on which he could call, than Simon had possessed, and the local lords were far more reluctant to oppose him directly than the northern upstart de Montfort. Louis VIII's reign was a brief one, but it was the crucial period in the Albigensian Crusade. Southern resistance continued, and had to be dealt with by the government of the young Louis IX, but the fate of the Albigenses and the South was settled by the decision to focus royal attention on the situation.

The tremendous climax of the Albigensian Crusade was reached in the dramatic siege of Montségur in the Pyrenees, its square keep standing on a five hundred feet high Pyrenean peak, some twelve miles from Foix. As the royal forces closed in, Montségur became the last refuge of the Cathars, the main centre for the *perfecti*, the leaders of the heretics, with their strict puritanical life, celibate and vegetarian. Raymond VII, trying to regain status with the powers that be, had besieged it half-heartedly in 1241, but abandoned the attempt. Montségur's armed garrison, though not Cathars themselves, made a daring raid against the inquisitors who were already bringing torment into the region, killing a number in their beds at Avignonet. The armed garrison at Montségur numbered some twenty knights and a hundred sergeants; together with a determined local citizenry, and the fanatical Cathars, they made a formidable defending

10 Moissac and Muret, see Sumption, pp. 151–2, 166–9; *Chanson*, i, pp. 266–76; and on Muret, Oman, i, pp. 453–67; *Chanson*, ii, pp. 129–33.

11 Sumption, p. 198; *Chanson*, iii, p. 206, ll. 23–4: *una peireira . . . /E tiravan la donas e tozas e molhers*. There is also a famous carving of Simon's death showing men and women operating a traction trebuchet, reproduced in Rogers.

force. As elsewhere in this crusade, the women were prepared to participate, and again we find them manning engines on the walls. The fortress held out through the winter of 1243, as the crusaders tightened their grip, battering the walls, one trebuchet aimed against the eastern tower, was commanded by the Catholic bishop of Albi himself. Finally someone betrayed the Cathars, and Basques among the crusading army were able to find an entrance by climbing the difficult way in and knifing the guards. The barbican was taken, and finally the garrison surrendered, against the wishes of the Cathars, who knew that only death awaited them. The garrison was allowed to go, but unless they were prepared to recant the Cathars were to be executed. Some two hundred refused to abandon their faith, and were burnt on a great pyre at the foot of the castle which had been their last stronghold, yet one more example of the inhumanity of man to his fellows which can be so ironically inspired by religious belief.[12]

Saint Louis

Louis IX was perhaps the greatest French king of this age, but he was so successful in keeping order that there were few sieges in France itself. His less successful efforts on crusade we shall cover in a later chapter. There were some threats early in his reign, while he was still a minor. Henry III of England made two rather feeble attempts to recover some of the lost Angevin Empire. during the second of which, in 1241, Louis countered the invasion by attacking Fontenay l'Abattu, one of Henry III's chief castles in France, held for him by the Bastard of La Manche. The English were forced to retire to Taillebourg, where they were beaten in battle trying to defend the bridge. Henry took refuge in Saintonge, but as Louis closed in, fled from there too, going without food and drink for two days in the hasty escape. His efforts had been even less glorious than his father's, if less disastrous in their consequences.[13]

Philip the Fair

On the whole Philip IV also kept good order within his realm. The two areas within France that saw most conflict, were both regions which had maintained independence to a late stage, and Philip's warfare was a consolidation of monarchical power in these border areas to the north and the south, Flanders and Aquitaine. In Aquitaine, Philip IV himself provoked a quarrel with Edward I of England, whom he outmanoevred in diplomacy.

12 Sumption, pp. 236–41; Brown, *Castles: A History and Guide*, p. 150.
13 On Louis IX, see Labarge, *St. Louis*.

Edward I was also involved in the struggle in Flanders. A detailed account of affairs in Flanders was written by an elderly Franciscan friar:

> One day, when I was not very busy, it occurred to me that since I enjoy reading and hearing stories and true facts about old times, and can write quickly, and since I had at my disposal a number of small pieces of parchment of no great value, I might describe the battles and various perils, troubles, oppressions, expeditions, sieges, passive and active conflicts, which had happened in our land of Flanders.[14]

A fascinating conflict developed between the monarchy and the new urban forces in Flanders, with their ever-increasing resources, and their own militias, and sieges played a vital rôle. Philip IV's capture of Lille in 1297 'with much toil and expense', intimidated others to surrender. Throughout the war the rebels were hindered by a fifth column of royalists known as the leliaerts, after the royal symbol of the fleur de lys; but at Courtrai, which the French attempted to relieve, the Flemings faced the king in battle, and to Europe's surprise, the royalists were beaten by the 'weavers, fullers and the common folk and infantry soldiers of Flanders', an early example of the power which infantry was to have in the late medieval period. The castle surrendered three days later.[15]

But Philip recovered from this humiliation, and the Flemings found themselves in difficulties trying to resource their efforts at a string of sieges at Lille, Lessines, Tournai, and Zierikzce. In 1304 Philip besieged Lille again, and stuck to it, despite the onset of winter, though it proved difficult to get supplies through as the roads worsened. Lille agreed to surrender by September if no aid came. With only three days to go, a Flemish force set out; Philip dug trenches before his position, but on this occasion battle was avoided by negotiation.

The degree of disorder in Flanders was considerable, as demonstrated by an incident in 1308. The men of the abbot of the Cistercian abbey of Ter Doest besieged a man in a church tower at Lisseweghe near Bruges. One of the abbey's lay brothers called William of Saeftingen had killed the cellarer and fled to the tower for refuge; he was then defended against the abbot's men by 80 citizens of Bruges under the leadership of Johann Breidel. The rescued man was carried off to Bruges, because William had fought alongside the citizens in the great battle of Courtrai. Later he was excommunicated but then pardoned in order to become a Hospitaller in the Holy Land.[16] Even the wealth of the French monarchy could not bring settled peace to Flanders for long, and troubles would break out again with the onset of the Hundred Years War.

14 On Philip IV, see Strayer, *Philip the Fair*; the quotation is *Annales Gandenses*, p. 1.
15 On Lille 1297, and weavers and fullers, see *Annales Gandenses*, pp. 3, 30.

England

Much of England's war effort in this period arose from the conflicts with France. As with France, the monarchy's resources increased, and internal wars tended to decrease. There were of course serious problems for several of the monarchs arising from political opposition, but only rarely did this break into full-blown war. At the beginning of the period John and Henry III both faced serious the rebellions which led to Magna Carta, and to the reforms of the de Montfort barons. But even under these kings who lacked the greatness of others, the manipulation of royal resources during a siege shows the advantage which kings should have possessed.

An important siege within England marks each of these reigns: that of Rochester by John in 1215, and that of Bedford in 1224 by Henry III. Whatever John's failings at Château-Gaillard, his efforts at Rochester show that he was capable of co-ordinating royal power in England to good effect when he chose. Rochester had been occupied by his opponents, and John, in fighting mood, approached the town along the banks of the Medway. There was a strong garrison of 95 knights and 45 men-at-arms, but there had been no time for long-term planning, and provisions were short. John collected materials for a major siege, food, drink, and weapons, including picks from the smiths at nearby Canterbury. He assembled a considerable force, which included a large number of mercenaries; they even occupied the cathedral and used it for stabling.[17]

A relief force was formed under Robert FitzWalter, but could not break through, and returned to London where the troops diced, drank, and 'it is needless to say what besides'. John now concentrated on taking the castle. He was in some danger when a crossbowman asked William of Albini's permission to shoot at him, but the latter refused, saying that it was God's task to kill the king, and not man's. John brought up five engines, including 'a strange contrivance', and also sent in miners. The latter were able to use the fat from forty pigs to fire their mine.[18]

The outer walls were mined first, and then the rectangular keep at its south-east corner. The tower cracked and fell outwards. The siege has left its mark on Rochester Castle, and today one can easily pick out the mined turret; the original turrets, like the keep itself, were all rectangular, but the ruined turret was replaced by what in the thirteenth century had become more fashionable, a round tower. Reistance continued for a time within the

16 Siege of Lille; incident at Lisseweghe: *Annales Gandenses*, pp. 33–4, 91–2 & n. 1.

17 On John, Warren, *King John*; on Rochester, Warner, *Siege*, pp. 136–7; *John Lackland*, pp. 248–51; Wendover, ii, pp. 146–9; Walter of Coventry, ii, pp. 226–7.

18 On 'needless to say', Norgate, *John*, p. 250; Wendover, ii, p. 149: *et caetera quis nesciat exercentes*. On the strange contrivance, Norgate, *John*, p. 251. On the crossbow and pigs, Warner, *Siege*, pp. 136, 137.

keep, which possessed the feature of an internal dividing wall, but eventually the castle surrendered. John wished to execute the whole garrison, and ordered that gallows be set up for that purpose, but one of the mercenaries in his own army, Savaric de Mauléon, argued that this would provoke similar actions by the barons in the war, and that his mercenaries would desert, so in the end only a few crossbowmen suffered the ultimate penalty.[19]

The lesson of Rochester is that in this age a king, even with John's shortcomings, could call on considerable power in war, and had every advantage over a baron or a vassal even if the king himself was in trouble when matched with his royal rival in France. Much the same point is demonstrated in the next reign, when one compares the success of the royal forces at Bedford with their unhappy fate in the attempted invasions of France.

Bedford castle was held by Fawkes de Bréauté, previously a favoured mercenary captain under John, who had been rewarded with the care of this important castle, having taken it for John from its previous holder, William de Beauchamp. After John's death there were complaints about Fawkes, who had used the castle as a base for unwarranted raids, such as a night attack on St Albans in 1217. Matters came to a head when Henry de Braibroc, the justice appointed to hear complaints against Fawkes at Dunstable, gave thirty judgements against him, and imposed a £100 fine. The judge was set upon, taken prisoner, and incarcerated in Bedford castle, an example of blatant lawlessness which could not be ignored. Henry III ordered that the judge be released, and when this was ignored, prepared to besiege Bedford.[20]

The king sent orders throughout the counties to collect iron, hides, stones, food and drink, as well as all the specialists required for a siege including masons, miners, carpenters. The bishops were required to send one man from every sixty acres to assist with the engines. From the Close Rolls one can obtain very detailed information about Henry's requests, and begin to see the enormous effort involved in a major siege, and the expense. There were orders for screens used as protection, bolts, leather for slings, ropes, tools, hammers, mallets, wedges, tents, wax, charcoal, planks, greyhounds, wine, pepper, saffron-the list is almost endless. Among the interesting orders are those for specific materials or specialists from particular places, for example iron from Gloucester, miners from Hereford, picks

19 On the castle, Brown, 'Rochester Castle'; on Savaric, Chaytor, *Savaric de Mauléon*, p. 30; on the hanging, Wendover, ii, p. 281.

20 On Bedford, Warner, *Siege*, pp. 144–46; Wendover, ii, pp. 278–82; *VCH* Bedford, pp. 10–11; Coggeshall, p. 176; *Dunstable Annals*, pp. 86–8; *Rotuli Clausarum*, p. 610; Fowler, 'Munitions'. For a more rounded view of Fawkes de Bréauté, see Carpenter, *Minority*; p. 363 n. 12 on missiles found in the moat; and pp. 361–70 on the siege. He insists that I have omitted the more important siege of Dover.

from London. Transport was arranged for engines to be brought, including the dismantling of some in Northampton along with a tower, which were then to be sent to Bedford. One order was for *diversas machinas, petrarias, mangonillos, berefridum cum balistis*, that is for engines, petraries, mangonels and a belfry with balistae. The Dunstable Chronicle speaks of the making of two towers higher than the tower of Bedford itself, and a cat for mining. As Matthew Paris claimed, Henry 'spent much money before it was taken'. No one but a king could call on such nation-wide resources.[21]

The garrison was commanded not by Fawkes himself, who was elsewhere, but by his brother William. The siege commenced on 22nd June, 1224. Two engines were set up against the eastern tower, two against the western tower, and others to north and south. The barbican was taken first, and then the main curtain was breached by mining, though many were killed in the effort. The outer bailey was occupied, then the inner. The garrison retreated to the keep: the familiar pattern of a defence which entailed giving way line by line. The great keep was now also mined and its walls cracked. The besieged yielded: Henry de Braibroc the royal judge was sent out, together with the women, and the royal flag was raised as the sign of surrender, but it was all to no avail, Henry III was in no mood for mercy: William de Bréauté and eighty of his men were hanged, though William's wife was allowed to go free, and the fortunate Fawkes de Bréauté, later captured at Coventry, was simply exiled to Rome. The castle was destroyed, its ditches filled, the walls halved in height, and the motte became the site for a manor house, and later for a bowling green![22]

Matthew Paris is a gossipy chronicler, but he often gives fascinating details, such as his picture of the occasion when Henry III commissioned him to write. Henry was visiting the monastery at St Albans, and during dinner the king ordered Matthew to come and sit on the step between the throne and the hall, instructing him that he should record the events of the time, cordially inviting the monk to join him for breakfast. Matthew tells the tale of a minor siege in Galwey during the reign of Henry III.[23] Roger earl of Winchester found himself besieged in the castle where he resided, and which he had obtained by marriage to the daughter of Alan of Galway. He had been taken by surprise and was without sufficient provisions to withstand a siege. The incident is instructive about attitudes, and also the value of attack. Roger decided that he would rather die an honour-

21 Diverse machines from Coggeshall, p. 206: *diversas machinas, petrarias, mangonillos, berefridum cum balistis*; compare *Rotuli Clausarum*, p. 617, on petraries, mangonels and a belfry. Towers from *Dunstable Annals*, p. 86: *duae machinae ligneae*; spent much money from Matthew Paris, ed. Giles, iii, p. 389; *Chronica Majora*, vi, p. 67: *maximam impenderunt pecuniam*.

22 On the bowling green, Warner, *Siege*, p. 147. I am told by Cath Roe that the bowling green is no longer there.

23 On meeting the king, and Galway, Matthew Paris, *Chronica Majora*, iv, pp. 644, 653; and ed. Giles, ii, pp. 242, 249–50.

able death in battle than be starved to death, and chose to make a desperate sortie against considerable odds. The sortie worked and his enemies fled so that he was able to escape.

Siege warfare played a rôle in the baronial wars of this period. Henry III was an ineffective king; his failures in France, his unwise and unsuccessful acceptance of the throne of Sicily added to his problems at home. His brother-in-law, Simon de Montfort, son of the Albigensian crusader, became leader of the baronial opposition in England. The barons defeated Henry in battle at Lewes, and for a year ruled England in his name. But in the end royal power recovered, and again resources could be marshalled to conclude the war, after Henry's son Edward had defeated and killed Simon in the battle of Evesham. Simon's son was pursued to his castle at Kenilworth and besieged there. Engines were pushed over the dry ditch to the north, but it proved difficult to get in close enough to be effective, and the defenders were able to destroy the engines. At first terms were refused, but after the defenders had suffered a bout of typhoid, surrender was agreed.

Edward I

Although Edward had shown military ability in winning the battle of Evesham, not much had been expected of him in early days; it looked as if he would follow in the steps of his father and grandfather. He was guilty of violent, unpredictable and irresponsible conduct. Matthew Paris forecast with some gloom: 'If he does these things when the wood is green, what can be expected when it is seasoned?' But Edward I proved to be one of the great kings of England, and one of the great kings of his age. His rôle in the barons' wars, and his crusade, gave him experience before he came to the throne. He had played the leading part in the sieges at Northampton in 1264 and Kenilworth in 1266.[24]

Edward proved to be a master in the art of castle warfare. His interest in castle building indicates his capacities, employing Master Bertram and Master James of St George on the great Welsh castles which were constructed at this time, with their advanced design.[25] His wars in Wales, Scotland and France involved numerous sieges. One of the most interesting to us, although it is one of the least in importance, is the siege of Caerlaverock, because it happens to have been recorded for posterity in a very detailed account, *The Song of Caerlaverock*. Edward I besieged this castle in July of 1300. It merited only a line in Langtoft, and about the

24 On Edward I, the major work is now M. Prestwich, *Edward I*, and see p. 3; the quotation is from Matthew Paris, *Chronica Majora*, v, p. 598.

25 The importance of Master James has long been recognised, but for Master Bertram, and their relative rôles, see A. Taylor, 'Master Bertram'.

same in the *Lanercost Chronicle*, so were it not for the *Song* we should take little note. It caught the imagination of the writer, probably the Franciscan, Walter of Exeter. The siege occurred during one of Edward's Scottish campaigns, lying just nine miles south of Dumfries. Edward spent a few days during the summer campaign dealing with the castle and its garrison of sixty men.[26]

The weather had been wet, and rain formed sheets of water in the plain. Edward ordered specialists to come from Carlisle, including smiths and carpenters. Master Richard was commissioned to make a cat, a belfry and a battering ram. From Dumfries he brought wood, vices and various things for the engines. Specialists were paid, including diggers, and Master Adam the carpenter, who received 4d a day.[27]

The English army set out from Carlisle on their best horses, with pennons flying. From a distance the whole countryside was covered with the men, the horses, and the wagons with their provisions and tents. One squadron was led by Prince Edward, the later Edward II, bearing arms for the first time. But Caerlaverock, with its great eastern tower, gate-tower, moat and drawbridge, thought itself strong enough to resist this mighty force. The Irish Sea lay to the west, and water almost surrounded the castle, and there was also difficult wooded land to the south. It could only be approached with any ease from the east, hence the positioning of the main tower.[28]

It would need some effort to take this castle, so the English set up their camp, tents with their cords and pegs, and huts. Provisions were brought up by sea. Now the engines came into play, and within one hour many were killed, shields broken by stones, helmets crushed to powder. The English raised a great shout at every hit. The engines were pushed to the edge of the ditch, and the king demanded to be allowed in by the bridge; the defenders responded with a hail of stones. Now Adam de la Fride was instructed to make a mine, and one of Edward's lords struck at the gate with a hammer. The attack by the engines was the most damaging, and at last the garrison showed a pennon as a sign of wishing to discuss terms, though one of those holding it was himself struck in the hand and the face by an arrow. But orders were given to stop the attack, and terms were agreed, the garrison being granted life and limb.[29]

There was development in this period, not only in the size of royal resources, but also in the improved administration of these resources; in

26 *Siege of Caerlaverock*, ed. Nicolas; see also Peter Langtoft, ii, p. 326; and *Lancercost Chronicle*, p. 194.

27 *Siege of Caerlaverock*, p. xv.

28 Renn, *Norman Castles*, p. 127.

29 *Siege of Caerlaverock*: on engines, p. 59: *Engin leve et balancie*; for its movement, p. 71; for the hammer, p. 77; an *espringaut*, p. 81; a *robinet*, p. 83; three engines, and the pennon, p. 85.

the ability to raise large armies, but also to supply them, to assemble all the necessary specialists, and to transport everything and everyone to the spot in time.

At Stirling in 1303 Edward raised thirteen great engines; the defenders could only find one, and the beam of that broke. The English engines demolished battlements and houses, and one called 'Ludger' knocked down a whole wall. Edward's power was such that he could ignore requests for terms and demand unconditional surrender. Wherever he went Edward was able to bring up engines from the nearest base, or make new ones on the spot, as he did at both Bettws and Castell-y-Bere in Wales, the latter surrendering after ten days' battering. For Stirling in 1304 Edward assembled a siege train at Berwick under Reginald the engineer. Here, as often, the great engines were given nick-names, such as 'Segrave' and 'Warwolf', the latter of which the king was so eager to see in use, that he refused terms until after it had been given a chance to operate. Edward had the power to take his enemies' castles with relative ease; Llewelyn's brother David had to abandon Hope (castle) in 1282, because its walls were too slight. But the great castles which Edward himself constructed, were almost too powerful to be taken: Harlech resisted rebellion successfully in 1294–5, with a garrison of only twenty. In the end his ability to hold on in France, against a more powerful enemy, also depended on his success in constructing fortifications, in this case the fifty or so *bastides* which he raised.[30]

Edward II was one of the least successful kings of medieval England, the first since the Norman Conquest to be deposed, but he was no mere cipher. He could still call on the resources which his father had developed, even if he used them to less effect. His power was far from negligible, and a recent biographer believes that he became a tyrant, instituting 'ten years of terror'.[31] With Edward II it was often lack of effort, will or ability rather than lack of resources that let him down. His failure to give adequate protection to Carlisle against the Scots, led to complaints from its citizens in 1318. They declared that Robert the Bruce had destroyed all the growing crops and taken many of their belongings, depriving them of the use of their mills. Even such aid as had been given was unsatisfactory; they complained that the sheriff of Cumberland, in digging a ditch, had encroached on the prior's ground, and that he had burned priory houses outside the wall to clear the ground. The troubles at Bristol earlier, when near anarchy seemed to reign, appear to have been fueled by royal incapacity to act promptly, thus allowing the citizens to riot, to attack royal mills, to attack the castle, obstruct tax collection, and build barricades in the

30 On Stirling 1303 and Ludger, see n. 1 above; Prestwich, *Edward I*, for Bettws, pp. 194–5; for Stirling 1304, pp. 499–502; for Hope, p. 189; Harlech, pp. 215–16; bastides, p. 308. See also *EHD*, iii, p. 610 and *Flores Historiarum*, iii, pp. 118–20, 315–20.

31 On Edward II, see Natalie Fryde, *The Tyranny and Fall*; the quote is p. 2.

streets. But when the king did belatedly take action and besiege the city, bringing up mangonels, the walls were soon breached and order restored.[32]

The *Vita Edwardi Secundi* was probably written by a royal official, and shows that even under Edward II baronial rebellion was not easy. It was aimed more against his unpopular ministers and favourites than directly against the king, as in the siege of Cardiff against the Despensers in 1320, which led to their exile, and again the siege of Bristol against them when Edward's queen, Isabella, invaded England together with her lover Mortimer to bring Edward's rule to an end.[33] This was followed by the capture of the two Despensers, father and son, and their barbarous executions.

Edward III

Edward III was established as king in the hands of his mother and Mortimer, but once old enough to act, he assembled support and overthrew their regime. His exploits in France in the first phase of the Hundred Years War will be examined in the following chapter, but we may here look at his Scottish wars, when he took up the task his grandfather had attempted, but in less promising circumstances, following the disastrous defeat of Edward II at Bannockburn in 1314. Edward III was not ultimately successfull in his attempt at conquest in Scotland, but he had victories along the way, and the abilities he demonstrated both helped to mould the English armies for the French wars, and also to establish Edward as a respected leader with the English barons. Thus he was able to bring back firm control within England itself.[34]

To be fair to Edward III, he was not guilty as Edward I had been, of provoking the warfare in Scotland. The Scots raided over the border in his early years, and their invasion in 1346 was an attempt to profit from his activities in France, coming as an unwelcome diversion of his resources. It is during Edward's earliest Scottish campaign that one hears of the English using *crakkis of war*, thought to be one of the earliest references to the use of cannons.[35] Early on Edward tried to operate indirectly in Scotland by giving encouragement to those disinherited Scots who wished to recover their own in 1332, and by supporting the disaffected Edward Bruce against his brother Robert. It was Edward Bruce who commenced the siege of Berwick two months before Edward III himself arrived. Immediately the

32 On Carlisle, *EHD*, iii, p. 610; on Bristol, *Vita Edwardi Secundi*, pp. 70–5.

33 For Cardiff and Bristol, 1326, see Fryde, pp. 44, 190.

34 On Edward III, the major work is now Ormrod, *Edward III*; on Scotland, R. Nicholson, *Edward III and the Scots*, remains useful.

35 On the guns, see Nicholson, p. 33; Hogg, *English Artillery*, p. 196; Oman, *Warfare*, ii, p. 213.

pressure of royal strength began to tell. Forty oaks were felled to make engines, and carried on ships, together with 691 round stone balls. Edward also possessed a number of the new weapons known as *gonnes*, and was supplied from York with saltpetre, charcoal and quick sulphur. The Scots tried to divert Edward by raiding into England, but he was not to be moved, grimly erecting a gallows on which to hang the now forfeit hostage, Thomas Seton, before the eyes of his parents; he ordered the hanging of two hostages a day until Berwick surrendered. The Scots attempted to relieve Berwick, but were beaten two miles away in the battle of Halidon Hill in 1333. Froissart says that the besieged were in such straits that they could no longer drink wine, but had to make do with water! One suspects their plight was somewhat worse, and at last they surrendered. Edward was able to enter Berwick, and other places yielded after this victory.[36]

But as with Edward I, so with his grandson, there might be military victories, but the Scottish corpse would not lie down, and rebellion rose in the very next year. Edward, like his grandfather was persistent, and organised a new campaign at once, making Roxburgh his base, and in 1335 a greater force than ever crossed the frontier. A great engine was taken by ship for use against Rothesay castle, requiring eight workmen to assemble it.[37] With Edward engaged in the French war, his people won a great victory at Neville's Cross in 1346, where David II was taken prisoner. Even so, in the long run, Edward had to abandon plans for the conquest, and Scotland retained its independence; greater resources allied to military ability were not always enough. It is a foretaste of a trend in the later middle ages in Europe, which would see several great nations humbled by relatively poor but highly motivated national armies.

The Holy Roman Empire

Frederick II is the dominant figure in imperial history of this period, perhaps the last really great medieval emperor; after his day, the empire would never be the power it had been, its unity cracked, its universal claims seeming ever emptier, its central authority in decline. It is true that the beginnings of this process are apparent well before Frederick II's time, and that in some ways his own reign and its aftermath accelerated such developments, but for all that, Frederick rides the period as a majestic, fascinating and powerful ruler.

Perhaps the image of him as *stupor mundi*, the wonder of the world, has been dented by recent interpretations, but few would deny his place among

36 Berwick, Nicholson, p. 121; lack of wine, Froissart, *EHD*, iv, p. 60.
37 On Rothesay, Nicholson, p. 221.

Mining and fire

the great medieval kings.[38] Frederick may have been less powerful in Germany than say Philip Augustus in France, or Edward I in England, but nevertheless the resources of the empire were tremendous, so that even access to a part of them gave great strength. His conciliatory attitude towards the German princes ensured that his chief worries would be elsewhere, from the papacy, the cities of Italy, and from his own family. Like other great kings of this age, in his homeland, whether one views that as Germany or Sicily where he had grown up as his mother's heir, he was predominant, and order was generally well kept.

Frederick had cause from very early days to realise the importance of fortification. His own life was in danger when the papal representative, Anweiler, besieged and took Palermo. At that time Frederick may well not have held on to Sicily, let alone gone on to become emperor of Germany. The boy with his tutor William had been forced to hide in the basement, betrayed by their own castellan. When discovered Frederick was enraged by the situation and by fate, tearing off his cap and clothes, and scratching his own flesh till he bled. In the end Frederick's supporters triumphed and he became ruler of Sicily and began to make his play for the empire which his father, Henry VI, had ruled.

His very first effort to claim the throne in Germany, showed the young Frederick the importance of defended strongholds, in the race to win

38 The major recent work on the great emperor is D. Abulafia, *Frederick II*, who sees Frederick as less of a wonder. See also biographies by Kantorowicz, Masson and Van Cleve.

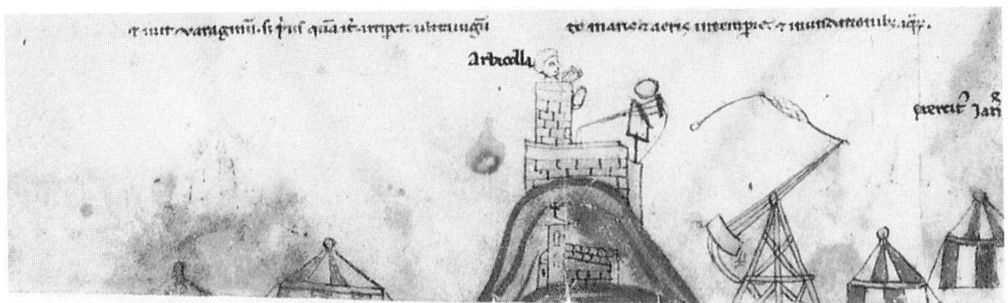

The siege of Savone, 1227, with trebuchets

Constance from Otto IV. At first, on his arrival, Frederick was refused entrance, but he used the fact of having papal support to persuade the citizens to open their gates. They let him in only hours before Otto IV turned up to try and gain the city. Apart from being an important stepping stone on the way to the imperial throne, it also gave Frederick the advantage over his rival of a decent meal that night. Probably Philip Augustus' victory over Otto IV at Bouvines in 1214 was the main event in settling the fate of the empire. Frederick went on from Constance to capture Aachen in 1215, and there he was crowned.[39]

Italy

Frederick II's hold on Sicily was strengthened by his victory over the Saracens in the island in 1222, the climax being his eight-week siege of Iato. Ibn Abbad finally surrendered and came before Frederick in the latter's tent, falling on his face to ask pardon. Frederick booted him with his spur, ripping open his flesh, and a week later had him hanged at Palermo, an example of the limitations to Frederick's supposed toleration with regard to Islam and its believers. One interesting effect of his victory in Sicily was the deportation of some two thousand Moslems to a fortress

39 Chronicles have far more on siege engines and techniques in Italy than in Germany, which may reflect the predominance of Italians in this field.

on the mainland at Lucera in Apulia. There Frederick built himself a new town, with a palace, and there he kept a harem. This act is partly responsible for Frederick's reputation as having views before his time. Almost certainly such unusual ideas as he did hold came simply from his experience of growing up in Sicily, with its population of Greeks and Moslems as well as western Christians. Otherwise it has been shown that Frederick was not especially favourable to any but Christians, though he might use his knowledge of Islam in his own interest, as during the course of his crusade. In his household the only Moslems to make progress were those who had converted to Christianity.[40]

As emperor, his campaigns into northern Italy were marked by a series of important sieges, denoting failures as well as successes. The first of these was at Vicenza in 1235, where he demonstrated his perennial strengths of energy and ruthlessness. The attack was pressed with vigour, the walls scaled, the town sacked and burned. Speaking to his lieutenant, Ezzelino da Romano, Frederick said this is how to show authority, and taking out his sword, proceded to hack off the blades of grass and heads of poppies in front of him.[41]

But Frederick was not always able to demonstrate his power in the way he wished, and the strength of the defences of the Italian towns, linked to his own problem of organizing materials against them, much of which had to be brought from distant Germany, combined to frustrate his ambitions. In 1238 Ezzelino advised Frederick to concentrate his attention on Brescia as a prelude to attack on the greater enemy, Milan. Frederick took the advice, but must have regretted it. At first he acted without any great urgency, only pressing in August a siege which had started in July. He probably hoped, vainly, that he could gain what he wished without having to make an all-out effort. Frederick had been sent the noted Spanish engineer, Calamandrinus, to help with his engines. The unfortunate engineer was kept in chains to prevent him from escaping, so it is hardly surprising that when he was captured and released by the citizens of Brescia, and then tempted with a house and a wife if he threw in his lot with them, he changed his allegiance. It was a sore loss to Frederick, since not only did he lose the engineer's vital services, but his enemies benefited from them, and new catapults soon appeared on the city's towers.[42]

Frederick threw everything at the city: engines, rams, catapults. He tried mining; it all failed. One night his German miners were caught while sleeping at their posts, and many of them killed. No siege illustrates better the evil results that could stem from losing key specialists. Frederick was reduced to the same barbarous methods employed by his predecessor

40 On Iato, 1222, and Moslem converts, see Abulafia, pp. 145, 148.

41 Vicenza, 1235, and the poppies, Abulafia, p. 129.

42 On Brescia and Calamandrinus, see Cleve, *Emperor Frederick II*, p. 415, and Kantorowicz, *Frederick the Second*, p. 464; *Annales Placentini Gibellini*, p. 479.

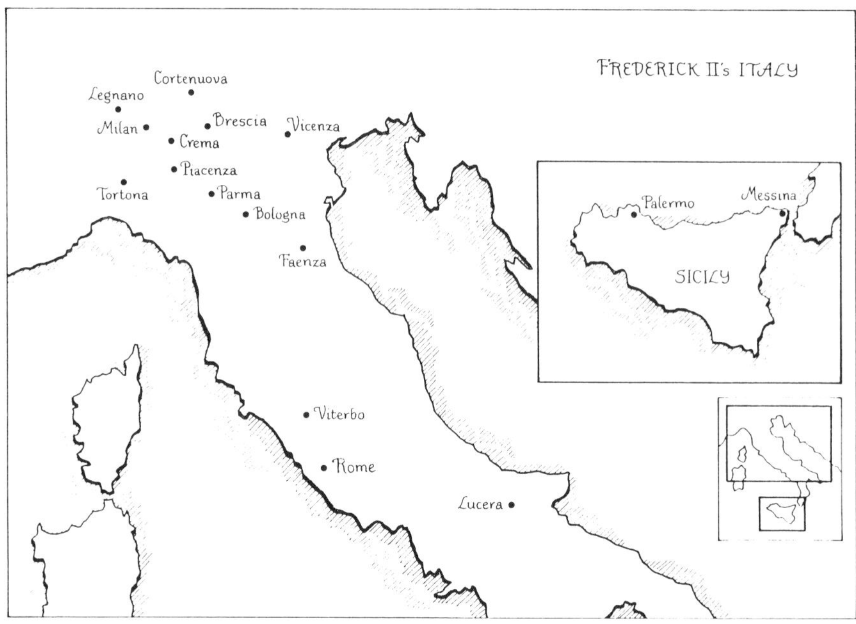

Barbarossa, of tying captives to the engines in an attempt to protect the machines. As then, so now, it failed. The citizens lowered prisoners down the walls in front of Frederick's rams.[43] One interesting development at Brescia was a sort of early germ warfare. In the city a virulent disease broke out among the animals, and some of the suffering creatures were driven out of the city to mingle with the beasts belonging to their besiegers, and so to pass it on. Added to this the weather worsened and finally Frederick ordered his own engines to be burned, and abandoned the siege. It was a significant defeat.

The siege of Faenza in 1240–41 was a success for Frederick, but so lengthy and costly that it must have given his enemies heart; Faenza after all was not the most powerful of the opposing cities. As with Brescia and Milan, so here Frederick saw it as a prelude to attack on Bologna. He set the siege with determination, constructing a camp of wooden huts with a trench encircling them, the usual sign that he was there to stay. One problem Frederick faced was finding the precious metal with which to pay his men, and he was driven to producing leather tokens with an imperial stamp on them, which could be redeemed for cash later. It was during this lengthy siege that Frederick found the leisure to while away his hours by checking Master Theodore's translation of Mos Moamyn's treatise on falconry. At last the blockade began to bite, and the citizens tried to reduce the number of mouths to feed by sending out the women, the young and

43 Kantorowicz, p. 464.

the elderly. Frederick offered little hope, declaring that the city had previously insulted his mother when pregnant, and had been responsible for an attempt at assassination when they put to death a man dressed as himself. At last, though desperate to hold out, famine caused the city to surrender after eight months. Frederick had the walls destroyed, but was more merciful than the citizens might have anticipated, allowing their lives as he showed them what he claimed were 'the outstretched arms of inexhaustible clemency'.[44]

The siege of Viterbo in 1243 was a new humiliation for Frederick, despite his magnificent arrival, riding a showy, red horse. He managed to enter after filling the ditches with barrels of earth, wood and turf, but the citadel would not surrender. Frederick tried hurling Greek Fire, with disastrous results, since the wind changed direction and caused his own engines to catch light. In the end Frederick abandoned the siege. As Matthew Paris saw it: Frederick 'retired basely', his reputation shattered.[45] Such sieges in the end sapped his strength in Italy, so that despite his great victory in the battle of Cortenuova, he was ultimately beaten by the resistance of the towns and their fortifications. One could hardly find a better war to demonstrate that battles were not always the deciding factor.

Towards the end of his life Frederick became engaged in the siege of Parma in 1247. The city had become papalist and was held by the pope's brother-in-law, Bernard Orlando Rossi. Enzio began the siege and was later joined by Frederick, swearing that he would not leave till it was taken. He built a veritable town for his men, intending it to have even a cathedral and a zoo, the whole complex being unwisely named Vittoria. Frederick had some successes, on one occasion capturing some citizens in an ambush 'like birds caught in a net'.[46] There was fighting in the streets, when the citizens were reduced to blocking the way with chains, and rolling casks to frighten the horses. According to Matthew Paris the city suffered because it had once insulted an English bishop passing through on pilgrimage, and things only improved when the city decided to placate his ghost by paying for a church to be built in London. With Frederick off on a hunting expedition, the citizens made a sortie against Vittoria. They captured many valuables including a famous hunting manuscript, and the person of the judge of the imperial palace, Tadeo de Suessa. The latter had his hands cut off and was left to die in a cell. Again Frederick had to abandon a key siege into which he had put much effort and expense. The citizens exulted in destroying his temporary city of Vittoria; the pope declared that Victory had been vanquished.[47]

44 Faenza, on falconry, Abulafia, p. 268; on clemency, Kantorowicz, p. 547.

45 On Viterbo, Matthew Paris, *Chronica Majora*, iv, p. 267: *turpiter*; ed. Giles, i, p. 465.

46 Birds in a net, Matthew Paris, ed. Giles, ii, p. 365.

47 On the pope, Matthew Paris, ed. Giles, ii, p. 263; the quote is from *Chronica Majora*, v, p. 15: *Victoria, victa fuisti.*

Frederick had been a great emperor in many ways, but he had failed to keep Italy within the imperial fold. His last years were marked with tragedy, the rebellion and death of his son Enzio, the betrayal of his chief minister Piero della Vigna. The latter had served him for some twenty years but was now accused of conspiring against the emperor, was tried, sentenced and blinded, and beat out his own brains against the pillar to which he was chained. When Frederick himself died in 1250 the pope proclaimed: 'let heaven and earth rejoice'.[48] Without Frederick himself, his territories split up, his family squabbled amongst itself. Germany fell to other families, Sicily to other nations, and Italy was divided amongst its own cities.

48 Abulafia, p. 408.

CHAPTER SEVEN

Trouble in the West, 1350–1500

Stability in the West, which had been hard won by the great kings, was disrupted in the last two centuries of the middle ages. Old threats to peace emerged in new guises: most often through the power of over-mighty vassals, who in this period Keen has called the super-nobility, sometimes in alliance with external enemies.[1] The greatest conflict of this age in the West was the Hundred Years War, which saw a combination of these two threats, given substance by a very old cause of trouble, a succession dispute. In one sense it was a rebellion against the king of France by very powerful vassals, including the duke of Burgundy and the king of England. In fact both of these vassals ruled their lands in France virtually independently of the monarch, and they were internal vassals and external powers at the same time. Essentially the war was an international conflict between two monarchies, England and France, seeking to dominate western Europe, dragging principalities around them into the struggle: Burgundy, Flanders, the Iberian powers. Meanwhile, in the Holy Roman Empire civil war was followed by a failure to maintain imperial authority over towns or nobles, and the later middle ages saw the disintegration of the empire.

The political situation of the later middle ages was worsened by the succession of inadequate men to the thrones of England and France. In France the end of the Capetian dynasty weakened the monarchy, at least for a time, allowing the kings of England to dispute the authority of the early Valois. In addition, the succession of the feeble-minded Charles VI, allowed the unity of France to crack asunder. In England Richard II brought upon himself rebellion, and eventually removal from the throne, and death. The usurpation of Henry Bolingbroke as Henry IV created problems for the new Lancastrian dynasty throughout its existence. Henry VI proved to be the English counterpart to Charles VI, perhaps inheriting the mental instability from his grandfather. In England there also appeared

1 Keen, *Chivalry*, p. 246.

over-powerful vassals in the duke of York, and after the Yorkists in their turn had usurped the throne, in the earl of Warwick.

The backcloth to the political struggle was the disruption which would have occurred anyway, brought on by the economic difficulties from the Black Death and the agricultural depression, followed by population decline and social change, which came near to revolution in mainly abortive peasant risings. At the same time as central authority was seriously called into question, the actual forces of war available were increasing in size and strength, armies grew larger, there were more trained troops available, artillery became more powerful, more flexible means of raising and using resources were developed. Campaigns could last longer, involved more people, and so became ever more destructive. One insignificant campaign could devastate hundreds of villages, and cause thousands of deaths. Bouvet thought that 'no man who did not know how to set places on fire was worthy of the name of soldier'.[2]

There were those who came to rely for a living on the occupation of war, who feared peace. The late middle ages saw many parts of the West under threat of disorder from such men, who formed roaming companies, made up of experienced and hardened soldiers, able at times to hold towns and princes to ransom. Captain Bascot de Mauléon explained the dilemma of the unemployed soldier to the chronicler Froissart, over drinks in the Moon Tavern. Bascot had fought under the Captal de Buch at Poitiers, but was put out of work when the Peace of Brétigny was made in 1360.[3] This was when he, like many others in the same situation, offered their services to any who would pay them, surviving by bandit-like activities in the meantime. It was one of the problems that arose from the increasing professionalism of war. There was only a thin line between commoners employed as captains, seeking to improve their lot fighting for a king, and mercenaries in a company, as war became more and more a commercial enterprise. Men like du Guesclin, Surienne or La Hire, with their military ability and knowledge of artillery, were always in demand.

It was an age of some disorder, to deal with which, in the end, was forged an even more powerful state, that could harness the greater military force to its own ends. The efforts of such as Louis XI in France and Henry VII in England, brought in a new age of nation states. As Commines said of Louis XI's armies, they had become so large that few princes could attempt to match them. There emerged permanent armies, permanent garrison forces, powerful artillery trains. The artillery of the Bureau brothers restored French confidence, and underwrote the success of Charles VII in the last stages of the Hundred Years War. Between 1449 and 1450 their artillery

2 Damage from one campaign, Kaeuper, p. 82; Bouvet quote is from Allmand, *Hundred Years War*, pp. 48–9.

3 Froissart, ed. Brereton, pp. 280–81.

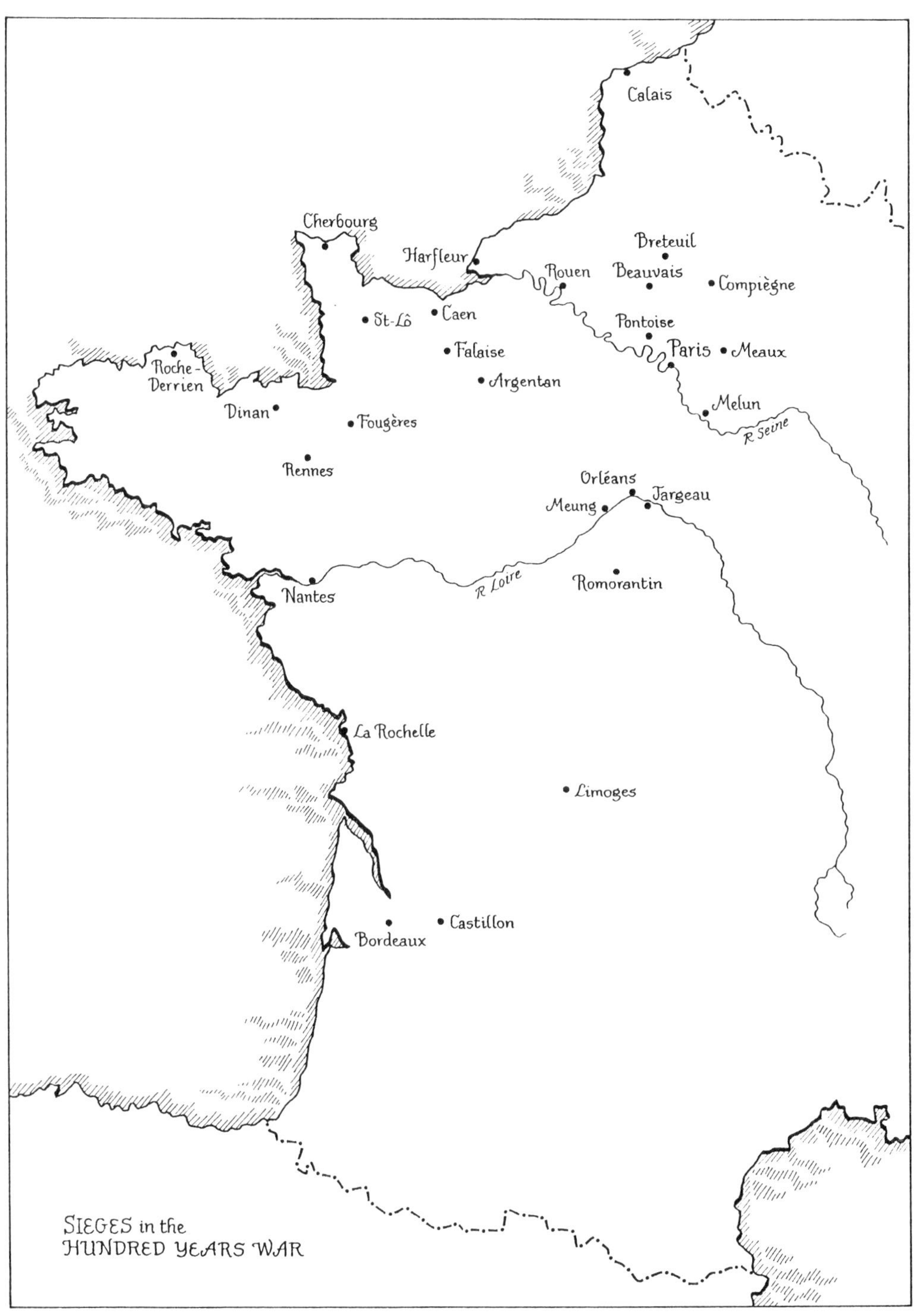
Calais
Cherbourg
Harfleur
Rouen
Breteuil
Beauvais
Compiègne
St-Lô
Caen
Pontoise
Falaise
Paris
Meaux
Roche-Derrien
Argentan
Dinan
Fougères
Melun
R Seine
Rennes
Orléans
Jargeau
Meung
Nantes
R Loire
Romorantin
La Rochelle
Limoges
Castillon
Bordeaux
SIEGES in the
HUNDRED YEARS WAR

was responsible for success in no less than sixty sieges; it was becoming difficult to stand out against such force.[4]

The Hundred Years War: Edward III

The Hundred Years War is the key conflict in this period, drawing in many western princes over a long period of time. Its beginnings lay in the ambitions of Edward III to recover something of the lost territories of the former Angevin Empire. His opportunity arose through the unexpected deaths of the last Capetian kings. The war, when described briefly, is usually marked by its great battles: Crécy, Poitiers, Agincourt, and so on, but in truth it would be more fairly characterised by its great sieges: Calais, Harfleur, Caen, Rouen, Meaux, Orléans. Indeed, like so many medieval battles, the last and decisive battle of the war, at Castillon in 1453, arose from a siege. Sieges played a greater rôle than battles in the whole war, apart from occurring in vastly greater numbers. After the early defeats on the battlefield, the French deliberately avoided such conflicts, and not surprisingly, therefore, for a long period of the war there were virtually no battles at all. The slower but surer gain of towns and castles was the main feat of the French movement to final victory. In most cases the famous battles were unsought by the victors: the English tried to avoid Crécy, Poitiers and Agincourt. Sieges formed the main objectives in the stategic planning of Edward III and Henry V.[5]

Edward III's earliest efforts were not especially glorious, despite the new tactics which had been hammered out in Scotland. Sieges at Cambrai in 1339, and Tournai in 1340, were both abandoned. There were a few successes in the south, but then came the great campaign of 1346 during which the battle of Crécy was fought. Edward III was able to land without trouble because many French knights were engaged in besieging Aiguillon, which they eventually had to abandon. Edward mopped up towns in western Normandy: Barfleur, Cherbourg where he could not take the castle, Valognes, Carentan, St-Lô. He then approached the major stronghold of western Normandy at Caen, where the Odon meets the Orne. The citizens panicked at Edward's approach by both land and water; the knights locked in the great tower watched the carnage below, as Edward stormed the Old Town. Their leaders surrendered to Sir Thomas Holland, apparently in fear of how they might be treated by common archers. Citizens resisted from housetops, throwing down planks and stones, which only made Edward furious and provoked him into ordering a general massacre from which

4 On large armies, Commines, ed. Jones, p. 380; on sixty sieges, Oman, ii, p. 404.

5 For general reading on the Hundred Years War, see Allmand, *Hundred Years War*, Seward, *Hundred Years War*, Perroy, and Burne, *Crecy War* and *Agincourt War*.

Edward III's attack on Caen

course he was persuaded only with difficulty. It was the first major land victory of the war for the English.

Edward then aimed for Calais, which would be a great gain for the English, establishing a base for further efforts. There can be little doubt that such was his objective. He did his best to evade the larger French field army on the long march north, but was finally caught at Crécy, where he made the best of a bad situation, and won a great victory. Even so, Calais was not to be an easy picking, the battle did not give that much advantage. The garrison prepared to resist with all its ability, and the siege endured into the new year. Crécy made success possible, but Calais was the true test piece of the campaign. Without it Edward would have little to show for his efforts.

Calais was held by John de Vienne for Philip VI. It was a mighty stronghold, with double walls and a double ditch. As Edward closed in, the garrison sent out 1,700 poor, whom Edward allowed to go through his lines, even providing a meal, but then the circuit was closed. Even so, some

French ships managed to slip through with welcome provisions. Edward settled to the regular business of blockade, at the same time preparing for an assault by bringing over cannons from London, and building engines. It proved difficult to find suitable positions in which to place the latter, since most of the ground encircling Calais was sandy and marshy. Blockade seemed the most likely way to bring success, and Edward said he was ready to wait twelve years if necessary. He constructed a 'New Town' for the besiegers, consisting of hutted accomodation, with its own streets and shops and a regular market. Letters were sent round to neighbouring towns to obtain flour, bread, corn, wine, beer, meat and fish. The besieged did try to send out messages to the French king. One messenger was seen, and as he was pursued, threw his message into the sea tied to an axe. Unfortunately for his efforts, the next morning the tide washed the message ashore: it described the suffering and need of the citizens and begged for supplies. It said that they were eating cats and dogs, and all that remained was to eat each other: they would have to surrender if they did not receive supplies or relief. Edward III, with some wit, forwarded the message to Philip VI.[6]

The French king, smarting from his defeat at Crécy, was reluctant to risk a clash, and it was many months before a serious effort was made to relieve Calais. It says much for the courage of the defenders that they held out so long, but Edward's blockade gradually wore them down. At last the hoped-for relief army appeared. Every night on the walls the defenders lit a fire, smaller each night to indicate to the king their decreasing resources and hopes. Edward had carefully blocked every way through for the French; ships with siege weapons on board covered the route across the sandy dunes, and a guard tower watched the tracks over the marshes. The French did eventually take that tower, but suffered many casualties in the process.

A French embassy was allowed through to discuss surrender, and eyed the English fortifications with some despair, warning Philip on their return that it seemed impossible to get through. The French king challenged Edward to a fight, but the latter said he had spent much on his preparations, was near to success, and not willing to throw it away. He challenged Philip in return to break through if he could; Philip was not prepared to try, and abandoned the attempt at relief. The city had no real hope now: the French royal standard was thrown into the ditch in disgust, and peace was sought. Edward was in no mood to grant easy terms, he wanted unconditional surrender in return for his time, trouble and expense, indeed he wanted a massacre. Some of his men argued that it would be better to be merciful. If they were ever in similar trouble there would be no mercy. Edward relented, but the terms were still hard. He demanded six men for execution. The citizens assembled by ringing the bells, and six of the town's leading members offered themselves as a sacrifice, the first being

6 An account of the siege of Calais is in Burne, *Crecy War*, ch. 8, pp. 204–23. See also Longman, i, p. 28 for the message story.

their richest citizen, Eustace de Saint-Pierre. Stripped to shirt and breeches, with ropes round their necks, the six emerged. In the famous sequel, they were saved only by the merciful appeal of Edward's queen.

Calais had been the first really long siege of the Hundred Years War, though it was far from being the last. It set the tone for the conflict. The English victory had been hard won, but it confirmed the success at Crécy, and deepened the defeat and despair of the French king, deflating the morale of his subjects. It also gave the English an invaluable base for future invasion in the north.

Despite the appearance of cannons in the first half of the fourteenth century, the conventional siege engines, and especially the trebuchet, remained the major hope of breaking down walls. However, in the see-saw for dominance between weapons and defences, the early stages of the Hundred Years War was a period when defences predominated. The fortifications of major strongholds were very intimidating; walls, ditches, techniques of protection for defenders and means of shooting at attackers had all been improved to the point where a straightforward storming could be difficult, as the siege of Calais had demonstrated. It usually required very considerable resources in men and engines, and even then blockade might be the only answer.

Charles of Blois besieged Roche-Derrien in 1347.[7] He cleared the ground all around in preparation, which included felling the trees, and made use of an old but formidable earthwork to protect his men. He produced nine engines, one of which was very large and threw 300-pound stones. One such stone hit the governor's house, though the occupants survived. Even so, a relief force in conjunction with a sortie, was enough to save Roche-Derrien for the English, and Charles was wounded and captured. Later in the war Philip VI did take the place, and massacred the garrison.

Cannons made their mark first in sieges, but as yet they were only a minor element in the range of weapons. The Black Prince's attack on Romorantin employed cannons as well as Greek Fire, thus setting light to the thatched roof of a tower, which led to the surrender of the knights within. At Romorantin the Prince attacked with venom, after a friend had been killed early in the siege. The defenders resisted using pots of quicklime which inflicted very unpleasant wounds, but finally were forced into surrender.[8]

In 1356 King John of France captured Evreux, and besieged Breteuil. He brought up engines, including a belfry on wheels which was three stories high. It had 300 men on each of the three levels, with loopholes and enough room for all the men to use their weapons.[9] Peasants were ordered

7 On Roche-Derrien, 1347, see Burne, *Crecy*, pp. 87–99.

8 Froissart, in *Hundred Years War*, ed. Thompson, pp. 96–7.

9 Belfry, Froissart, ed. Brereton, pp. 120–1.

to collect wood and fill up the moat, the pile then being covered over with earth and straw to make a track for the belfry. It took a month to fill the moat, then knights and squires were stationed inside the engine, and finally it was wheeled across to the wall. The garrison used both Greek Fire and cannons to try and stop it. The engine was set on fire, and had to be abandoned to the triumphant cheers of the English, who shouted out that their enemies had not got as far as they expected after all. The remains of the great wooden structure were left in the moat. But in the end the pressure told, the other engines did a good deal of damage, no relief force appeared, and after threats that all would be killed if it were taken by storm, Breteuil surrendered.

Chivalry was not altogether dead even in the increasingly vicious fighting of the Hundred Years War. A curious incident occurred at Rennes in 1356, when being besieged by the duke of Lancaster.[10] One of the English attackers, John Bolton, found time to go hawking, and returned with a bag of six partridges. He approached the town walls, with his bag, and offered to sell them to any taker so that the ladies of the town could be fed. Olivier de Mauny took up the challenge, but rather than offer to pay, said he would come and get them for free. He swam the moat and fought a combat for the unusual prize. The ladies of Rennes observed the fate of their dinner from the battlements. Olivier was wounded, but won the contest and returned with the birds, releasing Bolton. But then Olivier himself became ill, Bolton learned of it, and persuaded Lancaster to give his former opponent a safe-conduct through the English lines so that he could see a doctor. Again, in this siege, the engines did some damage to the walls and when no relief was forthcoming, the place surrendered.

The long drawn-out conflict caused much damage, often deliberate destruction by the English to try and provoke a battle; as at Romorantin, when Geoffrey le Baker reckoned it 'ought to provoke the French to come'.[11] The fourteenth century was truly disastrous, with economic troubles from famine and bad weather, added to the catastrophic effects of the Black Death. Population dropped dramatically, and farms, especially on poorer soils, were abandoned. In the wake of this came peasant discontent and rebellion thoughout Europe. In 1358 the French peasants rose in the Jacquerie, the equivalent of the English Peasants Revolt. An episode at Meaux demonstrated the contempt for the peasants felt by the 'chivalric' nobility, when the count of Foix and the Captal de Buch saved some noble ladies under threat. The mob retreated before the professional soldiers, some 7,000 being killed like cattle, many thrown into the river. Meaux was burned down, and many ordinary folk were left to their fate within the

10 The Bolton story, in Longman, ii, pp. 17–18.

11 *EHD*, iv, p. 94.

walls. Froissart describes the event for his noble masters, seeing only the heroism of the nobles, not viewing it in any sense as an atrocity.[12]

The first major phase of the war was brought to a close by the Treaty of Brétigny in 1360. Edward III had recovered much of the territory of the former Angevin Empire, though he was prepared, for the time being, to relinquish his claim to the French throne. The disturbed economic, social and political conditions of the later fourteenth century did not allow a period of stability and recovery. Indeed, in both England and France it seems that the situation deteriorated.

There were no major battles to mark the continuation of the war after the peace treaty was broken: from 1369 the French deliberately pursued a policy of avoiding battle. If the English could not provoke the French to battle, they would make large scale destructive raids through French territory. The best remembered of these chevauchées was the Black Prince's campaign of 1370, which resulted in the destruction of Limoges. The condemnation of the Black Prince for the sack of Limoges at the time, was more from political opposition than offended sensibilities. If one condemns the Black Prince, then one condemns virtually all medieval siege commanders. The conventions of medieval siege warfare allowed free rein to a besieger when a town or stronghold was taken by storm, and the Prince perhaps had more cause than some to vent his anger. The bishop of Limoges had earlier stood godfather to his son Richard, but tamely handed over Limoges to the French without a fight. The Prince was determined to recover the city, and despite illness, was carried there on a litter. He used 'rough labourers' to make a mine, which he ordered to be fired at six o'clock in the morning, when a large section of the wall collapsed into the moat. Then the gate was attacked and flattened, so that the troops were able to burst in. The town was given over to massacre. In the pro-French version of his chronicle, Froissart criticised the Prince's activities, but it is difficult to distinguish the killings here from those that came after many successful storms both before 1370 and after.[13]

A less grim tale attaches to the siege of La Rochelle in 1372, held for the English by the uneducated and rather dim-witted, Philip Mansel. The outcome turned on the fact that Mansel was unable to read. The French mayor played a daring trick on him. He invited Mansel to dinner and produced a letter which he said he had just received from Edward III. He waved the letter to show the king's seal. It was indeed a genuine seal, but on an old letter, and Mansel was deceived. The mayor then pretended to read the letter, with instructions to Mansel from the king, that on the next day he must bring the garrison out of the castle and parade them in the town. The mayor baited the hook even more enticingly by giving a

12 Count of Foix and the Captal, Froissart, ed. Brereton, pp. 154–5.

13 On labourers, Froissart, ed. Brereton, p. 177; and on criticism of the Black Prince, ed. Jolliffe, p. 222.

promise that he himself was to provide all the back pay owing to the troops. The English garrison prepared for the parade, polishing their helmets, armour and swords, and turned out in the town square. The French had prepared an ambush, cut off the way back to the castle, and surrounded the English. Taken by surprise, the shame-faced garrison surrendered, and the mayor handed the town over to the care of du Guesclin and the French.[14]

Not only France and England but other parts of Europe suffered from the conflict, including Spain and the Low Countries. At Ghent cannons split the gate in half, and the count of Flanders had to hide in the house of a poor woman, under a child's bed in the loft, until he could escape.[15] The war spread into Spain, as France and England supported rival claimants in the war of succession for Castile: England favouring Pedro the Cruel, despite the fact that he was said to have killed his wife in order to have his mistress; France favouring his brother, Henry of Trastamara. National divisions were blurred as mercenaries from various countries sought employment at a time when the fighting in France had stopped. One such soldier of fortune, Bascot de Mauléon, captured Albi, by disguising himself and his men as women, with handkerchiefs over their faces and using falsetto voices so that they could get in. A problem of soldiering in Spain was the strong wine, which it was said, 'burnt their livers and lungs and all the entrails of their stomachs'. In Paris the soldiers of the companies, known to them as 'the English', were so unpopular that the citizens attacked them. Jean de Venette, the French chronicler, born of peasant parents, had seen the English burn down his own house, and wrote that: 'highways and roads were almost everywhere uncertain and dangerous, on account of freebooters and robbers'.[16]

But for a time affairs within both England and France were so troubled that the war between them petered out. In England the heir to the throne, Edward the Black Prince, died in 1376, so that instead of going to an experienced military commander, the crown went to the Prince's young son, Richard. Edward III himself had lost respect in his later years, when he is pictured as given up to plesure with his mistress Alice Perrers. She was said to use herbs to keep him 'in a state of unseemly sexual excitement'.[17] Whether or not she helped him on his way, Edward died in 1377. There followed the difficult minority and troubled reign of Richard II, beginning with the disturbances of the Peasants Revolt, and ending in the usurpation by Henry Bolingbroke as Henry IV. The latter's reign was also plagued with

14 La Rochelle and Mansel, Froissart, ed. Brereton, pp. 182–5.

15 Froissart, ed. Brereton, pp. 237–8.

16 Froissart, ed. Brereton, on Bascot and Spanish wine, pp. 289, 331. On 'English' companies, Longman, p. 36. The quote is Jean de Venette, *Chronicle*, p. 66.

17 Prestwich, *Three Edwards*, p. 286.

internal troubles, and a series of threatening rebellions which involved the Welsh leader Owen Glendower.

The throne of France went to Charles VI, who in 1392 suffered what sounds like a mental breakdown, brought on by over-work. He had been over-doing attendance at councils and suffering from headaches, when an accidental clash of steel occurred while he was travelling on a hot day. He believed himself, quite erroneously, to be under attack, and without provocation went for the unfortunate duke of Orléans. The latter was only saved by others having the presence of mind, and the courage, to take hold of the king from behind. For a time Charles recognised no-one, not even those closest to him, but gradually he recovered his wits, though never again his full authority. The situation in France became even worse in 1407, when the duke of Orléans was surprised in a sudden attack. He revealed his identity in order to save himself, saying: 'I am the duke of Orléans', at which they smashed his head in.[18] The kingdom of France looked as if it might be about to disintegrate.

The Hundred Years War: Henry V

A new phase in the war opened with the accession of the young, vigorous and ambitious Henry V. He meant to earn a new reputation for himself and his family, and victory in France was the most obvious means of doing so. There is little question, that as with Edward III, the main thrust to renewing the war came from England; politically such aggression in the middle ages tended to make good sense, so long at least as it resulted in success. The parallel with Edward III may be extended, in that Henry also won a glorious and much remembered battle, and also gained more concrete success in terms of power in France through a series of great sieges.[19]

In Henry V's case, his war opened with a major siege at Harfleur, in an attempt to win a new base. It is probable that from the first, Henry aimed not only at destruction or victory, but at conquest. His preparations were on a grand scale, and careful. Harfleur was a test of his planning and his ability to command; it provided evidence of the difficulties he had to overcome, and proved the necessity of massive organisation.

Henry landed in a beautiful dawn at the mouth of the Seine, near what is now Le Havre. By 1415 he had been king for only two years. Harfleur was known to be well defended, and it was no surprise that six weeks were required to bring about its capitulation. Henry had brought with him guns from the Tower of London and Bristol, siege towers, ladders, rams, chains, caltrops, carts, sea coal, wood ash, and 10,000 gunstones. He also had

[18] *Hundred Years War*, ed. Thompson: Froissart on Charles VI's illness, p. 395; and Monstrelet on the Duke of Orleans, p. 259.

[19] For general reading on Henry V: Seward *Henry V*; Harriss, *Henry V*.

smiths, engineers, carpenters, masons, miners and gunners. At Portsmouth he had collected provisions, which included bread, dried fish, salt meat, flour, beans, cheese, ale, clothes, shoes, and live cattle, sheep and pigs. In France he made further efforts to get hold of provisions, including 600 casks of wine from Bordeaux.[20]

On landing Henry fell to his knees and prayed; he saw himself as the scourge of God, with that streak of fanatical piety which lay behind his boundless determination. The English forces, under Henry and his brother Thomas, duke of Clarence, camped around Harfleur, while the English fleet closed off the harbour. Harfleur possessed two and a half miles of walls, and twenty-six towers, with drawbridges and barbicans at the gates, besides a moat and an earth rampart; the barbicans or bulwarks were made from tree trunks lashed together. The River Lézarde, which the French dammed, created marshy ground around much of the city, which, as Edward III had found at Calais, caused difficulty in placing and using engines.[21] In these conditions mining was equally hard, the mines could not be concealed and were easily countered. A relief force of three hundred men managed to get through. Even blockade was problematic, an English force having to travel over difficult country by a roundabout route in order to close the gap.

Both sides used cannons; the English 'gunnys' included *London* and *Messenger*, and began a bombardment which flattened houses within the town.[22] Breaches were made, but the French plugged them with barrels of earth, sand, stones, and planks. Henry himself supervised the firing, but it was not enough. The siege dragged on, the weather deteriorated to a chilling cold, and illness struck the English camp, worsened by an unwise diet of fruit, sour wine and shellfish. There were 2,000 deaths, including those of the earls of Arundel and Suffolk, and the bishop of Norwich, the latter tended by Henry in person. An attack on the south-west bastion, after a to-and-fro contest, brought the English their first significant gain. It burned for three days, and smoked for a fortnight. Then a French sortie damaged the English defences, but was seen off. An attempt at storm was resisted with boiling oil and boiling water, fat, fire-arrows, quicklime and sulphur powder. At last the defenders agreed to surrender in three days if no aid was forthcoming. It proved to be a humiliating agreement for the French, whose leaders were held to ransom. Henry began to fill the town with English soldiers, and encouraged settlers to cross the Channel. The house which became the 'Peacock Inn', was given to Richard Bokeland for his contribution in providing two ships for the invasion.

[20] The beautiful dawn is *Gesta Henrici Quinti*, p. 23; for the provisions for Harfleur, see Seward, *Henry V*, pp. 51, 60.

[21] On Harfleur's defences, Wylie and Waugh, *Reign of Henry V*, ii, pp. 32–3.

[22] Wylie and Waugh, p. 36; *Gesta Henrici Quinti*, p. 28: *in canellis suis, quas in nostro vulgari Gunnys vocamus.*

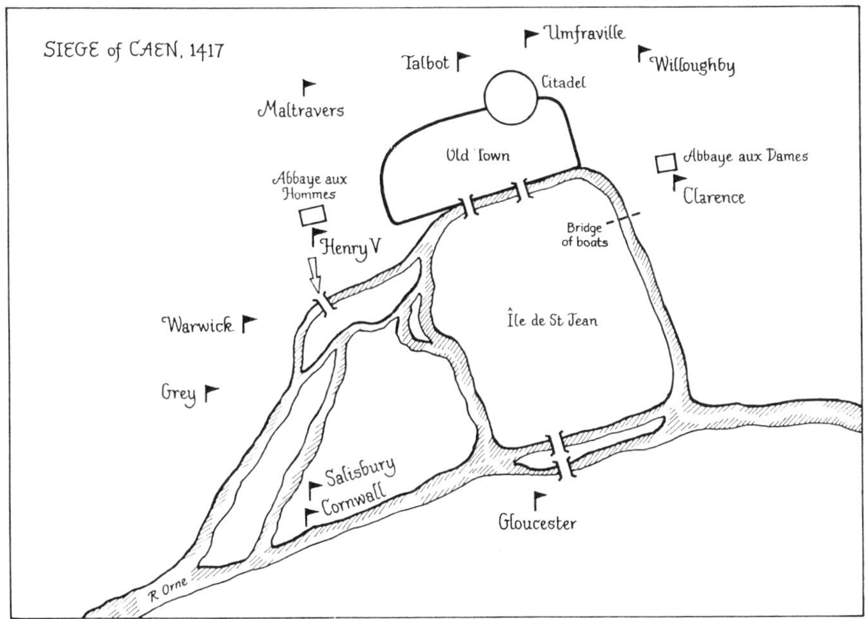

With Harfleur in his hands, Henry employed somewhat novel tactics as he made rapid progress through the Norman countryside. He made a series of agreements with the towns on his route, not for surrender, but giving an offer of 'protection', that is a guarantee against attack, in return for a neutral stance and provisions. For example, at Arques, Eu and Boves, he obtained bread and wine.[23] The success at Harfleur was followed by the unlikely victory at Agincourt, when Henry's depleted army was forced unwillingly to fight a battle. His triumph allowed him to plan an even larger campaign for 1417. His intention to concentrate on siege operations was made clear by orders for guns, trebuchets, engines, sows, leather bridges, scaling ladders, spades, shovels, picks, pavises and other necessities.[24]

This time he landed at what is now Deauville. Nearby towns were captured, and then the English moved on to their main objective, the 'capital' of western Normandy, Caen. The old town with its castle stands on a hill, with the 'new' town below on an island in the Orne. Henry took over the two great monastic buildings, which his distant predecessor William the Conqueror had built to compensate the church for allowing a doubtful marriage; they provided protection and a good base for operations. Henry himself took over the Abbaye aux Hommes to the east

23 Wylie and Waugh, ii, p. 38: *boyling cawdrens*. On Arques, Eu and Boves, *Gesta Henrici Quinti*, pp. 61, 63, 69.
24 Seward, *Henry V*, p. 98; *Brut*, p. 382.

of the city, and stationed guns on the roof. Caen had powerful walls, improved since the time of Edward III. There were twelve great gates, thirty-two towers, and ditches filled with water on three sides.

Henry brought up a collapsible bridge and used it to facilitate contact with his men over the river. He attempted all the usual methods of attack from bombardment to mining. The defenders placed bowls of water on the walls and were able to detect mining and counter it. Henry prepared for an attempt at capture by storm; on 4th September, after three masses had been said, the trumpets blared, and the English rushed forward. But their ladders proved to be too short; Sir Edmund Springhouse tried to scale one, but fell into the ditch, where the French dropped burning straw on to him, and he suffered a painful death.[25] Henry and his brother launched their attacks from opposite sides of the town, both succeeding in breaking in, so that they advanced to meet each other in the town's centre. 2,000 French were killed in the market. The horrors of medieval war are always likely to affront our modern sensibilities but, as with the Black Prince at Limoges, it was the normal right and practice of an army which had achieved a successful storm. The castle held out after the town was taken, and agreed separate terms of surrender.

Caen gave Henry an excellent foundation for his conquest of western Normandy, which he proceded to accomplish during the following year, taking Argentan in 1417, Falaise and Cherbourg in 1418. Falaise, where William the Conqueror had been conceived and born, required a lengthy winter siege. It possessed a powerful castle built on solid rock around the mighty rectangular keep of Henry I. Falaise was held by Charles VI's standard bearer, Olivier de Mauny. The weather was freezing, water turned to ice.[26] Henry provided his men with huts inside a trenched fortification. Artillery fire brought down the clock-tower. The town surrendered in January, but again the castle continued its resistance. There was some difficulty in positioning the artillery, and the solid rock was impossible to mine, but the blockade did the trick and the castle surrendered in February. Its Welsh captain was treated as a traitor, and hanged, drawn and quartered.

A letter from a soldier at the siege of Cherbourg in 1418, shows that the long campaign was beginning to take its toll. He wrote of 'the long time we have been here, and of the expenses that we have had at every siege that we have come to, and have had no wages since that we came out of England, so that we have spent all that ever we had'.[27] Henry's younger brother, Humphrey duke of Gloucester, commanded against Cherbourg. His troops had to forage in groups of three for wood and stones; some of

[25] Collapsible bridge, Burne, *Agincourt*, p. 120; bowls of water, Seward, *Henry V*, p. 104; short ladders, Wylie and Waugh, p. 59.

[26] Water to ice, Seward, *Henry V*, p. 108; *First English Life of Henry V*, p. 102.

[27] Cherbourg letter, Newhall, *English Conquest of Normandy*, p. 240, and n. 247.

Henry V at Rouen, 1418

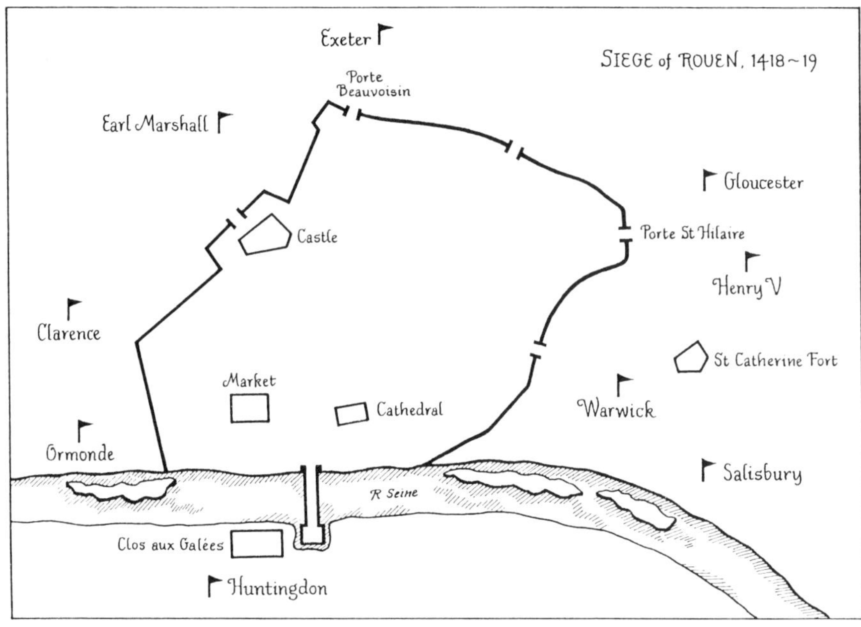

these were brought back on sledges which were floated down the river. The arrival of the English fleet decided the outcome; at first the French thought it was relief arriving, but when the ships were identified as English, they despaired and began arrangements for surrender.

By 1418 western Normandy was conquered, and Henry could turn his attention to the east, and to Rouen. First he needed to isolate the capital of the duchy against possible aid from the east. He allowed bands of Welsh knifemen to roam the area to the east of the city. Surrounding strongholds were taken. At Pont de l'Arche a diversion was arranged when English soldiers horsed about in the water to attract attention while a raid was made from another direction. Rouen was considered to be the second city of France; Henry made every effort to raise what was needed in order to take it. Every small ship available was loaded up in London and sent to France; from Harfleur by river came provisions 'for the refreshment of his army'. London sent 500 archers and a gift of £1,500, as well as thirty butts of sweet wine, 1,000 pipes of ale, and 2,500 cups for the army to use. Fastolf complained that the king's sieges 'consumed innumerable goods of his finance'.[28]

Probably the best account of the events at Rouen is found in the

[28] Rouen, as second city and things brought from Harfleur: *Calendar of Signet Letters*, pp. 197–8. Gifts from London, Allmand, 'Henry V the Soldier', in Harriss, p. 123. On Fastolf, Seward, *Henry V*, p. 170, Allmand, *Society*, p. 58.

Attack on Rouen

chronicle of John Page, who tells us: 'at that siege with the king I lay'.[29] He described the setting up of the camp as a blockade was closed round the five miles of walls, which had been strengthened with an earth bank behind them. There were no less than sixty towers and gates with bastions: every tower had guns, and every land-gate an engine to defend it. The bridge over the river had been deliberately made weak at the southern end, so that part of it could be easily dismantled in a crisis, and the southern end was also protected by a fortification.[30] The English set up five camps, with the king in a monastery to the east. No provisions were getting through, and the besieged began to suffer:

> They ate up dogs, they ate up cats,
> They ate up mice, horses and rats.

Thirty pence was charged for a rat, sixpence for a mouse. The diet was enlivened by vegetable peelings and dock roots. Girls sold themselves for a crust of bread.[31]

Henry, in contrast to the action of Edward III at Calais, refused to allow the ejected poor to go through his lines, and they were left stranded outside the walls, taking what shelter they could in the ditch, including children of two or three, begging for food because their parents had died. The siege endured over Christmas, when Henry did send the poor in the ditch some

29 *EHD*, iv, pp. 219–22, the quote is p. 220.
30 Rouen, gate defences, Seward, *Henry V*, p. 113; dismantled bridge, Wylie and Waugh, p. 119.
31 *EHD*, iv, p. 220; Seward, *Henry V*, p. 117.

food, but a grim Christmas it was. If Henry took prisoners, they were hanged.[32]

A Burgundian relief force came within twenty miles of Rouen, and then decided to abandon the attempt. The news that the dauphin Charles had taken the oriflamme and was preparing to bring an army, was cheered in the streets of Rouen, and the bells were rung, but prematurely; the dauphin never came, and Rouen finally surrendered in January of 1419. Henry entered, an impressive figure in black and gold on a black horse. The starving inhabitants were given food, while the garrison was searched to make sure they were not concealing valuables.[33]

Paris was now open: the fall of Rouen presaged the fall of all Normandy, and the complete victory of Henry in northern France. Charles VI proved no match for the vigorous young king of England, and his son the dauphin seemed to be struggling to survive. Everywhere English arms triumphed. La Roche Guyon surrendered after a three-month siege. The earl of Huntingdon and the Captal de Buch took Pontoise by a storm made at four o'clock in the morning.[34] The blackest moment for the French seemed to occur in 1419, at the bridge of Montereau over the River Yonne. Here a meeting had been arranged to cement relations between the duke of Burgundy and the dauphin. On the bridge which had been named as the meeting place, the duke was treacherously killed. The alliance was shattered, and Burgundy had little choice but to return to the English liaison. The stream of English victories became a deluge.

Allied once more to Burgundy, Henry besieged Melun in 1420, using *The London* and other cannons to batter the walls. A mine was constructed; Henry himself inspected it, and even fought hand to hand in it with the French commander, Lord Barbazon[35] Melun surrendered after four months, for lives and ransoms. Finally in 1420 Henry and the Burgundians were able to enter Paris as their own city.

Henry V's last great siege was at Meaux, a long winter siege from 1421 to 1422, and probably the cause of his death. Meaux was the last major stronghold to resist him in the north. Henry fired the district around in order to deny provisions to the garrison. It was of this event that Juvenal famously remarked: 'war without fire is like sausages without mustard'.[36] Meaux stood on either side of the River Marne. Its garrison included English and Irish mercenaries, as well as the notorious Bastard de Vaurus, who hanged his victims on an elm tree outside the town. It was said that

[32] On poor in the ditch and Christmas, Wylie and Waugh, iii, p. 136; on hanging prisoners, Seward, *Henry V*, p. 116.

[33] The bells, Wylie and Waugh, iii, p. 135; the black and gold costume, Seward, *Henry V*, p. 119.

[34] On 4 am, Seward, *Henry V*, p. 132.

[35] Melun mine, Seward, *Henry V*, p. 150.

[36] Sausages and mustard, Seward, *Henry V*, p. 186; Juvenal, p. 561.

the bodies of eighty unfortunates could be seen when Henry arrived, and that the Bastard had once tied a pregnant girl to it, and left her to the mercy of the wolves.[37]

Once again Henry chose an abbey for his winter quarters, this time St Faro, convenient for his prayers perhaps. Once more for a winter siege he built huts for his men. Warwick was sent to hold the southern bank, and a bridge of boats was constructed over the Marne to allow communications. The river flooded in the winter rains, making the camp unpleasant, and leaving in its wake an outbreak of disease. Henry himself fell ill, and probably never fully recovered. A more immediate victim was the son of Sir John Cornwall, whose head was shot off by a cannon ball. The defenders pushed a donkey up on to the walls, and beat it to make it bray, calling out that this was their king, meaning the unfortunate Charles VI, now in Henry's power, but they would find that Henry possessed no sense of humour, and had little liking for such jokes.

Guy de Nesle attempted a brave night-time relief in the new year, crossing the moat by a plank to scale the wall by a ladder, which was covered with cloth to minimise any sound. Unfortunately the man ahead of Guy dropped a box of herrings he was carrying as food for the besieged, knocking Guy off the ladder so that he fell into the moat to be captured by the awakened English.[38] As the siege was pressed, the French were forced to abandon the town and hole themselves up in the Market, the fortified suburb on the southern bank, breaking the bridge which led to it from the town. The river flowed round three sides of the Market, and with a Roman canal cutting off the fourth side, it was in practice a fortified island. Henry brought up a portable drawbridge on a wheeled belfry to bridge the river, and used a second small island as a new artillery base. He even constructed a floating tower on two barges lashed together.[39] Resistance was fierce, and mines were countered, but in the end the garrison had no real option but surrender.

Henry intended to move on to the siege of Cosne in his usual tireless fashion, but he found himself too ill to continue, and came to a premature death at the age of thirty-five. Perhaps he had bitten off more than he could chew; his claim for the French crown undermined the English hold on western France as a separate entity, a more limited ambition might have left a more lasting legacy. But his early death would have created problems in any case, with the succession of his young and ineffective son, Henry VI.

37 The Bastard, Seward, *Henry V*, p. 186; Bourgeois, p. 171.

38 Seward, *Henry V*: on Cornwall's son, p. 187; on the donkey, p. 188; on Guy de Nesle, p. 190.

39 Seward, *Henry V*: on the portable drawbridge, p. 190; on the floating tower, p. 191.

The Hundred Years War: Charles VII

The fascination of history, as of life, lies in its unpredictability. Who could have foreseen the degree of Henry V's triumph: forcing a marriage to the daughter of the king of France, and winning recognition as that king's heir? Equally, who could have forecast his early death, and the ultimate success of the desperate and hunted Charles VII? One could argue for ever, and without profit, as to how far this recovery was due to Charles VII himself, or to his generals, or to his artillery in the hands of the brothers Bureau, or to the totally surprising emergence of the Maid, Joan of Arc. Of course all of these played some part.[40]

Our task is simply to examine the rôle of siege warfare in this French trail to victory in the Hundred Years War. It was indeed a considerable rôle, the French after 1369 deliberately preferred siege tactics to battle, and the policy endured. As the French proved more successful, so confidence returned, and they did fight and win a handful of major battles in the late stages of the war. But it is probably fair to suggest that most historians have seen the siege of Orléans as the most notable turning point of the war.

The death of Henry V had been a great blow, but it took some years before the depth of the loss became apparent. England retained good troops, adequate and even excellent commanders, so the change in direction of fortunes was not immediately obvious. Battles were still won by longbows, and towns besieged and taken by the English. For the dauphin Charles the picture remained gloomy for some years.

In besieging Orléans, the English made what proved to be the fatal error. The earl of Salisbury was a good commander, and Orléans was a major stronghold on what had become virtually the frontier in the war, the River Loire, dividing northern from southern France; but it is questionable if Salisbury had sufficient resources to maintain a major siege, and without Henry V it was far more difficult to raise what was needed. It was still difficult for a commander who was not a king; and the problem of providing of resources showed in the failure to establish a complete blockade. It would almost certainly have been better to abandon the attempt at an early stage.

Salisbury attempted to dig in from October 1428. The chronicler, Waurin, says that the English made underground houses, presumably pit dwellings, 'according to their custom'.[41] Beaugency and Jarzeau were taken in an effort to isolate Orléans. The town contained a garrison of 2,400, and perhaps ten times that many citizens. In addition to the walled city, there was a bridge over the Loire with a fortification at its southern end, known

40 For general reading, Vale, *Charles VII*; Vaughan, *Valois Burgundy*.

41 Waurin, *EHD*, iv, p. 241.

as Les Tourelles, as well as the fort of St Privé on an island in the river to the west, and a fort to the east at St Loup on the northern bank. The English established five fortified bastilles in an arc to the north-west, and one other probably to the north-east, but never completed the encirclement. They did however succeed in mining the defences at the southern end of the bridge, forcing the French to retreat, but they suffered a severe blow at the very start of the siege. Salisbury climbed up to make a reconnaissance from the captured tower, and a shot from a cannon was aimed at him from the town, which was either lucky or brilliant. He saw it coming and ducked, but it hit the window frame, throwing into the room an iron bar, which hit Salisbury and sliced off half of his face. He was not killed outright but survived only for eight days.[42] The successful use of guns by the French, and their accuracy, is underlined by a shot which hit an English boat on the river from a distance of about 1,400 yards. Even with the death of Salisbury, the English thought they could succeed. Talbot took over command, and a French supply train bearing herrings for the besieged was intercepted, when the force guarding it was beaten in battle.

It was at this critical moment that Joan of Arc emerged from the obscurity of her French peasant life. She was aged about seventeen, born of humble parents at Domrémy. Monstrelet says she had been a chamber maid in an inn. She had been brought up to feel hostile to the Burgundians, and hence to the English. She was also pious, vowing virginity at the age of thirteen, and hearing the voice of an angel from God, a voice which told her 'to raise the siege laid to the city of Orléans', and which gave instructions on how to do it, instructions which proved to be most effective.[43]

She came, wearing male clothing, to Charles VII at Chinon. There was some initial scorn, and she did not easily win friends by her blunt advice on how to live a godly life, for example telling the duke of Lorraine that he must reform his ways and give up his mistress with their five bastards. She was also subjected to a bodily examination to check her claim of virginity. It is hard for us to understand why she was given her way, presumably they were absolutely desperate, ready to turn to almost any hope, even to one of the several peasant prophets seemingly half-crazed, who were offering their services at that time. Joan was allowed to dress as a captain, and to join the relief attempt on Orléans. She sent a message to Henry VI, king of England: 'Render up to the Maid, who is sent by God to the King of Heaven, the keys of all the good towns that you have taken and violated in France'.[44]

Her first success was to enter Orléans, using a barge on the river, and then to ride around the city on a white horse. It was Joan who insisted on

42 Waurin, *EHD*, iv, pp. 241–2.

43 For general reading, Warner, *Joan of Arc*; Pernoud, *Joan of Arc*. For the chambermaid, Monstrelet in *Hundred Years War*, p. 298. The voice is from Pernoud.

44 Burne, *Agincourt*, p. 238.

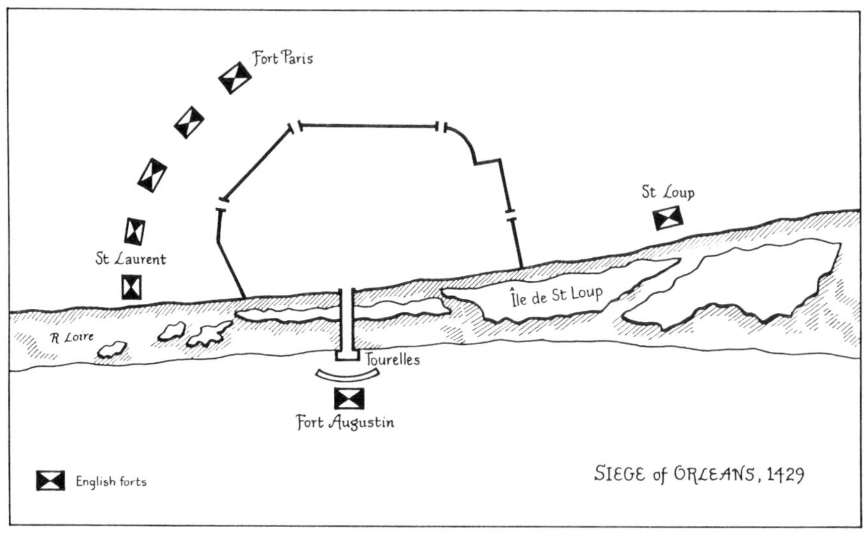

making the attack to recover the fort of St Loup, which succeeded, and Dunois also retook Les Tourelles. Joan's attitude was one of complete certainty that the English would be defeated, and as her prophecies began to be fulfilled with unexpected victories, her confidence became infectious; it was just the tonic which the demoralised French army needed. At last something was going right for them.

Joan of Arc had been wounded at Orléans during the attack on the fort. It is a wonder that her vulnerability did not lose her the magical awe with which she came to be treated. At the storm of Jargeau she was hit on the head by a stone, though her helmet saved her from death, and she kept on shouting encouragement to the successful French troops. She was wounded in the leg attacking the ditch at Meung, and left there till rescued in the dark. Monstrelet says she was wounded in the attack on Paris. Her attempt on La Charité had to be abandoned, and of course at Compiègne in 1430 she was dragged from her horse by an archer, taken prisoner by the Burgundians, and handed over to the English to be tried and then burnt to death at Rouen in 1431. Bedford saw her as 'the disciple and limb of the fiend called La Pucelle', while Henry VI accused her of practising 'inhuman cruelties', but as Monstrelet said, the English saw that Joan 'had completely altered their own fortunes'.[45] She had played a significant part in the revival of French hopes and the recovery of French morale. There was to be no looking back, now it was the English who were on the defensive and

[45] Joan of Arc, on Bedford, Oman, ii, p. 394; for 'inhuman cruelties' and altered fortunes, Monstrelet, in *Hundred Years War*, pp. 313, 304.

Joan of Arc directing siege operations

on the run. As it was suggested: 'The English used to say that we could dance better than we could make war. Now times have changed'.[46]

Once the change of direction had ocurred, the journey back to control by the French was as fast as had been Henry V's progress the other way. Many towns, where noted victories had been won by Henry V, were recovered by Charles VII, including Harfleur where Henry's triumphs had begun. In 1436 Charles regained control of Paris, whose citizens now showed their dislike of the English, whose rule had only ever been accepted because of the Burgundians alliance. That alliance itself had now come to an end, further strengthening Charles' position. In the streets of Paris the citizens shouted: 'Long live the king and the duke of Burgundy'.[47] Popular attachment was an important factor in this period, and it ran against England, as at Dieppe where the people rebelled against their English masters.

The fatal mistake made by the English was to allow, and even secretly to encourage, the attack made by Surienne on the Breton stronghold of Fougères. François de Surienne, known as *L'Aragonais* from his place of origin, was a mercenary captain in the pay of England, and he attacked Fougères in 1449. He had been put up to it by the duke of Suffolk, and believed he was acting on the wishes of Henry VI. The duke of Brittany had imprisoned his own brother Gilles, a boyhood friend of Henry VI, who had remained pro-English in the war. Surienne was an experienced captain, had served Henry VI since 1424, become captain of Montargis for the English, and been rewarded with a pension. Now he besieged and took

46 Barnie, *War in Medieval Society*, p. 30.
47 Monstrelet in *Hundred Years War*, p. 321.

Fougères in order to release Gilles. He sacked the town, and held it for seven months. The trouble was that England's weak position in the war was currently protected by a truce with France, and the attack broke that truce. The English government tried to wriggle out of the consequences by a cowardly denial of responsibility, leaving Surienne to shoulder the blame. Not surprisingly the latter in disgust at such behaviour returned his order of the garter, stalked off to Naples, and then took service with Charles VII. Suffolk's disgraceful behaviour did little good; the French were provoked to renew the war in earnest, and began preparations for what proved to be the final thrust.[48]

Rouen, again demonstrating the trend of popular support for the French monarchy, opened its gates to Charles VII, and gave him a magnificent welcome, which included presentation of the keys, and the construction of a mechanical stag which bowed its knees as the king passed.[49] Once more the English leaders acted without much credit, Somerset seeking a limited safe-conduct for himself.

Failure to pay garrisons was a cause of constant complaint, and undermined the strength of the English resistance. In the last years of the war, English response to danger was often inadequate and nearly always slow. Henry VI's government lacked authority and determination, and some of its chosen commanders shared those weaknesses, notably Somerset and Suffolk.

The brothers Bureau provided Charles VII with a large and effective artillery train. Town after town was either battered into submission, or else surrendered before it could be so battered. From 1449 to 1450 some sixty sieges were completed successfully by the brothers. In the north the battle of Formigny was almost a foregone conclusion, most of the main towns already being lost. At Cherbourg the French made novel use of their guns, placing them on the sands to get closer to the walls. When the tide came in, the guns were covered over, so that when the sea retreated again, the guns could be brought into use immediately. Avranches had been relieved by Talbot, but was then attacked by the Bretons. Here the wife of the English captain behaved with great strength of mind for her absent husband, donning trousers to encourage the garrison to resist, and when that proved useless, putting on a skirt to use her feminine charm in getting a good deal in the negotiations.[50]

Now the territories held by England in the south, retained even when the Angevin Empire had collapsed, were themselves under threat. French monarchical power had never been great in this region, but things were about to change; even Bordeaux was at risk. Fronsac, an important strong-

48 For the Fougères incident, see Griffiths, *Henry VI*, pp. 510–16.

49 Griffiths, p. 518.

50 On the Cherbourg guns, Griffiths, p. 521; on the Avranches trousers, Burne, *Agincourt*, p. 324.

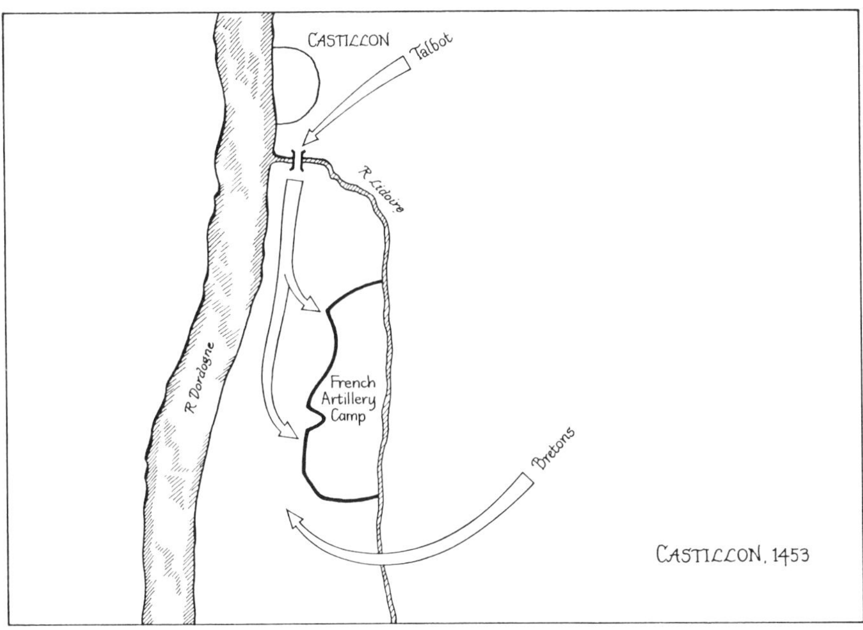

hold was besieged and quickly battered into surrender by cannons. The last major action of the Hundred Years War occurred at Castillon on the Dordogne in Périgord, thirty miles from Bordeaux. The French came to besiege it, placing their artillery at a distance from the town, out of range of the defenders' artillery, in a specially made park with irregular trenches for protection. These earthwork lines, however, were not designed at random, but provided something akin to bastions in a castle, forward positions which could defend the 'curtain', in this case with guns. Although there were said to be 300 guns within, it is probable that the majority of these were handguns, but it was still a well prepared camp.[51]

Talbot had apparently been told that success would be easy, and that the French were ready for flight. The old warrior was used to provoking fear at his arrival; he had a long history of success in the war, but for once he made a rash, a wrong, and, in the event, a fatal decision. He appeared at the front of the English relief force, brilliant in a crimson gown with white hair flowing in the wind from under a purple hat, and upon a white horse. He clearly meant the French to know that he was there! He wore no armour, because earlier in the war he had been captured, and released on condition that he did not bear arms against France again. He had always been a popular commander, and went out in typical fashion. Before the conflict he had set up a large cask of wine so that his men could drink. The English

[51] Castillon, in Burne, *Agincourt*, pp. 331–45; Monstrelet in *Hundred Years War*, pp. 338–40.

attacked with alacrity, and reached the earthworks, where hand to hand fighting ensued, but they suffered many casualties advancing into the gunfire. Defeat was made certain by the appearance of an army of Bretons, coming up to assist the French from the north. They crossed the river and joined in the fray decisively. Talbot's horse was hit by a shot from a culverin, and fell on top of him, pinning him to the ground, where a French archer finished him off with an axe. His body was found the next day with a tooth knocked out; the corpse was sent back to his home in Shropshire. The tomb was re-opened in 1860, and the skull proved that the account of a fatal axe-blow was correct.[52] On the day when Talbot's ancient corpse was identified, Castillon surrendered. Bordeaux soon followed suit. The south had been lost, France had been lost. The Hundred Years War was over, and all that England had to show for the long conflict was Calais which they would retain for a further century.

France and England After the Hundred Years War

The war had nearly exhausted France, on whose soil it had largely been fought; recovery was not easy, but it did occur. The king largely responsible for this was the unlikely, retiring, eccentric, almost sinister 'Spider King', Louis XI. His main success came from the downfall of Burgundy, which was the result of the rashness of Charles the Bold as much as of his own efforts. The great house of Burgundy, after a century of increasing power, suddenly collapsed, mainly to the benefit of France.[53]

The age is best chronicled by Philippe de Commines, a Fleming, godson of Philip the Good, duke of Burgundy, and who served both Charles the Bold of Burgundy, and Louis XI of France. The chronicler, like the king, seems to have been a rather secretive and devious character, probably acting for some time in the Burgundian court as a spy for the king. He did not always find favour from Louis, or from his son, and was for a while imprisoned in an iron cage to be exiled for ten years, which had the fortunate result of leaving him with time to write his memoirs.[54]

In the early years of Louis XI, the English threat may have diminished, but the erstwhile ally, Burgundy, posed a renewed problem and civil war broke out in France, the conflict known as the War of the Public Weal, according to Commines it was so-called 'on the pretext that it was for the public benefit'.[55] In 1465 Philip the Good of Burgundy besieged Paris, camping in the meadows by the Seine. But the Burgundians found it hard to close the blockade, and food was still brought in. The women of the city

52 Burne, *Agincourt*, pp. 341–2.
53 For general reading, Kendall, *Louis XI*.
54 Commines, ed. Calmette and Durville; English translation, ed. M. Jones.
55 Commines, ed. Jones, p. 62.

encouraged the soldiers to show off before them in knightly combats. In the serious fighting, the Burgundians had the greater artillery power, but in general the king was stronger because he had the support of the city itself. It was suspected that the king's moves were betrayed, and the Burgundians were, for example, forewarned of a night sortie, so that wagons were formed up and artillery ready. In the end peace was negotiated.

The city of Dinant had angered Philip the Good's son, Charles the Bold, by burning him in effigy, and making remarks about his supposed illegitimacy. The Burgundians laid siege to the town in 1466, a siege which lasted eight months, and was marked by escalating atrocities. Charles kept up fire into the centre of the town from bombards, so heavy that the citizens had to take shelter in their cellars. The bombardment did the trick, and the city surrendered, but Charles did not stop the killing, and some 800 were drowned in the Meuse.

Charles was clearly of a choleric character, and his anger was again aroused by the actions of the city of Liège, which he attacked, now in alliance with a reluctant Louis XI after the peace. Commines was at the siege, sleeping in the duke of Burgundy's room. As the chronicler said of this siege, but stating a general truth, the besiegers can nearly always afford to lose more men than the besieged, who cannot get reinforcements. The loss of ten defenders, he thought, was more damaging than the loss of a hundred besiegers.[56] Operations in the winter at Liège were difficult, with deep mud around the gates. The citizens made unexpected sorties through holes in the walls, and nearly captured the king and the duke while a group of their men were playing dice in the duke's room. The city was finally stormed by an unexpected attack on a Sunday. Ironically the duke killed one man of his own side with his own hand, to stop him plundering a church on the sabbath! The city was burnt, and Commines describes the dreadful sound of houses falling in a rush of wind and fire. He says that, the fire apart, the cold was so intense that men had lost fingers through frostbite, and soldiers found frozen wine, which they hacked out in chunks and carried away in their hats.[57]

The alliance between king and duke did not last long, and France and Burgundy were at war again by 1470, by which time Commines seems to be passing information to Louis XI. Artillery played an ever increasing rôle, and long resistance to it was becoming difficult. At Beauvais two Burgundian cannons made a great hole in the gate with just two shots, though they then ran out of stones. Commines thought Charles the Bold was too slow to exploit these initial advantages, and in the end had to abandon the siege, an early sign of the failures to come.[58]

56 Commines, ed. Jones, p. 151.

57 Commines, ed. Jones, p. 164.

58 On holes from cannons and Charles the Bold's slowness, Commines, ed. Jones, pp. 208, 209.

From 1472 Commines moved directly into the service of Louis XI. Sieges played a vital part in Charles the Bold's downfall. He overreached himself by making war on two fronts. Louis XI proved his master in diplomacy, and brought together the Holy Roman Empire and the virtually independent Swiss. Charles stayed too long, a year, at the siege of Neuss from 1474 to 1475, which he eventually had to abandon. His position here was worsened by a poor choice of position for his camp, which was flooded. After defeat at Granson, he besieged Morat and was again beaten by the Swiss in battle. By the time he besieged Nancy in 1476, his situation was becoming desperate, his army consisting of any quality of men he could raise. In 1477 the Swiss brought Charles to battle at Nancy, where he was killed. His naked body was indentified two days later in the frozen mud, half eaten by wolves, his helmet and head split by a Swiss halberd.[59]

It was at this time that Louis, who according to Commines was successful because 'he never risked anything', became disenchanted with the services of Commines, whom he felt did not do enough in Burgundy on his behalf. As Commines said: 'there is no prince so wise that he does not err once in a while'. One suspects that Commines' usefulness was much diminished by the collapse of Burgundy.[60] The lord of Craon made a series of successful and brief sieges through Burgundy on Louis' behalf. Two years later Louis suffered the first of a series of strokes. In his final years he retired into a reclusive existence at Plessis-les-Tours, dying in 1483. It might be claimed that Charles VII and Louis XI between them had brought into existence the modern kingdom of France.

In England, however, although not herself the battleground of the Hundred Years War, the aftermath seems to have been far more damaging, at least in the short term. Partly no doubt this was a result of discontent at the failure in the war. The Lancastrian government of Henry VI had been thoroughly discredited by inept action. The limitations of the king, the 'imbecile son' of Henry V as Commines bluntly called him, had been starkly revealed.[61] Criticism at home mounted, and found a focus in the opposition by the duke of York. Now the chickens came home to roost which had been hatched in 1399, when the first Lancastrian, Henry Bolingbroke, had usurped the throne. York sought at first to control Henry VI, and then to replace him. York's son Edward, after his father's death at Wakefield in 1460, succeeded in winning the throne, and Henry VI spent most of his surviving years under Yorkist guard before being put to death by Edward in 1471.

Sieges played only a small part in the Wars of the Roses between Lancaster and York. Perhaps, as Commines claimed when describing an English garrison on the continent which only had experience of warfare in

[59] Charles' death, 1477, Commines, ed. Jones, p. 306; Oman, ii, p. 271.

[60] For Louis XI avoiding risk, and princes erring, Commines, ed. Jones, pp. 380, 318.

[61] Commines, ed. Jones, p. 71.

England, they 'did not understand siege warfare very well'.[62] This may probably be ignored, since many Englishmen had a wealth of experience of sieges in France. The answer is perhaps more that fashions had changed, internal warfare in England had become less common, indeeed the Wars of the Roses themselves involved only a few weeks of actual fighting over a period of about half a century. Also probably because of the relative lack of warfare, English towns and castles had not been adapted to artillery methods to the same degree as their French counterparts, and were therefore even more vulnerable to an artillery battery. In other words, to expect much protection from walls in England at this time was being optimistic, and commanders facing a large army preferred to meet it in the field.

The point may be made by looking at the two battles fought at St Albans in 1455 and 1461. Both were in essence sieges, where the town defences were about as effective as cardboard. In both cases the defenders tried to fortify their position within the town with barricades, but they were flimsy efforts, and in each case the attacking side broke through without great difficulty. In the first battle the town was 'strongly barred and arrayed for defence', but the Yorkists broke in through the gardens to find Henry VI and his banner propped up alongside each other on a wall, the king with a wound in his neck. In the second battle the attackers simply went round the barricades, and found an unprotected route into the town.[63]

There were a few sieges in the north, which eventually brought the Yorkists control there. And in the west there was an interesting episode at St Michael's Mount, with its natural defensive position. According to Warkworth a few could hold the place 'ageyne all the world'. Edward IV ordered Bodrugan to besiege it, but the latter, with misplaced courtesy or perhaps something worse, during negotiations for surrender allowed provisions to go in, so that the resistance was able to continue. Bodrugan was replaced by Richard Fortescue, the sheriff of Cornwall; negotiations were reopened, and the place surrendered. The chronicler makes the interesting, if chauvinistic, remark: 'a castle that speaketh, and a woman that will hear, they will be gotten both', suggesting that negotiation by defenders in a siege is as good as surrender, a sure sign that the place is lost, and so far as sieges go, at least, our survey seems to bear him out.[64]

The most important siege of the Wars of the Roses was that of London by the Bastard Fauconberg, who led the Kentish rising of 1471. He was a cousin of the earl of Warwick, and had had some success at sea, committing

62 For warfare, see Gillingham, *Wars of the Roses*, and Goodman, *Wars of the Roses*. The quote is from Commines, ed. Jones, p. 295.

63 For the two battles of St Albans, see Burne, *Battlefields*, pp. 75–95. The quote is from Goodman, p. 23, from *English Chronicle*, p. 72.

64 *Ageyne all the world*, is Warkworth, from *Three Chronicles*, p. 26; and the proverb is p. 49: *a castelle that spekythe, and a womane that wille here, thei wille be gotene bothe*.

acts of piracy against Portuguese ships. He had meant to join Warwick, but by the time he was ready, Warwick was dead, killed in the battle of Barnet, so the Bastard went his own way, bringing ships and men against London. He became the focus for some local and economic discontents. The *Arrivall* says that most of his men came to rob and not to fight, and the well informed *Crowland Chronicle* calls them pirates and rogues. London was well prepared, with guns at the gates and along the Thames.[65] The Bastard tried to break in over London Bridge, but was held off. Some taverns near the Tower were hit and caught fire, but that was the extent of his success. He decided to withdraw and marched along the river bank to Kingston, but again abandoned the attempt to cross the river, probably because he foresaw difficulties in retreating from the northern side after hearing that relief was on the way under Edward IV. He tried a new direct attack from the southern bank on 14th May. He arrayed his guns along the river, but in a heated exchange of fire the Londoners got the better of it. The Bastard still proceeded with an attempt to storm the city, attacking at three points: London Bridge, and on the north at Bishopsgate and Aldgate. The men operating in the north had been ferried across the river in his ships, together with allies who had arrived from Essex, but they could not break in. Bishopsgate was set on fire, and the bulwark at Aldgate was captured, but then lost again. The Bastard's own attack from the south damaged sixty houses on London Bridge, which caught fire, but again the defences held. The Crowland author says later that the damage done to the Bridge could still be seen: 'where all the houses which had been built at vast expense between the drawbridge and the outer gate . . . were consumed by fire'.[66] The Bastard's men were beaten at all points and began a retreat, which under fire became a rout.

The Holy Roman Empire

The history of the Holy Roman Empire in the late middle ages is one of disintegration. Central power eroded, and a plethora of smaller units emerged. Whatever unity had once existed between Germany and Italy, and it had never been much more than a personal power connection of certain emperors, had now disappeared. An opportunity was given for the rise of lesser men, of national units, and of cities. On the whole it was a development which needed little siege warfare.

Possibly the most interesting military development was of militia in the cities, and the popular infantry armies of Switzerland and Bohemia. The

65 To rob not to fight is the *Arrivall*, from *Three Chronicles*, p. 181; pirates and rogues from *The Crowland Chronicle*, pp. 126, 128: *piratas . . . sceleratores*.
66 *Crowland Chronicle*, p. 128.

Fourteenth-century scaling

history of the Swiss has already been mentioned in the downfall of Charles the Bold, since Burgundy had been a threat to imperial regions, as well as to France. The great Swiss infantry forces had played the major rôle in Charles' defeat and death; and Swiss troops made excellent garrison troops and mercenaries, employed for example by the papacy.

Commines refers to what he sees as the difference between France and Germany: in the latter, the weaker central authority still allowed much local disorder, so that lesser men with moderate territories could act independently and defy authority. It had now become impossible in France for thirty knights in one small castle to stand against royal power, but it was not so in Germany, where punishment was seldom imposed for such actions, since the princes needed all the support they could get.[67] The number of castles in Germany increased considerably after 1300. In general Germany resembled France in an earlier age, and local disturbances were only too common. In one conflict in 1456, no less than sixty villages were burned in one day. It is no wonder that Germany witnessed numerous peasant risings in the fifteenth century.[68]

The most interesting siege developments in the late medieval Empire occurred in the conflict between the emperor and the Hussites of Bohemia. It is a neat microcosm of trends in the late Empire. Bohemia had gradually evolved as an independent unit, with its kings becoming imperial electors, and for a time ruling the Empire itself. Charles IV in particular used his

67 Commines, ed. Jones, p. 340.

68 For castles after 1300, and burned villages, see Du Boulay, *Germany*, pp. 69, 182.

imperial office to build up his own state, developing Prague and its new university, and hence he is known to history as the 'Father of Bohemia'.[69] The papacy recognised a new ecclesiastical province of Bohemia under the archbishop of Prague.

Matters were brought to a head through the preaching of John Hus, who became rector of Prague University, and a public figure through his popular sermons in Czech, which included criticism of the papacy. In the end this brought him excommunication. The emperor Sigismund offered Hus a safe-conduct to attend the Council of Constance in 1414 in order to debate his views, but the guarantee was ignored and Hus was arrested, tried, and then burnt to death as a heretic. Not surprisingly this treatment ignited the already unstable situation in Bohemia, and Hus' followers broke into armed revolt.[70]

As with the Swiss, the passionate and determined Czech infantry proved too much for imperial armies. The emperor Sigismund invaded Bohemia, but was humiliatingly beaten in a series of battles by the Hussite leader Ziska, at Vysehrad, Saaz and Deutschbrod between 1420 and 1422. On Ziska's death a new and equally impressive commander took over in Prokop. In the end, in 1436, the emperor was forced to agree peace, and Bohemia became virtually independent.

One of the main reasons for Czech success was their employment of a variation of defensive siege warfare on the move, through their use of the *wagenburg* or war wagons, which at short notice under threat on the march could be transformed into a kind of fort.[71] It was not entirely novel, but it was employed by them in conjunction with good artillery, and with great success. They formed a square or a circle, and entrenched their position, chaining the wagons together; they carried pavises on carts which were set up to cover the gaps between the wagons, and as general protection. They could resist attack, but also make quick and unexpected sorties from deliberately placed gaps at front and rear. They employed about half their force to defend the wagons in hand to hand fighting, and about half to fire guns. They used both handguns, and cannons which they carried on carts. Their military success saved Bohemia and the Hussite form of worship, which unlike most medieval heresies survived until it died a natural death by absorption in sixteenth-century protestantism.

Late medieval imperial problems are typified by the financial difficulties of the emperor Maximilian I, who established the house of Austria. He seems to have survived chiefly by making two profitable marriages, and then denying even pocket money to his second wife. According to Machiavelli, he listened to all advice and heeded none. As with many late

69 For general reading, and this viewpoint, see B. Jarrett, *Charles IV*; compare Du Boulay, *Germany*, pp. 36–42 for a more recent comment.

70 For Hus and the Hussites, see Lambert, *Medieval Heresy*, chs. 16, 17, 18, pp. 272–334.

71 Oman, ii, p. 364.

A fifteenth-century siege, from an Italian manuscript

medieval rulers, the strain of office told on him, and he took to carrying his coffin around with him on his frequent travels. He managed to win the Franche Comté from the French in the wake of the Burgundian collapse, but like Burgundy he fell foul of the Swiss.[72]

Italy

Italy, like Germany, suffered from the decline of imperial central authority, and saw a growth in the power of the cities. In Italy there followed the development of small states around many of the cities, a handful of which gradually won dominance over their neighbours. The late medieval and early modern period saw the amazing cultural flowering in Italy of the Renaissance, but socially and politically it proved a difficult time, with the city states vying against each other, and external nation states, particularly Aragon and France, seeking to profit from Italy's weakness. Hence it was ideal ground for soldiers of fortune, and the Italian *condottieri* became the typical warriors of this period.[73]

Historians have recently been at pains to contest Machiavelli's claim that Italian warfare at this time was bloodless, and that mercenaries wanted to save their skins first and worry about victory, honour and patriotism

72 Benecke, *Maximilian I*, p. 9 on Machiavelli, p. 10 on the coffin.

73 On fifteenth-century Italy, see for example Laven and Hay.

last.[74] At Anghiari some 900 were killed, not the one man that Machiavelli claimed. On the other hand, he was undoubtedly right to see the mercenaries in the companies as parasites sucking the blood of Italy. They were trained professionals who sought cash from ransom and pillage, as well as from wages, and the history of some of the great captains of the ages demonstrates only too clearly the depressing state of Italy in this age.

Some mercenary captains were of noble birth, some were men who rose through military skill, but all needed success to make the fortunes they sought. Their positions were as vulnerable as those of modern football managers; fail and they would be replaced by the newest soldier of reputation. Like modern managers, they might also be tempted by the glamour of their reputations to indulge in side benefits. Of Niccolo d'Este it was chanted:

On this side and that of the Po
All are the children of Niccolo.[75]

One notable captain was the Englishman, Sir John Hawkwood, son of a farmer, who had fought for Edward III in France and been knighted as a result. After the 1360 peace he sought employment where he could, joining the White Company which was hired by Pisa to fight against Florence. He tried to trick Florence by apparently abandoning the siege, and then returning suddenly to ram the gates, but the trick failed. Later he went over into the pay of Florence, and was given a good marriage, to the sixty-year old Domina, who was said to have gaps in her teeth and thinning hair, but was an illegitimate member of the Visconti family, and brought her husband wealth. Florence also, at his death, voted him a statue for his tomb because of the military services he had rendered the city. It was said of him that he managed his affairs so well 'that there was little peace in his day'.[76]

Another who rose from humble beginnings to become a captain, was the peasant who became count of Carmagnola. He was an expert in the use of siege engines, as demonstrated at Trezzo, and of artillery. Enemies at Milan, where he was employed by Filippo Maria Visconti, drove him into the arms of Venice, for whom he captured Brescia. But he fell foul of his new masters too, and was imprisoned, tortured with hot irons and coals, his arm broken, to be finally beheaded in public, on which occcasion his dog chased the severed head across the piazza as if it were a ball, licking the face. At least dismissed football managers have something to be thankful for!

Italian warfare could be cruel. The besieged countess of Forli, mother of Giovanni de Medici, held the citadel of Forli after her husband, Girolamo

74 Keen, *Chivalry*, p. 222.

75 On the Italian mercenaries, Deiss, *Captains of Fortune*; the verse is p. 22.

76 For Hawkwood, see Deiss, ch. 3; the quote is from Keen, *Chivalry*, p. 227; from Sacchetti, iii, pp. 91–3.

Riario, had been assassinated. Her children were paraded before her with the threat of being killed unless she surrendered. She lifted up her skirts and shouted down that the besiegers were fools, did they not realise that she could soon make more. In this case her Sforza relatives rescued her, and her children were not killed. She was besieged again in conflict with Cesare Borgia, when she dressed in plate armour to walk the battlements. She went up to the walls on the first day of the year of 1500 to watch the sun rise on a new century. A week later her enemies broke through the outer wall, and she retired to the citadel where she attempted to blow herself up with gunpowder. She survived to be captured and manhandled, but later was released and allowed to bring up her son, though the experiences had turned her hair white. Her son, Giovanni, himself became a noted captain, expert in the use of infantry and artillery. In 1524 he allied with the French invaders of Italy. At one council when a discussion was held about how to take a particular place, Giovanni became so impatient with the drawn-out arguments, which seemed to be ignoring his professional advice, that he advanced on the town and took it, then returned to find the meeting still in progress! It was the son of this Giovanni Medici who was to become the ruler of Florence.[77]

Late medieval Italy was a dangerous political quicksand; careers were made and broken in a moment, but military ability remained a constantly useful attribute, and skill in siege warfare was one of the most valued. Hence the great encouragement to military study, as may be noted for example in the drawings of Leonardo da Vinci. Commines, it must be said, found the Italians less skilled than the French, slower and not so well able to plan siege campaigns, though better at providing supplies.[78]

[77] For Giovanni de Medici, see Deiss, ch. 6.

[78] Commines, ed. Jones, p. 377.

CHAPTER EIGHT

Trouble in the East, 1200–1565

The geographical division between East and West in these two chapters is not precise, and it may seem an arbitrary decision which includes Spain in this particular section. Decisions have been taken, not purely on geographical grounds, but in thematic terms, according to whether the dominant cause of the particular conflict seems religious or political. The major theme of this chapter must be the religious conflict between Christendom and Islam in the late middle ages. A similar dilemma was resolved over the Albigensian Crusade, which although a genuine crusade, and therefore a possible candidate for this section, seemed primarily to be a western conflict involving political control of southern France between catholic powers. Another problem area is the Baltic and the northern crusades, which we have decided to include in the present chapter, though it was a political conflict for control in the northern area, but where a religious clash occurred, involving the local pagan peoples and the Christian orthodox Russians. We include Spain here, because although very obviously western by geographical definition, and also political to some extent, it seemed basically to be part of the broader clash between Christendom and Islam with which this chapter is chiefly concerned. In the final analysis the decision is not so very important, since the nature of siege warfare in the East and the West in this late medieval period is fundamentally similar.

In any case, to a degree, all these problematic conflicts were on the fringes of the greatest struggle of this period, which saw the end of the Latin Kingdom of Jerusalem and the fall of the Byzantine Empire. The early crusading movement, though not confined to Palestine, had certainly found its focus there. In the period from 1202 the focus becomes blurred, and attention moves from Constantinople to Egypt, to the Mediterranean and the Baltic. The variety of fields of conflict are well demonstrated by the activities of Chaucer's knight, who had been in Egypt, Prussia, Lithuania, Russia and Granada: a tour of the crusading world of his day.[1] Our subject matter is not

[1] Chaucer, ed. Benson, p. 24, ll. 43–67. ll. 48–9: *And therto hadde he riden no man ferre, /As wel in cristendom as in hethenesse.*

simply the thrust and response relating to various crusades, but includes the movement to the West of the Mongols and the Tartars, and finally the dramatic expansion of the Ottoman Turks.

A major theme of this work has been that although attitudes and enemies change, although defences are ever improved, and attacking methods forever being refined, the basic methods and conventions of siege warfare remain remarkably constant. There could be no better test of this view than a study of the late medieval clash between religions and cultures which we are about to examine, a period which also felt the full impact of the most revolutionary of the weapons we have had to consider, the cannon.

An enigma of the period is the growing viciousness of the religious wars, at the same time as a growing understanding of one's enemies. Runciman, with some justification, saw the crusades as 'a long act of intolerance in the name of God'.[2] As national identities and attitudes hardened, there is a plethora of evidence concerning that worst of human vices: racial, religious and national hatred of those who are different. The Latin Empire in the East condemned the 'machinations and slyness' of both Greeks and Turks. The Frenchman, Villehardouin, expressed a common view of the Byzantines: that no Frank could 'put much trust in the Greeks'. Barbaro, an Italian, saw these same allies as 'cowards', another only too common manner of expressing contempt, usually undeserved. The Moslem opponents of crusaders in Egypt saw the Franks as 'infidel dogs', abandoned by 'their devil', and in Palestine they saw the land, once the Kingdom of Jerusalem had been brought down, as 'purified of the Franks'. One finds false beliefs and propaganda used to denigrate opponents, another ploy which is only too familiar in the twentieth century. Thus Doukas the Byzantine claimed that the Turks indulged in sex, both natural and unnatural, with men, women and animals, and he accused the Sultan Bayezid of 'lascivious sexual acts' with boys and girls. Robert de Clari relished retailing details of atrocities committed by the Greeks, barbarians to his western viewpoint, who threw their enemies into the sea tied to stones, blinded them, had them tied naked to camels with their faces to the animals' rear, and had their flesh ripped off. Balbi, an Italian fighting for a Spanish master in the sixteenth century, still ridiculed Moslem worship, which he viewed being practised below the walls of a fort in Malta, with all its screaming. He quoted a Maltese Christian responding to offers of mercy with the proud claim: 'we would rather be slaves of St John, than companions of the sultan'.[3]

2 Runciman, *Crusades*, iii, p. 480.

3 On attitudes: 'machinations', *Chronicle of the Morea*, p. 267; 'no trust', Villehardouin, ed. Shaw, p. 74; on cowards, Barbaro, p. 50. On 'infidel dogs', 'devil', and 'purified': Ibn Wasil, Ibn al-Athir, and Abu l-Fida, in Gabrieli, pp. 292, 263, 346. 'Lascivious acts', from Doukas, p. 73; tying to camels, Clari, ed. McNeal, p. 55; and slaves, Balbi, p. 109.

The explanation for much of this is unfortunately, as is so often the case in history, a belief which can override all else, including compassion and even common sense. There is little doubt that on both sides belief was as strong as ever it had been in the First Crusade. Even defeat did not much dent an often fanatical trust in the rightness of one's case; defeat could always be explained as a punishment for sins. Thus St Louis saw the failure of his crusade to Damietta as a punishment for his own personal sins.[4]

What could demonstrate eagerness for the crusade more than the man described by Jacques de Vitry in the thirteenth century, whose wife shut him indoors so that he would not be won over by the preaching of a crusade, but who jumped from the window and went off anyway? Innocent III told the king of Denmark in 1209: 'to extirpate the error of paganism, and spread the frontiers of the Christian faith'. Such attitudes remained into the sixteenth century. James I of Aragon asked how it was possible to die more gloriously than in the service of God: 'I go to abase and destroy those who do not believe in Thee'. In Malta Francesco Balbi found comfort along with his comrades in the indulgence sent by Pius II: 'a pardon for all our sins . . . a relief for our souls'. He commented that men now knew that 'if they fell in the siege, they would find a place in heaven'.[5]

The later medieval period is, at the same time, marked by a growing knowledge and understanding of the ways and beliefs of the enemy. There are examples of men who knew both worlds. Frederick II's toleration of Moslems in Sicily has recently been questioned, but he certainly had contact with those who knew Arabic and Arab civilisation, and in Jerusalem he insisted that the calling of the muezzin should not be stopped in deference to himself.[6] During the conquest of Majorca by James I, there appeared a Christian knight who had been converted to Islam, and who acted as an interpreter, as well as a Jewish interpreter of Arabic. Like Frederick II, James I had some knowledge of Moslem ways, and claimed that he wanted to treat Moslems fairly: 'I had at heart to do them good'. He was annoyed when one Islamic enemy broke his word, commenting that 'up to that time no Saracen had ever broken faith with me'. He was equally concerned not to break his own word given to the Moslems; on one instance, when given provocation which allowed him to break an agreement, he remarked: 'God shields us from breaking the treaties made with the Saracens'. When he forced Moslems to become refugees, he said 'I was much grieved for the hurt I was involuntarily doing to them'. If some of this reads like crocodile tears, it is nevertheless interesting that James thought it important even to give the impression of sympathy to his

4 On sins, see Riley-Smith, *Crusades*, p. 161; compare Villehardouin, ed. Shaw, p. 89: repulsed 'for our sins'.

5 James de Vitry, from Mayer, p. 38; King of Denmark from Riley-Smith, *What Were the Crusades*, p. 19; James I, ed. Forster, p. 118; Balbi, p. 110.

6 On Frederick II, see above, ch. 6 n. 38. On the muezzin, Ibn Wasil in Gabrieli, p. 272.

Mongols torturing prisoners

enemy, and in fact his book gives the impression of a genuine feeling for his Islamic opponents. At one meeting for negotiation, he provided the representatives of the other side not only with tents, couches and food, but also with cooking pots so that they could prepare their food in their own manner.[7]

Joinville tells of a Saracen knight who took care of some of the Christian prisoners, carrying Raoul de Wanour to the privy because, with a hamstring severed in battle, he was unable to walk. At the siege of Rhodes, Suleiman the Magnificent expressed admiration of his opponent, the Grand Master Adam: 'It saddens me to cast this brave old man out of his house'. At the height of the siege of Malta, as supplies on both sides dwindled, we find men of opposing religions exchanging goods for items that were rare in their own camp: melons and oranges from the Turks, for bread and cheese from the Christians.[8]

In medieval times as in modern we are astounded by contradictions in the human make-up: the capacity for the most vicious hatred and the most tender compassion. The story of the late medieval conflicts of religion is full of atrocities, bravery and compassion. Perhaps the fascination is that what appears to us at first as a remote and alien world, reflects an unexpected mirror upon ourselves and those around us.

7 James I ed. Forster: on the interpreter, p. 152, though his house was later sacked (p. 178); compare the Christian who knew Arabic, p. 28, and the Jewish interpreter, p. 559. To do them good, p. 422; no Saracen broken faith, p. 471; God shields us, p. 480; refugees, p. 486; on tents and couches, pp. 559–62, and compare p. 365.

8 On Raoul, Joinville, ed. Corbett, p. 150; on Adam, Brockman, p. 153; on the exchange of food, Balbi, p. 164.

The First Fall of Constantinople

The first three crusades had seen the establishment of the Latin Kingdom of Jerusalem, and then its decline under the attack of Saladin. By the early thirteenth century the future of the kingdom itself was in question. The Third Crusade had saved Acre, but had not recovered Edessa or Jerusalem. The Fourth Crusade took an unexpected direction. We have become used to the facts, but they still have a capacity to shock. How could a movement which began with the intention of saving Christendom from the Turks come to the point where a crusade from the West attacked and took Christian Constantinople? The answer lies in the events, a chapter of accidents and empirical decisions, rather than in some long-planned and devious stratagem of Venice. In the end the results were accepted by the church, but had not been encouraged or intended.[9]

The calling of the crusade followed the usual lines. There were new threats and new opportunities in Palestine after the death of Saladin in 1193, when his territories were divided between his sons. The favoured target for a new crusade was Egypt, which the thirteenth-century West in general saw as the area where Christian attack could most damage Moslem power. Often in the later period of its existence, the Christian settlers in the kingdom of Jerusalem found themselves in a dilemma: they needed additional manpower, but they feared the consequences of crusades from the West, which usually disturbed the delicate balance of agreement and acceptance that had allowed them to survive. One truce had been made in 1192, and for the next century there was peace rather than war in eighty of the hundred years.[10]

Difficulties began with an over-estimation of the number of crusaders who would turn up in Venice, requiring provisions and transport. The chronicler Villehardouin, born of a noble family from Champagne, took part in making the arrangements and explains the problems. The organisers had to agree in advance on a sum to cover the costs to the Venetians, and then found that so many fewer people had arrived, that even a desperate collection of additional contributions from those who had come, left them 34,000 marks in arrears. Some crusaders had chosen to go by other routes, which annoyed Villehardouin and those who had agreed the terms, and who now found themselves in an embarrassing position.[11]

The Venetians were understandably displeased. The doge, the blind and aged Dandolo, said accusingly: 'you have used us ill'. He saw however that

[9] On the Fourth Crusade, see Queller, *Fourth Crusade*, and Godfrey, *1204*.
[10] On the Latin Kingdom, see Prawer, *Latin Kingdom*; Riley-Smith, *Feudal Nobility*; Richard, *Latin Kingdom*. For eighty out of a hundred, Richard, i, p. 201.
[11] On Venetian deal, see Villehardouin, ed. Shaw, pp. 33–43; ed. Faral, i, pp. 16–48, 58–64.

he had little hope of obtaining the promised cash, and so offered a deal to the French: Venice would allow the French to pay their debts from the gains made on the campaign, but before proceeding with the crusade the assembled forces, French and Italian, should attack the island of Zara, which was Christian and in Dalmatia, but was desired by Venice. Dandolo was not seen by most of his fellows on the campaign as anything but a brave crusader; Villehardouin certainly presents him in a favourable light, and he was to play a significant rôle in the military and diplomatic exploits of the expedition. His long experience included diplomatic missions in Constantinople, and Villehardouin found him 'very wise and able'. Leaving aside the morals of it, this force was to attack and take the great city of Constantinople, which had never previously been captured despite numerous sieges. It is clear that the Fourth Crusade would not have succeeded without the participation of the wily old doge. Dandolo spoke to the crusaders assembled in Venice, promising to go with them: 'I am an old man, weak and in need of rest, and my health is failing'. Fixing them with his blind but clear eyes, he brought many of them to tears.[12]

The crusade got under way, the colours of sails, costumes, armour and weapons making the sea shimmer, so that it appeared to be on fire. Dandolo was granted his first wish, and Zara was besieged for five days, with engines, ladders and a mine until terms were agreed, which gave half the spoils to Venice, and half to the French. Zara was a diversion, but had not delayed the crusade long. Some crusaders, including Simon de Montfort, protested at the direction the crusade was taking, but most consented, and although Innocent III had originally forbidden the attack on Zara, the accomplished event was accepted. The debts of the French and the hopes for profit of the Venetians combined now to direct the crusade against the wealthiest target possible. But in a sense this came about by chance in the form of a political crisis in Constantinople, which led to the disinherited Alexius IV seeking western aid to recover the throne he believed to be rightly his.[13]

Alexius's father, the emperor Isaac Angelus, had been blinded and imprisoned by his brother, Alexius's uncle, Alexius III, who had usurped the throne. Alexius IV had escaped to Italy, and now joined the crusade at Corfu, hoping to persuade it to travel to Constantinople and restore him to the throne. The possibilities of the situation appealed to the crusaders, and it was decided to give Alexois support.

The great city had never been captured by enemies through a long and

12 On Dandolo: 'used ill', Clari, ed. McNeal, p. 40; ed. Lauer, p. 10: *vous nous aves mal baillis*. For 'wise and able', which is used several times, see e.g. Villehardouin, ed. Shaw, p. 33; ed. Faral, i, p. 30: *qui mult ere sages et proz*. 'I am an old man', Villehardouin, ed. Shaw, p. 44; ed. Faral, i, p. 66: *je sui vialz hom et febles*.

13 On Zara, 1202, see Villehardouin, ed. Shaw, pp. 46–9; ed. Faral, i, pp. 76–86. On de Montfort, ed. Shaw, p. 54, ed. Faral, i, p. 110.

difficult history, as it stood against attacks from Arabs, Russians, and Turks. Now it faced a threat from the very crusaders who had set out to save it in the 1090s. It must be said, that from the beginning, relations between Greeks and Franks had been uneasy and often hostile. There had been little love lost between them, and little trust remained, but now the differences reached a new peak, as Christian French and Italians besieged Christian Greeks, albeit it on behalf of a Greek claimant to the Empire.

The crusaders captured Galata so that the fleet could enter the harbour, and attack could be made directly by land and water. The army was not large enough to blockade the city, and could only cut off one gate, success would have to come either through storm or through pressure to surrender. Villehardouin in a pre-Churchillian phrase believed: 'never have so many been besieged by so few'.[14]

The Franks fortified their camp with a palisade, and were able to fend off a Greek sortie. They suffered some casualties from the Greek engines stationed on the walls, and William de Champlitte's arm was broken by one stone. Preparations were made for a storm, dividing the land army almost equally between those who were to attack, and those who were to guard the camp: a sure sign of the lack of confidence among the westerners, and their fears. While the Venetian fleet approached the sea walls, the French attempted to scale the land walls. The Venetians had mangonels on their ships, and succeeded in making a landing, the doge having himself set ashore with his banner. His people rushed to follow, and a number of towers were taken. They started a fire in the city which was to last for a week, at one point it seemed to the crusaders that the whole world was on fire. Even so, the Greeks made a sortie against the camp, as anticipated, and the attack was abandoned. Constantinople had survived, but not for long.[15]

Alexius III took to flight during the night, and in the morning the westerners found that the city was theirs. Alexius IV entered in triumph and released his father from incarceration. Isaac and his son Alexius IV were seated beside each other on golden thrones, and crowned as co-emperors. However Alexius found that he was none too popular with his Greek subjects, who resented his alliance with the westerners, and there were riots in the city. Alexius decided on a bold move, rejecting his alliance with the crusaders, and relying on the support of the Greeks. The promises of rewards made to the westerners were broken, and payments to

14 For 'never so many', Villehardouin, ed. Shaw, p. 69; ed. Faral, i, p. 166: *que onques par tant poi de gent ne furent assegie tant de gent*.

15 On William de Champlitte, Villehardouin, ed. Shaw, p. 69; ed. Faral, i, p. 168: *brisie le braz d'une pierre*. Mangonels on ships from ed. Shaw, p. 70; ed. Faral, i, pp. 164–6, and compare Clari, ed. McNeal, p. 71. For world on fire, ed. Shaw, p. 83.

them stopped. Dandolo was furious: 'we dragged you out of the filth, and into the filth we will cast you again'.[16]

The crusaders prepared for a new siege against their former ally, but were forestalled by a coup within the city, led by Murzurphlus, a nick-name meaning black-brows. Alexius IV's brief reign was brought to an abrupt end and he was thrust into prison while Murzurphlus declared himself to be Alexius V. The old emperor Isaac is said to have died of fear, and his son Alexius to have been either poisoned or strangled. The news was shot out to the crusaders on an arrow. Preparations continued for a second siege, the coup made little change to their plans.[17]

Again the intention was an attack by land and sea. The Venetians had mounted on their ships not only engines, but also a contraption with ladders fixed high on the masts, which would enable them to climb on to the towers of the city. The Greeks in turn improved the walls, making them higher with wooden structures, up to seven storeys high according to Clari. Against the land walls, the French began mines and set up various engines including trebuchets. Some Greeks vulgarly provoked the French by baring their backsides to them, potentially a rather dangerous practice in a siege. The crusaders attacked in a hundred places at once, says Villehardouin, but were held off. Ships tied in pairs attacked the sea walls. One pair, the *Pilgrim* and the *Paradise*, managed to get in close enough to stretch a ladder on to one of the towers which they then captured. Some of the ships had to disengage from the towers to which they had tied themselves, for fear they might pull down the structures which now contained their own men, fighting hand to hand with the enemy. Several towers were taken, and now the gates were broken open to let in the land army. The crusaders unleashed an orgy of massacre and pillage, western Christian against eastern Christian, all by the book so far as medieval siege conventions are concerned, but a travesty of crusading ideals. In the chaos Murzurphlus fled the city.[18]

The crusaders had already agreed that, if successful, they would elect their own emperor. Their choice lay between Baldwin count of Flanders, and Boniface the marquis of Montferrat. Baldwin was elected, and his rival was given Salonika as compensation. Constantinople had fallen twice in two years to the westerners, and now the Byzantine Empire itself was subjected for over half a century to western rule under the Latin Empire.

16 Clari, ed. McNeal, p. 84; ed. Lauer, p. 59: *nous t'avons . . . gele de la merde et en le merde te remeterons*.

17 Villehardouin, ed. Shaw, p. 84; ed. Faral, ii, p. 22 ; Clari, ed. McNeal, p. 83; ed. Lauer, p. 60.

18 On 1204; the contraption, Villehardouin, ed. Shaw, p. 88; the trebuchets, *Chronicle of the Morea*, p. 91:(trimpoutseto); on backsides, Clari, ed. McNeal, p. 93; hundred places at once, Villehardouin, ed. Shaw, p. 89. On ships in pairs, and the *Pilgrim* and *Paradise*, see Villehardouin, ed. Shaw, p. 90; ed. Faral, ii, p. 44: *qui estoient liees ensemble; l'une avoit nom la Pelerine et li autre li Paravis*.

Despite papal disapproval of their acts, the crusaders were proud of their achievement, and Robert de Clari proclaimed it to be 'a righteous deed'.[19]

Robert was one of the many crusaders who marvelled at the wealth and the buildings of the great city. They were treated, as garrulous tourists, to some tall tales from the Greeks, who thus perhaps obtained some consolatory revenge. Robert could not read the Greek inscriptions, but was told that the words on one statue of two women, meant that the one pointing her hand outwards was saying 'from the West will come those who will capture Constantinople'; but with the hand which pointed to a 'vile place', she indicated: 'here is where they will be put'.[20]

Murzurphlus was captured, blinded, and thrown down from the top of a marble column, so that 'every bone in his body was broken'. The Latins set up their own precarious empire. Their engines proved very effective in the series of sieges which ensued, as they extended control over Athens, the Morea and the islands. Ladders were used in the capure of Corinth, and trebuchets brought surrender at Korone and Arkadia. Land plus sea attacks of the sort which had won Constantinople, were also effective at Nauplia and Monemvasia, the latter enclosed in siege 'as a nightingale by its cage'. Here the trebuchets operated night and day, and the citizens were reduced to cannibalism before surrendering.[21]

In order to capture Arakhoron, Geoffrey de Bruyères had his men pretend to get water while they noted how the entrances were laid out, and how many guards there were. He himself pretended illness in order to be taken inside out of sympathy. He got chatting to the castellan in a tavern, and having made the man drunk, stole the keys to the castle which he then took over.[22]

However the Greeks held on to Epirus, Nicaea and Trebizond, and mounted a growing threat to the Latins. In 1261 Michael VIII Palaeologus from Nicaea recovered Constantinople from Baldwin II. The two sieges of Constantinople in 1203 and 1204, are as significant in their way as that of 1453. Byzantium and Constantinople were irreparably damaged. The Greeks recovered Constantinople in 1261, but they never recovered their former authority, nor could the old belief in the invulnerability of the city be sustained. Where the Latins had led, the Turks could hope to follow. The Greek Empire suffered in the fourteenth century from economic problems including the loss of a third of the population from the Black Death, and a series of civil wars which saw, for example, John V dethroned three times. Glass 'gems', replacing the real thing in the imperial crown, symbolised the empty splendour of the late Byzantine Empire.

[19] Clari, ed. McNeal, p. 94.

[20] Clari, ed. McNeal, p. 110; ed. Lauer, p. 88, whose modern French translation omits the rudest phrase: *De vers Occident veuront chil qui Constantinoble conquerront et li autres ymages tendoit main en un vilain lieu, si disoit; Ichi asses plus que nous ne vous poons mie aconter . . . .*

The siege of Damietta, 1219

Frederick II

The change of target in eastern crusading marked by the Fourth Crusade was further emphasised by the Fifth Crusade, which after several similar abortive ventures, finally set crusaders in Egypt, against a city which from now on became a major focus for crusading endeavour, Damietta. The leading military figure in this venture was the sixty-year old John de Brienne, who later became the father-in-law of the emperor Frederick II. John had been encouraged to leave France after an embarrassing affair with Blanche, the countess of Champagne. In 1210 he had married Maria, the heiress to the kingdom of Jerusalem, and thus himself been crowned as king. But he lacked wealth, and won respect only by his martial abilities. At Damietta he lacked the authority to use these to the full. The crusaders surveyed their problems: the Saracens had built a chain across the Nile, from the east bank to a tower on an island close to the west bank, backed up by a bridge of boats. Damietta therefore blocked the way forward for the Christians. At one point the crusaders hauled their own ships overland to the upper Nile, with the men still on board.[23]

The crusaders made a first attack against the tower which secured the chain. They employed an idea, similar to that used by the Venetians at Constantinople, of two ships tied together and a revolving ladder. The first attempt failed, but eventually they captured the tower, and broke both the chain and the bridge of boats. Al-Kamil, however, shook their confidence with an attack upon their own camp, though it was repulsed. The camp was protected with a trench 'in their usual way' according to an Arab

21 On Murzurphlus' bones, Villehardouin, ed. Shaw, pp. 99, 109. On expansion in Greece, *Chronicle of the Morea*, pp. 111–60, Corinth on p. 111, Arkadia and Korone on pp. 118, 122; Nauplia and Monemvasia, p. 156. The 'nightingale' is p. 156.

22 *Chronicle of the Morea*, pp. 301–4.

23 For the Fifth Crusade, see Frederick II reference above, ch. 6 n. 38; also Runciman, *Crusades*, iii, pp. 150–204; Riley-Smith, *Crusades*, pp. 145–51; Philip of Novara.

source, but the attempt to improve communications to the sea by digging a canal was never completed. Then the Christian camp was flooded out by a storm, which washed up piles of dead fish. Even the ditches dug to contain the water overflowed; inevitably disease followed, an illness which turned the skin black, caused the legs to swell, and flesh to grow in the mouth. It killed off large numbers. The winter was hard in every way. The crusaders' response was to blame their own sins for the failures; a three-day fast was observed on bread and water only, while gambling, dice, alcohol and prostitutes were forbidden; the chastened Christians processed barefoot.[24]

The Egyptians were not finding life in Damietta very comfortable either. The army that came to relieve the city was forced to depart. The hard winter was followed by a baking hot summer. Stones from the Christian engines were answered by Greek Fire from the walls. The Saracens were somewhat surprised at the appearance of one representative from the other side, the famed but grubby Francis of Assissi; to them he appeared as an insane simpleton to be humoured.[25]

A surviving will graphically portrays life in the Christian camp. Bazela Merxadrus, a citizen of Bologna, drew up his will in the tent he shared with his fellows. He left his share in the tent, and the furnishings that belonged to him, to his wife Giulietta, for 'as long as she is in the army'. To one comrade he left two sacks of biscuit, two measures of flour, plus wine and wheat together with a pair of trousers, a shirt, and money for his part of the bread and wine which the group shared.[26]

The ordinary soldiers in the Christian ranks were becoming discontented with the lack of action, and took upon themselves to make an unco-ordinated attack, which was only saved from becoming a major disaster by the efforts of the aged John de Brienne. Al-Kamil made a surprisingly generous peace offer, which included control of Jerusalem to the crusaders, but though John de Brienne was in favour of acceptance, he was outvoted, a decision which the crusaders were soon to regret.

In November of 1219, they did finally storm Damietta after an eighteen-month siege, and there followed the expected looting. Over-confident, they now rejected a second peace offer, which again included the handing over of Jerusalem. The victors were far from agreed about future operations. A number of unwise decisions were made by the papal legate, Pelagius, which led to the disillusionment of John de Brienne with the enterprise, and to a disastrous defeat for the Christians in battle, followed by the loss of the hard-won Damietta in 1221.

24 Fifth Crusade: contraption, Oliver of Paderborn, pp. 179–82; Runciman, *Crusades*, iii, p. 152; Riley-Smith, *Crusades*, p. 147. On protection of the camp, Ibn al-Athir in Gabrieli, p. 259. On the disease, Runciman, *Crusades*, iii, p. 156; Riley-Smith, *Idea*, p. 167, and p. 168 on prohibitions.

25 Runciman, *Crusades*, iii, pp. 159–60.

26 Riley-Smith, *Idea*, pp. 174–5; the quote is p. 174. From *Annali Bolognesi*, pp. 419–20.

John de Brienne's daughter Isabella married the Holy Roman Emperor, Frederick II, in 1225. John de Brienne was caught out in a second sexual scandal, this time with one of his own nieces. Frederick ignored the rights of his father-in-law, with whom he quarreled, and proceded to claim the kingdom of Jerusalem for himself, even after the early death of his young wife at the age of sixteen. On the whole, Frederick II's involvement in the kingdom was an unhappy one. He did obtain in 1229, through negotiation, an apparently successful agreement, which brought Jerusalem into Christian hands. But no-one showed the expected gratitude: the Christian settlers in the kingdom feared they could not hold on to Jerusalem, the pope was furious because the whole campaign had been carried out while Frederick was still under excommunication for delays in going, and the Saracens were enraged at their own leader's generosity. Frederick himself was even pelted with offal and dung for his troubles, while at Acre.[27]

He left behind him a vitriolic situation, which deteriorated into a civil war between his supporters and the Ibelin family. Yet Frederick had regained Jerusalem, which he himself was able to visit. It was very unfortunate, from the viewpoint of the kingdom, that this particular agreement was so controversial and unacceptable, since Frederick's methods almost certainly offered the settlers their best hope of survival,through negotiation and agreement with the Moslems leading to peaceful co-existence.

St Louis' Crusades

With the crusades of Louis IX, king of France, interest again centred on Africa, and in the first place upon Damietta. Louis was among the most devout of all the leaders to take the cross, a great king with very considerable resources. His first crusade has been called 'the best organised of all'. We also possess an excellent account of his first crusade by someone both close to him and present at the event, the chronicler Joinville. He was obviously fond of Louis, and admired the man who never spoke ill of anyone, was ready to wash the feet of the poor, and out of sympathy set up a house for former prostitutes. Joinville says that Louis never swore, and that he himself copied this practice, to the extent of forbidding all swearing in his house, on pain of a clip round the ear. It was Louis' queen who asked Joinville to commit his memories of the king to writing. Yet the best organised crusade, made by the most devout crusader, was among the most disastrous in the history of the movement.[28]

27 Runciman, *Crusades*, iii, p. 192; Riley-Smith, *Crusades*, p. 151; Ernoul, p. 466.
28 On Louis IX see Labarge. On his crusades, see Runciman, *Crusades*, iii, pp. 255–92; Riley-Smith, *Crusades*, pp. 157–61, 173–5; and Jordan, *Louis IX*. 'Best organized' is from Riley-Smith, *Crusades*, p. 161; Joinville's remarks on Louis, ed. Shaw, pp. 1, 6, 121 (dice), 209–10 (swearing).

St Louis at Damietta

Louis sailed from his own newly-built port of Aigues Mortes in 1249, after assembling an impressive force and provisions. Accounts for 1250 show the size also of the work-force, including carpenters, miners, labourers and engineers. There were 15,000 men altogether, including 1,800 knights. They arrived at Damietta in June, when the landing was accomplished successfully, using the special landing craft which Louis had ordered to be constructed. Louis set up his red tent outside the city, whose defences had been improved by digging trenches, and by widening the river. Louis had engines brought up ready for a bombardment. In the initial fighting the Saracens' use of Greek Fire gave some problems, setting light to engines, clothes and horse trappings. They used fire-bolts tipped with Greek Fire, which were said to look like 'stars falling out of heaven'.[29] In fact the Moslems very soon abandoned Damietta, so that Louis had apparently won a rapid and remarkable victory, but appearances were deceptive. Nevertheless, finding the gates left open one morning, the Christians were able to enter the city without any resistance.

From Damietta the crusaders advanced towards Cairo. The Moslem leader Fakr ad-Din was taken by surprise while in his bath having his beard dyed; he scrambled out, but had not time to put on armour, and was killed.[30] From here on the story became one of disaster for the crusaders. At Mansourah in 1250, they met a tougher opponent in the Mamluk Baibars, by birth a Kipchak Turk; made a slave, he had been bought for the Mamluk guard. At Mansourah he set a trap for the crusaders, and caught them by

[29] Joinville, ed. Evans, p. 93.
[30] Ibn Wasil in Gabrieli, p. 290.

surprise. The count of Artois, and William, the English earl of Salisbury, were killed in the fight.

Dysentery and typhoid hit the Christian camp, and the crusaders decided they must return to Damietta. The going was hard, and St Louis himself became desperately ill. Joinville thought that the illness was caused by eating eels, which had been feeding on the corpses of the killed.[31] The symptoms sound very similar to those met by the troops who suffered illness during the Fifth Crusade: flesh which became black and dry, gums which became bad to the extent that flesh had to be cut from the gums so that men could eat, the execution of which operation made them cry out like women in childbirth. The army was trapped and had to surrender; the Saracens had captured St Louis himself and he was chained up in Mansourah. They sought an enormous ransom, and the surrender once again of Damietta. Only the efforts of Queen Margaret kept the Italians from abandoning Damietta, and thus losing the only bargaining counter they had; she had to promise to provide food for them.

Baibars killed the sultan, and himself assumed power. The crusaders would find him a difficult opponent. King Louis, once released, went on to Jerusalem, and decided to stay in the kingdom for some years to help in its defence, investing large sums in improving fortifications. The fate of his first crusade had not dented Louis' enthusiasm for crusading. He took the cross again in 1267, and set out on a second crusade in 1270. Joinville comments with some feeling: 'I was not there, thank God'.[32] Louis seems to have been persuaded by his brother, Charles of Anjou, to aim against Tunis, apparently on the grounds that, with a little pressure, its ruler was prepared to convert to Christianity. Thus Charles gained an unintended revenge for the way Louis had treated him on earlier occasions, as when rebuking him in public on board ship for gambling, throwing the dice and tables into the sea. The whole business of the new crusade was badly conceived; the emir showed no intention of changing his religion. Once again the king became seriously ill, and both he and his son died, Louis himself muttering over and over 'Jerusalem, Jerusalem'.[33]

The End of the Latin Kingdom

In addition to his victories in Egypt, the Sultan Baibars was successful in Palestine, and the remnant of the Latin Kingdom crumbled before him: Caesarea, Athlit, and Arsuf. Safed surrendered on an offer, though the captives were then beheaded, and the man who had negotiated the surrender for the Latins decided to save himself by becoming a Moslem. A

31 Joinville, ed. Evans, pp. 87, 90.
32 Joinville, ed. Evans, p. 223.
33 Runciman, *Crusades*, iii, p. 292, from William of St Pathus, pp. 153–5.

Frankish ambassador coming to Safed, found skulls encircling the place. Jaffa was taken, and Beaufort. After 171 years in Frankish hands, Antioch was captured, the attackers closing the gates so that the inhabitants could not escape, all being either enslaved or killed. There was a brief respite at Krak in 1271, when rain affected the engines, but not for long.[34]

In that year Edward I of England arrived in the Holy Land with a small force. He had intended joining St Louis' crusade, but that had already collapsed, and Louis was now dead; so Edward journeyed on to Acre. He had entertained thoughts of alliance with the Mongols against Baibars, but nothing came of it. He was himself in danger, when a member of the Assassins made an attempt on his life with a poisoned dagger, but Edward was able to kick the weapon away. The best he could achieve from his expedition was a truce. His most recent biographer sees the visit as having more significance for Edward's own personal development than for any contribution to saving the Holy Land.[35]

Baibars is said to have died in 1277 from drinking too much fermented mare's milk, but the Franks could gain little hope from the event. After a short interval Qalawun, Baibars' lieutenant, seized power, and aimed at finishing off the Latin Kingdom. Qalawun won a life-saving victory for Islam against the Mongols at Homs, and could then concentrate on the weak Latins. The rising in Sicily, known as the Sicilian Vespers, which saw the defeat of Charles of Anjou, deprived the kingdom of its last hope of outside help.

It is not known if the Franks recognised the symbolic significance of Qalawun's attack on Hospitaller Marqab, where by mining he brought down the Tower of Hope. In 1289 Qalawun besieged and stormed Tripoli, one by one the great names of the Latin Kingdom were being snatched from Christian control. The Italians in Acre foolishly rioted, and provoked Qalawun by attacking innocent Moslems in the city, as well as some local Christians, who were thought to be Moslems because they wore beards. But Qalawun himself, though he set out against Acre, died on the way, so the honour of striking the last blow was left to his son al-Ashraf. The latter collected numerous engines and an army of 220,000, men before the final attack in 1291. He carried so many provisions and weapons that the journey from al-Akrad, which would normally have taken eight days, needed a month.[36]

Only a handful of westerners arrived at Acre to help in the defence. Those who would not be able to fight, the elderly and the young, were sent

34 Runciman, *Crusades*, iii, on the convert, p. 321; on the skulls, p. 323; on rain-affected engines, p. 333.

35 On Edward's crusade, see Prestwich, *Edward I*, ch. 3, pp. 66–85; the incidents here are pp. 66, 82.

36 Runciman, *Crusades*, iii, on the attack in Acre, p. 410; on al-Ashraf's preparations, p. 412. On the size of army, Richard, ii, p. 426.

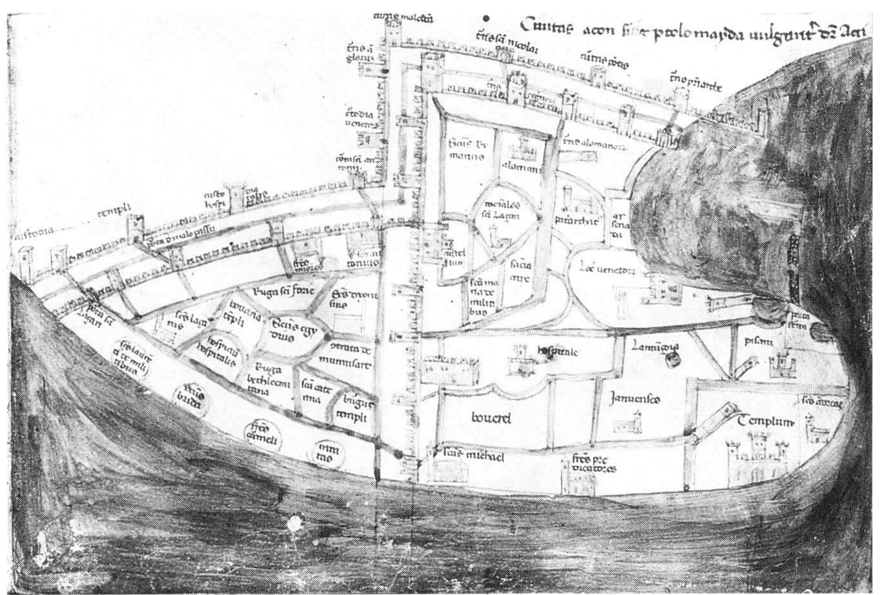

A fourteenth-century plan of Acre

to safety in Cyprus. The bombardment began, and included exploding shells which sound not unlike bombs. Among the engines brought with such effort from Syria were two called *Victorious* and *Furious*.[37] Belfries were built and mines dug: it was said there were a thousand engineers against every tower. The Christians did their best to resist, and a ship with an engine mounted on it managed to bombard the enemy camp. Two sorties were made, during one of which a knight came to an unfortunate end, when he fell into a latrine, and was suffocated. The Franks themselves had to set fire to King Hugh's Tower before abandoning it. The Moslem mines were fired, and two sections of the wall collapsed. The outer wall was taken, and then the towers. Among those killed was the Grand Master of the Temple. Patriarch Nicholas managed to find a boat, but was so generous in allowing others to clamber on board, that they all sank and drowned. The Catalan, Roger Flor, was more practical and, having commandeered a galley, charged exorbitant rates to take anyone who could afford it to safety. So many females were enslaved in this crusader city of delights, that the price of a girl in Damascus dropped dramatically.[38]

The city of Acre was abandoned. Decades later the place was found to be deserted, apart from a few peasants picking a living among the ruins. The remaining fortifications of the kingdom soon fell, except for the

37 On the Moslem engines, Richard, ii, p. 426; Runciman, *Crusades*, iii, p. 412; Abu l-Fida in Gabrieli, p. 344.
38 Runciman, *Crusades*, iii, on Roger Flor, p. 419; on the cost of girls, p. 420.

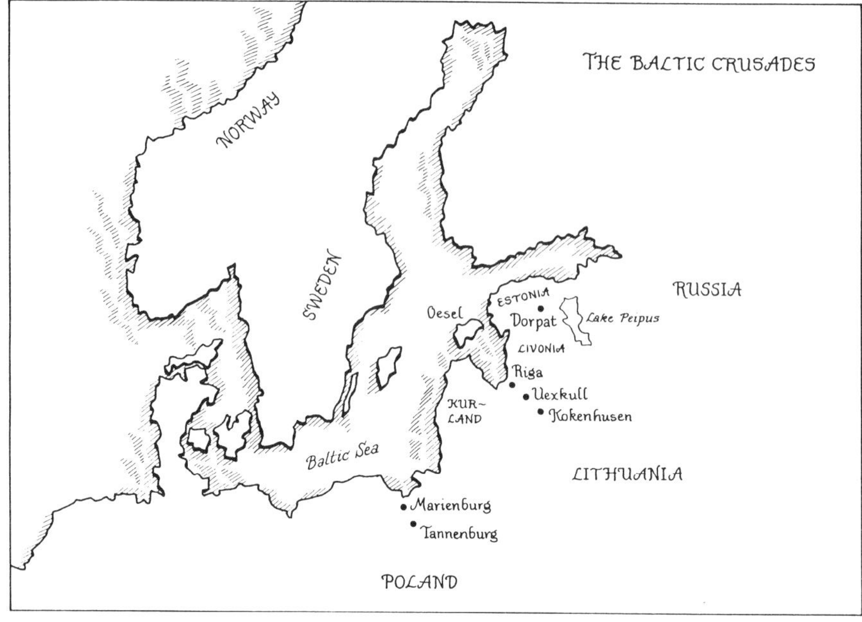

off-shore island of Ruad, which the Templars retained until 1303. The Latin Kingdom had come to its end. All the suffering and heroics of generations of crusaders from the first siege of Antioch and the taking of Jerusalem, through the years of Frederick Barbarossa, Richard the Lionheart, Innocent III, Frederick II, and St Louis, had ended in nought. The fervent wish of the Arab historian Abul-Fida was: 'God grant that they never set foot here again'.[39]

Crusades in the North

In the meantime other crusades had been called in various regions and with varying results. Among the more interesting were the northern crusades, called initially against pagans, as German Christians moved north and east in the years of economic expansion.[40]

The warfare which resulted from these crusades reminds one of the earliest medieval siege warfare, since it was small scale, and fortification had changed less in the far north of Europe, with isolated hill-top forts made of logs and clay. But victory for the crusaders was never easy or even assured, partly because few recruits could be attracted, and even fewer

[39] For Acre deserted, Runciman, *Crusades*, iii, p. 421; for the quotes, Abu l-Fida, from Maalouf, pp. 247, 259.

[40] On the Northern Crusades, see Urban, *Baltic Crusade*, and Christiansen, *Northern Crusades*.

could be persuaded to stay on for more than a brief campaign. On one occasion loyal Letts were taught to shout like Germans to give the impression there were more of the latter than was the fact. Both recruiting and warfare was made more difficult by the hard conditions, in an area where the sea froze over throughout the winter, and where broad, swampy areas were hung with fog. In the campaign of 1219 men lost noses, hands and feet through the bitter cold. Henry of Livonia, who probably came from Germany and settled in the north as a priest, wrote: 'snow covered the land, and ice covered the waves . . . the waters were as hard as stone'.[41] Henry had gone to Livonia in 1205 in the household of Bishop Albert von Buxhovden. At Ymera he helped to aid the priest baptising the Letts, and stayed on for the rest of his life, building and using his own church at Papendorp.

A mission from the West had established a church at Uexkull in 1180. The locals accepted conversion in exchange for being shown how to build western-style fortifications. The Semgalls thought at first that they could simply pull apart the new fortifications, as was their usual practice in war, for they had never come across cement. Instant conversion was not always to endure, and later many of the new Christians reverted to paganism with a sort of reverse baptism ceremony, when they entered the water to 'scrub off the faith'.[42] The Christian settlements became the basis of a new state around the recently established port of Riga, from which they sought to extend both Christianity and control. From 1202 a new military order, the Swordbrothers, was formed, based on the model of the Templars. Members of the order were trained in garrison duties, and in operating siege engines, which says much about the type of warfare in which they expected to engage.[43] They played a major rôle in the military efforts until their demise.

Interest in the region from Russia and Denmark complicated the situation, though the Mongol invasions served to divert Russian efforts. Loyal Livonians and other local populations allied with the Christian settlers, and there developed what was, in part, a nationalistic war against the Lithuanians and the Estonians. Western methods gave the crusaders an advantage in the initial stages: with the use, for example, of belfries, crossbows and various stone-throwing engines. On occasions the ice and snow, rather than being a hindrance, came in useful for putting out fires, which the enemy had started in order to destroy the wooden structures.[44] At first the winter was a bar to campaigns, but from 1211 the crusaders began to see that the frozen rivers could be used instead of roads for the advance into Estonia. Progress was frequently halted, though, by pagan revivals and rebellions.

41 Henry of Livonia, ed. Brundage, p. 239.
42 Urban, p. 37; compare Henry of Livonia, p. 34.
43 Urban, p. 56.
44 Urban, p. 81.

The locals were not without cunning in siege warfare. At Odenpah they threw the corpses of captives in the water in order to pollute it. At Dorpat in 1224 the defenders used fire wheels, probably an idea taken from the Russians. In this siege, the expertise of the Christians showed to good advantage, as they constructed a belfry from large trees, and under its cover made a hole in the rampart into which the tower itself was pushed. They bombarded the enemy with red hot iron, and with fire pots. But before long the locals learned from the methods of the westerners, and copied them. At Terwenten the crusaders captured a Christian who had earlier been taken prisoner by the pagans, and saved his life by showing them how to make and use crossbows. Before long the local forces were using much the same structures, towers and engines, as the crusaders.[45]

Here as elsewhere religious belief often stimulated heroic acts. Henry of Livonia was probably himself the priest he described, standing on the ramparts of the fort at Beverin during its siege, to 'pray' on a musical instrument. The Christian rôle of the crusaders was often underlined, for example by the use of the bell at Riga which was rung only in time of war.[46] The Teutonic Knights developed an interest in the northern wars, and took over from the Swordbrothers. The Knights conquered Prussia, and the Danes moved into Estonia. But from the 1230s there were serious problems for the crusaders. Alexander Nevsky won victories against both the Mongols,and then against the Knights in the battle of the River Peipus in 1242. As western methods lost their technological lead, so victory and dominance became more difficult. The Knights continued to be significant in the area to the fourteenth century, with their headquarters at Marienburg, attracting crusaders from many parts of Europe. At Tannenberg, however, they were defeated by the Poles and Lithuanians, and thereafter their importance diminished.

The Reconquest of Spain

The recovery of Spain by the Christians had always fitted into the picture of crusading attempts against Islam, but had rarely won the degree of interest, outside of Spain, which was shown in Palestine and the East. Spain came increasingly to depend upon its own Christian population to carry the fight forward.[47]

By 1200 Spain was still a patchwork of fairly small states: Portugal to the

45 Henry of Livonia, ed. Brundage: on Odenpah, p. 159; on Dorpat, and the belfry, p. 225. Henry of Livonia, ed. Arbusow & Baur, p. 202: *turrim ligneam fortissiman . . . octo diebus*; p. 204: *de quo rotas ignibus impletas*. For Terwenten, see Urban, p. 237.

46 Henry of Livonia, ed. Brundage, on the priest, p. 85; on the bell, p. 97.

47 A good, brief account of Spain in this period, is MacKay, *Medieval Spain*; see also Bisson, *Medieval Crown of Aragon*; Watt, *Islamic Spain*; and Lomax, *Reconquest*.

west, al-Andalus to the south, Navarre and Aragon in the north, Castile and Leon, Catalonia. The thirteenth century saw a significant move into Moslem territories by the Christian powers, probably the key period of the whole *reconquista*. In 1212 the Christian victory at Las Navas de Tolosa brought about the collapse of the Almohads. In the century which followed, the efforts of Ferdinand III of Castile and Leon, (1217–52) the conquests of James I of Aragon, known as the Conqueror (1213–76), and his efforts in alliance with his son-in-law, Alfonso the Learned of Castile and Leon, achieved permanent success. Cordoba was taken in 1236, Seville in 1248. James took the Balearic Islands, and James and Alfonso together won Murcia and Valencia. As so often, siege warfare was behind most of this advance.

The most intriguing of this trio of great rulers is James the Conqueror. Almost uniquely among medieval rulers, he wrote down an account of his own achievements, in Catalan, in *The Book of Feats*.[48] For once we can truly see into the mind of a medieval ruler. He rather glosses over his amorous exploits, and no doubt gives a rather one-sided view of his negotiations, but it is a genuine insider view, and it also includes detailed accounts of sieges. James emerges from his work as a very human king, with faults as well as virtues. Where else would one learn of a medieval king ordering his tent to be left in place because a swallow had nested in it, and he did not want it disturbed until the young had flown? On the eve of a fight in which his life might be lost, he confesses that his only offence is against his wife, Berenguela, and from now on he promises to live with her 'as a man ought to be with his wife'. He also has his moments of vanity, as when he shows off the paces of his mount, allowing it to curvet, and telling himself that the people would say he was not so old after all.[49]

It is interesting to note how much of his book is concerned with the provision of supplies, both in collecting and distributing them; and his personal involvement in negotiations, including times when he kept information to himself. For once we hear something of the reasons behind the chosen strategies and tactics. It is a work that deserves to be far better known than it is among military historians.

James I was born in 1208 in Montpellier, in what is now southern France. His mother and father, by his own account, had little love for each other, and he thought it a miracle that they had got together long enough for him to be conceived. For a time he was the ward of the Albigensian crusader, Simon de Montfort, who had fought against James' father in the battle of Muret, in which Pedro had been killed. The pope managed to

48 The English translation ed. J. Forster, is mainly used here; for the original Catalan see James I, *Cronica*, ed. De Casacuberta. A useful modern work on James and Alfonso the Learned is Burns, *Worlds*.

49 James I, ed. Forster; on the swallow, i, p. 322; on Berenguela, ii, p. 549; on the horse, ii, p. 650.

James I of Aragon planning the attack on Majorca

extricate him from Simon's control, and placed him in the hands of the Templars, who provided the boy with his education. Experience in war and in the world came early: at nine he was in full armour, he was storming castles at twelve, and at thirteen he was married to the first of his three wives. James had nine legitimate children, and several illegitimate. One of his daughters married Alfonso the Learned.[50]

Probably James' most enduring achievement was the conquest of the Balearic islands from 1229, an account of which figures prominently in his book. He was invited to dine with Pedro Martel, a citizen of Barcelona and a trader. As the meal drew to its close, James questioned Pedro about Majorca. Martel said he had been there once or twice, and described it to the king, suggesting that he should conquer it from the Moslems. James took him at his word, and set about immediate preparations, seeking promises from his magnates and cities for aid. The archbishop of Tarragona said he was too old to bear arms himself, but offered a contribution. The bishop of Barcelona, more aggressively, promised 'to pursue the enemies of the faith and of the cross'. A fleet of over 150 ships was gathered, some designed to carry horses and engines: 'a fine sight, the sea seemed white with sails'.[51]

They approached Majorca, with sails lowered so as not to be sighted, cloaks shading the land-side of the lanterns. Despite a bright moon, they successfully came ashore. James climbed a hill to view the city of Majorca: 'the finest city I had ever seen'. He settled down to an alfresco meal by a stream, noting that 'there were already stars in the sky'. Preparations were made to besiege the city; a large number of engines were landed, and three belfries were constructed, two of which were for mining. Friar Michael preached a sermon which encouraged everyone to help, and all the soldiers

50 On his parents, James I, ed. Forster, p. 100. See Burns, *Worlds*, p. 7 for Simon de Montfort; p. 8 for James' early exploits.

51 On preparations for the invasion of Majorca, James I, ed. Forster, i: on the dinner with Martel, p. 98; on the archbishop, p. 108; on the bishop, p. 110; on the fleet, p. 113.

including the knights brought wood and stones for the engines, the knights 'putting their own hands to everything', and carrying stones on their saddles.[52] James had much to say about how he brought stores by sea, and also obtained additional supplies by making deals with the Saracens on the island for water, barley, kids, poultry and grapes.

The Christian camp was protected with ditches and a palisade with two great gates. The bombardment commenced; one Saracen leader, Infantilla, was killed, and his head thrown back from an engine. A later source claims that 412 heads were returned in like manner; the same work has the Saracens hanging Christians alive from the walls, to stop James' trebuchets, but James apparently continued to shoot, aiming so well that the captives were not hit! Four towers were brought down by mining. The moat was filled with layers of earth and timber, which took fifteen days. When the enemy counter-mined in the moat, James sent for a powerful windlass crossbow to use against them. He also at one point had the moat filled with water to put out fires.[53]

Negotiations were begun by the Saracens through a former Christian knight, who had converted to Islam. James says he was himself prepared to agree the suggested terms, but that he was outvoted and accepted the majority decision. So the siege continued through a cold Christmas. James had now to borrow from the merchants in his camp, in order to keep up the supplies, promising payment after the town was taken, a reminder that commanders may often have been faced with similar equations, which must have played an important part in the nature of the settlements made. James suffered three sleepless nights, and consoled himself with a New Year's Eve mass, for an attack on New Year's Day. It was growing light as James' army advanced for the storm attempt. According to James, St George appeared to give them encouragement. The infantry forced their way through one of the breaches already made, and the knights followed them in. The city was taken, and gradually the pockets of resistance in the rest of the island were mopped up. James claimed that 20,000 were killed altogether.[54]

Minorca was captured in 1232, largely by a trick, lighting fires to make it look as if a much larger force had landed than was the case, and bringing a quick surrender. The archbishop of Tarragona undertook the final part of the conquest of the Balearics, by winning Ibiza on James' behalf.[55]

52 On Majorca, James I, ed. Forster, i: for the city, p. 135; for the stars, p. 136; for the three belfries, p. 140; for the knights giving aid, p. 141. James I, ed. Casacuberta, i, II, p. 52: *e denant si en ces seles aduyen en los cavals les pedres per als fenevols*.

53 The siege of Majorca, James I, ed. Forster, i: on the Infantella's head, the 412 heads, and hanging Christians, p. 143. James I, ed. Casacuberta, i, II, p. 54: *en la fonda del almajenech*. On mining four towers, filling the moat, and the windlass crossbow, ed. Forster, pp. 147–9. James I, ed. Casacuberta, i, II, p. 62: *una balista de torn*.

54 On negotiations, sleepless nights and 20,000 killed, James I, ed. Forster, i, pp. 151–72.

55 For Minorca and Ibiza, see James I, ed. Forster, i, pp. 211–21.

The fight against the Moslems continued on the mainland, where James' main ambition was the conquest of Valencia, which was accomplished during the twenty years after the taking of the Balearics. One of his key victories was in the capture of Burriana by siege. He constructed engines and a tower. James suggests that his engineer was at fault in using the tower before it was properly protected by a screen, with the result that it was badly damaged and had to be abandoned.[56]

It has been shown that James depended considerably for his successes on assistance from his own cities, and their militia, but these local troops could also create problems. At Burriana they helped in the construction of 300 hurdles to fill the ditch, but many wished to go home when the time came for bringing in their crops. James managed to retain sufficient forces to continue. One sortie led to the wounding of one of James' main supporters, Bernard Guillem. James himself treated the man: 'I took the lint, dipped it in water, and put it in the wound', which was then bound up with a squire's shirt. James ordered his people to bring up a mattress and a bolster for Bernard to sleep on. A storm attempt was made to a fanfare of trumpets. An engine had badly damaged one tower, and a few troops broke in, the first man receiving five leg wounds, but in the end the attack had to be called off.[57] However it proved sufficient persuasion, and the defenders called for a parley which led to surrender.

In general James shows himself to have been a cautious commander. He abandoned the attack on Gillera because he only had food for five days, and heavy seas were delaying the arrival of further supplies; the land route took too long, and he had insufficient stone-cutters to build a platform for the engines. Before Boatella he refused permission to attack forty peasants working in a bean field outside the town, on the grounds that irrigation canals made the ground dangerous for horses, and it was simply not worth the effort and risk. Even with a surprise attack, James believed caution was wise: 'many surprises fail through over-hasty attack'. He abandoned the attack on Alfama because again his supplies were inadequate, having only food for one day and no meat, since they had provisioned themselves only for a single day for a battle. His opponents had enough to last them ten days in 2,000 loads of corn. His sons complained that James' caution was ruining the campaign. He retorted that the kingdom had been won by his methods, but it would very soon be lost by theirs.[58]

Supply arrangements at Muntcada are of interest. It seems that James

[56] For Burriana, James I, ed. Forster, i, pp. 257–82; on the engine, pp. 262–5. James I, ed. Casacuberta, i, III, p. 76: *lo castell d.anar*.

[57] James I, ed. Forster, i: for hurdles and crops, pp. 274, 270; on the lint, p. 276; on the five wounds, p. 280.

[58] On James' caution, ed. Forster: Gillera, i, p. 301; Boatella, i, p. 372; surprise attacks failing, ii, p. 548. James I, ed. Casacuberta, ii, VIII, p. 10; *car moltes celades se fan que son perdudes en lo segle per ravata d.exir*. Alfara, and the answer to his sons, ed. Forster, ii, pp. 554–5.

himself decided to take on the task of going back to arrange for further provisions, and took orders from his commanders before setting out: for bread, wine, barley, sheep, and salt meat; he also intended to get an engine for himself. James says that he paid his own men for food which they brought back from raids: sheep, goats and cows, so that it could be distributed to the army, a fascinating glimpse into the way raids operated in financial terms. In this emergency, James commandeered supplies which he himself had loaded on to ships, ready to send to the garrison in Majorca; he also ransomed prisoners in order to get ready cash with which to pay the merchants. He worked out that after these efforts he had flour for three months, wine for six months, and salt meat and barley for two months. He also kept an eye on how his subordinates organised their own supply problems, and on one occasion was furious with Bernard Guillem, whose life he had earlier helped to save, for spending money on hiring knights, which should have been spent on food; again the balance of such calculations must have always been vital to commanders, but here for once we are told about it.[59]

James may have been cautious, but he was also determined. Puig de la Cebolla, the Hill of the Onion, proved difficult to take. His men told him that if he left the siege to deal with other matters which needed his urgent attention, the siege was bound to fail. Their demand annoyed him: 'no people are so arrogant as knights are', but he realised the truth of their remarks. He says he was very worried about what to do, and turned in his bed a hundred times that night in a hot sweat, despite the January weather. His decision was to vow to them that he would not go far away, and would not cross back over the River Ebro until Puig was taken. The place was important because it offered a base for attack on Valencia, his final ambition. As James wrote: 'I intend having the hen and the chicks too'. In the end his determination paid off, and Puig surrendered. James picked off other places around Valencia: Boatella was captured, and Cilla.[60]

The siege of Valencia in 1238 is another great set piece in James' book. A relief fleet from Tunis threatened to save the city, but although James made preparations to deal with its intervention, they proved unnecessary, since the fleet decided not to risk landing. The Saracens lit torches and beat drums; the Christians, not to be outdone, replied by throwing torches into the moat: 'so that the Saracens might understand that we cared little for their bravado'. James received supplies by sea: bread, wine, barley, cheese and fruit. In the camp one could buy and sell provisions 'as in a city'. James also arranged for the transport to the siege of spices and drugs

59 James I, ed. Forster, i: for Muntcada, pp. 302–8, 322; for Majorca, pp. 311–12; on Bernard Guillem, p. 320.

60 On Puig, James I, ed. Forster, i: arrogance of knights, p. 350. James I, ed. Casacuberta, i, V, p. 18: *car e.l mon no ha tan sobrer poble con son cavallers*. Turning in bed, ed. Forster, i, p. 349; the chicks, p. 356.

from the apothecaries of Montpellier and Lerida, 'for the sick as well as the sound', again something that must have been common, but which rarely gets a mention.[61]

James was himself wounded at Valencia: 'I happened to turn my head towards the town in order to look at the Saracens', when a bolt from a crossbow struck him on the forehead. It must have pierced deep and he was lucky to live, breaking off the shaft so that the blood ran down his face, which he wiped off with a laugh, so as not to worry his army; but when he returned to his tent, he tells us, his eyes became swollen till he could not see.[62] He still insisted on going out for his routine ride round the camp at the end of the day. An offer of surrender was turned down at first, but finally terms were agreed, and James had to supervise the tricky business of distributing the spoils and the lands. James hoped to get a promise that all those who benefited from the distribution would stay with the army for a year, but after protests, he had to settle for an arrangement with a four-month rota system.[63]

The latter part of James' military career was mainly spent in alliance with his son-in-law, Alfonso the Learned. One bone of contention between them, though, was control of the city of Xativa. James had determined that he would control one of the loveliest sites he had ever seen, with 'the most beautiful orchards round the town and castle', and 200 flat-roofed cottages, and pretty villages on its outskirts. It proved difficult to find a base camp with the necessary water and defensive capability, and eventually he had to settle for a position at some distance. Dams and mills round about were destroyed, but he found his army was not large enough to cut off all the enemy's water supply. He placed his own tent in a garden by the river, with a wall enclosing it. Pressure proved sufficient, and Xativa surrendered. When Alfonso expressed a desire to be given Xativa, James wrote: 'I could not be king of Valencia if Xativa were not mine', and refused.[64]

James agreed to assist Alfonso in the conquest of Murcia. He assembled at Valencia some 3,000 loads of corn, 20,000 sheep, and 2,000 cows, but though he had expected 2,000 knights only 600 turned up. In the end he took with him provisions for three weeks, bread, wine and barley carried by the beasts of burden, with shields and armour on top of the mules, but the knights carrying their own lances. James advanced to besiege Murcia in company with Alfonso. James went ahead to select the camp site. Again the emphasis which he gives to this rôle is of great interest. He wrote: 'in battle kings should be in the rear, but in quartering their army they should

61 On Valencia, 1238, James I, ed. Forster, i: on bravado, p. 328; on provisions as in a city, and drugs, p. 379.

62 James I, ed. Forster, i, p. 380.

63 James I, ed. Forster, ii, p. 406.

64 The quotes are from James I, ed. Forster, ii, pp. 434, 466.

be foremost, in order to place their men better'.[65] A guide suggested a spot which they agreed on in the end, though James was worried because it was rather close to the walls, and within crossbow range. With the capture of Valencia, James' main work of conquest was over.

After this heady period in the reconquest, further advance was rather intermittent. For a while Iberia was distracted by involvement in the Hundred Years War and with a succession dispute in Castile, where the French supported the eventual victor, Henry of Trastamara, and the English his brother Pedro the Cruel. Castile and Portugal emerged from this period as stronger powers.

The mid-fourteenth century saw some further advance, when despite a Moslem victory at Algeciras, the town was finally taken by the Christians in 1344. Thereafter little advance was made until the end of the fifteenth century; then the combination through marriage of Aragon and Castile in the persons of Ferdinand and Isabella brought new triumphs. Muley Hasan, the sultan of Granada refused to pay tribute, and Granada, with its famous Alhambra fortress, was besieged from 1490. Isabella herself accompanied her husband to a number of his sieges, appearing at Moclin on a mule. Ferdinand saw the conquest of the last part of Moslem Spain as a siege war, and promised to pick out the seeds of the pomegranate (Granada's symbol), one by one.[66] Isabella attended the siege of Malaga, where strict moral conduct was enforced upon the Christian army, which was forbidden to gamble, swear or consort with prostitutes. Engines, mines and towers were all employed, and the Aragonese fleet blockaded the harbour. The relief force from Almeria was defeated. A Dervish fanatic tried to stab Ferdinand and Isabella together, but another couple were his unfortunate and mistaken victims. The assassin was captured and killed, and his body catapulted back into the city. Malaga surrendered unconditionally, and many were enslaved, including fifty girls who were sent to the queen of Naples. Renegados, Christians who had converted to Islam, were tied to stakes and used for target practice by the victorious knights.[67] Others were executed, and some 450 Jews were ransomed. Granada itself surrendered, and the citizens were allowed to continue in their Moslem worship. Boabdil was given a safe-conduct, together with a small kingdom, which he later abandoned in favour of a life in Africa. The Alhambra became a palace for the Christian monarchs, Ferdinand and Isabella.

65 James I, ed. Forster, ii, p. 557. James I, ed. Casacuberta, ii, VIII, p. 22: *car en la batayla den esser lo rey en la reraguarda, mas en albergar la ost, lo rey hi deu esser, que vaja primer en assetjar cos meylors.*

66 Trevelyan, *Alhambra*, p. 49.

67 Trevelyan, pp. 52–3.

After the Fall of the Kingdom of Jerusalem

With the end of the Latin Kingdom, the Byzantine Empire had, more than most in the West, to fear the irruption of the Tartars from the East under Jenghiz Khan. Westerners were interested in the methods of war of these fearsome invaders. Plan Campi described them in this way:

> They conduct sieges as follows. When they come to a fortress, they surround it, or even circumvallate it, so that no one can come out. They shoot arrows and operate machines night and day without interval, working in shifts so that some can rest. They can dam rivers, and divert the water in force against a wall, or they can mine, or sometimes build a wall all round the besieged in order to starve them out. They always ration food so that each man receives a measured amount.[68]

It was said that they besieged one fortress for twelve years. They entered Europe in the 1220s, burning and taking Vladimir, Kiev and Cracow. In their clashes with western forces, their siege methods seem to differ little from those with which we are familiar. They were described as having a great variety of engines, and being able to aim well with them. They were of course accused by westerners of barbarous atrocities, such as killing prisoners in order to boil them down for fat, which could then be used for throwing fire into cities. According to an English chronicler, they were no good on foot because they had short legs. They also ate frogs, snakes and men, and drank human blood, so that their teeth always looked bloody![69]

A further example of germ warfare occurred at Schwanau in 1332, when the men of Strasbourg put bodies in barrels with the rubbish, and hurled them into the city. A similar, and even nastier story came from the Crimea. A group of Genoese merchants were besieged in the town of Caffa. Some of the besiegers brought the plague with them. They put diseased corpses into their engines and hurled them into the city. The Genoese were terrified into flight, and were thus one further means of spreading the dreaded Black Death towards the West.[70]

Jenghiz Khan had been born in 1167. His father was poisoned when he was only ten, but Jenghiz survived to become khan in 1194. It was said that, initially, the Mongols were 'unused to attacking fortified places', and that they learned the art of siege warfare in China, which they then proceded to conquer. Certainly their advance to the west, as we have seen, showed them well versed in siege techniques. Jenghiz Khan conquered the

68 Oman, ii, pp. 320–21. On the Mongols, see Morgan, *Mongols*, Holt, *Crusades*; Chambers, *Devil's Horsemen*; Runciman, *Crusades*, iii, pp. 237–54; Maalouf, pp. 235–46; Sinor.
69 Matthew Paris, ed. Giles, iii, p. 450, from the additamenta.
70 Contamine, p. 104; Gottfried, *Black Death*, pp. 36–7; though the author queries the chronicler's accuracy.

largest empire the world had seen, and established the Yuan dynasty in China. James I of Aragon saw the Great Khan as 'the highest king in the world'.[71] His descendants moved into the Middle East from the 1220s, taking Baghdad in 1258 after making two bridges of boats, and bombarding the great city. The epileptic Hulagu had the caliph strangled and the population massacred. Aleppo fell, then Damascus, and their progress seemed unstoppable, until Baibars' victory at Ain Jalud.

The Latins in the East had felt genuine hope at the Mongol advance, with possibilities of alliance, and even of the conversion of the Mongols to Christianity. Some Mongol leaders married Christians, and showed sympathy to them. But co-operation was intermittent. When Bohemond VI allied with them, he was excommunicated, and in the end the opportunities were lost. By the time the Mongols showed themselves in a position to aid the Latins, the kingdom had collapsed, and the Mongols themselves were, in the end, converted to Islam.

Tamberlane, or Timur, generally known as the Tatar, was a Turco-Mongol, born in Samarkand in 1336. His great empire also extended into the old crusading lands. He took Baghdad in 1392, and shortly afterwards entered Syria, where he sacked a series of cities. He succeeded, where his predecessors had failed, in defeating the Mamluks, and even captured Bayezid, in a battle near Ankara in 1402, after which the unfortunate prisoner was carted around in an iron cage.[72]

The Mongols may have offered temporary hope to the Latins, but they also appeared as a threat to the weakened Byzantine Empire. Timur did distract the Turks from Constantinople for a while, but again the hopes proved transitory. In the last resort, it was not the Mongols but the Ottoman Turks, who brought about the downfall of the Eastern Empire. Christian strength in the Middle East, such as it was, depended on the sea and on Mediterranean links with the West. Gradually the Turks won over the coastal ports and islands, and with them control of the eastern Mediterranean.[73]

Ottoman power began with the establishment of a small border state, not much more than a brigand territory, founded by Ertughrul in the late thirteenth century. Under his son, Osman, who gave his name to the new power, and then his grandson, Orhan, they began to threaten, and eventually to take over Byzantine territory. At first the Ottomans seem to have lacked knowledge of siege warfare and equipment, and could only succeed by blockade, which was often a very lengthy process. Nonetheless great and ancient towns fell to them: Ephesus in 1308, Nicaea in 1329. Osman's grandson, Suleiman I, took Adrianople in Thrace, and turned it into the new Ottoman

71 On Mongol tactics, see Runciman, *Crusades*, iii, p. 242; Morgan, *Mongols*, pp. 65–6, 91. On the highest king: James I, ed. Forster, ii, p. 579.

72 For Timur, see Runciman, *Fall*, pp. 40–2; and *Crusades*, iii, pp. 463–64.

73 Runciman, *Fall*, pp. 22–47.

The Mongol siege of Baghdad, 1392.
Miniature from the Saray-Album, late fourteenth century

capital from 1366 until the acquisition of the even more prestigious Constantinople. Thessalonika fell after a four-year blockade, and gradually Constantinople was isolated, as the Turks took over the Balkans.

This threat to eastern Christendom sparked a late burst of crusading activity, no longer concerned with Palestine, which had been lost, but with defence against the Islamic Ottomans. Interest in eastern crusades had certainly declined in the West, though it had not not altogether vanished, but some of the eastern European states, closer to the Ottoman threat, continued to respond.[74]

There were still some efforts directed towards Africa. Peter I of Cyprus made great efforts to get support in the West, with little result, though a force did assemble at Rhodes, and Alexandria was taken in 1365. When the Christian fleet arrived, it was allowed into harbour, in the belief that it was a trading fleet. The town was stormed, and the citizens massacred, but the project seems to have been unwise, and the success short-lived, provoking retaliation in the form of persecution of local Christians, and harming Italian trade. Another short term success was the taking of Gallipoli, by Amadeus of Savoy, only for it to be lost again soon after. In 1426 Cyprus itself fell to the Egyptians.

In 1390 Enguerrand de Coucy was engaged in the siege of Barbary, against Tunis and the barbary pirates. The force went under the guise of a crusade, with blessings from both the pope and the anti-pope. Despite bad weather the crusaders reached the pirate base at Mahdia, a walled city some 200 miles from Tunis. Here a belfry was constructed, but the effort petered out after a ten-week siege, and was ended by a negotiated agreement.[75]

The crusade to Nicopolis in northern Bulgaria in 1396, sought to block the Turkish advance into Europe, and a large army, possibly the largest ever assembled against the Moslems in the crusading period, moved eastwards under Sigismund of Hungary. A few towns were taken, and the army advanced to Nicopolis, the Ottoman stronghold on the Danube. The crusaders did not, however, possess engines, though they did produce scaling ladders and start digging mines. A Turkish relief force, drawn away from Constantinople, arrived under Bayezid, and the Turks won a famous victory, after which 3,000 prisoners were killed.[76]

When the Turks captured Smyrna, each of them had to carry a large stone and throw it into the water, to make dry land of the sea, so that the walls could be approached and scaled. Some made it up the ladders, other 'took the descent to Hades'.[77] Christians, trying to escape in boats, found their co-religionists beating their hands with cudgels to prevent the boats from becoming over-crowded.

In 1444 armies from Serbia and Hungary, under John Hunyadi and the Albanian Skanderbeg, set out against the Turks. They besieged Varna, but

[74] On late crusades, see Riley-Smith, *Crusades*, ch. 9, pp. 208–40; Runciman, *Crusades*, iii, pp. 427–68.

[75] On Barbary and Mahdia, see Tuchman, *Distant Mirror*, ch. 22, pp. 458–77; Riley-Smith, *Crusades*, pp. 230–31.

[76] On Nicopolis, 1396, see Riley-Smith, *Crusades*, pp. 231–32; Froissart, ed. Jolliffe, pp. 372–75, 378–85; Runciman, *Crusades*, iii, pp. 458–62; Atiya, *Nicopolis*.

[77] Doukas, p. 98.

Murad came with a relief force, and defeated them in battle at Kossovo. The papal representative, Caesarini, had shocked both sides by refusing to observe an agreed truce, on the grounds that an oath given to infidels was not valid. This was the last major military effort of the crusading movement to come from Europe. The droll tale of Pius II, 'the last crusader', insisting that in his dying moments he attend the assembly of his crusade at Ancona, and having to be shielded from the knowledge that virtually no one had turned up, symbolises the dying moments of the movement that had played such a great part in medieval history.[78]

The decline of crusading enthusiasm, and the advance of the Ottoman Turks, predicted the downfall of Constantinople. By 1450 what survived of the Byzantine Empire seemed to have no hope of countering the might of Turkish power, and yet the siege of Constantinople in 1453 became one of the great set piece sieges of history, and might well have ended in Turkish failure, or at least in yet another agreement. It was a far closer contest than the situation might have led one to anticipate.

The Siege of Constantinople, 1453

The Greeks had recovered Constantinople from the Latins in 1261, but the last two centuries of the Byzantine Empire were years of civil war, problems and desperate crises. From the 1390s Constantinople was in a position of virtually constant siege, in that the city had become an island in the midst of Turkish controlled territories. Bulgaria had been conquered by 1393, the Peloponnese by 1394, Belgrade was captured in 1440. The Moslems made many attempts against the city, including a siege by Bayezid in 1396, which was, however, diverted by the crusade of Nicopolis. The city was besieged by Musa at the beginning of the fifteenth century, and again by Murad II in 1422 for eleven weeks, though his attempt was made without engines, and was abandoned because of supply problems.

The Black Death hit Byzantium hard, and in its last period as capital of the Byzantine Empire, Constantinople was relatively empty: like a group of villages within the walls each separated by uninhabited stretches. The emperors found it difficult to make ends meet, and even sold the lead off the roof of the imperial palace for ready cash. John V at one point needed to be rescued from a debtors' prison in Venice, and the imperial crown was studded with jewels made of glass. There were few periods of political stability. Andronicus II was forced into exile, and spent the last part of his life in a monastery. John V Palaeologus was deposed three times: by his father-in-law, his son, and his grandson; he became virtually a vassal of the Turkish sultan. John VI Cantacuzene had to abdicate, and also ended his

[78] Runciman, *Crusades*, iii, pp. 467–68; the quote is the heading for p. 467.

days in a monastery, probably about the best end a late Byzantine emperor could hope for. Order was dubiously aided by the employment as mercenaries of the Catalan Company. Civil War was endemic, and at one moment there were four emperors in Constantinople at the same time: two ruling and two in prison, who both escaped to seek Turkish aid.[79]

There were also longish periods when the Empire had to cope without its emperor, while he went off on travels to the West, seeking assistance against the Turks. Manuel II was an absentee emperor from 1399 to 1402. One rather desperate ploy, used on more than one occasion, was to promise union of the Orthodox Church with the Roman Church in return for the hope of aid. This proved more harmful than helpful, since it was greeted with hostility at home. In the period before the final fall, after one such agreement, the church of Santa Sophia itself was boycotted for five months in protest. The last emperor, Constantine XI, came to the throne in 1448, on the death of his brother. His weak position was clear from the first moment, he had to be crowned at Mistra, and by the local metropolitan, since initially he lacked power in the capital.

On the other hand, Ottoman strength had continued to grow. Their sway had been gradually spread, mainly through blockades and siege war. They seem still to have lacked adequate engines, but the Christians could rarely raise a field army to dispute their threat. It may have taken four years, but still Thessalonika fell, and so did a great slice of Europe to the west of Constantinople. By 1453 Turkish knowledge of siege warfare had improved considerably, through the employment of western advisers, in particular their grasp of the manufacture and use of artillery. One great triumph was to attract over to their side the services of the famous Hungarian cannon expert, Urban. This too was the result of Byzantium's poverty, the emperor being unable to pay the wages which Urban thought he was worth. The Turks offered not only pay, but also all the resources he required to build new and enormous guns; he was responsible for the famous giant cannons employed against the Christians with such devastating effect.[80]

The Turks had also developed a new type of force, which proved surprisingly effective, the Janissaries, or 'new troops'. These had their core in a kind of royal bodyguard. What is surprising is that they were selected from Christian children, originally slaves, and educated and trained as if they were the children of the sultan, and of course as Moslems. They developed a fierce loyalty to their master, and became the most reliable and feared troops of the age. They had been founded only in the time of Murad I, but

79 A good, brief account of later medieval Byzantium, is Nicol, *End of the Byzantine Empire*; see also Browning, *Byzantine Empire*.

80 The many sources on 1453 available in print and translation, include; Sphrantzes, Barbaro, Doukas. A useful collection of sources is J.R.M. Jones, *Siege of Constantinople*. The classic modern account is in Runciman, *Fall*.

already by the rule of Mehmet II (1451–81), were recognised for their great abilities.

Mehmet, the sultan who brought about the final fall of the Byzantine Empire, young, aggressive, and ambitious, was himself the son of a slave girl. George Sphrantzes, the Grand Chamberlain of Byzantium, a close friend of Constantine XI, was dismayed at the accession of the hostile Mehmet. Sphrantzes left an account of the fall of Constantinople, the only account from within the walls written by a Greek. He would survive the siege, and become a slave of Mehmet's Master of Horse, and later lived on in Greek Corfu. He was in a good position to record events as seen by both sides. He believed Mehmet was 'an enemy of the Christians', a view shared by the chronicler Doukas, who called Mehmet more crudely, a 'blood-thirsty beast'. Before Mehmet, the sultans had on the whole been developing more tolerance towards Byzantium as their fear of the Empire diminished, but Mehmet reversed such policies.[81]

Mehmet was something of an intellectual, who rarely laughed, and enjoyed having read to him histories of Rome. He was interested in geography, and ordered the making of a map of Europe, over which he cast longing eyes. He is said to have forecast: 'there will be one empire in the world, one faith for all'. Dolfin thought him sober, and 'not given to lustful desires, which seems to be in opposition to the common western view of a debauched drunkard. Another writer thought him 'full of wild enthusiasm'. In the capital at Adrianople, he was said to go about dressed as an ordinary soldier, but would order the execution of anyone who recognised him! He is described as having a great hooked nose and brightly coloured red lips, so that he resembled a parrot eating cherries.[82]

Mehmet was responsible for the decision to build the Roumeli Hisar fort on the European shore of the Bosphorus at its narrow point, which was a declaration of intent and virtually a declaration of war. Its Turkish name symbolically, meant 'cut-throat'. Byzantium protested formally, but was helpless to stop the Turks completing a base which so dangerously controlled the straits. Shipping could only expect a free passage now with Turkish permission. A Venetian ship, attempting to run past the fort, was shot at and sunk, and those who managed to swim ashore were beheaded. Niccolo Barbaro, a Venetian surgeon, who 'happened to be in the unfortunate city of Constantinople', says it was built 'for the express purpose of taking the city'. Mehmet's response to the protest over the fort was blunt: 'beyond the ditch she (that is Constantinople) owns nothing. I can do what I want in my own land'; he offered to flay alive any messenger who brought further

81 The quotes are Sphrantzes, p. 311, Doukas, p. 190.

82 From Jones, *Siege*: Dolfin on Mehmet, p. 127; Leonard of Chios on enthusiasm, p. 15. Doukas on Mehmet in disguise, p. 201; on description, Runciman, *Fall*, pp. 55–8.

Constantinople, 1453

protests. Doukas says that the Christians trembled, for they saw that the end of the city was at hand.[83]

Mehmet assembled probably the largest army every brought against Constantinople, and a tremendous artillery train, far more powerful than anything the city had previously faced. Sphrantzes says there were 420 ships and 258,000 men; they used 1,000 pounds of gunpowder a day.[84] The Turks collected provisions from all around, goats and sheep were driven from their villages.

At least the city had time to look to its defences, already very powerful. There were a hundred towers, four miles of land walls, with an enormous ditch, and nine miles of sea walls.[85] Repairs were made, concentrating on the outer wall, but one Italian thought that the walls were still in a poor condition and the towers dilapidated 'because of the laziness and negligence of the Greeks'.[86] The Italian galley crews were drawn in to help with the last-minute improvements, using flags to mark the sector of each group at work. The ditches were cleared; provisions were hurried into the city from all around, though the new fort reduced the amount which could be brought from the Black Sea. But ships from Chios arrived with wheat, wine, olive oil, figs, carob beans, barley and pulses; supply was not to be the decisive factor. The emperor had ordered a great boom to be placed across the harbour, made from great round pieces of wood joined by chains, stretching across the Golden Horn to a tower at Pera.

What Constantinople most lacked was manpower, with such long walls to defend. Appeals to the West had brought a pitiful response. A few Italians came in, and played a major part in the fight, especially the 700 well-trained men from Genoa and Rhodes who arrived in 1453 with Giustiniani. Altogether, according to Sphrantzes, from the results of a census which he himself took, there were 4,973 fighting citizens, and 2,000 foreigners.[87] But, as Leonard of Chios wrote: there were 'scarcely enough to defend the circuit of the city . . . which I observed at close quarters with my own eyes'.[88] Constantine knew he could not man both walls, so decided to make the outer wall the main line of defence.

Mehmet had careful plans made of the city and its defences, traced with ink on paper, marking the best places to dig trenches, to place artillery batteries, and to attempt scaling.[89] He decided that the Lycus Valley, and the stretch called the Mesoteichion, was the weakest part of the land walls, and himself camped opposite this point, which he chose to make the chief

83 Chalcocondylas, in Jones, *Siege*, p. 42, on cut-thoat. Barbaro, p. 9; Doukas, pp. 194–5.
84 Sphrantzes, pp. 48–9.
85 On walls, see Tsangadas.
86 Riccherio, in Jones, *Siege*, p. 120.
87 Sphrantzes, pp. 48–9.
88 Leonard of Chios, in Jones, *Siege*, pp. 26, 12.
89 Doukas, p. 202.

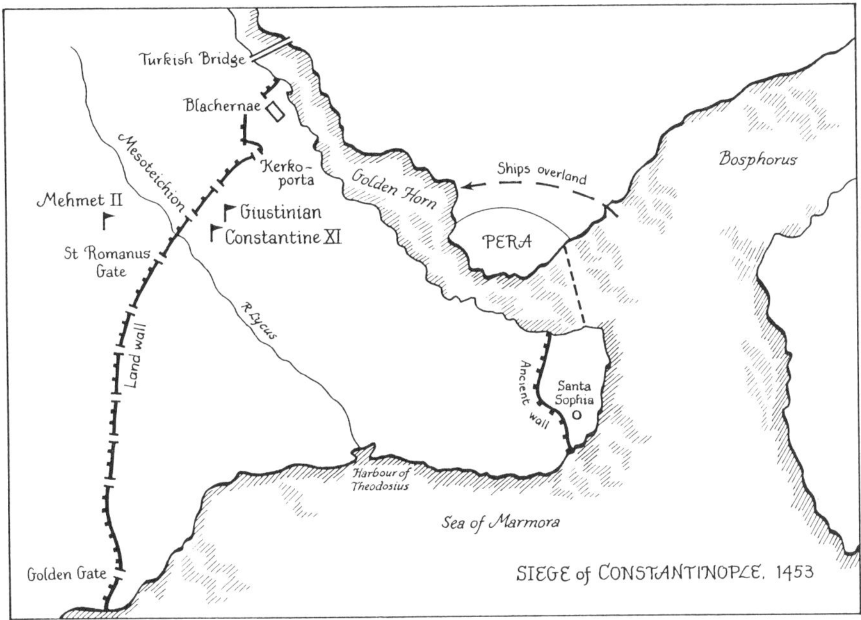

target for a massive bombardment. He established himself in his red and gold tent, with the Turkish army stretched out on either side of him. And so the great siege commenced. Mehmet had his cannons dragged into position, including the large guns made to Urban's designs, and started a six-week bombardment. The wall was breached first in what had always looked the most vulnerable area, between the Lycus Valley and the Golden Horn, near the Charismian Gate, crumbling down into the ditch. Efforts were made by the Turks to fill the ditches, so many pressing forward to the work that some fell in and were buried, thus assisting in an unintended manner. The Greeks patched the damage as best they could, with beams and barrels of earth; chains of people passed materials in baskets. Two small outposts outside the walls, Therapia and Studius, were attacked and soon taken, together with an island in the Sea of Marmora. Prisoners captured by the Turks were impaled: 'fixed by the fundament upon sharp stakes, which pierced them to the top of their heads'.[90] On 18th April the first storm attempt was made, the Turks crossing the ditch in force, but failing to break in.

An interlude was provided by the arrival of a small squadron of Genoese galleys. The intermittently rough conditions hampered the Turks, and they could not get their cannons to bear down steeply enough in order to hit the ships when they were close in. Both sides watched the battle at sea: the Christians from the walls, the Turks from the shore. Mehmet himself

90 Tedaldi, in Jones, *Siege*, p. 5.

became so excited that he rode into the waters, urging on his fleet. When the wind rose, the Christian vessels were able to break out, and were let in through the boom under cover of dark. Mehmet's admiral, the Bulgar Balta, despite receiving an eye wound in the conflict, was sentenced to death by Mehmet for cowardice. However others had the courage to speak in his defence, and the sentence was commuted to that of the bastinado, beating with rods on the soles of the feet and the belly. Doukas says he was stretched out by four men and beaten a hundred blows by a golden rod with a heavy end.[91] Many died under this punishment, but Balta was released, and lived the rest of his life in obscurity. The naval battle had come at a lucky time for the Greeks, for the Bactatinian Tower collapsed at just this moment, but with attention directed elsewhere, it was possible to carry out emergency repairs.

A feature of this siege, and a credit to Mehmet's perseverance and ingenuity, was the decision to take ships overland so as to by-pass the boom, and get into the Golden Horn. Even the Greek Sphrantzes saw this as 'a marvellous achievement, and a superb stratagem'. The Venetians had tried something similar at Lake Garda, and possibly a renegade Christian gave the idea to Mehmet. The way was cleared, and a track laid down on planks greased with sheep and ox fat. The ships were dragged from the water using pulleys and lifted into wheeled cradles, pulled up to the top of the hill, and then allowed to run down, 'with sails hoisted and oars moving', a man holding each yardarm, with sea songs being played on trumpets: 'they transformed the land into the sea'. The Turks fired cannons, so that smoke hung over Pera and obscured the view of that neutral Christian settlement, one shot falling on Pera itself, which the Turks claimed was an accident. The Venetian Barbaro thought that the Genoese of Pera could have prevented this whole move, and he is probably right, but they kept their heads down.[92]

The Golden Horn now held some seventy Turkish ships, which the Venetian Coco offered to try and put out of action that very night in a sea attack. It seems that the plan was betrayed, and the Turks were ready; Barbaro again accused the citizens of Pera of guilt for the betrayal.[93] Coco's party were captured without doing any damage, and next day they were executed in view of the city walls.

Attention returned to the main problem of breaching the walls. The Turks tried many mines, fourteen altogether according to Tedaldi. An important rôle in countering these was played by a man described as a German, but probably a Scot called John Grant, an expert in the use of Greek Fire. When mines were discovered, the Turks encountered were

91 Doukas, p. 56.
92 On ships carried overland: Sphrantzes, p. 56; Chalcocondylas, in Jones, *Siege*, p. 46. On Pera, Barbaro, p. 37.
93 Barbaro, p. 47.

blasted with fire. One captured Turk revealed the site of other mines, which were then destroyed. They continued to probe in all directions, digging trenches under the protection of shelters, and 'making openings in the earth' for their guns.[94]

Constantine XI toured the defences regularly, in the company of George Sphrantzes. The emperor had imperial treasure melted down in order to pay the troops. Meanwhile the Turks built wheeled towers, and prepared for a new major storm attempt from all sides, land and sea, including now from the harbour. The Greeks knew their chances were slight, and resorted to one of the oldest ploys known in siege war, appeal to God. They made a procession through the city and round the walls, carrying icons, while the bells were rung. The emperor spoke to his commanders to encourage them. He demanded that they should all be ready to die fighting for their families, and reminded them that they were the descendants of the heroes of ancient times. After a gap of five months, a last Christian service was held in Santa Sophia. But there were bad omens: a strange light in the sky, thunder and fog, and the icon of the Virgin fell from its frame. At night Constantine went up to a tower on the Blachernae walls, Sphrantzes with him. Turkish fires lit the Lycus Valley, and the Golden Horn, while the enemy brought up artillery by the light of torches.[95]

Once the defenders were in their places on the outer wall, the gates were ordered closed behind them: there was to be no retreat. The attack began in the early morning dark, at 1.30, to the fearsome sound of cymbals, pipes, trumpets and shrieking: 'screaming their war cries incessantly in an attempt to terrify us'.[96] Everyone in the city turned out to give a hand, including women and nuns. Mehmet made his attack in carefully orchestrated waves, saving his best troops to last. The first attack was made by the bashi-bazouks, irregular troops of mixed background, Turkish, Greek, Frankish. More reliable men stood behind them with orders to kill if anyone fled, using clubs and whips tipped with steel to drive back into the fray any who returned. The first attack reached the walls, but after two hours of attempting a breach, this wave was called off.

There followed a bombardment, and then the second wave of troops were sent in, the Anatolian Turks. Urban's great cannon had flattened the temporary stockade blocking an earlier breach, creating a cloud of smoke and dust. Troops entered the breach, but became isolated, and were killed or driven off; forty carts were not sufficient to carry away the dead. After two hours the second attack was called back. As it grew light the Greeks

94 From Jones, *Siege*: on 14 mines, Tedaldi, p. 5; on making openings, Chalcocondylas, p. 45.

95 Sphrantzes, p. 74; Doukas, p. 221.

96 Sphrantzes, p. 70.

could see the stones hailing in from the engines: 'as though a dark cloud covered the sun and sky'.[97]

Now came the climax, the attack of the Janissaries. For the Turks it had to succeed, and Mehmet himself advanced to the edge of the ditch. Two events decided the last struggle. The first was the wounding and retreat of Giustiniani; it is likely that dispute will always rage over his conduct, but it is difficult to judge after the event. The man was badly wounded and died about a week later, how can we be sure what mind he was in, and whether cowardice, weariness, or simply a muddled brain motivated him? He had been wounded on an earlier occasion by a splinter from a cannon shot. His actions to this point had been consistently brave, and his intelligence and qualities of leadership, had impressed everyone, including the emperor. His command in the vital and vulnerable sector of the defences had been the key to the successful defence. Now the gates were opened and he was taken away, giving a poor example to the troops and breaking morale. It was said that he 'trembled at the sight of his own blood'. Possibly his resolve had been dented by a quarrel with the leading Greek minister, Lucas Notaras; Guistiniani had requested that guns be moved from the sector under the command of Notaras to his own more vulnerable area. Notaras had refused, and Giustiniani had been angry to the point of drawing his sword on the Greek. At any rate, Giustiniani was wounded by a cannon or by lead shot, according to Riccherio fired by his own side, and his men decided to take him away. Constantine appealed to him to stay put, but the appeal was not heeded. The opening of the gate and the retirement of Giustiniani 'sapped their will to win'. Others followed, and retreat became rout.[98]

The second significant event seems to have resulted from an error, though treachery cannot be ruled out. During the attack, a sortie had been made from a small postern at the Kerkoporta in the Blachernae wall, and for reasons now unknown, the gate had not been closed afterwards. The Turks discovered it, and were able to effect an entry. In conjunction with Giustiniani's retreat, the appearance of Turks within the defences proved decisive. The giant Hasan had the honour of being the first on the walls, though he was killed for his trouble. Others soon followed and before long the outer wall was taken.

Exactly what happened to the emperor Constantine is uncertain, but he was probably killed in the crush as the flight got under way, either fighting or running. One account says he was wounded in the shoulder, and died from the wound. A body wearing socks, with eagles embroidered upon

97 Sphrantzes, p. 75.

98 The 'cowardice' and wounding of Giustiniani: for 'trembled', Leonard of Chios in Jones, *Siege*, p. 36; from own side, Riccherio, in Jones, p. 122; Doukas, p. 222 has lead shot in the arm; Riccherio in Jones, p. 121 says it sapped the will; Sphrantzes, p. 77 has him wounded in the legs and losing courage. For the quarrel with Notaras, Leonard of Chios in Jones, pp. 29–30.

them, was later identified by the Turks as Constantine.[99] A massacre followed the entry: blood ran like rain, and bodies floated in the water like melons. Some resistance spluttered on. The crews from two Cretan ships held out at the Horaia Gate, and were finally allowed to surrender on terms, with permission to take their property and sail away. Some others escaped to Pera by water. Mehmet had promised the traditional three-day sack, and the troops were allowed their way. He commented gloomily: 'what a city we have given over to plunder and destruction'.[100] On entering the city in the afternoon, he did rebuke one of his men for tearing up pavements, pointing out that he had given them the property and the people, but the city itself was his. Turks dressed themselves in the rich robes of clerics, gold cloths were draped over dogs, wine was guzzled from holy chalices. At last the orgy of looting ended, calm was restored. The wounded city, according to Doukas, was 'desolate, lying dead, naked, soundless, having neither form nor beauty'.[101]

Constantinople soon recovered as a city. The Ottomans commenced a programme of repairs and re-building, which soon restored ancient glories. But from the Christian viewpoint, the city was lost for ever. The podesta of Pera in a letter back home to Italy wrote: 'in one day all our labours went for nothing'.[102] Constantinople was now a Moslem city. The Byzantine Empire, with its continuous history from Roman times, apart from a few minor surviving outposts, was at an end. Without it the world would never be the same, it has rightly been seen as symbolic of the ending of the medieval era.

Rhodes

The siege of Constantinople was the great event, but before Europe settled into a new shape, there were a number of lesser but often significant fights. Two of considerable moment, fill the rôle of postscript or epilogue to our narrative of medieval sieges: the great sieges of Rhodes and Malta. The final siege of Rhodes brought an end to Christian power in the eastern Mediterranean, and the saving of Malta drew the limits to Turkish expansion.

99 On Constantine XI's death; Leonard of Chios in Jones has the crush, as does Riccherio, who also says he fled: pp. 37, 122. Chalcocondylas in Jones, p. 50, has him retreating like a 'commoner'. But Sphrantzes, p. 78, has him on a horse, and Barbaro says he hanged himself, p. 68. Doukas, p. 224, has him killed by two Turks who did not recognise him, p. 232 later bringing the head to Mehmet, whose skin was peeled off and filled with straw. Sphrantzes, p. 81, has embroidered shoes. See Runciman, *Fall*, pp. 143–4.

100 Runciman, *Fall*, p. 152.

101 Doukas, pp. 234–5.

102 Giovanni Cornellino, from Jones, *Siege*, p. 135.

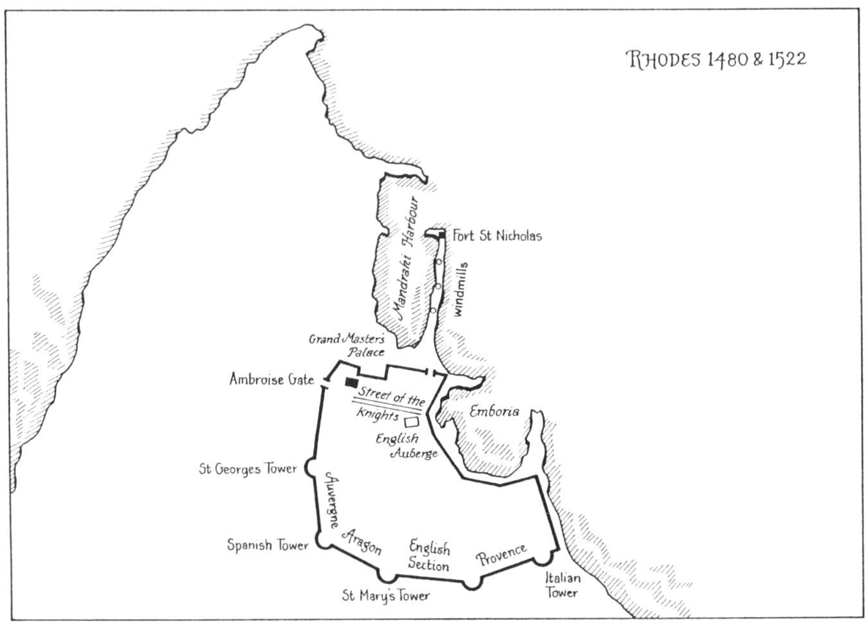

Both Rhodes and Malta were well defended islands held in turn by the last great military crusading order, the Knights Hospitallers. Rhodes, with its position near the coast of Asia Minor, blocked the sea route around the fringe of the Mediterranean coast, and had become a thorn in the sultan's flesh. The Knights had moved there in the early fourteenth century, with assistance from Genoa. It is said that the town of Rhodes was captured by the ploy of dressing in sheepskins and entering with returning flocks. One of the main harbours is still called Mandraccio, or the sheep-fold. The Knights had turned the island into a fortress base for their naval activities, making attacks on Moslem shipping. The career of a Knight came now to include a period of service in the galleys. Each of the eight Langues, or 'tongues', English, Spanish and so on, built its own auberge; their fortified houses still dominate the incline within the old city, known as the Street of the Knights. Each langue also defended its own tower and sector of the city walls, such as the English Tower in the south.[103]

Rhodes underwent two great sieges: the first in 1480, when the Knights saw off their Turkish attackers, and the second in 1522, when the Knights were ejected once again, and had to seek new quarters. The 1480 siege was not the first attack made against the Knights: in 1440 the Egyptians had lost twelve of the seventeen ships they sent against the island; and again in 1444 they called off a siege after forty days.

Peter d'Aubusson, the hero of the 1480 siege, himself left behind an

103 See Brockman, *The Two Sieges*; Luttrell, 'The Hospitallers'.

The Street of the Knights, Rhodes

account of the events.[104] He had been born in France, and fought for Charles VII against the Swiss, coming to Rhodes at the age of twenty-one, where he joined the langue of Auvergne, becoming its prior, and later Grand Master of the whole order. At one point during the siege, he was hit in the head by a cannon splinter, and only saved from death by his helmet, while the man standing next to him was killed. This was only one of several wounds received by d'Aubusson.

104 Brockman, pp. 58–60.

Attack on the tower of St Nicholas, Rhodes, 1480

After the siege of Constantinople, Mehmet sought to come to terms with the Knights on Rhodes, but without success. An attack was planned, and landings were made in 1479, but the Moslems were driven off, only to return in force in 1480. 600 Knights held the island, with some 1,500 mercenaries and other troops. They were well provisioned, with grain, oil, wine, cheese, salt meat, altogether enough for two years. Even so, the great Turkish fleet engendered fear, as they watched it approach: 'the sea was covered with sails as far as the eye could see'.[105]

105 Brockman, p. 66.

The Turks landed, and began to set up their guns and engines. They offered terms to the Christians, as had to be done under Islamic law, but did not even receive the courtesy of a reply at this early stage in proceedings. One ship from Sicily managed to run the blockade, and bring in welcome food and reinforcements. A heavy bombardment made an impact, within days several towers and the Grand Master's palace were in ruins. The Italian, Giacometti de Curti, in a letter written to his brother shortly after the siege, said that the ground trembled under his feet.[106] The famous mole, now marked by three picturesque windmills, was used as part of the defence, with a trench dug along its top. St Nicholas was supposedly seen riding along the mole on a white horse. A deserter from the Turks, Master George, reported that they had sixteen large guns, and twenty-two stone-throwing engines. Later he advised the Christians where to site their main guns; these sites were immediately made targets by the Turks, and the Knights decided that Master George was betraying them to show the Turks where to aim. Whether or not this was the case, the unfortunate Master George was hanged.[107]

The Tower of St Nicholas was badly cracked, and chosen as the target for an attempt by storm in June. The defenders used every available weapon to hold off the Turks: guns, crossbows, Greek Fire. They succeeded in blowing up one Turkish trireme. In the end the attack was called off, and the Moslems decided to switch their attention to the southern walls, which the Grand Master had done his best to repair and strengthen. They laid down such a heavy bombardment, that the only safe place within the walls was in cellars.

A belfry was brought up against the mole, and from 13th June there was a new non-stop attack for four days. The Turks then constructed a bridge from the shore to the mole, with a swing pontoon aimed again at St Nicholas, but the Christians destroyed it with their guns. Several successful sorties were made, and a group of Italians returned with heads, which these civilised westerners had taken, and which were fixed like trophies on the towers. The Turkish attack on 27th July was decisive: it was held off, and the Turks fled, the sultan's standard being captured in the pursuit. 'There were corpses all over the city, on the walls, in the ditch, in the enemy stockades, and in the sea'. Of the fourteen British Knights in Rhodes, seven had been killed.[108]

In the period between the two sieges of Rhodes, the defences were repaired and strengthened. By 1522 Villiers de L'Isle Adam had become Grand Master, and Suleiman the Magnificent was now sultan. Adam had been born in Beauvais, and been a captain in the Genoese galleys; he was elected Grand Master in 1521, at the age of fifty-seven. His opponent,

106 Brockman, p. 67.
107 Brockman, p. 82.
108 On the 1480 siege, Brockman, pp. 76–90; on the belfry and the corpses, p. 88.

The defences at Rhodes looking towards the English sector

Suleiman, was Mehmet II's grandson, and the architect of tremendous Ottoman advances in Europe. Rhodes seemed but one further minor gain, when he demanded its surrender in 1522.

The sectors of the wall held by the Knights of England and Aragon were the focus of the new siege, to which the Turks brought a far larger number of cannons, indicative of the direction of siege warfare in this late period. The situation inside Rhodes was not helped by some internal squabbling, when some young Knights set about a group of slaves returning from the walls, and killed twenty of them. Early in September the English Tower was brought down by a mine, though the attacks which tried to take advantage of it were held off. Before the end of the month the Tower of Aragon suffered a similar fate, but this time was captured, only to be recovered.

Throughout the siege the women in the city played an important rôle: carrying gunpowder up to the walls, helping to lug guns, bringing up food and water, and nursing the wounded. The mistress of an English Knight (Knights were supposed to be celibate), when her lover was killed, put their children to death, donned his armour, and fought on the walls till she was herself killed. Rhodes fell when the citizens of the town pressed the Knights to surrender. Suleiman was able to enter on 27th December. By the agreement the Knights were allowed to leave the island and seek a new home.[109]

109 On the 1522 siege, Brockman, pp. 128–53.

The siege of Rhodes, 1480

Malta

The Knights who left Rhodes were eventually given new accomodation in Malta by the Holy Roman Emperor Charles V, in 1530. The comparison with their former home was not a happy one. Francesco Balbi, the Spanish arquebusier who was at the siege, says that when they saw Malta the Knights 'wept, remembering Rhodes'. Balbi was among the Spaniards stationed in St Michael's fort in Malta, and very soon after the siege wrote 'a true account of everything that happened from day to day in the siege, as I myself saw it'.[110] The Knights found Malta barren and rocky, but after their failure to hold Rhodes, they had little alternative other than to accept the new offer. They received a cold reception from the Maltese nobility, whom the Knights in turn decided were not sufficiently aristocratic to be awarded Knightly status within the order. In the siege, however, the ordinary local population fought with great bravery alongside the Knights, in defence of their Christian religion and their homes. Malta did possess two excellent harbours, and the Knights chose to make their headquarters not at the capital Mdina, but in the small fishing village of Birgu beside the best harbour in Malta, Grand Harbour.

By 1565, Suleiman the Magnificent, the conqueror of Rhodes, was over seventy, a great ruler of a vast empire. Despite their removal from Rhodes, the Knights continued to plague Moslem shipping in the Mediterranean. Commander Romegas had recently made one such attack, provoking Suleiman's anger. He called Malta 'that cursed rock', and saw the Knights as 'those sons of dogs'.[111] He determined now to concentrate his vast resources on taking the tiny island; Malta's hopes of survival looked slim indeed. Suleiman sent to the task two of his leading commanders: Mustapha Pasha to lead the land forces, and Piali Pasha to lead the navy. The sultan ordered his ally, the vastly experienced corsair Dragut, king of Tripoli, to join the invasion force. Dragut had raided Malta half a dozen times in the past, and knew its layout well. Suleiman ordered his commanders 'to work together in harmony', but even great sultans cannot always get what they want. Suleiman's aims had become more grandiose with the years. Vienna had not succumbed, but he had not given up hope of Islamic domination of western Europe, and saw Malta as the base for an attack on Sicily, and then Italy, till 'we should extend our sway to the limits of the known world'.[112]

Malta was commanded by the venerable Grand Master of the Knights, Jean Parisot de la Valette, born in 1494 in Provence. He had joined the

110 On Malta, see Bradford, *The Great Siege*. The quote is from Balbi, pp. 12, 189.
111 Suleiman's words from Bradford, pp. 14, 18.
112 Suleiman quotes from Balbi, p. 33.

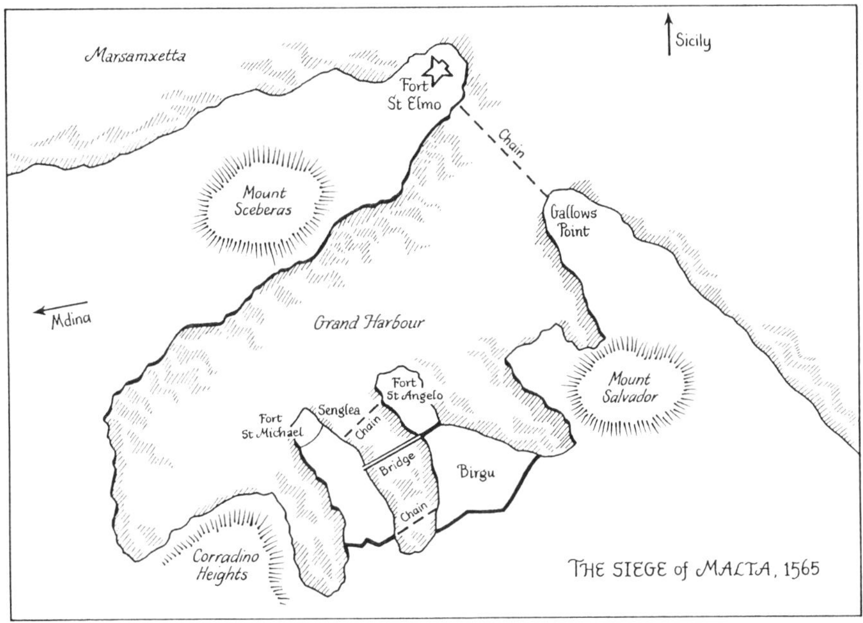

Knights at the age of twenty, and had never returned home. Valette had been taken prisoner by the Moslems in 1541, and become a slave in the galleys for a year, until released in an exchange deal. When twenty-eight he had fought in defence of Rhodes. He was a tall and severe man, marked by a hard life, who had become Grand Master in 1557. Yet during the siege, he would walk about his fortress accompanied by a jester, brought to the island by one of the recently arrived Knights. The jester was expected to perform a useful function, and ran messages, but he also kept Valette amused with merry tales, though, says Balbi, there was little to laugh at. Valette had done much to improve the defences since his election as Grand Master. He proved an even tougher opponent for the Moslems than his valiant predecessors. He was capable and shrewd, and had laid in considerable store of provisions, filling the underground chambers with grain, and collecting water in clay bottles. He even had great piles of earth, a relatively precious commodity in Malta, dug up and brought inside the defences, ready to fill any breaches. Houses which would give the Moslems aid or hinder Christian movement, were demolished, and Christian prisoners in the cells were released to help with the defence.[113]

The great Moslem fleet left Constantinople in March: 181 ships and 30,000 men including 6,000 Janissaries. They arrived at Malta in May after various delays. Realising how difficult it would be to obtain necessities on the island, they brought hides, sacks, tents, powder and shot, lead, ropes,

113 On Valette, Bradford, pp. 29–35.

spades, picks, shovels, iron bars, wood, cannons, raisins, dates, honey and oil.[114]

Piali Pasha believed that he needed control of Marsamxetta Harbour in order to shelter his fleet, so it was decided to begin the siege by attacking the star-shaped fort of St Elmo on the imposing headland between the two great inlets of Marsamxetta Harbour and Grand Harbour. This appeared on the face of it to be a simple task, St Elmo being a small fort, cut off from the other defences and overlooked by the heights of Mount Sceberas, but it proved to be a fatal decision. The capture of St Elmo could be no more than a preliminary skirmish. Victory would depend upon taking the two main defences of Senglea and Birgu, which lay on parallel headlands jutting into Grand Harbour. St Elmo proved a hard nut to crack, and delayed other operations for a vital period. The fort was well provisioned, with biscuit, wine, cheese, salt pork, vegetables, oil, vinegar, and even cattle which had been kept it its ditch. The Knights denied the enemy fresh water from a nearby pool, by throwing salt in it. The defenders performed feats of courage almost impossible to envisage, fighting on under a tremendous bombardment, even the badly wounded refusing to abandon their posts. A member of the garrison had to be almost dead to drop out of the fighting. They sent one message back to Valette: 'Do not send further reinforcements, since they are no more than dead men', but still on several occasions volunteer relief forces crossed the water to St Elmo and almost certain death.[115] At one point the younger Knights in St Elmo requested permission to abandon the hopeless defence, but Valette refused, appealing to their honour, so they fought on.

Only late in the day, after the arrival of Dragut, did the Turks take steps which were vital to the capture of St Elmo. Now at last they cut off the route taken by reinforcements from across the water, by setting up a new battery. An earthwork in front of St Elmo, the ravelin, was also captured, and the Turks then built a mound, or cavalier, behind it on which were placed guns aimed directly into the fort. Balbi says there were twenty-four large guns, and the Turks fired more frequently than was the Christian practice. The attack on 16th June 'seemed like the end of the world'.[116]

The defenders kept to their task. They made great use of fire weapons, including Greek Fire in pots, exploding bullets, and fire hoops which caused havoc by catching alight the Moslem robes. Dragut the corsair had said: 'I have felt in this island the shadow of the wing of death'.[117] While supervising a new trench, he was hit by a rock splinter from a cannon shot, and wounded severely in the head. He was saved from immediate death by

114 On provisions, Balbi, pp. 33, 39, 117.
115 Bradford, pp. 109, 236–7.
116 Balbi, on 24 guns, and end of the world, pp. 62, 81.
117 Bradford, p. 125.

his turban, but survived only a few days. The loss of his experience and advice was a severe blow to Turkish hopes.

Time and again, against impossible odds, the garrison of St Elmo held off storm attempts. Thousands of Turks were killed in the desperate attempts to scale the walls, in face of a barrage from cannons and handguns. The defenders fought to the last, blocking breaches with anything that came to hand: mattresses, blankets, old sails soaked in sea water. By the end of June, with the new battery preventing further reinforcement, the fate of the garrison was sealed. Balbi says that by 22nd June there was not a single officer left alive in the fort, and only about a hundred fighting men altogether. Confession was made by men 'who know that the next day will be their last on earth', to two priests who had stayed in the fort throughout. The bell in the fort was tolled. Even on the last day there was a desperate struggle before the Turks finally broke in on 23rd June. A few Maltese leaped into the sea and escaped, and a few prisoners were taken by the corsairs, but otherwise all were slaughtered. Knights' heads were placed on stakes, facing their comrades in the forts across the water. Some bodies were beheaded and floated over the sea, fixed on crucifixes. But says Balbi, grimly, 'they had little reason to rejoice', and Valette showed no sign of weakening. He ordered that all the dogs in Birgu and Senglea be killed because of the noise they made at night, and because they consumed valuable food.[118]

Now the focus switched to the two major fortifications, and Mustapha Pasha doggedly began to move the guns to new sites. It is amazing that Malta held out so long without the arrival of the expected aid from outside. Ironically, before the siege began, the governor of Spanish Sicily, Don Garcia, had visited Malta, and offered to leave a force behind, but had been turned down by Valette, until they knew for certain what would be Suleiman's target. Once the siege had begun, it was obvious that Malta desperately needed relief from Sicily, not far away to the north. But now Don Garcia delayed and prevaricated. His motives are uncertain, probably his chief reason was fear of defeat in Malta, and its likely effect on Sicily. Days passed, weeks, and even months. A very small relief force did arrive, and with great good fortune, in foggy weather, managed to land unopposed and get through to Birgu. It consisted of only 700 men: useful, but not enough. Valette became convinced that the outcome would have to be decided without help from Don Garcia.

The two remaining fortifications stood on either side of what is now Dockland Creek: the fort of St Angelo on the tip of the headland behind the village of Birgu; and the fort of St Michael on Senglea. With St Elmo taken, Piali Pasha had finally been able to enter Marsamxetta Harbour. Now the Moslems tried the same trick used at Constantinople, dragging

118 Balbi on no officer, last day, little reason to rejoice; pp. 88, 89, 91.

ships overland to get them into Grand Harbour, whose main entrance was blocked with a chain. Within a few days some hundred ships were dragged across, but the effect proved less decisive than at Constantinople. Valette had a barrier built at the edge of the shore, on piles in the water, to block any landing. Entry to Dockyard Creek was still prevented by a chain across its neck, and guns made St Angelo impossible to attack directly. However, Senglea and French Creek were now vulnerable. The Turks sent men with axes to hack down the new barrier at the edge of the water, but they were met by strong Maltese swimmers, who won this strange aquatic conflict.

The bombardment on St Michael's began from the batteries established on nearby heights. Again the effect was murderous, showing the great impact of cannon by this period; part of the wall soon collapsed. The Turkish cannon power at Malta was probably greater than at any other siege we have witnessed. The impact of the weapon can hardly be better illustrated; breaches were made every time the Turks set up a new major battery, yet breaches could not always win sieges. It must be noted that the fire of the defenders, using guns from prepared positions behind the protection of walls, was even more murderous: more Turks died at Malta by far than Christians. The cannons of the Knights played a vital rôle in the next attack. Now they were in Grand Harbour, the Turks planned a landing against St Angelo, and sent ten ships loaded with a crack force of Janissaries. They were not aware of a battery placed at sea level below St Angelo, which had played no part in the siege until this point. As the ten ships headed towards land, the battery opened a deadly fire, which sank nine and drove away the tenth with the very first salvo. Not only did this halt the immediate threat, which was considerable, but it persuaded the Turks against further use of their fleet in Grand Harbour. Some Turks did swim ashore, to receive 'St Elmo's pay', that is, they were killed in revenge for the killings at St Elmo. Balbi took part in a sortie, which did hold on to a few prisoners in order to question them. He says documents and cannabis were found on the corpses.[119]

Nevertheless there was still much to fear, and St Michael and Birgu came under fire from the land. Slaves, chained in pairs, were made to build new stone barriers in the streets, to give some protection inside the fortifications, and many of these unfortunates were killed at the work. The defenders received information from Christian slaves among the Turks, who while pretending to shout abuse, gave news about Moslem shortages of men and powder.

The major bombardment of Senglea began in July. The delay in taking St Elmo, and the time needed to move the guns, had taken their toll of the days. The time had been well employed by Valette, in improving his defences by building inner walls. When the Turks breached the outer wall,

[119] Balbi, p. 117.

they found themselves entering a trap, caught in the space between two walls. Even so, the situation was desperate, and men prepared for inevitable death. On two occasions, Valette himself went armed, to defend a critical breach, once despite having been wounded in the leg by a splinter. His nephew Henry was killed during a sortie, but nothing seemed to daunt the fierce old man, who declared that 'if necessary we must bury ourselves beneath these ruins'. The bombardment was relentless, said Balbi: 'there was not a single safe place in Birgu or in St Michael'.[120]

The Turks constructed belfries. One of these was destroyed by novel means: secretly a hole was made in the wall, but the last stones were left in place. Then, when the tower had come close, the gap in the wall was opened, to reveal a cannon behind it, loaded with chain shot such as was used at sea to cut through masts. The tower was shot to pieces, and collapsed.[121] A second tower was captured by a sortie, and then used by the Knights against their enemy. An explosive device, which is perhaps best called a bomb, was thrown into the fortifications, but the defenders were quick enough to pick it up and throw it back, so that it exploded among the Turks, doing much damage.[122]

At a critical moment, the floating bridge, which had been constructed to allow communications between Birgu and Senglea, was ordered by Valette to be destroyed, so that the men in Senglea, like those in St Elmo before them, would know that there was no retreat. Both forts were under attack, and Balbi in St Michael described the Turkish storm attempt of 15th July, when the Turks came on in their scarlet, crimson and gold, weapons gleaming, men at the front reading from the Koran: 'they certainly made a fine sight, almost beautiful, if it had not been so dangerous'. Wine, water and bread were put on the walls, since defenders could not leave, even to eat and drink. Desperate measures had to be taken: gaps were filled as best they could, with earth wrapped in the cloaks of dead slaves. In the crisis at the Tower of Castille, Valette took up helmet and pike, and later snatched an arquebus from one of the soldiers, which he fired, calling 'let us all go and die there'.[123]

New hope was given to the Christians by a further error on the part of Mustapha Pasha, provoked by an attack made from Mdina. It clearly angered the Turks, because their camp was attacked, and the sick and wounded were slaughtered. Mustapha decided to turn aside from his main effort, and march on Mdina, which caused further delay, and proved fruitless. As the Turks approached the impressive site, the citizens of Mdina tried a classic ploy; everyone who could, peasants, the elderly, the wounded, and women, dressed in military costume, and paraded along the

120 On burying ourselves, Bradford, p. 184; on no safe place, Balbi, p. 126.
121 Bradford, pp. 185–6; Balbi, p. 155.
122 Bradford, p. 187.
123 On the fine sight, and going to die: Balbi, pp. 111, 144.

walls, so that the garrison looked much larger than in fact it was.[124] The trick seems to have worked, but surely only because Turkish morale by this time was low. Mustapha decided against the new attack, but time had been lost, and Turkish morale was further dented.

Knights from distant parts of Europe, including the unfortunately named Louis de Lastic, had not reached Malta in time to aid the defence, but had gone to the court of Don Garcia in Sicily to join the relief force. They pressed him to make a move, shaming him into action. Belated though it was, the arrival of the relief force was decisive. After yet more delays because of weather, the relief landed on 7th September. The Moslems were tricked into believing this force was larger than it was. An 'escape' was arranged by a slave, who gave the Turks false information on numbers.[125] On the same day as the landing, the Christians were able to stand on the walls in safety, for there was no one to fire on them.

The long summer, the high death rate, the determined resistance, problems with resources and health, had all taken their toll. The Turks began to embark. Even now all was not over, for Mustapha realised the actual size of the relief, and decided that, rather than return to Suleiman, he would disembark and fight. Some troops went ashore, but for most the heart had gone out of their fight. Landing again, after having boarded ship to escape the hell of Malta, must have seemed like the last straw. Some, including Mustapha himself, fought bravely, but they were defeated and retreated in some disorder to the ships. Many died in St Paul's Bay, leaving such a stench that it was some time before anyone could approach the place.

The siege was over. 'Never', says Balbi, 'I feel, did music sound so sweet to human ears as did the peal of our bells on this day'. Malta became a legend in Christendom, 'the island of heroes'.[126] Some 30,000 men had died there. When Suleiman received the news, he stamped in rage upon the unfortunate messenger; his dreams of world domination were ended. As for Valette, he lived to build a new city on Mount Sceberras, with a better position and better defences than those he had had to defend, a new city which was named after him as Valetta. Malta of the Knights survived until 1798, when it was taken by Napoleon, but its great moment had been in 1565, when the Moslem advance had been held. After Malta, came the Christian naval victory at Lepanto. The Ottomans settled for a lesser vision than that of Suleiman the Great. Medieval Europe under siege from barbarian Huns, vikings, Mongols, Tartars, Turks and many others, had emerged, not exactly unscathed, but in a form which is recognisable to modern eyes. Present day Europe was forged in the fires of medieval sieges.

124 On Mdina, Bradford, pp. 197–9; Balbi, p. 151.
125 Bradford, p. 168.
126 On music so sweet and the island of heroes; Balbi, p. 168; Bradford, p. 221.

CHAPTER NINE

Medieval Siege Weapons

Siege Towers

Siege towers, or belfries, were a common feature in major sieges throughout the middle ages; they were used by the Romans, and appear, for example, in the early medieval sieges at Paris and Verdun. Vitruvius claims that mobile towers were invented by Polydus, a Thessalian, for Alexander the Great; and that Ceras the Carthaginian made rams on platforms with wheels, and a cover protected by ox hides; at the very least it may be said that such structures were familiar to Vitruvius himself.[1] It may be, however, that most early structures were mobile rams, or 'cats', that is a roofed platform or hut, rather than a high tower with several platforms; but high towers were not unknown. Belfries required a good deal of planning and expenditure, and could normally only be produced by the wealthiest and greatest military leaders. Their usefulness continued throughout the middle ages, and they were, for example, used by John II at Breteuil in 1356, and taken by Henry V on his Agincourt campaign. The Turks also used siege towers against Constantinople in 1453, that made by Zagan Pasha being higher than the great wall of the city; and again towers appeared at Birgu during the siege of Malta, as late as 1565.

The functions of such towers were complex, and could vary considerably, for example, Richard the Lionheart dined in his tower at Messina, on his way to the Holy Land.[2] More commonly they had two basic purposes: to cover operations from within the lower reaches of the tower against the wall; and to provide a bridge from the upper storey, from which the top of the wall might be reached. Many other weapons might be employed from a belfry: mangonels and all kinds of throwing engines, crossbows and ordinary bows, spears and hurling weapons, but most commonly the tower gave cover to a ram at ground level, or even more usually covered mining operations. For example, towers at Tyre and Damietta contained stone-

1 Vitruvius, ii, pp. 343–4.
2 Ambroise, pp. 69–70; ed. Paris, col. 30, l. 1087.

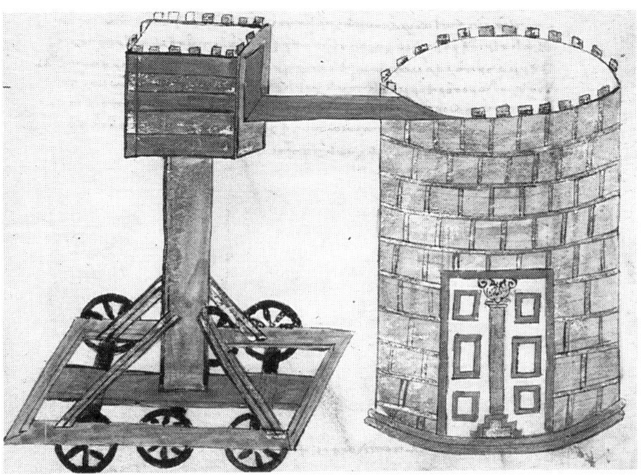

Bridge from a siege tower

throwing engines, and one at Durazzo held a ram; a tower at Nicaea was used to cover mining operations.

These belfries were normally made of wood, were wheeled, had several storeys, and were protected on the outer surface against fire and weapons, often with ox hides. The structures described by Abbo in use against Paris, were roofed towers made of oak, and had sixteen wheels.[3] At least some of these gave shelter to rams, which were tipped with metal, and operated by cords and chains. They were protected by deerskins, and held sixty men. Two of the vikings responsible for making these were hit by a balista, and thus 'suffered the fate they had prepared for us'.[4] Richer, describing the siege of Verdun, also says that oak was used, great oaks felled at the roots, and laid out on the ground. From these four beams of thirty feet in length were chosen to make a rectangular base, with other beams used as ties. A similar rectangle formed the top of the tower, top and bottom joined by transverse beams. There were several storeys, and again the lower one housed a ram, which was swung back and forth on ropes, and was sheathed in iron. Richer says that this engine was on three wheels, which allowed it to be manoevred.[5] William of Tyre, writing of a tower used during the crusades, also speaks of oak beams. James I of Aragon described a tower made for him at Majorca: it had two supports for each side, together with two beams to make it steady; there were two platforms, one half way up, and one at the top, to be used by crossbowmen and slingers. It was covered with hurdles. A tower used against Mahdia in 1390, had three storeys and wheels, and was constructed on a forty-foot square frame.[6]

3 Abbo, p. 30.
4 Abbo, p. 32.
5 Richer, ii, pp. 135–7; compare, i, p. 143.
6 William of Tyre, ed. Babcock and Krey, i, p. 159; ed. Huygens, i, p. 203: *machina*

A wheeled tower

The Anglo-Norman tower at Lisbon had collision mats, made of osiers, all round, to give it protection; ox hides were placed with the tails dangling, so that when water was poured from above, it dripped from the tails over the whole engine in order to put out fires. A tower at Sidon, in 1110, also had matting and fresh ox hides over it, and at Acre a tower was covered with skins soaked in vinegar and mud. Belfries made by Frederick Barbarossa in Italy were apparently covered in iron for protection, which must have considerably added to their cost. James I of Aragon described a tower which he had made on wheels, covered 'like a house' and pushed forward by poles; it was protected by three thicknesses of hurdles, with a roof of hurdles and brushwood, covered with earth, which he says was against the hits of stone-throwing engines. A Turkish tower in 1453 was protected by earth, by layers of bullock and camel hides inside and out, and by 'turrets and protective barricades on top'; the earth was used not only against fire, but also to soften the impact of cannon balls. We are also told that movement inside this tower was by ladders, which must have been normal. The description here makes the point that these ladders were concealed inside to protect the users, as if they were normally fixed outside.[7]

quercinis. James I, ed. Forster, i, p. 260; James I, ed. Casacuberta, i, III, p. 72: *lo castell de fust haura ii vases de cade una pert..e fer los ha ii solers*. On Mahdia, Tuchman, p. 473.

[7] On Lisbon, *De Expugnatione Lyxbonensi*, p. 147. On Sidon, Ibn al-Qalanisi in Gabrieli, p. 28. On Acre, Ibn al-Athir in Gabrieli, p. 198. On Italy, Otto of Freising, ed. Mierow, p.

One Anglo-Norman belfry at Lisbon was eighty-three feet high, and another even larger at ninety-five feet. A tower at Acre had five platforms, filled with soldiers; and the one at Ma'arrat had knights on the top platform preparing to cross over the bridge, as well as Everard the Huntsman blowing loudly on his horn to encourage them. The towers at Tyre and Acre were forty, fifty and sixty cubits high; a cubit is usually said to be six feet, which would make the largest an impossible 360 feet, suggesting, perhaps, some exaggeration here; but this may be the Egyptian cubit, which makes the highest about 103 feet, and seems possible. In any case, towers obviously could be large, since one of the main considerations was that they should overlook the walls, and at Tyre it was said: 'one could look down into the city below'.[8]

Such a large structure, high enough to at least equal the height of the wall being attacked, needed a considerable quantity of wood, and this might be difficult to obtain in some regions. In the siege of Banyas, in the Holy Land, the Damascene allies of the Christians sent for 'tall beams of great size', which had been laid aside in advance for the purpose. These were then dressed by carpenters, and joined together with iron nails. Timber often had to be brought from considerable distances. At Jerusalem, a local Christian told the crusaders of a supply of suitable wood some seven miles away, which, although not of the most desirable kind, was brought back on camels and wagons. Because of such difficulties, it was sometimes necessary to improvise. At Jerusalem wood from houses was used, and at Tyre the masts and rudders of beached ships; Amaury I also used ships' masts for his engines at Alexandria. The structures at Jerusalem had to be made from small pieces of wood joined together. Another answer, if planning was careful, was to have ready-made structures brought from elsewhere: thus Richard the Lionheart brought machines from Sicily and Cyprus to Acre, the king and his nobles themselves unloading the vital parts of the tower, and carrying them about a mile: 'not without perspiration'. The crusaders, in the early stages of the movement, were awed by the height of the walls they had to deal with, but responded by making towers of a size which in turn amazed the Moslems. Richard the Lionheart's tower at Acre had steps to climb to the top; a tower at Tyre had five platforms, and one at Damietta had seven. In the West, John II's belfry at Breteuil in 1356, consisted of three storeys, with room for 200 fighting men on each platform, and loopholes for their bows; it was also manned by knights and squires, and was padded with leather against bolts and stones.[9]

302. James I, ed. Forster, i, p. 140; James, ed. Casacuberta, i, III, p. 52: *E axi con el anava, fahian de pals forcati e ficats . . . axi con manera de casa.* On 1453, Sphrantzes, p. 52.

[8] On Lisbon, *De Expugnatione Lyxbonensi*, pp. 135, 139. On Acre, Ibn al-Athir in Gabrieli, p. 198; on size, p. 32. On Everard, *Gesta Francorum*, p. 78.

[9] On Banyas, the camels, and Alexandria, see William of Tyre, ed. Babcock & Krey, i, pp. 109, 351, ii, p. 337. On Tyre, Ibn al-Qalanisi in Gabrieli, p. 35. On Richard,

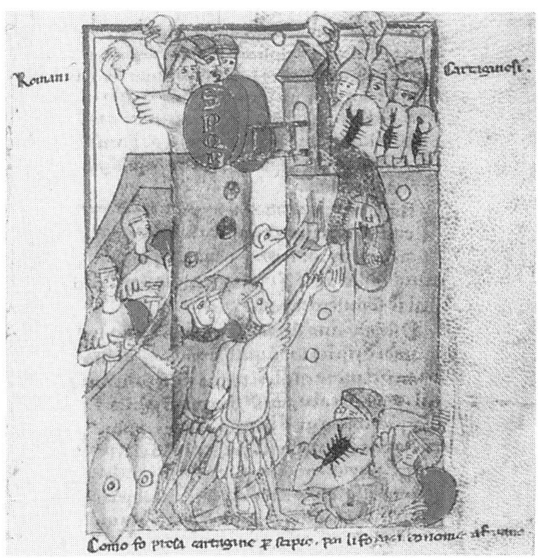

A belfry in action

Skill was obviously required in the design and building of the great towers, and it was one of the major tasks of the engineers, so often employed in siege warfare. At Nicaea, on the First Crusade, a Lombard specialist was given the task, because of his 'marvelous skill', and was well paid for his efforts. At Jerusalem, shortly afterwards, men with axes and carpenters had to shape timber and hew it, boring holes and fitting planks together. Sailors, used to working in wood on board ship, were often useful in siege construction, as at Jerusalem where they felled the trees, smoothed the timber, and fitted the beams together for the engines, with the speed of experienced carpenters. Frederick II thought highly of the value of the engineer, Calamandrinus, and had him kept in chains, so it is hardly surprising that the engineer, when promised his freedom, together with a house and a wife, went over to the enemy. King John employed Master Urric in Normandy in 1201: 'to make engines', and in 1229 we find St Louis paying several masters to look after his engines; one of his masters of engines, the Gascon Jean de Mézos, was knighted in 1254. Engineers were well paid, and often featured in royal accounts. Those working the largest of the engines for the crusaders at Carcassonne, were paid a massive twenty-one pounds a day, presumably to cover the teams working under them. At Caerlaverock, Edward I paid Master Richard for making a cat and a belfry; and John de la Dolyve and Robert de Woodhouse, for their part in

Ambroise, ed. Hubert & La Monte, p. 201; and on Breteuil, Froissart ed. Luce, iv, pp. 194–5: *un grant berfroit a trois estages, que on menoit a roes . . . en cascun estage pooient bien entrer deus cens hommes . . . breteskies et cuiries . . . en ce bierefroi entrerent grant fuison de bons chevaliers et escuiers.*

making engines. The importance of engineers is also demonstrated by the responsibilities which were given to them. For instance, Reginald the engineer was delegated by Edward I to assemble his whole siege train at Berwick in 1304. James I of Aragon wrote of his own engineers, including Nicoloso, who made a trebuchet and a 'castle of wood' in Majorca. The value of these men is further shown by the efforts of the enemy to shoot them down. There was, for example, great rejoicing at Lincoln, when an engineer on a tower was hit and killed.[10]

The career of Master Bertram has been reconstructed, and will serve as a useful indication of how such a man might advance.[11] He was born in about 1225, and became a royal engineer for Henry III of England. In an early record, Bertram *le Engynnur* was one of six such men, rewarded by the king for his services. By 1276 we find him in England, employed in making engines at the Tower of London. He himself took the trouble to go and choose the oaks from Odiham, which were to be used for his work, and had them brought to London by water. In 1278 we find him supervising the engines at the Tower, and bringing oak, beech, and elm from Reading, Windsor, and Fulham. He was also in charge of the engines at sieges in Wales, at Dolwyddelan, and in 1283 at Castell-Y-Bere, when he is referred to as *machinator*, and *ingeniator*. Master Bertram is also now known to have designed and built some of Edward I's earlier Welsh castles, before his death in 1284.

The men on board the towers were mainly soldiers who could shoot or hurl missiles, particularly archers, but one also finds knights, especially when it was time to try and cross the bridge from the tower to the wall, as for example from Godfrey of Bouillon's tower at Jerusalem, with its draw-bridge on top. Crossbowmen were the main fighting force aboard the Christian tower when it was pushed forward against the Estonians. Men were also needed to operate the various throwing engines which might be carried by the tower, such as the mangonel on the roof of a tower during the Third Crusade, or to operate the ram if it had one, or to dig the mine under cover of the tower.[12]

Towers were generally built on the spot, by individual leaders for their

10 On the Lombard, William of Tyre, ed. Babcock & Krey, i, p. 164; on Jerusalem, Orderic Vitalis, v, p. 164; William of Tyre, ed. Huygens, i, p. 400: sailors: *multam habebant experientiam*. On Calamandrinus, Kantorowicz, p. 464, and see ch. 6 n. 42. On Urric, and St Louis see Contamine, p. 106, and on the latter, Taylor, pp. 291–4. Caerlaverock, p. xv, and see ch. 6. n. 29. On Reginald, see Prestwich, *Edward I*, p. 501. On Nicoloso, James I, ed. Forster, i, p. 257; ed. Casacuberta, i, III, p. 72. On Lincoln, *Guillaume le Maréchal*, in *EHD*, iii, p. 89; and Carpenter, p. 39.

11 Taylor, 'Master Bertram'; calls *machinator* and *ingeniator*, pp. 301, 314.

12 On Jerusalem, William of Tyre, ed. Babcock & Krey, i, p. 367; Raymond of Aguilers, (English), p. 127. On Estonians, Henry of Livonia, ed. Brundage, p. 105. On the tower, Ambroise, ed. Hubert & La Monte, p. 155; compare Durazzo 1081, William of Apulia, iv, pp. 249–51.

own forces, and there might be an element of competition over the size and ingenuity of one's own machine. Sometimes the structure could be put together quickly, at Antioch it seems to have been done in a few days, at Banyas 'it seemed as if a tower had been suddenly erected in the very midst of the place'; but often it took valuable time, eleven weeks at Tyre to make two towers and a ram. The tower built at Dorpat in 1224, was made from large trees as high as the fort, and took eight days to make; the same period was required by James I of Aragon's engineer, Nicoloso, to build a tower in Majorca. According to an Italian, the Turks in 1453 built one tower overnight, taking only four hours, so that it appeared next morning: 'on the lip of the ditch'. One suspects that some prefabrication was employed here; in any case, the writer says that it would have taken the Christians a month to build such a tower.[13]

Towers often were built in advance and transported, as by Richard I to Acre. Edward I had a tower made of wood and hides brought to Bothwell, and then transported to Stirling on thirty carts. For Wales in 1287, the same king provided an escort of twenty cavalry and 450 infantry, to bring an engine on four-wheel wagons dragged by forty oxen, or sixty oxen over the more difficult terrain. St Louis in 1242, used 1,600 carts to carry his engines and provisions, and they stretched back over three miles of the highway. A tower at Orléans, during the Hundred Years War, required twenty-six carts to carry it, which given the similarity to the number required for a large engine by Edward I, and the probable reliability of the two sets of figures, provides some indication of the amount of material used.[14]

Movement into position of these enormous structures was a major problem. For them to be effective, they had to be manoevred as close as possible to the walls. The Turks in 1453 dropped earth and rubbish into the ditch to fill it, and also specially made hurdles. For all the ingenuity with wheels and pulleys, this was always a weakness of the belfry. The men having to move the bulk forward inch by inch were open to attack from the walls. It was also difficult to move such towers on anything but even ground, and only too often, after all the effort of construction and pushing, the towers would get stuck in wet ground. At Carlisle, for example, the ground was marshy, and men had to haul out the engines with ropes. It was important not only to fill the moat, but also to make a flat way over which the engine could be pushed. James of Aragon speaks of making a special track, which was greased for ease of movement. This ingenious contraption also made

13 For Antioch, Banyas and prefabrication, see William of Tyre, ed. Babcock & Krey, i, p. 210; ii, p. 109; i, p. 360. On Tyre, Ibn al-Qalanisi in Gabrieli, p. 32. On Dorpat, Henry of Livonia, ed. Brundage, p. 223. On Nicoloso, James I, ed. Forster, i, p. 259; ed. Casacuberta, i, III, p. 72: *a viii jorns*. On 1453, Barbaro, p. 52.

14 On Acre, Ambroise, ed. Hubert & La Monte, p. 201. Prestwich, *Edward I*, pp. 493–4. On St Louis, Matthew Paris, ed. Giles, i, p. 422. On Orléans, Payne-Gallwey, p. 314.

use of rings driven in to the ground near the walls, and the use of a pulley and cables, so that the workers were moving away from the danger, as they pulled the tower towards its objective, though the device seems to have failed. James blamed his engineer for this, because he insisted on using the tower before screens for proper protection had been put in place. James wanted to get mats from his ships to hang down from beams at the top, against stones. They heaved on the ropes, as sailors do, but the engine stuck half way. James says it was thirsty work, and that he himself had never drunk so much wine and water in one day. The enemy engines hit the tower ten times during the rest period for food, and over a hundred times during the night, so that it had to be pulled back to safety.[15]

Siege towers were also made of wood, and for all the covering with hides and so on, they were vulnerable to fire, and often were destroyed in this way. There was also a limit to how solid, and therefore heavy, such towers could be, and it is clear that they were not the most stable of structures, so that another weakness was attack from engines throwing heavy stones. There are many examples of towers collapsing, and thus endangering the lives of those on board. At Verdun, an engine was rocked by attaching hooks to it and pulling, so that the men inside fell out, to be attacked and killed. Odo I's siege of Montboyau, against Fulk Nerra, saw the collapse of a great wooden tower, simply from faulty construction, leading to the death by crushing of those inside; the tower was later burnt in triumph by the citizens. A belfry used by the Swordbrothers in the Baltic region, simply blew over in the gusty northern winds. A tower at Nicaea fell apart under the weight of rocks thrown on to it; the joints in the structure gave way, and all the men inside were killed. At Arsuf, Baldwin's tower was knocked right over and wrecked, and a hundred men in it were either injured or killed. Once on fire, a belfry became a death trap, and efforts to douse fires were an important part of the job of those on board, sometimes bravely risking their lives by climbing up to put out the flames. Fire could, on occasion, simply rush up through the storeys, and consume all within. Although the equation has not often been made, it seems likely that the development of effective cannons tolled the death knell of siege towers. The compact size and great impact of the cannon, made it a very useful defence weapon. Wooden towers had little hope of surviving close fire from cannons, as happened at Malta, when a hole was opened in the wall so that a cannon could destroy a belfry, using chain shot such as was used in naval warfare to bring down masts.[16]

15 On 1453, Leonard of Chios in Jones, p. 18. On Carlisle, *Lanercost*, in *EHD*, iii, p. 266. On Lisbon, *De Expugnatione Lyxbonensi*, p. 136. James I, ed. Forster, i, pp. 261–5.

16 On Verdun, Richer, ii, p. 139. On Montboyau, Halphen, p. 43. On Nicaea and Arsuf, William of Tyre, ed. Babcock & Krey, i, pp. 159, 435; compare Dobrel's Fort in Henry of Livonia ed. Brundage, p. 127. On Malta, Bradford, pp. 185–6; Balbi p. 155 and above ch. 8 n. 121.

It was often necessary to fill a moat or ditch, in order to get the tower to the wall, and this is one of the most frequently witnessed scenes in a siege. At Montreuil-Bellay, in the 1150s, Geoffrey V of Anjou brought the citizens from the nearby fair at Saumur, and used them to drop stones into the deep ditch. The wooden towers were then pushed forward, and Greek Fire thrown from them. At Jerusalem, Count Raymond and the other leaders offered a penny for every three stones dropped into the ditch; and at Acre, a woman who was helping to fill the ditch, was severely wounded, and knowing herself to be dying, made a last request that her body be thrown into the ditch to help with the work.[17]

The effort to move a tower towards the wall is a crucial feature in many sieges. At Lisbon, on the Second Crusade, the progress of the tower is described in detail, by the priest who probably himself made a sermon of dedication from on board the new structure. It was moved forward ninety feet on the first day. On the second day it was moved on further, and also at right angles in order to approach the wall near the Porto do Ferro. There were archers and crossbowmen on board, and overnight it was protected by a force which included a hundred knights. Behind it came a smaller engine, a cat or penthouse, made of woven osiers, in which were young men from Ipswich, who had to keep it in position.[18]

Pushing the tower forward was a dangerous business, and usually the task of fighting men; at Ma'arrat, for example, knights gave a hand. At Jerusalem poles were attached to the belfry, for the men pushing it to grasp. The towers, of course, possessed wheels; those at both Ma'arrat and Jerusalem had four; but they still needed even ground. At Laon, Hugh Capet employed a skilled engineer to build a tower, but the effort was wasted because they could not pull it up the hill. It was said of the tower at Jerusalem that it could not operate up and down slopes: 'always needing level ground if it were to be pulled along'. At Damietta, the Franks chose a poor position for their tower, being unable to approach the walls because the incline was too steep. At Shrewsbury, when King Stephen constructed a belfry, and aimed it against the gate rather than the wall, fires were lit, so that it could be pushed forward under cover of the smoke.[19]

In the earlier middle ages, the belfry was apparently chiefly used to reach the top of the wall, and to cover a ram. In the later middle ages, its most

17 On the fair, John of Marmoutier, p. 217: *et suppositis rotulis tracte muris admoventur . . . Hi vero qui in turribus ligneis erant, sagittarum granine premissa, grecum jaculantur ignem.* On Jerusalem, *Gesta Francorum*, p. 91. On Acre, Ambroise, ed. Hubert & La Monte, p. 163.

18 *De Expugnatione Lyxbonensi*: *cattus Waliscus*. Again the measurement is in cubits and therefore uncertain.

19 For Ma'arrat, *Gesta Francorum*, p. 78. For Jerusalem William of Tyre, ed. Babcock & Krey, i, p. 362; Orderic Vitalis, v, p. 164: *Talis enim machina nequit ad decliva conduci, nec contra montuosa dirigi, se semper aequam expectat planiciem ut possit conduci.* On Laon, Richer, ii, pp. 175, 179 & n. On Shrewsbury, John of Worcester in Stevenson, ii, pt. 1, p. 357.

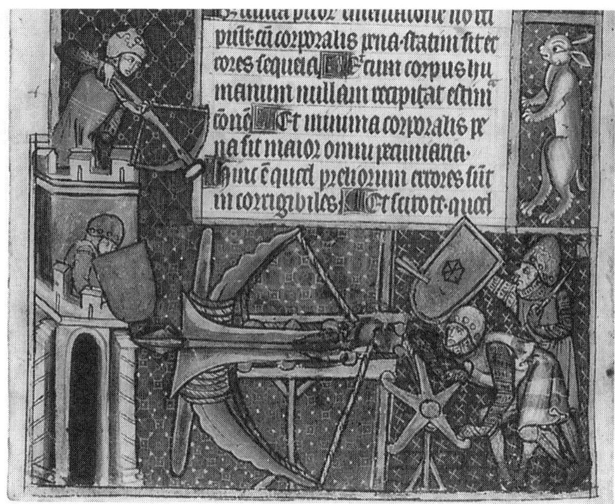

A balista operated by winch

common use was to cover mining operations, as for example in the north against Dobrel's fort. The Rigan tower against Loal was built: 'so that they could dig at the fort from below, and fight more readily with the enemy from the top'. On the northern crusade, indeed, the tower seems usually to have been pushed not only up to the wall, but actually dug into it, no doubt because of the relatively primitive fortifications found there. Two of the three belfries, which James I of Aragon made at Majorca, were used for mining operations. The Moslems at Constantinople used their towers to cover mining: 'the Turks inside the tower were excavating earth, and casting it into the ditch, and kept on heaping up earth in this way'.[20]

Hurling and Shooting Engines

Hurling and shooting engines, like siege towers, were well known from Roman times onward, some from even earlier. The *balista*, for example, was a kind of large crossbow. Its operation depended on the tension created by drawing back a string, exactly as a bow is drawn; the larger the machine, the more advanced the machinery for drawing back the string had to be. Such machines could also be operated by making springs out of twisted ropes, creating force by torsion, as had been done in antiquity. *Balistae* were commonly used to shoot arrow-like missiles or bolts, and were only useful against personnel, not against walls. The ancient world possessed the mathematical and mechanical knowledge to develop the mechanisms

[20] On Loal, Henry of Livonia ed. Brundage, pp. 127–8. James I, ed. Forster, i, p. 140. On Constantinople, Barbaro, p. 53.

necessary to operate machines, and to use them with accuracy. At least sometimes, they made models to test out the operation. Throughout our period, *balistae* were known and used, for example early on they appear in the hands of Arabs, Franks and Saxons, but whether torsion was employed is not clear.[21]

Often it is difficult to know from the sources, when a structure is mentioned, whether it was a siege tower or a form of stone-throwing engine, or indeed some other machine, since the words 'engine' and 'machine' were often used indiscriminately. Towers were of great significance, mainly for breaching, mining or climbing walls, but stone-throwing engines were much more common. They varied from the small machine, which was chiefly used against people, to large mangonels, and the prince of the stone-throwers, the trebuchet, which was mainly employed in breaking through walls. The early and common types may have used torsion from twisted ropes, which created a spring, or tension as in a bow. The trebuchet, which was a later development, worked on the principle of a pivot operated by a heavy counterweight. But, as with siege towers, so with throwing engines, skill was required in design and manufacture. Joinville tells us that the count of Eu possessed a model engine, whose capacity he demonstrated at the dinner table, breaking pots and glasses with it. We hear of something similar in England, where the sons of Edward I were given model castles, and the young Alfonso received a miniature siege engine.[22]

Chroniclers were not always precise in their use of terms for the types of throwing machine, but various names appear in our sources. Abbo refers to catapults and *fundae*. Anselm de Ribaut was killed at Arqah by a stone from a *tormentum* which hit him on the head. At Jerusalem there were *tormenta* and *petraria*, at Acre there were *mangonelli* on the roof of a Christian tower. The Moslems used *balistae* at Nicaea on the walls to throw stones, at Jerusalem to throw combustible materials, and at Ma'arrat to hurl beehives. There are many other names used for the same or similar weapons, such as fonevols, springalds, paterells, brigoles, algarradas, calabres, chaabla, manganas, and *fundae*, and in chroniclers' usage these terms often seem to be interchangeable.[23]

The catapult, or *balista*, was normally made on the same principle as a crossbow, though even in this case medieval chroniclers could use the term

21 On engines in the ancient world, see Oman, ii, pp. 43–54; Soedel and Foley, 'Ancient Catapults'. I am grateful to Ted Crawford for drawing this article to my attention.

22 On the count of Eu, Joinville, ed. Evans, p. 177; on Edward I's sons, Prestwich, *Edward I*, p. 127.

23 On Arqah, Jerusalem, Nicaea and Ma'arrat, see Raymond of Aguilers (Latin), p. 109: *de lapide tormenti in capite percussus est*; pp. 149, 43, 97. On Acre, Ambroise, ed. Hubert & La Monte, p. 155. On the combustibles, Imad ad-Din in Gabrieli, p. 173. On others, e.g. *Chanson de Croisade*, p. 66: *peireiras e calabres*; James I, ed. Casacuberta, i, III, p. 74: *fenevol, algarrades*; ii, VIII, p. 52: *brigola, fonevol*. Abbo, pp. 28, 22: *balista, funde*; p. 42, ll. 364/5: *mangana quae proprio vulgi libitu vocitantur/Saxa quibus jaciunt tormentorum*.

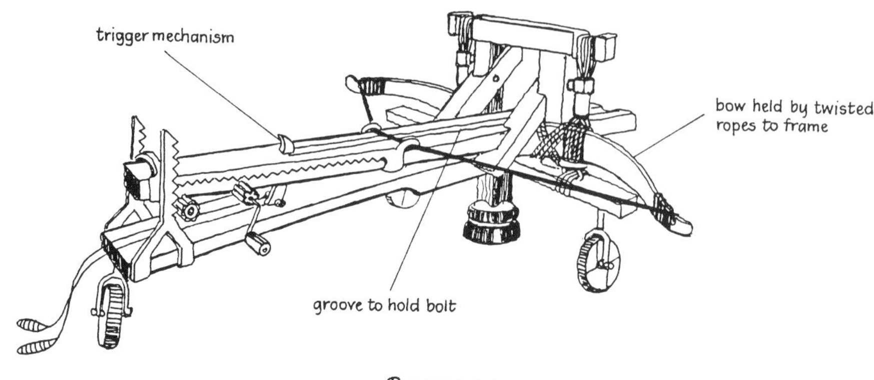

BALISTA

more loosely. The Arab attackers of Nicaea in 727 used a form of catapult; a stone from one of them killed a young groom, Constantine, smashing his head and face. The vikings used a *funda* at the siege of Paris, a bolt from which transfixed seven Danes, who were then taken off to the kitchen on the 'spit'. Whether or not one wishes to take this story at face value, it certainly implies a weapon of some size which shot large bolts. St Louis had machines of this type at Damietta, what Joinville refers to as swivel crossbows; and James of Aragon used weapons to shoot bolts, to which fire was attached. Two late medieval weapons of this type survive in the Paris Musée de l'Armée.[24]

The word 'mangonel' seems to have developed as a diminutive from *manga* or *mangana*, itself a word for a stone-throwing engine. The fact that it was a diminutive seems to argue against it being an enormous machine. The term may derive from the Greek (mangano), meaning crush, or squeeze, which also provided the origin for the Arabic term for an engine: al-majanech. If so the word means 'crusher', or 'mangler'. William of Tyre thought that manganas were lesser engines, and William the Breton similarly said that mangonels threw lesser rocks than petraries. Mangonels are usually described as engines which possessed a long arm, or beam, with a fixed cup at one end. The beam was drawn backwards and held in place; it was attached to twisted ropes, so that on release, the torsion caused the arm to revolve upwards until it smacked against a cross beam. The stone or missile was placed in the cup, and when the arm hit the bar, it would be released at the target. The ancients possessed weapons of this type, and

24 On Nicaea, Theophanes, pp. 97–8. On vikings, Abbo, pp. 22, 56, 84, 94. Joinville, ed. Evans, p. 61. For the museum, Finó, 'Jet', p. 26.

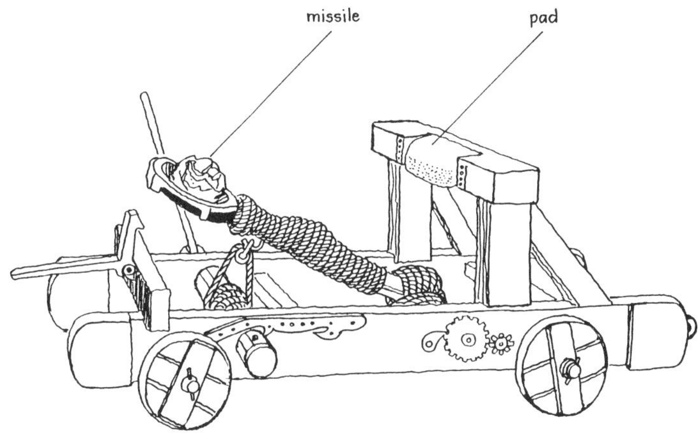

MANGONEL

they were certainly used in the fourteenth century. There is however no certain proof for their use in the early medieval period. The word mangonel is frequently used, but often as a term meaning little more than 'stone-thrower', which is precisely the origin of the word *petraria* or petrary. Thus, although 'mangonels' were used at Paris against the vikings, and written about by Paul in his eighth-century *History of the Lombards*, we cannot know for certain what they were.[25] Often chroniclers speak of engines using more than one term, such as mangonels and petraries, which certainly seems to imply that more than one type existed, but in the earlier period, there is no evidence which conclusively demonstrates what these different types were. Occasionally one gets a hint, for example the springalds referred to in the *Lanercost Chronicle* had staves with sockets for casting stones, which suggests a type of mangonel. In this book, mangonel is taken to mean the type of weapon with a cup fixed on the end of its arm, but clearly we cannot take every medieval reference to a 'mangonel' as being like this.[26]

It is argued by some that torsion weapons were not used by medieval armies, at least until the fourteenth century. Direct evidence for them in the earlier medieval period in not strong; but evidence for any specific type of thrower is weak until about the twelfth century, with a lack of both illustrations and detailed descriptions. This is complicated by the loose way in which medieval chroniclers used descriptive words. It is unwise, for

25 William of Tyre, ed. Huygens, i, p. 403: *alii vero minoribus tormentis, que mangana vocantur*; William the Breton, ii, p. 54. On Paris, Abbo, p. 42, see above n. 23. Paul the Lombard, p. 189: *quam vulgo dicimus mancolam*.

26 Double terms, e.g.; James I, ed. Casacuberta, i, p. 80: *fenevol e l.almanganel*; Villehardouin, ed. Faral, i, p. 166: *de perrieres et de mangoniaus*. *Lanercost*, in *EHD*, iii, p. 266.

example, to think that *catapulta* always has the same meaning. Historians who dismiss the medieval possession of torsion weapons, believe that only a lever type or trebuchet was used, though the early evidence for these machines is equally uncertain. Since the Roman world and the later middle ages both possessed torsion weapons, and since a variety of throwing engines appear to have existed throughout the middle ages, we are prepared to accept the probable existence of torsion engines, but without insisting that *mangonellus*, *tormentum*, or any other single term necessarily implied a torsion weapon. What, for instance, should one make of *tormenta mangeranum*? Jacques de Vitry in 1143 described a variety of throwing- engines as bein *cum cornu*, with horns, which is certainly suggestive of the double arms required for torsion machines. It is possible that the 'fonevols' used by James I of Aragon, were torsion engines. I have not been able to discover the derivation of this unusual word, but the two main possibilities are either from the Latin *funis*, meaning sinew or cord, which certainly brings to mind the idea of torsion; or from the word *funda* meaning sling. Either, or indeed both are possible – the word like many others may have come to simply mean an engine. However, the survival of a charter of Count Raymond of Toulouse of 1190 mentioning a *frondevola* probably tips the balance in favour of a derivation from *funda*, French *fronde*.[27]

There is also evidence which hints at the early medieval existence of the pivot-type of engine, an early form of trebuchet. These early machines were operated by a crew of men pulling on ropes to provide the force later supplied by a counterweight. An Arabic source dating from 683 referred to a 'long-haired' engine, which probably relates to the dangling ropes.[28] Our contention is that historians may have underestimated the skill and knowledge of the early middle ages, and that in all probability Roman techniques for torsion engines were never lost, and the new pivot-style of engine was pioneered in this period.

As in other areas of medieval warfare, there were experts in making and using engines, and they were invaluable. Sailors were expected to be good at using, as well as building, engines, as was often demonstrated by Italians during the crusades. At Tyre the Christians used 'experts in the art of throwing missiles', and these included an Armenian Christian from Antioch with particular skill at hitting selected targets, who was given a

27 For views, see Rogers, microfiche pp. 15–47; historians concerned include Schneider, Köhler, Huuri, Finó. Köhler favours the use of torsion, Huuri of the pivot. On the *balista*, see Schneider, p. 96, but meaning made of horn; Ducange, under *balista*. On the fonevol, James I, ed. Casacuberta, ii, VIII, p. 52; and Ducange on the count of Toulouse under *frondevola*: *in faciendis petrariis et frondevolis*.

28 Hill, 'Trebuchets', p. 100: siege of Mecca 683 called *Umm Farwa*, 'mother of the hair'; and 708, 'The Bride', needing 500 to operate; Baghdad, 865 *arradas*, needing ropes to pull, presumably traction trebuchets and the origin of James I of Aragon's algarradas.

salary from the public purse, and thus enabled to 'live in his accustomed magnificence'. Robert of Bellême, who though a magnate is said to have been skilled in developing fortifications and engines, at Bréval, in the early twelfth century, produced stone-throwing engines which were on wheels: 'hurling great stones at the castle'. Thomas the Carpenter, Philip IV's Master of Engines, in 1301 was receiving 100 *livres tournois* per annum.[29]

The best information that we can get on types of early crusading throwing engines, comes from a twelfth-century Arab source by Mardi ibn Ali al-Tarsusi, which gives fascinating, if not always easily comprehensible, details of different types of engines.[30] The word mangonel itself is thought to have come from Greek, via Arabic, to the West, and although this work refers to a Frankish mangonel as one type, there are clear similarities between the weapons known in the West and those described in this source. Mardi ibn Ali believed that the Arabic mangonel was 'the surest and most reliable', and also praises the Turkish engine, which needed little attention, and was not over-elaborate. He deliberately did not give all details, since 'the operation of the mangonel involves secrets which must be well kept'. Such work required expert operators, who had to master the necessary theoretical knowledge, for example concerning the trajectory of a stone thrown from the cup. The cup on the arm of a Turkish mangonel could be moved to alter the trajectory; this weapon had a range of 240 to 360 feet. The degree of flexibility of the arm was important, since a slightly flexible arm gave greater range. Mardi ibn Ali believed that cherry was the best wood for this, or failing that a close-grained wood such as cedar. The operator, he wrote: 'should part his legs, adjust the cup with his hands, and sit down while pulling the cup with all his might.' The words suggest a mangonel with a fixed wooden cup, rather than a trebuchet with a sling, but the following section casts doubt on this interpretation.[31]

Mardi ibn Ali described a number of other weapons, including the Arabic mangonel, which was made on a triangular frame, with two equal sides, and a base which was shorter than the sides. It had an axle at the top, with a roof to protect the operators, and there were cords attached to the cup. The Persian mangonel had a power of 50 pounds; its base was shaped in a cross. This appears to be a complicated machine, using both tension of a crossbow for the initial power, perhaps as a kind of trigger, and then a counterweight. It involved a machine of the crossbow type, in which the

29 On sailors: William of Tyre, ed. Huygens, i, p. 400; Ibn al-Qalanisi in Gabrieli, p. 34; *De Expugnatione Lyxbonensi*, p. 147; Ambroise ed. Hubert & La Monte, p. 167. On Venetians, and the Armenian, William of Tyre ed. Huygens, i, pp. 596, 598; the latter with *arte in dirigendo machinas*. On Bréval, Orderic Vitalis, iv, p. 288 and n. 6: *ingeniosissimum artificem adduxit . . . Hic machinas construxit . . . super rotulas egit, ingentia saxa . . . proiecit*. On Philip IV, Finó, 'Jet', p. 41.

30 Lewis, *Islam*, pp. 218–23, includes the illustrations; Rogers, microfiche, pp. 36–8; Cahen, pp. 103–63.

31 Lewis, *Islam*, pp. 218, 219.

operator 'takes the bow and shoots and releases the shaft'; but it is interesting that a net of stones is used to draw the bow, which indicates a move towards the trebuchet; and Mardi ibn Ali recommended that a hole be dug to the depth of the cords for the net holding the stones. The enigmatic drawing strongly suggests a type of trebuchet. Since the writer says that the cup for this should be 'the same as for the Arab mangonel', and the picture seems to show a sort of hanging cup rather than a cup shaped in the arm, one is left in some doubt as to the actual difference between them, since this drawing looks more akin to a trebuchet sling, albeit using a hanging cup rather than the sling generally used in the West. Some historians believe that all these Arab descriptions are of types of trebuchet. The mangonel which Mardi ibn Ali described as being Frankish, or Roman, presumably meaning Byzantine, was similar to his Arabic mangonel, in that it had a triangular frame, but with the top beams continuing, rather like the top of a wig-wam, and with a base which was longer across than the two equal sides. Like the Arabic mangonel it worked with a cup and cords.[32]

A major problem exists with this Arab material. There is no doubt that we are dealing with throwing machines. From the descriptions, we might well take it that here are a variety of mangonels. But most of the illustrations seem to be *not* of mangonels, but of trebuchets, that is, they depend for their action on a pivot and the use of a counterweight, a matter we shall return to in due course. A fourteenth-century manuscript provides a mangonel, with a beam operated by torsion, a cup, and a man operating the beam with a winch.[33] Those historians who dismiss the use of torsion in the medieval period until this time, argue that it may have been re-developed from Renaissance interest in the classical past. It remains equally possible, and equally unproveable, that torsion had continued in use throughout the middle ages, but we have inclined to the latter view simply because it is a more likely explanation. There is no good reason why Byzantium should have lost the skills of ancient Rome in warfare any more than in any other area; and the fact that the word *manga* has a Greek origin is also suggestive. We cannot be certain how the mangonel operated, but like the petrary, it threw stones, sometimes of considerable size. When the torsion machines appear in the later medieval illustrations, they are commonly called mangonels.

The positioning of engines at a siege was tremendously important. Defenders constructed towers and positions on the walls, so that engines could be aimed against the attackers; projecting towers were especially significant. For the attackers, it was vital to assess the main targets, whether individuals on the walls, or the weak points in the defences. On several occasions, one finds the besiegers making efforts to improve the

32 Lewis, *Islam*, pp. 221, 220, especially fig. 4.

33 Schneider, Tafel 1, f. 3; Tafel 2, f. 6. Milemete, ed. James, figs 69a, 78b.

effect of their attack, for example, the Franks at Brissarthe against the vikings, built mounds on which they placed their engines. Edward I used the same idea at Edinburgh, building mounds for several engines. It was also important to give protection to engines: James I of Aragon explained how at Balaguer, guards were placed night and day, and they had to fight off a sortie by men using faggots soaked in grease to try and fire the engines; they set light to the palisade which James had built as a protection, but the engines were saved. At Gillera, James says he surveyed the site to choose the position for his fonevols, which had been transported there by sea. He found a site on a hill, which was at about crossbow range; there, he says, they could be screened and guarded.[34]

By the twelfth century, it was common to use engines in groups or batteries; in the case of Rouen in 1174, it required an eight hour shift system to keep the machines going day and night. The number of engines built and used, increased greatly through the twelfth century. At Chinon Philip Augustus collected 400 cords for petraries. The engines used by James I of Aragon, which he called fonevols, at Lisana threw 500 stones in one night, and 1,000 in the daytime. St Louis against Damietta had eight engines made by his Master Engineer, Jocelyn de Cornaut; and Joinville says that the Saracens had sixteen engines.[35]

The missiles hurled by these engines varied enormously, in both size and material, though large stones were the most common. Any large, weighty, or unpleasant object might serve: metal, inflammable material, heads, corpses, dead animals, dung. Charles duke of Lower Lorraine, at Laon in the late tenth century, had smiths prepare projectiles for his machines, which were therefore presumably made of metal; and Edward I at Edinburgh used lead: sending in 'an unbearable rain of metal'. At Montreuil-Bellay, in 1151, Geoffrey V of Anjou used a mangonel to hurl pots filled with Greek Fire against the place, fixing the pots to the arm of the engine; three houses were set alight as a result. The Saracens at Damietta, also hurled Greek Fire from their engines, producing a tail like a lance, and making a noise like thunder: 'as a dragon that flew through the air'. William the Lion, king of Scots, used an engine at Wark to throw fire, but the wind unfortunately changed direction and blew the flames back in the faces of his own men. At Museros, James I of Aragon shot spindles with lighted tow attached, and at Carolstein, in the later middle ages, 2,000 cartloads of manure were hurled. In the case of Auberoche, in 1345, where the French employed four large engines brought from Toulouse, an

34 For Brissarthe, Regino, ed. Kurze, p. 92. On Edward I, *Chronicle of Bury St. Edmunds*, p. 132, made mound, *quasi montulum*. On Balaguer and Gillera, James I, ed. Forster, i, pp. 87, 299; ed. Casacuberta, i, I, p. 106, i, IV, p. 20.

35 For Rouen, William of Newburgh in *EHD*, ii, p. 382. For Chinon and Damietta; and the latter, Joinville, ed. Evans, pp. 129, 203. Contamine, p. 106. For Lisana, James I, ed. Forster, i, p. 26; ed. Casacuberta, i, I, pp. 36–7.

Heads used as missiles from an engine

unfortunate pageboy, carrying a message for the English, was taken prisoner, and thrown back inside from an engine, with his letters tied round his neck; the knights inside 'were much astonished and discomfited when they saw him arrive'. It seems that mangonels were still being used by the Turks at Rhodes in 1480, to hurl 'carcasses', that is, clay eggs containing a mixture which ignited on impact. At about the same time, during Ferdinand and Isabella's siege of Malaga, a Dervish prisoner tried to stab the two of them, but picked on another couple to attack by mistake; his body was cut up, and catapulted back inside.[36]

Aim could be quite accurate, and one often hears of individuals or specific targets being hit. At Tortona in 1155, one of Barbarossa's engines was struck by a machine operated from within the town. When Saix in Spain was besieged by the Christians, an enemy engine hurled a great stone from the roof of a tower, and hit Don Artal on the helmet, knocking him from his horse and killing him. It is not certain what type of engine was a brigole or brigola, it was probably a trebuchet, since James I or Aragon described one with a beam, cords and a box, the latter suggesting a container for the counterweight. At any rate, according to him, the

[36] On Laon, Richer, ii, p. 173. On Edinburgh, *Chronicle of Bury St Edmunds*, p. 132. On Montreuil-Bellay, John of Marmoutier, pp. 217–18: *mangonelli conto innectitur*. For Damietta, Joinville, ed. Evans, p. 61. For Wark, Jordan Fantosme, p. 94, ll. 1260–5. For Museros, James I, ed. Forster, i, p. 310; ed. Casacuberta, i, IV, p. 38: *E nos faem fer segetes en semblanca de filoses, e metia hom dins estopa ab foch ences; e tiraven les losl balestes*. On Carolstein and Auberoche, Payne-Gallwey, p. 272. For Rhodes, Brockman, p. 45; and Malaga, Trevelyan, p. 51.

Saracens possessed one at Licana, where its cords became tangled with its beam, and they could not disentangle the cord in order to lower the beam. A Christian fonevol was then brought forward to aim against it. The first shot missed; then says James: 'I myself went to take charge of it, shot and hit the brigola so hard that its box was broken'; the master of James' fonevols, with another shot, broke 'a beam on one side of the brigola'.[37]

Although not as powerful as fully-developed trebuchets, mangonels or petraries could do severe damage to walls, and were sometimes used for this purpose. It was a mangonel of Frederick Barbarossa's which hit the upper fortifications at Tortona in 1155, so that they broke into three parts as they collapsed, killing three knights standing below. It is of course, by this period, always possible that what is called a mangonel might in fact be a trebuchet. Henry of Livonia calls the engines which were used in the north paterells, and says they were smaller machines. This term does not seem to appear in any other source. The most likely derivation for it is from the Latin *patera*, meaning dish or cup, suggestive of the spoon-like arm of mangonels. They threw rocks, and when used at Mesoten, the first shot demolished a hoarding, the second broke the logs in the rampart, and the third breached the rampart, and brought the enemy to a peace negotiation. The mangonel was also useful as a smaller machine, which could be employed from defensive positions, for example on walls and towers, or even from on board ship, as by the Venetians in the attacks on Constantinople during the Fourth Crusade. James I set up an engine against Muntcada, putting the cords to it, and next day used it against a tower, killing many inside; within five days the place surrendered; while at Museros, his fonevol carried away three or four battlements.[38]

Trebuchets

It is not certain when the counterweight trebuchet was developed; and this remains uncertain despite the many scholarly arguments, since neither definitive descriptions, nor conclusive illustrations, have so far been produced, before the thirteenth century. Historians have differed wildly in their claims for the date of the introduction of the trebuchet, from the

[37] For Tortona, Otto of Freising, ed. Mierow, p. 141. For Saix, James I, ed. Forster, i, p. 404. For details on the brigola, the tangle and the hit; James I ed. Forster, ii, pp. 581–2; ed. Casacuberta, ii, VIII, p. 52: *e la corda de la lur brigola envolve.s entorn la pertxa*; p. 54: pertxa is the beam, caxa the box.

[38] On Tortona, Otto of Freising, ed. Waitz, p. 124: *Ferunt quadam die lapidem vi tormenti ex balista, quam modo mangam vulgo dicere solent*. On Fellin, and Mesoten, Henry of Livonia, ed. Arbusow & Bauer, pp. 83, 162: *ducentes secum machinam minorem sive paterellum et balistas*. For Muntcada, James I, ed. Forster, i, pp. 309, 310; ed. Casacuberta, i, IV, p. 36: *meterem hi les cordes*; p. 38: *e tolch dels deuteyls de la torra, de iii fro a iv*.

period of the siege of Paris, to the thirteenth century.[39] The trebuchet could hurl heavier objects further, but recent theories have depended upon effects rather than the mechanism, and the latter is the crucial point. Evidence which refers to ingenious new machines, and to the degree of destruction they caused, may be indicative, but cannot be conclusive, and it seems best at present to consider this an unresolved problem. The most that can be said, is that the evidence from the twelfth century provides a good case for its introduction then, although one has to wait for the thirteenth century for conclusive proof.[40]

One of the puzzles in this period is to know what were the Balearic *fundae*, mentioned in connection with the siege of Lisbon. Both sides are said to have used them, for example the crusaders set up one against the Porto do Ferro, operated by knights and their companions, and one on the right bank of the Tagus, operated by sailors. We are told that these were worked by men in groups of a hundred, which obviously indicates large engines, and that they hurled 5,000 stones in ten hours. Richard the Lionheart was on one occasion described as moving faster than a Balearic sling, and this may denote speed in operation rather than frequency with which it could be used. The speed with which they could be re-used rather suggests a smaller machine; on the other hand the idea of speed through the air might denote a counterweight trebuchet. The most likely explanation, given the large numbers needed to operate the machines, and the speed through the air of the missile, is that these were indeed early counterweight trebuchets. But this is hardly the incontrovertible evidence some have taken it to be. It may be that 'Balearic' was confused with the Latin term to throw, *baleare*, itself derived from the Greek βαλλω (ballo), to shoot or throw, in which case it may be an old confusion, dating back to Julius Caesar. Engines are described as 'balearic', meaning simply hurling-engines; but they are sometimes described in such a way, both in ancient and medieval times, that it is clear the writer had in mind the geographical term, and presumably believed that the engines had some association with the Islands. It might, of course, have originated as a pun. Although the geographical link may indeed have some significance, we should take it that the basic meaning of a Balearic sling, was of a hurling-engine. The fact that a crossbow could be described as an *arcus balearis*, suggests that this type of mangonel operated on the catapult principle. Large engines are also met in the East. 'God's Stone-Thrower' at Acre, was built from common funds, and was again a major project. Richard's engines were said to be able to 'hit the mark at an incredible distance'. The fact that stone-throwing engines were dismantled and transported by sea for Richard suggests that they were large and valuable. The Moslems also

[39] See above, n. 27.

[40] In addition to works in n. 27, see also Hill, 'Trebuchets'; Gillmor, Clephan, and Berthelot.

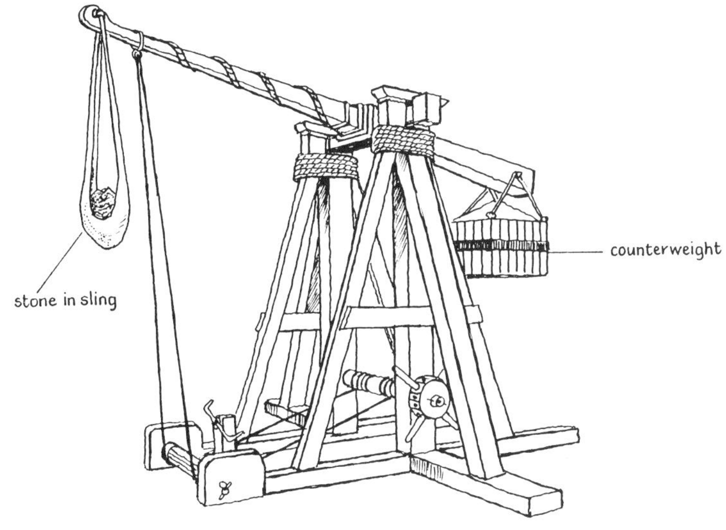

COUNTERWEIGHT TREBUCHET

possessed stone-throwers, of which, according to at least one writer from the West: 'the like had never been seen', able to smash the Christian engines from a great distance, hurling large rocks which sunk a foot into the ground, broke marble columns in two, and took two men to load into the sling. Often we find these engines capable of breaking down walls, though mining was perhaps even more effective, but at Nicaea, for example, two engines used persistently against a section of wall over several days caused it to crack.[41]

One major controversy over siege weapons of the middle ages, is when and where we should look for the invention of the trebuchet, which unlike practically all other large engines or machines was a medieval rather than an ancient innovation. There can be no doubt of its arrival by the thirteenth century, when there are records in words and in pictures; but historians are still divided over its origins. As so often, much of the difficulty lies in defining our terms: recent writers have talked in terms of more than one type of trebuchet, and although this is correct, it has perhaps blurred rather than clarified the picture. The main problem is with the sources: medieval chroniclers were casual in their use of terms for weapons of war, as they were for types of fortification; one word would do as well as

[41] *De Expugnatione Lyxbonensi*, p. 135: *fundis Balearicis*, pp. 143, 163. On Richard, Howden, iii, p. 252. Ducange on *Balea*, also see Clephan. God's thrower is Ambroise, ed. Paris, col. 127, l. 4760: *Periere Deu*. On distance, Archer, p. 87; on like not seen, Ambroise, ed. Hubert & La Monte, p. 160. For Nicaea, William of Tyre, ed. Babcock & Krey, i, p. 161.

another. Otto of Freising, for example, refers to a mangonel as a kind of *balista*.[42]

It seems most useful, first, to try and define what we mean by a trebuchet. It was certainly an engine used for hurling stones. Clearly in the middle ages the word trebuchet implied a pivot. It was from ancient times associated with the word for a balance, and is an old word in England for a ducking-stool. Its main distinction was in possessing a large beam on a pivot, with the pivot placed, not in the centre, but towards one end of the beam. The shorter end of the beam had a large container attached to it, which was filled with heavy materials such as earth or stones or lead. The longer end of the beam had a sling attached to it, in which was placed the projectile, which might be a large rock. The longer end was winched down, and held in position by a catch; the release of the catch allowed the heavy-weighted end to drop, and caused the longer arm to rise. As the long arm rose, the sling, laid flat in a channel, moved up and in an arc, with the effect of making the long arm even longer, so that the projectile when released from the sling would have maximum impetus. The sling itself was made so that one end was attached permanently to the beam through a hole in that end of the sling, while the other end was tied on, and would come loose at the moment of release. A reasonable comparison might be with a bowler in cricket: the long beam moved, but the sling was like a fast bowler's arm on the end of it, making it longer and also whirling it round at greater speed. Although the counterweight is usually emphasised as the distinctive part of the trebuchet, the sling was equally important in giving impetus, and just as distinctive, and our chroniclers more often noticed the sling than the weight.

A more careful examination of sources than has been possible in this survey, might produce useful conclusions from the use of the word for the sling. It seems convincing that if an engine possessed a sling then it was a type of trebuchet. This does not answer conclusively the vital question of when the counterweight was introduced, but is as good a hint as we can find. The long sling used on the trebuchet was more effective because of the sudden force provided by the heavy counterweight. There is one unfortunate complication: the double meaning of the word sling, which can denote the weapon we usually associate with David against Goliath, as well as the attachment to the trebuchet, with the result that a 'slinger' in medieval warfare might be operating either! Oddly, it has usually been translated in the first sense, whereas the latter is likely to have been more common. We can here give no more than a few hints, but, for example, the *fundae* of throwing engines are mentioned at Nicaea and Jerusalem during the First Crusade;and the word is often transferred to the engine itself, as at

42 Practically no word for these can be safely taken to mean anything more precise than 'engine' from the diverse uses made of terms by chroniclers. Otto of Freising, ed. Waitz, p. 124: *balista, quam modo mangam vulgo dicere solent.*

A trebuchet with winch and sling

Lisbon during the Second Crusade. The implication is that all these weapons, of whose type we were uncertain, should probably be seen as trebuchets.[43]

Peter de Ebolus portrays a trebuchet being used in Italy at the turn of the thirteenth century, usually quoted as the first certain evidence of its existence, but in fact it is a traction trebuchet, without a counterweight.[44] We find the appearance of a new word for these engines: *trebus*, *triboke*, *trabuchetum*, *trabocco*, and so on, words which become increasingly common from the 1220s. The engineer, Villard de Honnecourt, drew plans of a trebuchet in his notebook in about 1270. The elevation plan is lost, but the design shown from above survives, and shows the shape of the frame, and the positioning of the sling; 1,296 cubic feet of earth were required to fill the counterweight container, and there was a winch to lift it. The German engineer, Konrad Kyeser, at the end of the fourteenth century, also left drawings of a trebuchet. and part of his work was devoted to siege engines.[45]

The evidence points to the appearance of the counterweight trebuchet in the West in, or by, the early thirteenth century; but some historians

43 *Funda* can mean either sling or engine. On Nicaea, *Gesta Francorum*, p. 15. On Jerusalem, Peter Tudebode, p. 139: *in funda cuiusdam ingenii, quod petrera vocatur*; thrown *tanto impetu* that the body broke up. Compare Jordan Fantosme, p. 92: *la piere de la funde*; Ambroise, ed. Paris, col. 95: *metre/En la funde*. Abbo, p. 22, l. 87: *funde lacereque baliste*. On Lisbon, see n. 41 above.

44 Peter de Ebolus, f. 109; in Finó, *Forteresses*, p. 155, fig. 39; Zaky, fig. 20.

45 Villard de Honnecourt, see Hahnloser, Taf. 59; Finó, 'Jet', p. 33; *Album*, f. 30. For Kyeser illustrations, see Kyeser, ii, ff. 32v, 43, 43v, 48, 128v.

A traction trebuchet operated by pulling on ropes

have made claims for an earlier origin. This is partly because they have been convinced by uncertain kinds of evidence. The fact that Charles the Bald is described as possessing a 'new weapon' at Angers in 873, is hardly sufficient to conclude that it must be a trebuchet. It has also been claimed that a trebuchet was used at the siege of Paris, but again Abbo's original words give no indication that the engine was of any particular kind; the likelihood that it was a counterweight trebuchet is not great. One line of argument which has caused difficulty, is the argument from impact: that if an engine can do sufficient damage to a wall, it must be a trebuchet. There are some grounds for this, in that counterweight trebuchets could do more damage than previous engines, which indeed led to their increasing use. But to see a trebuchet, every time a source says considerable damage was done to walls, is clearly mistaken, particularly when we note the tendency of medieval chroniclers to exaggerate. This test on its own is inadequate evidence for the existence of counterweight trebuchets. It is, however, possible that the traction trebuchet had been used throughout our period.[46]

There is evidence, which one might call circumstantial, for the appearance of the counterweight trebuchet in the twelfth century. The evidence concerning Robert of Bellême, who brought up 'a most ingenious invention' at Bréval, is of the same kind we have already dismissed. But William the Breton's comment about an engine which could throw larger stones

[46] On Charles the Bald, Gillmor, p. 6; Finó, 'Jet', pp. 27, 37; *Chroniques des Eglises d'Anjou*, pp. 133: *nova et inexquisita machinamentorum genera applicantur*. Abbo, p. 32: uses a variety of terms, impossible to translate precisely: *fundae*, *balistae*, *falaricae*, *catapultae*, *manganae*.

A trebuchet on triangular supports

than a mangonel deserves consideration, even if he does call it a petrary! William speaks of rocks being thrown, which four men could not lift, and it is difficult to envisage anything smaller than a trebuchet being capable of this. It is probably another example of inexact use of terms, since Jean de Garlande contradicts this comment by suggesting that petraries were a lesser type of throwing machine! By the time of Jean, trebuchets were known, and he indeed declared that *trabuceta* were the best weapons to use against walls.[47]

The early version of the trebuchet, which worked on the principle of a pivoted beam, that is, the man-powered or traction trebuchet, was operated by a crew pulling on ropes, which were attached to the short end of the beam, in other words by using manpower rather than a counterweight. Such machines date back as far as ancient China. No doubt it can be argued that such an engine used the technique required for the later counterweight machine, but its impact upon walls could not possibly have equalled that of the trebuchet proper. References to engines which are compared to long hair in their appearance, are probably of this type, the ropes for pulling would give the appearance of dangling hair.[48]

The meaning of the word 'trebuchet' itself may give some clue; it seems certainly to have the sense of tripartite, but in what sense? There are links in the use of the word with stool, and with balance, both of which may provide some help. The idea of a balance is clear enough, with the pivot giving both the appearance and the function of a balance. As for the link with stool, this is also possible; it may be that the word referred to the appearance of the frame of the trebuchet, as having three legs. Several of the early illustrations show a triangular-shaped frame, which seems the most likely explanation, since the large frame would certainly draw the attention of the ordinary spectator. However, when in 1212, Otto IV besieged and took Weissenburg, it was said that he used a 'three-armed machine called a *Triboke*'. Here the tripartite meaning seems to derive from

47 On Bréval, Orderic Vitalis, iv, p. 288. William the Breton, ii, p. 541; and see Rogers, microfiche, p. 45; and n. 24 above; also Finó, 'Jet', p. 35. On Garlande, see Contamine, p. 103: *Trabuceta sunt etiam tormenta murorum*.

48 See above, n. 28; Hill, 'Trebuchets', p. 100.

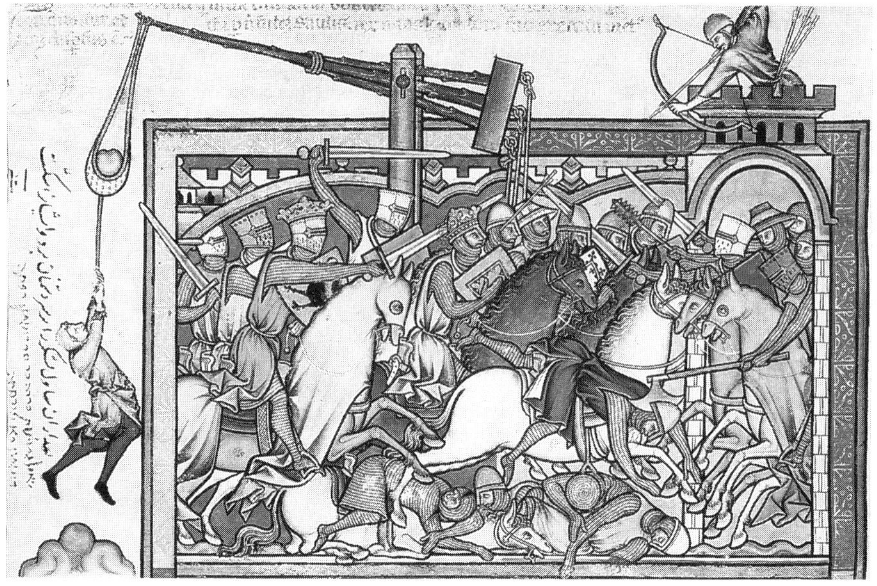

Trebuchet with the arm made from three beams

the beam. Otto at Weissensee, also used for the first time, so it was said, an engine called the 'Tribok'.[49]

It seems that the engines used in Greece by the crusaders, immediately after the taking of Constantinople in 1204, were trebuchets, and these were made by the Venetians. James I of Aragon in his conquest of Majorca used various kinds of engines, including trebuchets, referred to as *trabuquets*, which were made by sailors from Marseilles: 'after our own fashion, out of the yards and spares of ships'; he also possessed a trebuchet brought by sea, which had the greatest range of any engine there. Later he mentions that Nicoloso the engineer had made his engine in Majorca; whose place of origin is given as Albanguena, which has been thought to mean the Auvergne. James says that the Saracens also possessed trebuchets.[50]

One test of the existence of early trebuchets in the records, is the mention of its sling. It is also very likely that some of the references to 'slingers' in the armies, indicate men operating trebuchets. Early references to an engine by a name such as *funda*, which probably implies a sling

49 Contamine, p. 104; Schneider, p. 28; *Annales Marbacenses*, p. 82: *instrumenti bellici quod vulgo tribok appellari solet*; compare p. 54: *quod ebenhoe dicitur*.

50 *Morea*, p. 91: τριμπουτσετω (trimpoutseto); pp. 111, 118, 122, 130, 306. Another possibility could be drawn from Lynn White Junior's explanation of the revolving prayer wheel, containing the Tripitaka, the Buddhist scriptures: i.e. that the word was transferred to the rotating wheel, and from that to the rotating beam of the trebuchet – odder things have happened to words. James I, ed. Forster, i, pp. 139, 140, 257; ed. Casacuberta, i, I, p. 50: *e la I trabuquet que nos aduxem per mar tirava pus luny que reguns dels lurs*.

include those mentioned above: from Barcelona in 800-1, Paris in 885, Nicaea in 1097, Jerusalem in 1099, and Lisbon in 1147, though doubtless many others are there to be found. One interesting example is the stone-thrower used by William the Lion, king of Scots, in the rebellion against Henry II in 1174. At Wark, King William ordered up an engine, whose maker had claimed that it would demolish the gate and win the bailey 'in no time at all'. In the event the machine was a flop, and the first stone 'barely tumbled out of its sling', to hit one of William's own men. The fact that this weapon possessed a sling, almost certainly means that it was a trebuchet; the fact that it did not work well, adds to the impression that this was a newish kind of engine, perhaps with a counterweight.[51]

Egidio Colonna, who worked for Philip IV of France in the late thirteenth century, described four different types of trebuchet in use by his day.[52] The first possessed a fixed container for the counterweight, and the last was a man-powered trebuchet. His other two 'types', were simply different ways of aiming the machine: the first, which he calls the *biffa*, had a counterweight, which could be moved backwards and forwards along the beam, to alter the range; the second had a fixed container counterweight, and also a second movable weight, employed as a flexible range-finder. By 1350 trebuchets were to be found at virtually every major siege.

It is interesting how often clerics were associated with siege engines, including trebuchets. The archdeacon of Paris designed Simon de Montfort the Elder's largest trebuchet at Penne d'Agenais, which was mainly responsible for his success there. During that same crusade, the bishop of Albi acted as engineer at the climactic siege of Montségur, preparing the trebuchet for use against the eastern tower. Of course clerics were more likely to be involved in a crusade, and may simply have been playing their rôle of magnates; but it might also be that the ability to draw up plans, and the mathematical knowledge necessary to make engines operate, required a good education, and clerics were more likely than others to have received it.[53]

The range and impact of a stone from a trebuchet was considerable. Experiments carried out by Napoleon III, using reconstructed trebuchets, showed that a machine could hurl a twenty-five pound weight some 200 yards. Care had to be taken over the choice of projectile; it was important that it be both heavy and hard. At Castelnaudry, Raymond VI found the local stone was too soft, and that it, rather than the wall, broke on impact; he had to send to a distance to obtain suitable stone. Metal was therefore sometimes used, such as lead, but it was expensive and difficult to

51 On Barcelona, Ermold, p. 30, l.347; on Paris, Abbo, p. 22, l. 87; on Nicaea, *Gesta Francorum*, p. 15; on Jerusalem, Peter Tudebod, pp. 136, 139; on Lisbon, *De Expugnatione Lyxbonensi*, pp. 135, 143; on Wark, Jordan Fantosme, p. 92.

52 Finó, 'Jet', pp. 28–9; Hill, 'Trebuchets', p. 105.

53 Sumption, pp. 148, 239.

transport. Lead might also be used for the counterweight in the trebuchet, and Edward I's son was reduced to stripping church roofs in order to obtain enough of it for his engines.[54]

A recent experiment with trebuchets was made in 1989 in Denmark, through the Museum of Falsters Minder.[55] The researchers began with a series of models, and then constructed a full-scale trebuchet, with which a series of experimental throws was made, altering the variables, including the angle of the sling and the weight of the missile. They calculated that it required a twenty-seven ton counterweight to cast a 1,000 kg stone. They found that the heavier the missile, the earlier the sling burst open. When operated, it went 'with a strange singing sound'. For example, a 15 kg concrete ball, operated by a one-ton counterweight, released at an angle of 70 degrees: 'accelerated away in a curved trajectory' to a distance of 120 metres; the longest shot with a ball of this weight was 180 metres. They claimed that their accuracy was as good as that of a modern mortar, and that the machine was both reliable and accurate.[56]

The significance of trebuchets, towers and engines is demonstrated by the common practice of giving nick-names, showing the degree of attention which an army gave. Thus we hear of towers called *Malregard* or *Malvoisin*. Edward I, at Stirling, had engines called *Segrave*, *Vicar*, *Parson*, *Warwolf*, and *Gloucester*. A delivery memo from Thomas de Cotynge to Richard de Bremesgrave at Berwick refers to *Segrave*, *Vernay*, *Robynet*, and *Forster*, as well as the great engine called *Warwolf*, two made in Brechin, and one from Aberdeen; together with staves, hammers, cords, lead, and round stones. It took five carpenters and fifty labourers to construct *Warwolf*. Nick-names for engines were not confined to the Christians; in the late stages of the history of the Latin Kingdom, the Moslems brought up two large engines which they called *The Victorious*, and *The Furious*; they also knew their mangonels as 'black oxen'. At Rhodes, as late as 1480, there was an Italian trebuchet given the name *The Tribute*, apparently as a response to the Turkish demand for payment of tribute. This same kind of army affection saw the sling with its stones on the trebuchet earning the graphic, if vulgar, sobriquet of the 'bollocks'.[57]

In the end, the effect of trebuchets was tremendous, and they became the favoured weapon for demolishing walls. They could cast heavy projec-

54 On Napoleon, Hill, 'Trebuchets', p. 110; Finó, 'Jet', p. 34. See also Hansen, p. 10; I am grateful to my friends Ted Crawford and Matt Bennett respectively for directing me to this article, and providing a photocopy. On Castelnaudry, Sumption, p. 141; on the roofs, Prestwich, *Edward I*, p. 501.

55 Hansen, 'Reconstructing a Medieval Trebuchet'.

56 Hansen, p. 14.

57 Ambroise ed. Paris, col. 127, ll. 4745–6: *li reis aveit Male Veisine, /Mais en Acre ert Male Cosine*. On Edward I, *Calendar of Documents*, iv, p. 370; *EHD*, iii, p. 610. On the Moslem engines, Runciman, *Crusades*, iii, p. 412; Ibn l-Fida in Gabrieli, p. 344; Richard, p. 426. On the Tribute, Brockman, p. 83; on the bollocks, Contamine, p. 195 and n. 10.

Trebuchets in action

tiles a considerable distance, and with great force. When three suitable stones were finally found for the engine at Castelnaudry, the first demolished a tower, the second destroyed a chamber, and the third shattered on impact, killing many men. On Ibiza, the archbishop of Tarragona, acting on behalf of James I, had ten stones hurled by a trebuchet against the castle, at which it surrendered.[58]

The fourteenth and fifteenth centuries saw important changes in the effectiveness of cannons, though throwing machines including trebuchets remained useful. By the fourteenth century, monarchical resources increased; defences had become so good, that storming them became more difficult, and blockade had to be relied on against major sites, as, for example, by Edward III at Calais. Conventional methods remained dominant through much of the Hundred Years War, but towards the end of that war, and in the period which followed, guns came into their own. Froissart, in the fourteenth century, saw the common weapons as 'engiens, canons, trebus, espringales, brigoles et ars'; and trebuchets were still the main

58 On Castelnaudry, Contamine, p. 104; *Chanson*, i, p. 216; compare Henry of Livonia ed. Brundage, p. 181. On Ibiza, James I, ed. Forster, i, p. 221.

weapon used to break down walls.[59] At Orléans in 1420, the citizens tested out their trebuchet by throwing a bale of hay. It was still thought: *trabeta sunt etiam tormenta murorum*(trebuchets are the throwing-engines for walls). The conquest of parts of Greece, which followed the taking of Constantinople in 1204, was largely achieved by sieges, and by the frequent employment of western trebuchets: as at Corinth, Korone, Arkadia, and Nikli. These machines were made for the crusaders by Venetians.[60]

By the later period, trebuchets were undoubtedly powerful weapons; the stone which hit the governor's house at Roche-Derrien, weighed 300 pounds. At Cyprus, in 1373, it was claimed that twelve stones weighing a hundredweight each were thrown. Engines remained effective; they allowed the English to take Moncontour in nine days in 1371. Henry V ordered 'two of the best engines, called brides', for his Agincourt campaign, which were almost certainly trebuchets; and trebuchets and other engines were taken on his next expedition too. Trebuchets still proved useful at Burgos in 1476, and at Rhodes in 1480, where some 22 stone-throwing engines were employed, as against ten large guns. It must be said, however, that the Italian trebuchet here, was seen as old-fashioned, and they could only find one man, a sailor, who knew how to operate it.[61]

Cats and Mining

Mining was a very old method of attacking fortifications, either simply by burrowing under them in order to come up on the other side, or by weakening the foundations so that they would collapse. Vitruvius makes it clear that the Romans not only used mining at sieges, but also had means of combating mines, for example, by deepening defensive ditches, and using water to flood enemy mines. For the same reason, Vitruvius recommended the building of deep and solid foundations for defence.[62] The normal method of mining aimed at undermining the foundations of a wall or a tower, by digging a tunnel beneath the foundations, supported on timber props. At the chosen moment, the props would be set alight, so that the structure above would collapse into the tunnel. Thus we see King John at the siege of Rochester, making available the fat from forty pigs for his mine.[63]

59 Froissart, ed. Luce, xv, p. 19; compare p. 80.

60 On Orléans and the quote, see Contamine, pp. 195, 103. For Greece, *Morea*, pp. 111, 118, 122, 130, 306.

61 On Roche-Derrien, Burne, *Crecy*, pp. 90–1. On Cyprus, Payne-Gallwey, p. 314. On Montcontour, Longman, ii, p. 189. On Henry V, *Calendar* ed. Kirby, p. 197. On Burgos, Finó, 'Jet', p. 43. On Rhodes, Brockman, p. 70, called 'palms'.

62 Vitruvius, ii, p. 367.

63 See above, ch. 6, n. 17, 18, 19.

Mining with picks

Mining was necessary because the throwing engines were not always sufficient to break down a wall. The vikings at Chester in 918 used hurdles on props to give them cover while they mined the wall; and later they improved their covers by adding hides to the roofing. The cat, or Welsh cat, was useful for this purpose; it was basically a mobile shelter for miners to begin their operation. It was said that the name came from the way it was moved, creeping like a cat up to the wall. Iron nails were used to attach it to the wall. A Welsh cat was used at Lisbon, under the wings of a mobile siege tower; it was made of woven osiers, and inside was a group of youths from Ipswich, who had to keep it in position behind the tower. The cat which Simon de Montfort, the crusader, produced at Toulouse in 1218, was particularly large, holding 400 knights, and 150 archers; it was made of wood, iron and steel, with a platform, a door, and a roof.[64]

These roofed, mobile protective structures were called by many names, such as sows, mice, or weasels, and were often used to cover mining operations, as at Berwick, where the sow 'had been brought up to the wall to mine it'. Henry of Livonia described the use of a sow at Mone: 'under which they dug at the fort, until they came to the centre of the rampart'; they then removed the sow, and pushed a tower into its place. The sow

64 On Chester, *Fragmentary Annals*, p. 170: *do ronadh na cliatha, t ro bhadar no sloigh fotha ag tolladh an mhair*. On Lisbon, *De Expugnatione Lyxbonensi*, p. 162. For Simon de Montfort, Contamine, p. 102; *Chanson*, iii, p. 156: *una gata; Que.lh soler e las alas e.l trau e.l cabiron/E.lh portal e las voutas e.l fial e l'estaon/Son de fer e d'acer*. compare *Chanson*, i, p. 166, l. 26: *la gata aprobjeron ins el fons del valat*; to the edge of the ditch, in order to fill it.

Mining under cover of a mantlet

seems to been named from the image of a sow suckling her piglets-the men crouched underneath, mining the base of the wall. William of Tyre described one of these being used at Nicaea, made by a Lombard expert, with a device inside to attach it to the wall. This one had a roof with a particularly steep pitch, which gave added protection against stones thrown down on to it. The Germans and Flemings also made a sow at Lisbon.[65]

Mining could be a very precarious business. The wall at Acre fell at an unexpected, twisting angle, and nearly killed the miners. At Aleppo Joscelin, count of Edessa, did not take sufficient care, and was nearly buried alive; he was seriously ill, but when his less bold son refused to go to Cresson, Joscelin had himself carried there on a litter. On arrival he raised his hands in praise of God, and fell dead. At Tortona the citizens counter mine led to a fall in the imperial mine, and some of the miners in it were suffocated.[66]

Mining proved effective at sieges throughout our period, and, if

65 On Berwick, *Lanercost*, in *EHD*, iii, p. 272: 'brought up to the wall to mine it'. On Mone, Henry of Livonia, ed. Brundage, p. 241: 'under which they dug at the fort'; ed. Arbusow & Bauer, p. 218: *porcum fingunt, sub quo castrum fodiunt, donec ad medium vallum perveniunt*. William of Tyre, ed. Huygens, i, pp. 208–09: *quidam Longobardus natione accedens ad principes, videns quod omnium artificum eluderentur argumenta . . . huius artis professus est se habere periciam; machinam miro construit artificio . . . murum eam possent applicare*. On Lisbon, *De Expugnatione Lyxbonensi*, p. 143.

66 On Acre, Ambroise, ed. Hubert & La Monte, p. 205. On Aleppo, William of Tyre, ed. Babcock & Krey, ii, p. 52. On Tortona, Otto of Freising, ed. Mierow, pp. 135–6.

anything, became more common, and more important, in the later period. But, for example, we hear of a successful mine at Bergamo in 894, which brought down the wall, so that the Franks were able to enter. Less successfully, the vikings used picks to try and mine the walls at Paris in 885. Barbarossa used 'a quite unusual device' for his mining at Tortona, but unfortunately the chronicler does not describe it further.[67] Mining was significant in the sieges of Rochester, Bedford, Château-Gaillard, and Carcassonne, all in the early thirteenth century. It is probable that this period saw a burst in mining activity, at the time when the trebuchet was in its infancy.

Mining retained its importance, and techniques were developed. It became important to detect enemy mines, and then try to counter them; hand to hand contests often followed. At Caen, the defenders used bowls of water placed at suitable points, if the water moved, it would warn of mining activity. At Rhodes, in 1522, a system of bells was set up for the same purpose. Still, with Henry V, mining tools formed an important proportion of the things assembled for a campaign: shovels, scoops, and props; and Henry V himself fought hand to hand inside a mine. Tedaldi claimed that no less than fourteen mines were begun at Constantinople in 1453, and all from a considerable distance. Barbaro says that one mine, which was discovered, began half a mile away from the walls, and went right under the foundations; the men had dug into the ground: 'the earth being supported above with stout props of good wood'. At Sebastea, the mine began a mile away, so as to escape attention. Smoke and evil-smelling objects were part of the armoury of the defenders against these tunnels, as well as water for flooding. At Constantinople, both sides employed specialists for mining: the Turks brought men from Novo Brod, and the Christians used the Scot, John Grant. One counter mine here came upon a mine, held up by props, already smothered with pitch ready to fire.[68]

Mines could also be quite complex, with several tunnels, or as at Malta, one above the other, obviously hoping that this might catch out the enemy. They continued the mine while a parley was being held, but a Christian noticed the earth moving. The Knight who discovered the mine was rewarded by the presentation of a gold medal. At Lisbon, we hear of a particularly elaborate mine being constructed, extending inside the city to forty cubits, with branches off, thought to be the first known medieval gallery mine.[69]

67 On Bergamo, *Annales Fuldenses*, p. 117. On Paris, Abbo, p. 22. On the device at Tortona, Otto of Freising, ed. Waitz, p. 125: *sed etiam inusitato satis utens artificio cuniculos versus turrim*.

68 On Caen, Seward, p. 104. On Rhodes, Brockman, p. 128. On Henry V, Wylie & Waugh, p. 32. On 1453, Tedaldi in Jones, p. 5; Barbaro, p. 50, and see pp. 55–8; Doukas, p. 89; Leonard of Chios in Jones, p. 17.

69 On Malta, Balbi, pp. 132–4; on Lisbon, *De Expugnatione Lyxbonensi*, p. 143 and n.; Köhler, iii, pt. I, p. 127.

Various kinds of shelter are met with, including screens. Henry of Livonia described what sounds like a very simple protection indeed, a mantlet made with two planks and a staff, 'like a pastoral staff', to support it. *Gregory's Chronicle* mentions, during the Wars of the Roses, the invention of a kind of screen made like a trellis, which could be squeezed out or pushed in, to make the size required. The same chronicle refers to pavises carried like doors, which could be folded up, and which possessed loopholes for shooting through.[70]

Rams and Bores

The battering ram is one of the most ancient of all siege weapons, and one of the most effective. The simplest form of ram was simply some large, heavy object, such as a tree trunk, carried against a wall or gate. Usually in the middle ages, the ram was strengthened with a metal head, and the beam and its operators protected by a roof. This might be a simple roofing over the ram, it might be a wheeled vehicle within which the ram rested, or it might be an elaborate siege tower in which the ram dominated the ground level storey. The smaller protective shelters were similar to those used for mining, and given similar names: weasels and mice, with their implication of gnawing holes, could have been used for either, but probably usually refer to boring or ramming operations. Normally the ram was swung within its protecting cover by ropes or chains. Bores and picks differed in that they possessed a pointed end with the purpose of breaking up the joins of a wall, but they performed basically the same function as rams.

Vitruvius described a Roman ram operated on rollers, and pulled backwards and forwards by ropes; and the Byzantines, who continued Roman techniques, used rams, for example, in 711. Gildas says that the Anglo-Saxon invaders of Britain possessed rams; and Leudegisel, in the Merovingian age, had rams with sheds and wheels, carried on wagons. Attila the Hun used battering rams against Orléans, making the walls rock, before it was saved by Aetius.[71]

Rams were made at Lisbon, Jerusalem and Tyre, amongst other places, and commonly, by this time, seem to have been incorporated into siege towers, in the lower part. One ram at Acre had iron bound round it, and another was a ship's mast with iron placed over each end. At Tyre, a Moslem officer developed an anti-ram device, catching the head of the ram with hooks using ropes from the wall, and then pulling on these to

70 Henry of Livonia, ed. Brundage, p. 97; *Gregory's Chronicle*, in *EHD*, iv, p. 288.

71 Vitruvius, i, pp. 51, 345–7. On 711, Theophanes, p. 76. Gildas, p. 27: the major towns were laid low by the repeated battering of enemy rams. On Leudegisel and Attila, Gregory of Tours, ed. Krusch & Levison, i, pp. 359, 48: *Interea iam trementibus ab impetu arietum muris iamque ruituris; maximo arietum inpulsu.*

overturn the whole engine. A kind of counter-ram was developed at Tyre as well, consisting of a beam swung on pulleys using a winch, which could be aimed against the siege tower if it came close to the wall. The defenders also used pulleys to hoist up containers with dung so that they could empty it over the Franks in the tower; manning that particular tower must have been a signally unpleasant task! The ingenious efforts against rams at Tyre were provoked by the crusaders' frequent use of them, and several were smashed to pieces. They were over forty cubits long here, with iron blocks at the end of the beam, one of which weighed over twenty pounds. These rams were placed within structures, to which they were attached by ropes. At Beaucaire, during the Albigensian Crusade, the citizens designed a noose, in which to catch the crusaders' ram, and then heave it over. There was a tendency, as with many siege weapons, to make larger rams in the later period, as did the king of Aragon at Peniscola.[72]

Scaling

Ladders must be one of the oldest means for effecting entry to a fortification, and go back well beyond the Romans. In the middle ages, as walls got higher, and ditches deeper and broader, ladders often had to be quite long, but they always remained useful. At Boulogne though, in 1351, the besiegers broke into the lower town, but when they tried to scale the walls into the inner town, found that their ladders were simply not long enough, and had to give up. Not only wooden ladders, but folding ladders, rope and leather ladders are met, for example, Fredegar describes the Franks as using rope ladders; but at Tortona, one of Barbarossa's men made do with a simple axe, which he used to make footfholds for himself.[73]

On the crusades, the expertise of sailors with ladders is sometimes mentioned. At Antioch Bohemond had a rope ladder made of hemp, which had hooks at boths ends: to attach to the top of the wall, and to fix securely at the bottom. At Jerusalem it was ordered that every two knights should between them produce a ladder for the common use, giving some idea of the numbers that were required. At Constantinople in 1453, the Turks had no less than 2,000 long ladders ready for their storm attempt.[74]

Ladders, however, are fairly frail structures, and easily spotted. Defenders naturally tried to push them away, and even when they possessed claws to

72 On Acre, Ambroise, ed. Paris, col. 102, ll. 3825–7: *un moton faire . . . s'ert bien ferrez/E mult estreitement serrez*. On Tyre, Ibn al-Qalanisi in Gabrieli, pp. 32–3. On Beaucaire, Sumption, p. 186; and Peniscola, James I.

73 On Boulogne, Burne, *Crecy*, p. 233. Fredegar, p. 79: *restium funibus*. On Tortona, Otto of Freising, ed. Mierow, pp. 137, 135.

74 On ladders, Ambroise, ed. Hubert & La Monte, p. 167. At Antioch and Jerusalem, William of Tyre, ed. Babcock & Krey, i, pp. 255, 369. On 1453, Barbaro, p. 59.

Scaling a wall, note the wedge supporting the ladder

grip the wall, this could be done. A ladder at the siege of Llanstephen was pushed away, and the climbers fell into the ditch. At Pontorson, in the Hundred Years War, a scaling ladder was pushed away from the wall by none other than the sister of Constable du Guesclin, Julienne, who was also a nun! Ladders could only bear a limited weight, and often broke under the strain of too many enthusiastic attackers clambering on to them. In the fourteenth-century siege of Smyrna, Doukas' grandfather climbed half way up a ladder, then took off his helmet to see how far there was to go, only to be hit between the eyes by a crossbow bolt, so that he fell to his death.[75]

The use of the conventional ladder for scaling, was demonstrated in a highly unconventional manner by Marshal Boucicaut, during the Hundred Years War. With a touch of showmanship, he displayed his considerable athletic prowess, by turning a somersault in full armour, and then, still in armour, climbing a scaling ladder to the top, without using his feet, by a series of arm jerks; he followed that up, by taking off the mail, and doing the same thing again, with one hand![76]

In addition to ladders, bridges were often made to assist the attackers in reaching the top of the walls. The Venetians were adept at attaching such structures to ships, often with ingenious means of swinging ladders or bridges round to the required position, as on the Fourth Crusade. The *grue*, or crane, used at Neuss seems to have been something like a modern building crane, able to lower a bridge into position.[77] Towers later often

[75] On Llanstephan, *Brut Y Tywysogion*, p. 122: *Ac yn dilesc ef a'e wyr hwynt a ymhoelassant yr ysgolyon hyny syrthawd.* On Pontorson, Contamine, p. 242. On Smyrna, Doukas, pp. 69–70.

[76] On Boucicaut, Contamine, pp. 216–17; Boucicaut, pp. 219–20.

had a drawbridge attachment near the top, which could also be lowered when the tower had been pushed close enough to the walls.

Combustibles

Fire in various forms was used in a large number of sieges. When the Hungarians attacked Pavia, in 924, they simply threw torches over the walls, and with effect.[78] Fire was also used attached to arrows, or in containers. Often some such material as tow was set alight for these purposes, but the most effective medieval combustible was surely Greek Fire.

Greek Fire, said to be invented by Kallinicos, was developed by the Byzantines in the seventh century, and used primarily at sea. We have seen the major rôle it played in the defence of Constantinople, against enemy fleets, as against the Rus in 941.[79] It was difficult to put out and, later at least, exploded on impact. The Byzantines used it both from a siphon which threw the flame direct, or from catapults. In time it was also used on land, in various ways.

The Turks used Greek Fire more frequently than the crusaders, and this suggests that they were more familiar with it. The Byzantines may have been slow to pass on its secrets, fearful, as they often were, of the intentions of the Franks against themselves. They may also have been unwilling to pass on large amounts of the necessary ingredients. Nevertheless crusaders picked up recipes and the use of Greek Fire, and we find it appearing in Anjou in the mid-twelfth century, probably through the services of Fulk the king of Jerusalem, and father of Geoffrey V, the first to use Greek Fire in the West, so far as we know.[80] It was also used by Richard the Lionheart, the grandson of Geoffrey V, at the end of the century, himself of course with crusading experience.

The Turks used Greek Fire at the sieges of Nicaea, Ma'arrat and Acre, among others. At Acre it is mentioned that they hurled it in containers. At Nicaea the Christians had used oil against it, at Sidon water and vinegar, and at Acre mud. At Jerusalem the Moslems used some kind of special weapon for hurling what seems to be Greek Fire, multiple flame-throwing balistas. We also hear of a Moslem from Damascus at the siege of Acre offering the defenders his own special recipe of Greek Fire, which proved effective where others, although containing naptha, had failed against the Frankish siege towers; now the flames roared up through the

77 On Fourth Crusade, Villehardouin, ed. Shaw, pp. 87–90. On Neuss, Contamine, pp. 211–12.

78 On Pavia, Liutprand, pp. 74–7.

79 See above, ch. 1 n. 16.

80 See Bradbury, 'Greek Fire'.

platforms, and the previously jubilant Franks danced to another tune. As the Frankish Ambroise lamented:

they burned,
And all their might to ashes turned.

The Franks also used Greek Fire, and Ambroise described an incident at Acre, where it was hurled in a container, and hit an unfortunate Saracen, breaking and pouring over him: 'so that his genitals were burned'.[81]

A twelfth-century Arab source gave a recipe for Greek Fire, including naptha, olive oil and lime, which had to be distilled several times. Other combustible recipes were given, using tar, resin, sulphur, and dolphin fat, all of which had to be cooked. The writer mentioned that naptha was the vital ingredient for use in war. His method of use was to heat in an earthenware pot, cover it with felt, and hurl it: 'it will never be extinguished'.[82]

The first known use of Greek Fire in the West, as we have mentioned, was by Geoffrey V of Anjou, at Montreuil-Bellay in 1151, when the inflammable material was closed in an iron jar, and thrown by a mangonel. In this case it was used against wooden repairs to the defences, and against houses inside. 'The contents were expelled by the impact, and the discharged matter caused a fire'.[83]

Various other fire weapons are heard of, including fire wheels. These were used on the Baltic Crusade, when they were described as 'wheels filled with fire'. They also appeared at Malta, where for such a simple device, they proved extremely effective because they set alight the robes of the Turks. Here, one commentator described them as hoops dipped in brandy and rubbed with oil and gunpowder; another as being invented by the Knight, Ramon Fortuyn, and consisting of barrel hoops with caulking material over them, dipped in pitch until they were as thick as a leg, then set alight and thrown at the enemy. Even at this time, fire was still a much feared weapon, and the Christians placed large barrels of water on the walls, ready to jump into should their clothes catch fire.[84]

[81] On Acre, Ambroise, ed. Hubert & La Monte, p. 149; compare Abbo p. 57. On Nicaea, Orderic Vitalis, v, p. 138. On Sidon, Acre, Jerusalem, the recipe, see Gabrieli, pp. 28 (Ibn al-Qalanisi), 198, 199 (Ibn al-Athir); 173 (Imad ad-Din). On the quote and the genitals, Ambroise, ed. Paris, col. 92, ll. 3429–32: *Li Turc le feu grezeis jeterent/Es treis chastels que alumerent, / . . . / Quis virent toz ardeir en cendre*; and col. 99, ll. 3697–9: *Desur ses choses necessaires, /Si qu'il ot ars les genitaires/Del feu grezeis*.

[82] Lewis, *Islam*, pp. 222–3.

[83] John of Marmoutier, pp. 218–19.

[84] Henry of Livonia, ed. Brundage, p. 225; Balbi, p. 76 and Bradford, p. 115.

Cannon in action, with crossbows shooting fire-arrows, from a German manuscript firework book, about 1400

Miscellaneous Weapons

Quite primitive and simple materials could make effective siege weapons, from boiling water or oil, to large rocks or heavy objects dropped from a height. Gregory of Tours says the Franks used rocks, flaming barrels of pitch, and boxes filled with stones. At Bergamo in 894, the defenders were forced to resort to pulling the stones from their own wall, to drop on the heads of the attackers. Still at Malta, in the sixteenth century, ordinary rocks could be important: Balbi says that stones taken from demolished houses, 'proved as useful as any other kind of ammunition'. At Crema, the citizens fighting off Frederick Barbarossa, dropped iron weights which were red-hot and barbed. At Chester in 918, when attacked by the vikings, the defenders, clearly in desperation, mixed ale with water, which they boiled in cauldrons and poured on the enemy, so that 'their skin peeled off'; later they also dropped beehives on the unfortunate attackers. The Parisians under siege by the vikings dropped heated wax and pitch. And, of course, the ordinary weapons of war, such as spears and bows, could prove exceedingly useful. A summons of 806 to the Franks demands spades, axes, picks and stakes; and a capitulary of 813 calls on the warriors to bring pickaxes, hatchets and stakes. It is not certain when the first *archères*, or arrow-loops, were built into fortifications, but they became common. Early examples usually consisted of two solid blocks of stone built into the wall, with a narrow gap between them. In this way, the archer could shoot out, from a large space behind the loop, but there was only a slim chance of enemy arrows coming in, and the method of construction did not weaken the wall. Battlements were also constructed in order to give protection to archers and other soldiers.[85]

At Barcelona, in the time of Charlemagne, we find the old Roman *testudo* being tried, that is, the tortoise, which provided a cover either with shields, or with some structure, under cover of which the walls could be approached. The vikings used this method against Paris; and the *testudo* was also used at Bergamo in 894, when it was described in more detail: 'holding their shields above their heads like a roof'. The same device continued in use, and is described, for example, during the First Crusade, as 'a roof of shields'. Count Raymond made use of a *testudo* at Nicaea; and even as late as the siege of Malta, Balbi says the Turks found a *testudo* useful, though in this case as in many others, some kind of constructed mantle seems to be implied.[86]

85 Gregory of Tours, ed. Krusch & Levison, p. 359. On Bergamo, *Annales Fuldenses*, p. 123. Balbi, p. 122. On Crema, Otto of Freising, ed. Mierow, p. 303. On Chester, *Fragmentary Annals*, p. 172. On Paris, 806 and 813, Oman, ii, pp. 81–2. On the *archères*, Viollet-le-Duc, p. 40 and n.k.

86 On Barcelona, Ermold, p. 31. On vikings, Abbo, pp. 37, 39. On Bergamo, *Annales*

Dirty Tricks

The dirty tricks department was often active in crusading sieges. We have already mentioned the ingenious devices that were improvised for countering towers. An interesting addition to siege methods was used at Jerusalem. It may have been common, but is not commonly mentioned. In preparation for a storm attack, the Franks set fire to sacks and cushions and threw them into the city, thus making a smoke screen. Control of water supply was always important, and it was common practice to try and damage the likely sources for the other side by tainting water with corpses of men and animals and all manner of awful materials, as Barbarossa did at Tortona. A particularly sneaky trick was used against the Franks at Bostrum where, desperate for water, they found a well and let down buckets to draw up water, but Moslems were concealed in caves off the shaft, and cut the ropes as they descended. The Turks at Rhodes in 1522, used objects, again called carcasses, but this time giving off an unpleasant smell, and studded, so that when they scored a hit, the wounds became septic.[87]

The use of disguise is common in descriptions of sieges, though one at times suspects a degree of literary invention. Richer described two such tricks in the tenth century: at Laon, where the attackers joined foragers returning to the city, in order to get in; and at Mons in 956.[88]

One also hears of some novel weapons, such as the crow, which was used like a giant fishing rod to hook up men below, and was employed at Ludlow in 1139; while at Vatteville an artificial hand with iron hooks was used to capture a knight. In Italy, at Crema, Barbarossa used some kind of mantrap, 'like mousetraps only stronger'. At Malta, the Christians had weapons, called trumps, which were hand-guns, some of which threw Greek Fire, while others fired bullets. But one of the oddest ideas must be that of the sheriff of Essex under Henry III, who took forty cockerels, with the declared intention of tying combustibles to them so that they would fly inside; as it happened, peace was made, and the poor creatures escaped what would surely have been a most unpleasant, and presumably, fatal experience for them.[89]

Fuldenses, p. 123. On First Crusade and Nicaea, Raymond of Aguilers, p. 26; Orderic Vitalis, v, p. 52: *consertorum testudine scutorum se occultare*. Balbi, pp. 152, 160: a manta 'which was called a *testudo* by the ancients'. Compare William of Tyre, ed. Huygens, i, p. 206: *sub testudine*.

87 On Jerusalem and Bostrum, William of Tyre, ed. Babcock & Krey, i, p. 368; ii, p. 151. On Tortona, Otto of Freising, ed. Mierow, p. 135. On Rhodes, Brockman, p. 131.

88 Richer, i, pp. 275–9; ii, pp. 17–19.

89 On Ludlow, Warner, p. 97 and fig. 4; Robert of Torigny, ed. Stevenson, p. 712. On Vatteville, Orderic Vitalis, vi, p. 346: *ingeniosa manus unci ferreis*. On Crema, Otto of Freising, ed. B. Mierow, p. 302. On Malta, Balbi, pp. 82, 159. On cockerels, Prestwich, *Edward I*, pp. 58–9; though n. 131 suggests they were a ruse rather than a reality.

Cannons and Handguns

There was considerable development of fire power in the later middle ages, experiments in types of weapon, in size, in the materials used. A gun could be a vase or pot, a small hand weapon, or an enormous cannon which required dozens or even hundreds of men to move. Guns could shoot pellets, darts, and stone, or metal balls of various sizes. There were no recognised calibres, balls were made to fit the individual weapon. That there were various types and sizes is clear, but it is not always easy, or possible, to distinguish the contemporary meaning of the many terms used, such as cannons, bombards, culverins, veuglaires, serpentines, crapaudins, mortars, haquebuts, arquebuses, falcons, ribaudequins, guns.

One can reasonably make the division between cannons and handguns. Sometimes it is made clear, that by culverin was meant handgun, as when at Rouen in 1435 we hear of culverins *ad manum*. Sometimes the culverin was used on a tripod or stand, and was probably usually portable at least. When one hears of large numbers of guns, it is probable that they included handguns, as in the French artillery park at Castillon.[90]

Gunpowder seems to appear first in the West in the thirteenth century, and the development of useful guns depended upon the manufacture of gunpowder made from purified saltpetre. There have always been claims that it originated in China, and saltpetre was early known in Arabic Africa as 'Chinese snow', and in Persia as 'Chinese salt'; but if this is so, the Chinese do not seem to have developed guns at a date earlier than those found in the West, and used gunpowder for fireworks; though they did, by the thirteenth century possess something called 'heaven-shaking thunder'. Roger Bacon, in a letter of 1249, shows that he had been experimenting with gunpowder, and the fact that he hid the recipe in code, suggests that he was aware of its significance. His mixture consisted of seven parts of saltpetre, five of young hazelwood (charcoal), and five of sulphur. The *Liber Igneum* of Marcus Graecus, dating before the 1270s, contained thirty-five recipes for incendiaries and explosives, five of which use saltpetre; and the Arab writer, Hasan al-Ramah, writing in the late thirteenth century, has comments on the purification of saltpetre, essential if it were to be useful for guns. The Spanish attributed the invention of gunpowder to the Moors, who used it against Alfonso XI in 1343; and it has been claimed that the Mongols used gunpowder in Japan in the thirteenth century. The traditional view that gunpowder was first developed in the Far East, and then transmitted to the West by the Moslems, remains a possibility.[91]

90 On guns in general, see Oman, Vale and Hogg, and Contamine, pp. 138–50, 193–207. On Rouen and Castillon, Vale, pp. 134, 141, and the Musée de l'Armée, pl. 22.

91 On the Chinese, and the Mongols, Contamine, pp. 139, see also pp. 137–50. On thunder, Bacon, Graecus and Hasan see Oman, ii, pp. 207, 206, 209.

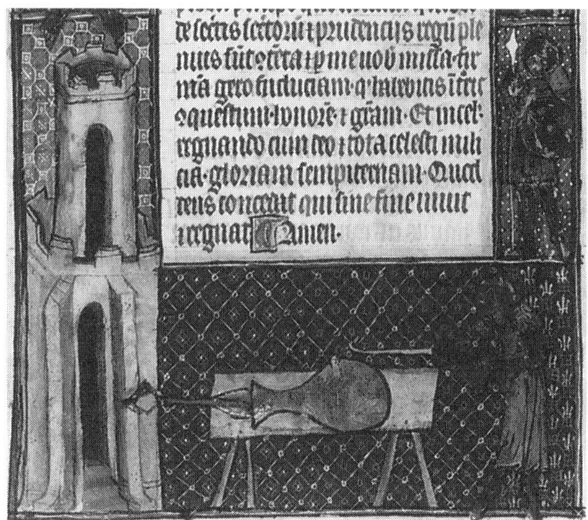

The cannon from the
Milemete manuscript, 1326

It used to be thought that gunpowder was invented by a German monk, Berthold Schwarz of Freiburg, in the early fourteenth century. The 'evidence', in the *Ghent Memorial Book*, is a later addition, and now discredited; the legend about the German monk first appeared in 1493, and was only added to the *Ghent Book* in the sixteenth century. Roger Bacon's claims, however, remain good; his work is as early as anything clearly demonstrated from elsewhere, and could well have been done independently. One point of interest is the difference between eastern and western methods of making gunpowder, at least by the sixteenth century. Balbi noted at Malta, that you could tell a Turkish shot, because the Christian smoke was 'different from theirs', with its thick, black smoke.[92]

The origins of guns remains obscure. As we have seen, the claims for named individual inventors, such as Schwartz, are not substantiated. All we can observe is a gradual emergence of weapons which are recognisably guns, made of metal and fired by gunpowder. This had occurred in the West by the early fourteenth century. One possibility is a gradual progression from weapons of a similar nature. Probably the use of combustibles, particularly Greek Fire, which may have incorporated gunpowder, and of machines to throw darts, contributed to the development of the cannon. The earliest representation in the West, in the Milemete Manuscript of 1326, presented to Edward III on his accession, shows a vase-shaped cannon, apparently of metal, which reminds one of illustrations of containers for Greek Fire; it holds a bolt which looks much like a crossbow bolt, of the kind shot by *balistae*. Yet it is unquestionably a cannon, with a touch-hole. Early references to the French use of *pots de fer* as, for example,

92 On Schwarz, see Contamine p. 138. Balbi, p. 164.

against Southampton in 1338, and the knowledge that early cannons fired bolts with iron feathers, points in the same direction.[93]

Gunpowder was known in the West by the thirteenth century, when explosive compounds are mentioned. There is a mass of evidence, of varying certainty, for the use of guns in the fourteenth century. This evidence also covers a wide geographical area, and makes it certain that guns were being used throughout Europe in the first half of the fourteenth century. Edward I used gunpowder at Stirling in 1304, and the use at Brechin in that year, may be the first known instance in the West. During his Scottish wars, Edward III was supplied with saltpetre and quick sulphur from York; saltpetre and sulphur had also been used in an explosive mixture by the Burgundian, Jean de Lamouilly. At Ghent in 1313 were kept *bussen met kruyt*, cannons with powder. Cannons were used at the siege of Metz in 1324, at Florence in 1326, and at Friuli one hears of *vasi e scioppi*. Guns were used by the English against the Scots in 1327, by Edward III in France as at the Battle of Crécy, and by the French, for example at Southampton in 1338, at Perigord in 1339, at Cambrai against Edward III, and at Aiguillon in 1345. The same period saw the use of guns elsewhere in Europe, notably in Italy: at Lucca in 1341 a 'thunderer' is mentioned; and 'an iron cannon to fire iron balls'. Brescia also possessed a 'tube for firing balls'. The Moors cast iron balls against the Christians 'by fire'; and in 1342 at Algeciras used 'thunder engines' which shot iron balls the size of apples. There survives an Arabic manuscript of the first half of the fourteenth century, which describes the loading of a *midfa*', or gun, using gunpowder, with instructions to load carefully or else the gun will explode. As the century progressed, possession of guns, and of large numbers of them, became a commonplace: Edward III had ten cannons at Calais, ten at Cambrai, and a hundred at the Tower in 1345, of which twenty-two were used in his 1346 campaign.[94]

The early guns seem to have been small, but there were soon experiments to develop their size and capability. The *pot de fer* was one type, but there were also guns which threw stones, perhaps what may be called bombards. This particular word came from the Greek *bombos* because of the noise made by the weapon, a loud hum, which also reminds one of descriptions of the hurling of Greek Fire. *Ribaudequins* seem to have been the most commonly used guns in the mid-fourteenth century. At the siege of Ghent, where 200 wagons were loaded with cannons and artillery, we hear of *ribaulds* mounted on 'high wheelbarrows, banded with iron, with long iron spikes sticking out from the front, which they are accustomed to wheel along with them'. At Bruges there is reference to 'new engines which men call ribaulds' (*niewen enginen die men heet ribaulde*). Ribaudequins were used to defend the gate at the siege of Tournai in 1340. Edward

93 Milemete, f70b, and compare f44b. On Southampton, Oman, ii, pp. 212, 215.
94 Contamine, pp. 138–40; Oman, ii, pp. 212–18.

III had made considerable use of them in the form of tubes clamped together, with touch-holes in close proximity, so that several could be fired at one time. In 1345 he took 100 from the Tower, and at Calais they were listed alongside the engines and trebuchets. Like most such weapons, there were attempts to increase their effect. At Verona in 1387 no less than 144 of them were placed together in three tiers, each tier in four sections, each section containing twelve tubes. A gunner was employed on each tier, and it took four horses to draw the cart which carried the contraption, standing some twenty foot high altogether. Although they were less important later, when more powerful weapons had been developed, they did not altogether lose their usefulness, and were still found at Meaux in the fifteenth century, placed side by side on battle carts.[95]

The earliest representation of a cannon, shows a pot-shaped weapon. Early tube-shaped cannons were often made from rods of wrought iron fitted round a core. White-hot rings were fixed round the whole, so that when cooled, they would shrink and thus bind the tube; sometimes melted lead was run between the joins. The core was then removed, leaving a hollow tube. A solid chamber was then made with a taper to wedge into one end. Gradually cast iron replaced wrought iron. No cannons from the earliest period survive, but a medieval example kept at Woolwich was taken from the moat of Bodiam castle. It dates from the fourteenth century, and is a small example of an early wrought iron cannon. Another was found in the Marne and taken to Meaux, probably having been used in the siege of that place in the fifteenth century. It consists of an octagonal tube with a round bore, and a breech block hammered in during casting. In the fourteenth century, cuprum, a kind of tough brass, was also used for making guns, as was latten, a brass-like yellow alloy.[96] But increasingly iron was the metal employed, and, by the mid-fifteenth century, usually cast iron. In the fifteenth century the same people were employed to make guns as to found bells.

The word 'cannon' comes from the Greek *kanun*, via the Latin *canna*, meaning simply a tube, though it was only one of several words used to describe early guns. Two men were making and operating *canones de metallo* in Florence in 1326. Words relating to thunder were sometimes used, as, for example, in the master of *tonnoire*, at Lille in 1341. 'Buss' was another common word for the early gun, as the *busa ferrea* at Aachen in 1346, or the *dunrebussen* at Deventer in 1348.[97]

Early cannons were generally tied to a wooden board or platform for use, which allowed for some tipping in order to aim and alter range; the Milemete cannon is placed on a sort of trestle. Froissart speaks of beams

95 On Ghent, Contamine, p. 199; Froissart, ed. Brereton, pp. 235–6. On Bruges and Verona, Oman, ii, pp. 216, 222.

96 On Bodiam, Hogg, p. 10; on Meaux, Seward, *Henry V*, p. 60.

97 Contamine, p. 139.

A cannon on a wooden frame

used to tilt cannons, and the raising and lowering of the wooden mounts by wedges. Even more primitive, but possibly safer and more effective, cannons might be simply placed on a slope, or on a prepared mound of earth. A wooden frame which could be adjusted was convenient, but it would also be damaged by recoil. Better mobility was ensured by the construction of trunnions in the fifteenth century, for example at Rouen in 1456 one hears of cannons carried on two-wheeled carriages. Commines, writing of the siege of Paris, said that there was effective fire from a distance of two leagues. He wrote: 'I am pretty sure that they had elevated the muzzles of the cannons very high'. Methods of cooling and cleaning guns between shots also sound remarkably like later usage, as at Harfleur, where the cannons were swabbed out with vinegar and water.[98]

Cannons could be loaded, either by a mobile chamber or thunder-box, or at the breech. The chamber was filled with powder, leaving a tube for the heated touch. The chamber was closed with a bung of soft wood, such as alder or willow, which would not explode, but would act as a wad between the charge and the ball. The bung would expand and pop out like a champagne cork, and this would prevent the chamber itself from exploding. A chamber consisted of a plug, an empty space for safety reasons, and three sections for powder. The mobile chamber was lifted into the breech by handles, with an iron rod to clamp it in, and was packed with tow. Mobile chambers in the lower end of the tube do not seem to have worked very well, perhaps because the clamping could not be firm enough, allowing premature ignition and a dangerous blow-out. In 1397 at Bologna one hears of a wedge being used to hold the chamber; while by the end of the fifteenth century, plugs were replaced by direct loading, using rods to ram down the muzzle.[99]

98 On tipping, Oman, ii, p. 223. On Rouen, Contamine, p. 144; Commines, ed. Jones, p. 101. On Harfleur, Seward, *Henry V*, p. 59.

99 Oman, ii, p. 221, and n. 6.

Cannon with a range-finder

For a while the ambition was to make larger and larger cannons, which would do more damage with a single shot and be ever more fearsome. The appearance of the great Turkish cannons at Constantinople in 1453, demonstrates that the belief in the advantage to morale of a really enormous gun was not misplaced. But there was also an increasing realisation that greater size did not necessarily signify greater efficiency, and certainly did not make for greater ease of use and mobility. Nevertheless in the meantime some truly monstrous weapons were built. Mons Meg made for Philip of Burgundy in 1449 weighed in at 15,366 pounds; Mad Margot in Ghent at 36,145 pounds.[100]

A chronological glance at the use of cannons in the West in the late middle ages demonstrates something of these changes and developments. Once they had arrived in the early fourteenth century, guns soon began to be used in some numbers, for instance the French had twenty-four made at Cahors for the siege of Aiguillon in 1345. At first, however, they do not

[100] Contamine, p. 142.

seem to have been very large, or to have been fired very frequently. The guns at Calais required only three or four ounces of powder each a day; the four guns made by William of Aldgate in 1353 cost only thirteen shillings and fourpence each, and could not have been large. Projectiles were more various at first, including lead shot, pieces of lead, and iron bolts, as well as balls of metal or stone. The French raid on England in 1338 involved less than fifty bolts with iron feathers, and a mere three pounds of gunpowder. Guns were not at first used for battering walls, lacking the necessary power, but were anti-personnel, as at Crécy, where Froissart describes the 'cannons which they (the English) had in the battle in order to frighten the Genoese'. Villani makes a similar comment of the same battle, remarking that the guns were 'for the purpose of frightening the horses', largely from the noise they made. In the fourteenth century wall battering was still the work of the conventional throwing engines, especially the trebuchet.[101]

In about the last quarter of the fourteenth century, there was a surge forward in the development of guns. It was the first period for the development of large cannons, which brought them into the picture as siege weapons. Larger balls, for example of 800 pounds, began to be used. But in this period efficiency was far from guaranteed. Larger guns were in demand for siege warfare, but the larger the gun, the greater the amount of powder, and the greater the potential for explosion. There was an increase not only in the size of individual weapons, but also in the number used, for example, thirty-two at St Sauveur in 1375 using 100 pound balls. Between 1382 and 1388 William Woodward in England made for the crown seventy-three guns: forty-seven at 380 pounds, five at 318 pounds, and one at 665 pounds. Men who made the individual stones for these weapons were paid wages of sixpence a day. Now cannons were reaching a power where they could be useful in sieges for demolishing walls, for example, at Andruch in 1377 the guns pierced the wall. By 1408 a treatise was able to claim that no wall could withstand cannons.[102]

The Greek chronicler, Doukas, describes the firing of Turkish guns at Belgrade in the fifteenth century in some detail. These were guns which fired quite small lead balls. The rear end of the tube was filled with a powder made of natron, sulphur and charcoal, and then ignited with a

[101] On Cahors, Burne, *Crecy*, p. 118. On Calais, Longman, i, p. 280. On William of Aldgate and 1338 bolts, Oman, ii, pp. 221, 215. On Crécy, Froissart, ed. Luce, iii, p. 416, the Amiens MS: *et le Engles demorerent tout koy et descliquierent aucuns c kanons qu'il avoient en le bataille, pour esbahir les Genevois*. Burne, *Crecy*, pp. 192–203, especially p. 195; Hogg, pp. 197–8; Villani, vi, p. 173: *e tali di sotto con bombarde che saettano pallotte di ferro con fuoco, per impaurire e disertare i cavalli de' Franceschi*.

[102] On Woodward and Andruch, Oman, ii, pp. 223, 225, 226. On St Sauveur, Allmand, *Hundred Years War*, p. 79; on 1408, Seward, *Henry V*, p. 99.

A battery of cannons

spark. 'The compressed air, of necessity, impels the balls', which could pierce mail and flesh.[103]

Really large guns were often a matter or morale or prestige. A commander liked to be able to drag one into position facing a stubborn town. Cities were often proud to produce monsters for their own princes. On more than one occasion guns presented by the citizens were named 'London'. Commanders often sent to places where larger guns were stored ready for use, thus the Captal de Buch besieging Montguyon sent to hire guns from Bordeaux.[104] More often a king or ruler kept guns in his own main strong-

103 Doukas, p. 178.

104 On London, Warkworth, in *Three Chronicles*, p. 60; Wylie and Waugh, ii, p. 36. On the Captal, Wylie and Waugh, ii, p. 359.

Cannon on a carrriage

holds for use on demand, as the kings of England kept a number in the Tower.

By the fifteenth century cannons had become essential siege weapons. Large was beautiful, and they were often made of cast iron, often employed in batteries, and frequently effective in shattering walls and breaking resistance. Long sieges became less common as the century progressed; royal resources were now poured into gun-making. In 1405 Henry IV used 8,000 pounds of iron for repairs to cannons, together with money to be paid as wages to gunners, for carriages for the cannons, and for the mounting of new weapons. There were also expenses on saltpetre, charcoal, and brimstone, on carts for carrying stones, and payments to masons to make them. At this time there was a forge for making cannons in Windsor Castle. We hear of Richard de Love, a mason in Gloucester, who made cannon stones for Henry IV, employing others in the work. It was at this very time that the future Henry V was gaining his early siege experience in Wales. For the siege of Aberystwyth in 1407 cannons were transported by sea, including the four and a half ton 'King's Gonne', together with saltpetre, sulphur, and some ready made-up gunpowder; at the siege itself two of the guns exploded during the bombardment.[105]

105 On 1405 and Richard Love, *Calendar* ed. Kirby, pp. 71, 141. On Aberystwyth, Seward, *Henry V*, p. 23.

Henry V proved to be a master of siege warfare, in which he had a whole string of successes, providing far more evidence for his ability in warfare than the one victory at Agincourt, fought when seeking to escape battle, for which he is chiefly remembered today. He was also a master in the use of artillery, though the cannon was still not guaranteed to bring a result, and blockade was generally the order of the day. Henry took sixty-five gunners and 10,000 gunstones to Harfleur, including some Dutch master gunners, and his cannons included half a dozen of the largest bombards ever seen. Guns had been made for the campaign, in Bristol and London, to add to the existing royal stock. The new guns included ones named *London*, *Messenger* and the *King's Daughter*. He also had built special structures made of wood and iron, which when pulled at the top would open at the base to allow a view of the town, so that a target could be selected, and the guns inside fired 'by the explosive force of ignited gunpowder'.[106] Trenches and earth ramparts were also made to protect the gunners. The impact of the bombardment was considerable, and the French put earth and dung on the roads to deaden the impact of the stones and prevent them from shattering. Special incendiary shells were used which added combustible material to the stone balls, and which played a part in the English victory by setting fire to the bulwark.

His 1417 expedition was equally well equipped with 'gonnez', with 'ordynaunce gadred and welle stuffyd as longyd to such a ryalle Kinge'. For Mantes in 1419, guns were taken by water in ships from Caen. Though the ships could not manage the largest of the guns, they did load 52,000 pounds of iron and gunstones from the wharf, as well as sea coal from the house of Jean du Pont, called the Ordinance House. Similarly for Meaux in 1422, Caen was used as the supply base; Henry ordered from there 10,000 pounds of iron, and sent for all the gunstones and saltpetre, coal, brimstone and iron at Caen and Harfleur to go via Rouen. The cannon in the museum at Meaux, which has a hammered-in breech block, is thought to have been used in Henry's siege. The use of cannons operated by skilled gunners, is seen as one of the main reasons for Henry's success in Normandy: 'there failed them no manner of skill or science'.[107]

In the last stages of the Hundred Years War, improved cannons began to have more effect on walls and on siege warfare. At Orléans in 1428, Salisbury demolished the suburbs, including twelve churches, for the distance of a cannon shot, though apparently he underestimated that distance, since he was then killed by such a shot when making reconnaisance from a tower. The Bureau brothers, Gaspard as Master of Artillery and Jean

106 On Harfleur, Seward, *Henry V*, pp. 52, 54; and the guns, Wylie & Waugh, ii, p. 36. On the structures, *Gesta Henrici Quinti*, p. 36: *vi pulverum ignitorum*.

107 On 1417, Allmand, *Hundred Years War*, p. 80. On 1419, Jean du Pont, and 1422, *Calendar* ed. Kirby, p. 199, 201. On Meaux, Seward, *Henry V*, p. 60. For the quote, Harriss, p. 75; *First English Life*, p. 80.

as Treasurer, played an enormous part in Charles VII's success; they were Parisians of humble birth, who made their fame and wealth as engineers for the king, particularly by the production and operation of cannons. At Harfleur in 1449, Bureau's first shot at the town went right through the rampart of the outer ward. In that year of 1449 to 1450 the French conducted sixty successful and brief sieges.[108] Bayonne surrendered as soon as the large guns, including sixteen bombards, made their appearance; the siege of Dax in 1442 lasted only three weeks, that of St Sever a month, that of Bourg in 1451 six days. The damage done by the guns to walls, and increasingly the knowledge that such damage could be done, brought many sieges to a quick conclusion.

By the time of the last battle of the war, at Castillon in 1453, the rôle of guns is clear. The French had developed the idea of using artillery parks, for example at Dax in 1442, at Mauléon in 1449, and at Guissen in 1449. At Castillon they made a park for 300 guns. Whatever the error of Talbot in attacking, there is no doubt that guns did the damage, holding off the English charge. Talbot's horse itself was brought down by one shot, which led to the death of its rider. It was said that each shot could go through five or six men, and never was there 'such a noise of culverins and ribaudequins being loaded'.[109]

The story was the same everywhere in the later fifteenth century: cannons and guns dominated the weaponry of warfare. Corned powder was developed in granule form, and was more stable than earlier gunpowder. One method of achieving this was, apparently, to use the urine of a wine-drinking man for the mixture, and then allow it to dry out. Powder mills were also invented in the fifteenth century, allowing easier production of powder on the spot. At the same time handguns became more efficient and more common, used for example at Castillon, by the Hussites, by Edward IV who employed 300 Flemish gunners, and in Italy. About a fifth of the Swiss infantry in 1470 were handgunners. It was also the period when handguns began to be shot like modern rifles, from the shoulder, as for example by the Hussites. The arquebus did not truly take over until the sixteenth century, but the necessary mechanism was developed in the fifteenth.[110]

Cannons were now essential for siege warfare, and could do great damage quickly. Edward IV's 'greet gonne', *Newcastle*, and another called *London*, were used against Bamborough, and the stones from the shattered walls 'flewe into the see'. By 1475 Edward possessed a large number of bombards, and had new ones made every day. Town defences came to rely

108 On Orléans, Waurin, in *EHD*, iv, p. 241. On 1449 and the sieges, Oman, ii, p. 226.
109 Thomson, *Hundred Years War*, p. 340.
110 On powder, Seward, *Hundred Years War*, p. 259 and Contamine, p. 197. On Hussites, Oman, ii, p. 229. On Edward IV, Warkworth in *Three Chronicles*, p. 35. On 1470, Contamine, p. 149.

on cannons. At Bourg-en-Bresse, when attacked in 1468, there was a veuglaire and a serpentine with its own loop, at each of the six town gates, as well as mobile culverins.[111] Castle defences were modified to take account of cannons: with lower towers, casemates, and ground level platforms outside the walls but inside the moat.

There were large and famous guns, such as Mons Meg and Mad Margot, already mentioned, or the one in 1476 inscribed: 'I am the Dragon'. But the monster guns were always exceptional, and the usual demand was for large numbers of ordinary cannons. Christine of Pisa thought that an average town defence required twelve cannons, but an average besieger needed 128. In 1431 the emperor took a hundred bombards against the Hussites; while Charles VIII laid out eight per cent of his military expenditure on cannons in 1489. Compared to the small amounts bought in the early fourteenth century, the vast amounts of powder now required show how much the use of guns had increased. Henry VI used a thousand pounds at Beaumont in 1425, and 3,000 pounds against Le Mans; while Philip the Good needed 17,000 pounds of powder against Compiègne in 1430. The Turks in Malta used 130,000 rounds, and 65,000 iron balls were afterwards collected.[112]

The improvements and growing importance of guns, did not mean that disasters could not still occur occasionally. James II of Scotland's royal gunner was killed in 1460 when the *Lion* exploded. The tale of Theuerdank, based on the life of the emperor Maximilian I, mentions a somewhat foolish inspection of artillery by the emperor, using a naked flame to provide light, though he did duck in time to save himself from the effects of the resulting explosion.[113]

By the end of the middle ages, enormous cannons could be built, and large numbers of guns brought to a siege. Cannons became the vital weapon in most of our late conflicts, as at Constantinople, Rhodes and Malta. The Christians were overwhelmed at Constantinople by the size of the great guns which Mehmet had made for him by his Dacian employee, Urban: 'greater than any which had previously been known'. Urban was an Hungarian cannon founder, who had come to seek work in Constantinople in 1452, but was dissatisfied with his pay. Mehmet could offer not only much more money, but also all the materials he needed to make the kind of guns he dreamed of. Urban promised him: 'the stone discharged from my cannon would reduce to dust not only those walls, but even the walls of Babylon'. One huge gun needed forty or fifty yoke of oxen and 2,000 men to move it. When his new monster cannon was tested, a warning was

111 On Edward IV, Warkworth in *Three Chronicles*, p. 60; for Bourg-en-Bresse, Contamine, p. 202.

112 Contamine, pp. 148–9; Balbi, p. 187.

113 On James II, Allmand, *Hundred Years War*, p. 100. On Theuerdank, Benecke, pp. 18–19.

issued, so that pregnant women would not abort. Urban supervised the careful loading of the shot, and measured precisely the amount of powder; the discharge made 'a piercing, air-rending sound', heard ten miles away. It shot stones a mile, which buried themselves six feet deep in the ground. These guns were also accurate, and the Turks used shots to find range, and could aim a triangle of shots to weaken a wall. Balbi says that the Turks at Malta, had one large gun of 180 hundredweight, two of 130 hundredweight, and four of 110 hundredweight; they also had special carriages on which to move them, with iron axles, and iron-rimmed wheels. He says they brought with them by sea 100,000 iron cannon balls, and 15,000 hundredweight of gunpowder. At Malta there were sixty-four large cannons, and during a bombardment, it was 'as if the end of the world was coming'.[114]

The large cannon at Constantinople shot balls weighing 1,200 pounds each, and the explosion 'made all the walls of the city shake, and all the ground inside'. The Turks also used large numbers of guns; there were fourteen batteries, each of four cannons. At Rhodes by 1522, there were up to eighty large guns, in batteries of three or four, and in one month, 1,316 balls were fired. In Constantinople a bombardment left a great pall of smoke over the scene. The shot from the larger cannons was 'carried with such devilish force and irresistible impetus', that the ground shook for miles around. There were enough cannons in the batteries to keep up fire day and night. One problem for defenders in this period, was that walls and defences were not built to take the vibration from really large guns, and so they could not quite reply in kind. At Constantinople it was reported that their own guns made the walls shake. There was also the problem of the recoil in confined spaces. At Malta the Knight, Romegas, did develop an attempt to make guns less damaging when used from the walls; he tried to reduce the impact of the recoil by placing 'a great heap of rope' behind the gun, which absorbed the shock. The Knights here also had made special gun embrasures in the defences.[115]

The Christians were also struck by the frequent use made of the Turkish guns, without the period they themselves would allow for cleaning out and cooling off. They were not surprised when the occasional cannon burst, but they were amazed by the weight of shot raining upon them. The metal would crack from air entering the pores, and therefore the guns were covered with felt. The Turks did in fact cool their weapons by soaking them in oil, which also helped to protect the metal. At Malta, Balbi reported that a large gun at Corradino exploded: 'probably because they had neither been cleaning it, nor allowing it to cool', and forty men were

114 On Urban and the pregant women, Doukas, pp. 200, 201. For the huge gun, Sphrantzes, p. 47. For Malta, Balbi, pp. 31, 33, 81.

115 The large gun, Leonard of Chios in Jones, p. 18; the 14 batteries, Sphrantzes, p. 48; Rhodes, Brockman, p. 127. On Malta, Balbi, p. 149.

killed. The Turks also made special earthwork protections for their cannons, with gaps to fire through. At Constantinople they constructed ditches and put up palisades; they also made special platforms, using rubble and planks. In Malta they built gun platforms, using 'wooden, triangular frames, which they filled with earth'.[116]

Handguns, like cannons, became more efficient, and were also produced in ever larger numbers. In Malta, the Turks proved to be better shots, perhaps because their very best troops, the Janissaries, were trained musketeers. Against the fort at St Elmo they fired up to 7,000 shots a day. Plate armour was also stronger by the end of our period. At Malta, Don Francisco de Sanoguera survived a hit by a musket ball, thanks to his bullet-proof breastplate, though a second shot in the groin killed him.[117]

At any rate, cannons and handguns had transformed warfare; sieges were now dominated by them. And yet, the methods of siege had not altered tremendously. Cannons were used as once throwing engines had been, to breach walls, but even by the time of Malta, enormous cannon power with the attackers need not always bring success. It is not our task to consider why siege warfare altered in the later period, but we might point out that it is a gross simplification entirely to attribute the change to the development of guns. As so often in the history of siege warfare, it is likely that political and social change was more significant.

116 On cleaning guns, Doukas, p. 216. On cleaning, Corradino and the platforms, Balbi, pp. 63, 107, 56. For Constantinople, Sphrantzes, p. 48.
117 On St Elmo, Bradford, p. 92. On Don Francisco, Balbi, p. 114.

CHAPTER TEN

The Conventions and Laws of Siege Warfare

The conventions and laws of siege warfare are of ancient origin. In western warfare, the most important additional factor of the medieval period, was a Christian input; but, when one compares western traditions with eastern, the similarities are more striking than the differences, and this can only be because these traditions, in origin, pre-date both Christianity and Islam. The clashes over religion, and between religions, which we have witnessed during this period, gave rise to passionate feelings, and sometimes atrocities, but there is an overwhelming recognition that conventions existed, and usually they were obeyed.

We need to recognise these conventions in order to understand, and properly judge, medieval war. Harsh action after a capture by storm, for example, was accepted as a convention of war. The breaking of one's word in an agreement, though it happened, and at times was justified by some on the grounds that an oath to one of another religion was not valid, was generally disapproved by those active in medieval war. There was undoubtedly a sense of what was honourable and what was not, and this was, for example, embodied in the medieval code of chivalry. There were also attempts to limit warfare by appeal to a higher good as, for example, developed in the Christian idea of a Just War.[1] Moslems similarly possessed ideas of honourable behaviour, and of a religious interpretation of war, though there was perhaps less division between the two in Islam. In Islamic law, an offer of surrender terms had to be made, before any storm attack, though it seems to have been done, at times, in a way calculated to invite refusal. Several writers through the period, in various places and times, referred to the 'laws of war', as something which all would, or at least should, recognise. Thus one finds such references in the twelfth-century West, or in fifteenth-century Byzantium. Doukas says that Timur captured Arsyngan: 'by the laws of war'.[2]

1 On the just war, the essential reading is Russell, *Just War*.
2 Doukas, p. 89.

William of Tyre wrote that 'war is waged differently and less vigorously between men who hold the same law and faith.'[3] One would expect this to be true, though William had little knowledge of the internal warfare of Christendom, and the surprising thing about the conventions and rules of siege warfare in the conflict between Christendom and Islam, is that, despite hostile attitudes, the agreements were strikingly similar to those made in the West between Christians. One does find atrocities, and examples when the codes were ignored, but men on both sides would also find this regrettable and scandalous. This is the more surprising in that there was every excuse to ignore agreements. The Christian church did not recognise oaths made to Moslems, and vice versa, yet by and large agreements were made and respected. Saladin was worried that if he did not stick to the letter of his agreement over Jerusalem, he would be criticised: 'if we interpret the treaty to their disadvantage, they will accuse us of breaking faith'.[4]

Often the agreements indicate a degree of trust between the two sides, and clearly, on the whole, it was expected that agreements once made would be kept. At Ascalon three days were allowed to carry out the agreement to vacate the place. When Ambroise accuses the Turks of attacking during a tournament, or when Saladin remarks about fears of criticism if he does not abide by the agreement, one can sense the belief that in general the other side is honourable, will abide by treaties, and follow the same code. Saladin's agreement at Jaffa could easily have been modelled on siege conventions in the West. He stormed the town, but the citadel resisted. He agreed to a one day truce during which the Franks might seek aid, but then, if still without assistance, they would surrender.[5]

The agreement at Banyas was a particularly interesting one, since the victory was won against Moslems by an alliance of Christians and Moslems from Damascus. The defeated stronghold had to promise an annual payment to the emir of Damascus. The citizens were allowed to go, or give fealty and stay. Here the Damascenes did the bargaining on behalf of the alliance. Another example of a growing understanding between the two sides was presented in the events at Damietta. Once the agreement had been made, the Christian attackers were allowed into the city for a market, again suggesting some trust. Such arrangements also demonstrate what is generally true of medieval siege warfare, that the conventions crossed boundaries of race and religion.[6]

3 William of Tyre, ed. Babcock & Krey, ii, p. 25; ed. Huygens, i, p. 606: *Aliter enim et remissus solet inter consortes eiusdem legis et fidei pugna committi, aliter inter discolos et contradictorias habenter traditiones*.

4 Imad ad-Din in Gabrieli, p. 162.

5 On Ascalon, William of Tyre, ed. Babcock & Krey, ii, p. 282. On the tournament and Jaffa, Ambroise, ed. Hubert & La Monte, pp. 179, 402.

6 On Banyas and Damietta, William of Tyre, ed. Babcock & Krey, ii, pp. 111, 368.

The Just War

The high middle ages has been seen as a period when the rules of war began to crystallise. There is some truth in this idea, but at the same time the period brings forward little that is new. Perhaps the most important development, broader than the laws of siege, is the working out of the just war theories which had already been broached, but which were now worked over by many leading intellectuals. Not that these theories necessarily reflect the realities of war; they tend to be out of step, either ahead of their time, or more often rationalisations following in the wake of practice.

The development of the just war theory probably grew in the wake of the increase in royal power, and added to that increase by stressing the significance of princely authority in war. Huguccio wrote that 'a just war is waged on the just edict of a prince'.[7] It assisted in making baronial opposition by force invalid, and so helped to keep order within the great realms. The question remained as to how one could define 'prince'; did it include, for example, the princes of Germany, in other words great nobles? There was certainly some blurring at the edges in the use of the terminology, but increasingly definitions of princely authority moved to include only the very greatest powers, and that again assisted the more powerful rulers.

It is unlikely that just war ideas had much effect in limiting warfare between princes; though such theories could not reasonably be interpreted as allowing two opposing princes *both* to have a just cause, and neither to be the aggressor. This however is a familiar fallacy, not unknown in modern war and religious theory. The theory does not so much prevent war, as make sure that each side fits its claims within the accepted framework; it does not so much restrict war, as encourage propaganda, make sure each party claims to have justice on its side. It may be that values were affected, and that one sees 'the diffusion of Christian values in a military society'; and it has been argued that casualties became lower as a result.[8] Perhaps among the knights this was the case, though probably mutual self-interest and the hope of a good ransom was as much responsible as the effect of Christian virtues. In any case, in the later medieval period, one sees often an increase in atrocities and ruthless behaviour; and the common man, the infantry soldier, rarely benefited from any Christian mercy. Treason could always be held up as the justification for any massacre. It is difficult for modern man to view the activities of the westerners on the Fourth Crusade as having much justice, or seeing the attack on eastern Christians as being a very Christian act; yet the Franks at Constantinople assembled, after taking the city, and declared; 'this war is just and lawful', and even saw it as 'a righteous deed'.[9]

7 Contamine, p. 282.
8 Contamine, p. 256.
9 Villehardouin, ed. Shaw, p. 85; Clari, ed. MacNeal, p. 94.

The just war also incorporated just conduct of a war, and this involved the code which was being worked out through the middle ages, and which in one aspect might be called chivalry. Several clerical authors show that they had a concept of what was permissible. Matthew Paris thought that when the victorious royalists cut off the head, feet and hands of the dead Simon de Montfort, they were breaking the rules of the knightly code. The author of the *Vita Edwardi Secundi* also believed in the existence of such a code of practice: when the castles of Despenser the younger were taken in Wales, the writer says the barons divided the spoils between themselves: 'contrary to the law of war', presumably meaning that if done properly others should expect a share. The same writer thought it wrong to build castles without a royal licence, a rule which kings had fought hard to have recognised in earlier ages; and also that it was wrong to defend castles against the king, another example of the way in which royal authority was becoming the expected norm.[10]

Writers on other occasions showed some general agreement on behaviour that was acceptable or not. An interesting example is found in the criticisms of Hubert de Burgh, earl of Kent, when he fell from favour under Henry III. The attacks on him were exaggerated beyond belief, and often nit-picking. He was accused of calling Henry III: 'squint-eyed', silly and impotent, more a woman than a man, and of trying to cut the king's throat with a knife. The accusations also included the charge that he had been paid to deliver provisions to royal garrisons at Niort and La Rochelle, and had cheated them by keeping the cash, and sending casks filled only with sand and stones, and thus was responsible for some of Henry's defeats in France. Another example of unacceptable conduct occurred at Seville, where the citizens allowed the king in, with a promise to surrender, and then closed the gates on him, though as a matter of fact he escaped through a postern. Even some practices which had generally been recognised as normal in siege warfare came in for criticism, mainly because of the changing attitudes of church and clergy. It had always been the thing to destroy provisions which the enemy might otherwise use, but Matthew Paris criticises this practice in Gascony, when vineyards were destroyed, as: 'old women's warfare, and not that of men'.[11]

The Code of Chivalry

The concept which dominates discussion of the conduct of war in the late middle ages, is that of chivalry; whether because of the belief that it was a

10 On Simon de Montfort, Matthew Paris, ed. Giles, iii, p. 356. *Vita Edwardi Secundi*, pp. 110, 116.
11 Matthew Paris, ed. Giles, i, pp. 237–8, 254; iii, p. 52.

major influence upon conduct, or because that belief is thought to be incorrect. On the whole, in recent times, chivalry has been seen as a significant factor in social and military behaviour. Of course, no one thinks that every action, of every medieval warrior, was guided by the code; it was an ideal more akin to a religion, than to a practical way of life for the average knight. And like religion, even among those who followed it, there were many who fell by the wayside; there were others who ignored it altogether. It was also a Christian concept, though warriors of other religions had their own codes of conduct, often sharing the same ideals, such as those lauded by Froissart: of courage, honour and loyalty. Criticism of those who fell short, in the chronicles, is often a good guide to the common belief of what chivalric conduct ought to be: criticism, for example, of failing to keep one's word, of not showing mercy, of not being loyal to one's lord.[12]

Undoubtedly chivalry was the code of a class which saw itself as superior. When chivalry was transported to the Morea after the Fourth Crusade, a local chonicler claimed that: 'a noble should not be a liar', in criticism of an individual knight guilty of the offence. He further commented on the gaining of keys to a stronghold by a trick, through getting the castellan drunk in a tavern: 'it was not fitting for you, as a noble, for treacherous purpose, to have even thought of it'.[13] Criticism itself may not be entirely objective; it was more common to criticise an enemy of one's patron, than the patron himself.

Criticism could also derive from social attitudes; chroniclers looking from an aristocratic milieu, might well comment unfavourably on warriors of plebeian background; thus one finds damning opinions expressed against the infantry forces of the Flemings or the Swiss, for killing rather than taking prisoners. Looked at from the plebeian angle, the chivalric code of mercy had not normally been applied for the benefit of the humble; prisoners were taken in order to obtain ransoms, the poor were commonly butchered. Chivalry was the code of a privileged social class, the knightly class, an hereditary noble class. Mercenaries, like infantrymen, had normally been treated with contempt in defeat. In the later middle ages, when the infantry and the mercenaries often found themselves in the ascendant, it is perhaps not so surprising, that they found less virtue in the chivalric code than those who had previously benefited from it. The different treatment of knights and commoners is often to be noted in medieval warfare. At Berwick, when food was short, the cavalry were given the flesh of the dead horses, the infantry got the bones.[14] In the distribution of spoils, there was a monetary recognition of social rank: a commander might expect a

12 Amongst recent work on this now popular subject are the important studies by Keen, *Chivalry*, and Vale, *War and Chivalry*.

13 *Morea Chronicle*, pp. 239, 306.

14 Prestwich, *Three Edwards*, p. 248.

proportion, say a fifth; an ordinary soldier would perhaps receive a few coins. As a result of the siege of Bilbais, in Egypt, an actual law or *assise* was agreed, restricting the role of knights in sieges, largely it seems in order to make risking one's life and one's horse a voluntary matter for knights.

Ordinary folk often came off worst in sieges, however little their rôle in the political making of the conflict or in the defence, as a result of the distinction often made between town and citadel. Frequently the town was stormed, while the citadel held out long enough to win terms of surrender. The lord and garrison in the citadel could often make an agreement, and thus escape with lives and property; while the citizens, as victims of a storm assault, were left at the mercy of the attackers. Even as prisoners, the fact of being worth a ransom would frequently obtain better treatment. As Paris of Pozzo wrote: 'a man may not torture a prisoner to extort money from him by way of ransom, but it is different in the case of peasants'.[15]

Knights certainly feared that they would not get the same chivalric treatment from commoners as from peasants, and would normally surrender themselves only to a recognised knight; as, for example, the two counts at Caen, who surrendered to the one-eyed Thomas Holland, because they recognised him from the days when they had all fought together in Spain. The duke of Suffolk, during the Wars of the Roses, finding that he had surrendered to a mere squire, knighted the man on the spot, and then accepted him as captor. Sometimes such precautions were proved to be well founded; as, for example, with the lord who called out his identity, expecting thus to save his life, only to be battered to death by enemies who had not recognised him, but hated the name.[16]

A chivalric code did however exist, and was frequently appealed to in the literature of the age. One of the Paston letters describes a good soldier as one who was: 'no brawler, but full of courtesy'. Froissart stressed the rôle of knights in protecting women, for example from rape; an attitude, in the view of Froissart, which distinguished the knight from other soldiers. The wife of John Lampert, at Avranches, played on the male deference to women: having donned trousers to lead the fight on the battlements, and having been beaten, she changed the trousers for a feminine skirt, in order to conduct the negotiations. Similarly at Castel Achard in the 1370s, the wife of the absent Guichard Achard, made an appeal to the duke of Berri and Bertrand du Guesclin because she was a lone woman, the 'widow of a living man'; she made a favourable arrangement with them for peace, on condition she remained neutral. Froissart praised the knights under Gaston de Foix for rescuing ladies in distress at Meaux, during the French peasant

[15] Keen, *Laws*, p. 243. The siege of Bilbais was referred to in a paper by Bill Zajac, part of his thesis. See Philip of Novara, ed. Köhler, pp. 82–4; and Prawer, pp. 74, 346.
[16] On Caen, Longman, i, pp. 244, 46; Froissart, ed. Jolliffe, p. 134. On Suffolk, Burne, *Agincourt*, p. 251; and see Contamine, p. 257.

rising, and apparently approved of the massacre of the poorly armed peasants which followed.[17]

Christian values could sometimes go beyond the usual responses to war. Sir John Cornwall was certainly exceptional in deciding, after a career of some honour, on the death of his son in France at Meaux, that Henry's war was not just; he returned to England, vowing never again to fight against Christians. Henry V himself obviously saw the Bible as one foundation of his code of war. When making terms with Harfleur, he based them on a reading of Deuteronomy, which includes such military advice as: 'when you advance on a city to attack it, make an offer of peace'; on surrender, 'all the people in it shall be put to forced labour'; if stormed 'you shall put all its males to the sword', but you may take the women, the dependants, and the cattle for yourselves, and plunder everything else in the city'; 'in the cities of these nations whose land the Lord your God is giving you as a patrimony, you shall not leave any creature alive. You shall annihilate them'. A reading of this makes clear how ancient are most of the conventions of siege war, how similar are the precepts in the Old Testament to those of the Romans, the barbarians, and the Christians of medieval Europe. It also makes one realise, how much of the code of chivalry may be based on Christian concepts arrived at by reading the Bible; it is unlikely that Henry V was unique in being so influenced. But certainly he did heed the Biblical injunctions, and indeed, when his terms were refused, he meted out punishment, also according to the rules of Deuteronomy.[18]

Honour in various forms played an important part in the chivalric code. At Marienburg the names of the visiting knights were inscribed on a Table of Honour, partly as encouragement for others to come and win the same privilege. It was expected that knights would keep their word, and in a manner unthinkable in normal modern warfare, prisoners would be released on promising to turn up on a certain day with their ransoms, or to return to captivity if they could not pay. Simon Burley proved himself no gentleman, by swearing that he would not escape, and then proceeding to do it. Even King John of France returned to captivity in England, as a matter of honour. Gilbert de Lannoy expressed a common belief: 'it is better to die honourably, than to live censured and dishonoured'. Thus medieval warfare is full of examples of men who fought on, knowing that there was no escape, but aware that they were acting with honour to the

[17] On the brawler, Goodman, p. 223; on Froissart, Barnie, p. 71; and Prestwich, *Three Edwards*, p. 207; on Lampet, Burne, *Agincourt*, p. 324; on Castel Achard and Meaux, Longman, ii, pp. 219–20, 33.

[18] On Cornwall, Contamine, p. 293; on Deuteronomy, *Gesta Henrici Quinti*, p. 34 and n. 3: *iuxta Deutronomium legis*; also pp. 36 and n. 1, 48, 154. Deuteronomy, xx, 1–17.

last. A knight would also respect courage and bravery in his opponent, and at times mercy was extended to a valorous enemy.[19]

An unusual incident at Rennes, in 1356, demonstrated many of the perceived virtues: a besieging knight, John Bolton, boldly challenged his hungry enemies on the battlements, waving at them a bag of partridges; a besieged knight, Olivier de Mauny, came down to fight him, swimming the moat and winning the contest to claim the birds. Bolton was wounded in the fight, but Mauny out of respect for the good show he had put up, released him; Mauny, it was said, loved honour more than silver. Then Mauny became ill, and in respect for his opponent, and from a debt of honour, Bolton arranged for Mauny to receive a safe-conduct through the lines, and be treated by an English physician.[20]

There are also numerous examples of the code being broken or ignored, or sometimes recognised but evaded. Talbot was a symbol of chivalric behaviour; he was captured, and promised not to wear arms again against the French, yet he appeared at Castillon, leading the English in the fatal attack. In order not to break his word, he appeared on horseback, but without armour, and of course was killed. Chivalry and *realpolitik* did not always mix: the English were quite prepared to support Pedro the Cruel in the Spanish succession struggle, though it would be hard to find a less chivalric ruler. He seems to have heartily deserved his cognomen, having, for example, killed his wife in order to go off with his mistress, allied with the Moslems, and been excommunicated by the pope. The same king's death demonstrates another example of ignoring the usual code: Pedro came to blows with his brother and rival, Henry Trastamara. Bertrand du Guesclin, the French Constable, saw nothing wrong in butting in on behalf of his own man, and grabbing Pedro by the leg, so that Henry could stab him to death. Another unchivalric action was carried out by the English commander, Thomas Dagworth, though A.H. Burne, with a touching loyalty, believed that Dagworth, was too chivalric to have done anything base, and used this as the only reason to dismiss a chronicle description of Dagworth's treatment of the wounded Charles of Blois. Charles had no less than seventeen wounds, but Dagworth threw him off his bed on to the floor.[21]

At times it was less the lack of justification than the sheer savagery of the act which earned disapproval by the chroniclers; as at Rouen, when English prisoners were hanged with dogs tied round their necks, or thrown into the Seine, tied up with dogs in sacks. Henry V, despite his high reputation in England, was a severe judge. His opponent Lord Barbazon,

19 On Marienburg, Riley-Smith, *Crusades*, p. 214; on Burley, Prestwich, *Three Edwards*, p. 208; on Lannoy, Vale, p. 15.

20 Longman, ii, p. 17.

21 On Talbot, Burne, *Agincourt*, p. 338. On Pedro the Cruel, Longman, ii, p. 139; on Dagworth, Burne, *Crecy*, pp. 97–9.

for fighting hand to hand against Henry during a siege, was afterwards imprisoned in an iron cage; indeed, Henry's treatment of prisoners was rarely merciful. Surrender for lives often meant being retained in confinement for ransom, often in dreadful conditions, and often resulting in death; as, for example, those kept at Paris in a ditch, fed only with straw and called dogs, which the French chronicler Juvenal thought was: 'a great disgrace to the King of England'. Nor was Henry often merciful to enemies during a siege, as with those, at Rouen, who were left to die in the ditch, after being turned out of the town. He was hardly less severe on his own men, having one deserter buried alive. Such actions could normally be described as within the rights of the situation, and hence even as just, but they were barely Christian, and hardly chivalric.[22]

Once surrendered, a knight was considered to be under the protection of his captor, and like the count of Foix might be allowed to hunt and lead a normal life, within certain limitations. Ill treatment of such prisoners was definitely against the code, but of course at times occurred. A notorious example is that of Henry Gentian, who found snakes introduced into his cell, and then had his teeth knocked out with a hammer in order to force him to agree to a larger ransom! Offences against the chivalric code were common. Every army contained some rogues, including at times sentenced criminals. Froissart said of the English army: 'it contains base knaves and evil-doers enough, and men of little conscience'.[23]

Word was often given and then broken; for example, when the Bastard Fauconberg was given a charter of pardon, and then executed. Chroniclers clearly thought that the sabbath should be treated as a day of truce; it was often a day used for negotiations. It was on a Sunday, that the leaders at Harfleur came before Edward III. And yet the sabbath truce was often broken, in order to make a surprise attack. At Liège the duke of Burgundy favoured such an attack, but was opposed by Louis XI, who however gave way. One suspects that this may be Commines explaining away the monarch's part in the unchivalrous decision. The citizens were certainly not expecting an attack, and had gone for their Sunday dinner: 'in every house we found the table set'. In the same attack, Burgundy killed one of his own men for robbing a church! No wonder we sometimes find it hard to fathom the medieval mind.[24]

The code also expected respect for messengers and heralds, under an understood truce, but this again might occasionally be broken. At Nesle the besieged citizens killed a herald of the duke of Burgundy; so Burgundy responded by pretending to negotiate and offer mercy, and then punishing

22 Seward, *Henry V*, pp. 116, 150–1, 187.

23 On the count of Foix and Henry Gentian, Keen, *Laws*, pp. 169, 180. On Froissart, Barnie, p. 71; Froissart, ed. Jolliffe, p. 136.

24 On Fauconberg, Warkworth in *Three Chronicles*, p. 42; on Harfleur, Seward, *Henry V*, p. 67; on Liège, Commines, ed. Jones, pp. 159–60.

his enemies by hanging and beheading, an act which even his own men thought cruel. The same duke ignored a safe-conduct given to the Constable St Pol, and handed him over to the French king for trial and execution, an act which Commines saw as shameful.[25]

The chivalric code continued to be applied, probably because all armies had some members of the knightly class at the helm, or because genuine Christian values could be held by commoners, as well as by knights. Few Christians can be saints, and few soldiers lived perfectly by the chivalric code, but this does not invalidate it as an ideal. Maurice Keen has written that 'if you scratch the paint from the picture of the knight errant, you will all too often find something rather different underneath'. Knights could commit atrocities as effectively as the next man. The earl of Worcester put his enemies to death in barbaric manner, with stakes through the anus, and heads placed on top, which one chronicler thought was against the law of the land, and certainly offended against chivalric Christian custom'.[26]

Mercenaries were sometimes of knightly origin, and despite their bad reputation, often gave much stress to honour. Sir John Hawkwood, the English captain in Italy, was a professional soldier who sought profit, but believed that loyalty was the honourable path, and refused bribes from the enemies of his employers when others accepted. Although he was a mercenary, his employers thought him worth the payment of ransom after his capture by Arezzo. Sometimes the paymaster, rather than the hired soldier, was responsible for unchivalric actions. Hawkwood, against his will, was ordered to act without mercy at Cesena by his employer, none other than Cardinal Robert of Geneva; the city was sacked, but Hawkwood did save a thousand women by sending them to Rimini. The problem for the mercenary lay in the fact that war was his livelihood; he might be redundant in peacetime, when in any case garrison service would not pay as well as armed war, with its possibility of ransoms and loot. The church, which had, to some extent, written the code of chivalry, sought peace rather than war between Christians, and tried to restrict the occasions of war. It was almost impossible to obey the church to the letter and be a mercenary, though, if it suited, the church itself would employ mercenaries. When Hawkwood was told about plans for making peace in the war he was fighting, he claimed: 'I live by war, and peace would be my undoing'.[27]

Those who offended against the code of chivalry, might also find themselves offending against the law, in the sense that they might be given legal punishment, as well as suffering social contempt. Cowardice broke the code of bravery and honour; there are several examples of men punished by being stripped of the honours of knighthood as a result. The count of Dammartin was hanged in his armour, because he was a vassal who had

25 On Nesle and St Pol, Commines, ed. Jones, pp. 204, 271–3.
26 Keen, *Chivalry*, p. 232; on Worcester, Warkworth in *Three Chronicles*, p. 31.
27 Deiss, *Captains*, p. 139.

been guilty of cowardice in his lord's service. Sir Ralph Grey was accused of disloyalty, though he had been an honourable warrior; he was told to: 'remember thee the law', and his spurs were struck off by the cook, his coat of arms reversed, and he was made to walk thus through the town, before being dragged to his execution. To some extent this kind of example represents the viciousness which crept into late medieval warfare. Disloyalty was a common charge, considered particularly bad if associated with the breaking of an oath; for example, Charles VII made such a charge against all the citizens of Bordeaux, on the grounds that they had 'broken their oaths and expressions of loyalty'. In 1433 Robert Stafford's crime was to have been absent from his post as captain when La-Ferté-Bernard was attacked. He was summoned to the parliament in Paris, at the time when the English controlled it, but managed to defend himself successfully, so that the original sentence against him was reversed. Another accused man, Thomas Catrington, fought a duel to defend his honour which had been impugned by the suggestion that he had sold St Sauveur-le-Vicomte.[28]

There were also attempts to control and regulate behaviour during a siege, and commanders often took less than their due in vengeance, probably most often for political reasons and for the sake of their reputations, in an age when mercy received praise. The view of a modern French historian, is that during the Hundred Years War: 'the English monarchy displayed implacable cruelty'. But commanders sometimes tried to control abuses; thus Edward III at Caen threatened that anyone guilty of arson, killing or rape would be hanged. The same king allowed 1,700 poor to go through his lines at Calais, giving them a meal and twopence each to help them on their way, which Jean le Bel thought: 'an act of great courtesy', the action of 'a noble nature'.[29]

Edward III does not seem to have been a naturally merciful man, and often needed persuasion to forego acts of vengeance. At Calais, Manny had to argue against putting all the citizens to death, suggesting that if, in the future, his own men were similarly in need of mercy, the enemy would follow the king's example. It was wise advice; escalation of retaliation has often dogged war, as it would in the Wars of the Roses. At Calais there followed the famous episode of the six burghers, reluctantly pardoned by Edward for the sake of his queen. One feels that modern interpretations of all this, miss Edward's main point, which was surely to make a dramatic propaganda show of his mercifulness. Several clerical chroniclers voiced admiration of mercy, and the church's view was certainly one which helped to shape such acts. Chartier in the fifteenth century described an act of

[28] On Dammartin and Catrington, Keen, *Laws*, pp. 31, 127. On Grey, Warkworth in *Three Chronicles*, pp. 60–1; on Charles VII, Griffiths, pp. 530–31; on Stafford, Allmand, *Hundred Years War*, p. 115.

[29] The quote is Contamine, p. 291; on Caen, Froissart, ed. Brereton, p. 76; on Calais, *Chronicles of the Hundred Years War*, pp. 74–5.

mercy as due to kindness: 'to avoid the shedding of human blood'. But mercy, like chivalry, though admired as an ideal, was not always approved in practice. Bodrugan who sent in provisions for the besieged at St Michael's Mount, was dismissed for his pains; and Bertrand de Chaumont, who felt pity for some of the French at Melun and allowed them to escape, was beheaded'.[30]

Henry V at Harfleur, like Edward III at Caen, made an order forbidding excessive measures against the defeated: no arson, looting, attacks on priests or women; and in an excess of puritanical Christian morality, he threatened to have the left arm broken of any harlot found within three miles of the camp. Henry V at times wished to appear as merciful; harsh and unrelenting though he generally was in practice. After Harfleur, he gave the poor five sous each when they were sent away. He was certainly merciless to those who offended him during the course of a siege, and frequently made exceptions to those granted their lives in a surrender. The gunners who hit his tent at Louviers, when he was standing outside it in conversation with the earl of Salisbury, were hanged when the town surrendered. At Rouen those excepted included: 'that person who spoke the foul words', as well as Alain Blanchard the leader of the crossbowmen; and, at Meaux, the twelve excepted included the hornblower Orace, who was publicly executed in Paris for insulting the king, presumably because he had blown raspberries down his instrument during the seige. Another exception in the same siege was the more deserving Bastard of Vaurus, hanged on the same elm which he had used as the gallows for his own victims.[31]

Even Henry V did not go so far in his ordinances as Charles VII, in preparation for his recovery of Harfleur, when he placed a ban even on swearing. But orders were of course often ignored; for example, Edward III's ban on burning at Carentan in 1346, or his ban on looting in 1360. Such was chivalrous behaviour: a mixture of the ideals of the honourable warrior, and of the Christian, put into practice by men with all the usual shortcomings of their kind. Keen has pointed to the significance of chivalric practice, in that it precedes the development of international law, by presenting an international code with at least some possibility of enforcement. Various national laws embodied part of the code, and the practice of warfare with its code and conventions of conduct, led to the development of some international understanding of what was acceptable. The idea of war crimes has developed from the concept that there were ideals of practice which could be offended against. The behaviour of the individual

[30] On Calais, Froissart, ed. Brereton, pp. 97, 106. Chartier in *EHD*, iv, p. 263. For Bodrugan, Warkworth in *Three Chronicles*, pp. 48–9; and Melun, Wylie & Waugh, iii, p. 209.

[31] For Harfleur, see Seward, *Henry V*, pp. 64, 68. On Louviers, Rouen, Meaux and the Bastard, see Wylie & Waugh, iii, pp. 113, 143–4, 350–2.

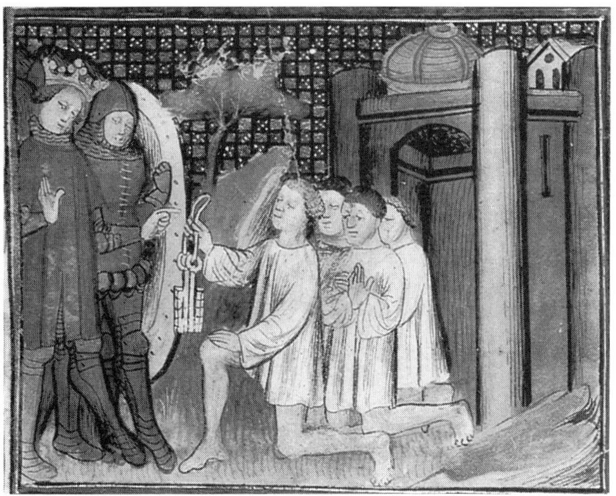

Edward III and the burghers of Calais

was affected by such considerations, as well as the general conduct of siege warfare, including, for example, arrangements over the division of spoil, ransom, and the making of treaties and truces. More than that, to some extent, proper practice became to some extent enforceable in courts of chivalry, as that held in England under Edward III in the White Chamber at Westminster.[32]

The Conduct of Sieges

Whether chivalric or not, the conventions for conducting a siege were well established by the late middle ages. It was expected that besiegers would, for example, convey their intention to besiege. It was common to throw a missile, such as a spear, at the gate, or later to fire a cannon shot, as a sign that war was declared: the siege had begun in earnest and siege rules now applied. For example, at Nancy, Charles the Bold fired a cannon, and, according to Commines, it meant that anyone trying to get in or out could be killed: 'according to the laws of war'. James I of Aragon was concerned that it was wrong to go against his vassal, Ramon Folch, who was holding a royal castle: 'how can I go there when I have not defied him?' Occasionally one hears of the beating of drums to signify the calling of a parley, as at Malta. The Moslems had a way of showing that if the terms they had offered for surrender were refused, the place was about to undergo all-out attack: they would hoist a black flag, as was done at Rhodes in 1480.

32 On Harfleur, Wylie & Waugh, ii, p. 53; on Carentan, Prestwich, *Three Edwards*, p. 200. On international law and the court of chivalry, see Keen, *Laws*, pp. 7, 27.

Fifteenth-century Flemish siege

White flags were used by both Christians and Moslems, with much the same meaning they still possess. At Rhodes in 1522, both sides flew white flags in order to call a negotiation for surrender. Flags and banners were also a symbol of possession, and the flying of the victors' flag over a captured stronghold was common, as at Acre on the Third Crusade.[33]

There was no protection for the poor citizens of a town under siege; the defenders would at times turn them out so that there were fewer mouths to feed. One might praise Edward III for letting them through at Calais, for it was indeed an act of mercy. The poor in such a position were, under the usual conventions, at the mercy of the attackers. When Henry V refused to allow the poor through at Rouen, and left them to die in the ditch, it was part of the normal pressure applied to the town, part of the punishment for refusing to surrender. Henry did send them food for Christmas, but even the English soldiers pitied their plight. Babies were hoisted up to be given baptism, but then lowered again; parents died, but children were still left to survive as best they could. When, in negotiation, the besieged asked that the poor be allowed through, Henry asked: 'who put them there?' We may not much admire such ruthlessness, but it was part of the normal siege code.[34]

Just as making an overt act of war to declare siege was usual, so was it to make a symbolic act of surrender, normally the handing over of the keys, as

33 On Nancy, see Commines, ed. Jones, p. 297; On Folch, James I, ed. Forster, i, p. 96; on Malta, Balbi, p. 90; on Rhodes, Brockman, pp. 84, 150; on Ascalon, William of Tyre, ed. Babcock & Krey, ii, p. 232.

34 On Calais, see above n. 29; on Rouen, Seward, *Henry V*, pp. 117–18.

Keys offered in surrender at Dinan

to Edward III at Calais together with the sword of peace; or, at Rouen, to both Henry V and later Charles VII. The Bayeux Tapestry depicts the surrender of Dinan through the handing of its keys to William the Conqueror. When Cordoba surrendered, the governor, Abn Hasan, handed over the keys; and still in 1453, when Pera yielded to the Turks, it was done by giving the keys. The victors often demanded more humiliating signs of surrender, as when at Harfleur Henry had the captain and others come out with ropes round their necks to hand over the keys, and then kept them waiting before he took any notice.[35]

Truces and agreements also had a code of practice attached to them. Truces normally meant a suspension of military activity, during which defences should not be improved, and siege engines should not be built or moved into position. Like all such conventions, they were at times broken, but the fact that they were generally respected is implicit in the actions of the people of Paris during a siege, when they emerged from the city to stretch their legs and have a look round the enemy camp. The Moslem leader, al-Ashraf, was naturally annoyed, when during negotiations, a stone from a Christian engine landed on his tent; not surprisingly, the negotia-

[35] On Calais, Geoffrey le Baker in *EHD*, iv, p. 89; on Dinan, *Bayeux Tapestry*, ed. Wilson; on Cordoba, Lomax, p. 146; on Pera, Tedaldi in Jones, p. 8; on Harfleur, Wylie & Waugh, ii, p. 56.

tions were brought to an end. An even more deliberate breaking of a truce occurred at Licana, when Don Ferris rebelled against James I of Aragon. It is clear that James himself was breaking the truce, but this did not temper his anger over the enemy doing the same! He says that he granted a truce 'while the engines were getting ready', only to find that the enemy were shooting a brigola: 'regardless of the truce'. Truces were, indeed, not always kept. The papal legate, Caesarini, on the Varna Crusade, deliberately broke a truce with the Moslems, on the old grounds that truces with the infidel were not valid; other Christians disapproved his decision. The sultan showed his contempt for the Christians breaking their word, by carrying the paper containing the truce agreement into battle, attached to a standard. The battle of Varna, which followed, was a disaster for the Christians.[36]

The giving of hostages was in essence an extension of the truce, to guarantee that its promises be kept. It was understood that if promises were broken, the hostage was at mercy for his life, though, needless to say, chroniclers on opposite sides might well dispute circumstances. Like so many of the aspects of siege warfare, the giving of hostages has a long history. For example, in 882, the vikings exchanged hostages with the western emperor, as part of an agreement. Commonly hostages would be important named individuals; thus, at Alicante, James I of Aragon asked for the the son of the kaid, and two of his nephews as hostages, though in the end they reached settlement without need of hostages.[37]

The fate of a hostage in the hands of the Holy Roman Emperors might well be an unhappy one: both Frederick Barbarossa and Frederick II tied hostages to their engines, in the hope of persuading the enemy not to shoot stones against them. The chronicler, Rahewin, writing about this at Crema, apparently saw nothing wrong in Barabarossa's treatment of the hostages. At Senlis, in 1417, the conditions were broken, and the count of Armagnac had his hostages executed: 'as the laws of war allowed'. Derval, in the hands of the English, agreed to surrender in forty days if no help was forthcoming, and handed over four hostages. The captain, Knollys, claimed that he was not a party to the agreement, and continued to resist, and so the unfortunate hostages were beheaded by the Duke of Anjou. On another occasion, the Duke of Burgundy executed six hostages at Liège, including the town messenger: 'whom he hated greatly'. Henry V, at Dijon, threatened to hang the hostages if the town did not surrender, and carried out his threat, which though not unique was against the usual conventions. More happily at Cherbourg the governor, Thomas Gonville,

36 On Paris, Commines, ed. Jones, p. 95; on al-Ashraf, Runciman, *Crusades*, iii, p. 417; on Licana, James I, ed. Forster, ii, p. 581; on Varna, Runciman, *Fall*, p. 19.

37 On the vikings, *Annales Fuldenses*, ed. Pertz & Kurze, p. 98: *datis ex utraque parte obsidibus*; on Alicante, James I, ed. Forster, i, p. 422.

agreed to surrender in return for the life of his son, who had become a hostage at Rouen in 1450, and both then sailed to England and safety.[38]

Keeping order among one's own men was often as great a problem as dealing with the enemy. In the cramped and dangerous conditions of a siege camp, quarrels were common, and could seriously harm hopes of success. Differences between commanders on the same side are often encountered, as during the First Crusade, or between Richard the Lionheart and Leopold V of Austria on the Third Crusade. James I of Aragon described an incident he had to deal with at Xativa. One morning, as he was walking down the hill, he saw Berto Squierdo having an argument with another man, whom he attacked with a knife 'in my very presence'. James followed Berto into the tent of Don Garcia Romen, grabbed him by the hair, and pulled him outside, where he had him arrested. Don Garcia then complained that the king had no right to enter his tent; but James retorted: 'the houses of my barons are not churches', and in any case this was only a tent provided by the king himself.[39]

Christian commanders often sought to control moral conduct in their camp, especially on crusade. A number of commanders issued ordinances, dealing with such matters as stealing, violence and general behaviour, and commonly prostitutes were expelled. On St Louis' crusade, one knight was discovered in a brothel; he was given the choice between being led through the camp by a whore while clad only in a shirt and bound with a cord, or the loss of his horse and his armour and expulsion from the camp. He chose the latter.[40]

The treatment of prisoners was, to some extent, part of a recognised code. Chivalry only catered for the capture of knights by knights, when reasonable treatment might be expected, though not always received. In effect, the treatment of prisoners related to the conventions on surrender agreements, which we shall examine in due course; prisoners who surrendered might expect some sort of leniency and their lives, though this was less likely to be guaranteed than in the case of a city's surrender, but simple capture during conflict left the prisoner in the same state as the inhabitants of a stronghold taken by storm, entirely at the mercy of the captor. Therefore, as in seizure by storm, captives might well be treated harshly, and were often executed, sometimes in bizarre or cruel fashion, in order to terrify those still resisting. Thus men were hanged before the walls, or indeed from the walls if taken by the garrison, beheaded, tortured publicly, even hacked to pieces and hurled by engine back into the city. The Oeselians, during

38 On Crema, Otto of Freising, ed. Waitz, p. 294. On Senlis, Keen, *Laws*, p. 130; *Chronique du Religieux*, vi, p. 194: *bellorum jura*. On Derval, Longman, ii, pp. 223–4; on Liège, Commines, ed. Jones, p. 124. On Dijon, Wylie & Waugh, iii, p. 209; on Cherbourg, *Chronicles of the Hundred Years War*, p. 336.

39 James I, ed. Forster, ii, pp. 438–40.

40 Joinville, ed. Evans, p. 153.

the northern crusades, tortured their captives in order to gain information, by sharpening pieces of hard, dry wood, and inserting them under the nails, or by tormenting every member with the point. The Christians, during St Louis' first crusade, were given the choice of becoming Moslems, or being beheaded. Joinville described tortures that were inflicted on the prisoners, including: 'the most grievous torture that a man can suffer', a device with folding beams bound by oxhide; a man was placed in it on his side, with legs between pegs, then they sat on the beams, which broke the bones in the legs at intervals of every six inches. He says they repeated this treatment every three days, so that the legs became swollen. Although Louis himself was threatened with torture, it seems to have been the poor who were the actual victims.[41]

The code of chivalry did not always protect the Christian prisoners of Christian captors; for example, when Bohemond VII, in the Holy Land, took captives during his conflict with Guy of Jebail, prisoners were blinded, and some buried up to their necks in a ditch and left to die. On the other hand, during the negotiations at Constantinople, during the Fourth Crusade, Villehardouin declared to the emperor Alexander: 'they will not do anything to injure either yourself or any other person without fair warning of their intention to commence hostilities, for they have never acted treacherously, that is not the custom in their country'. The Turks at Constantinople in 1453 impaled some prisoners, and beheaded others; and, as so often, there was a tit-for-tat progress of atrocities, Turkish prisoners being killed on the walls. When the Byzantines captured Turkish miners, they tortured them to gain information about other mines, then beheaded them, and threw the bodies over the wall.[42]

Many sieges were brought to an end by negotiation. The task was often performed for the western nations by clerics. It is probable that the more desperate the situation, the more likely it was to send lesser men who were seen as dispensable; insignificant ambassadors, perhaps better called messengers, were clearly taking their lives in their hands. In Malta, the Turks sent a slave to seek terms from the other forts after the fall of St Elmo. He was led through the lines blindfolded, 'as is customary'. The unfortunate man was then ordered to be hanged, but when it was pointed out that he was only a slave being forced into the task, Valette relented, and he was sent back with the reply that if any more messengers came, they would be hanged. However, at Constantinople in 1204, the chronicler, Villehardouin, himself participated in the making of terms to end the first siege. He described how for the Byzantines, English and Danish soldiers formed a

41 On the Oeselians, Henry of Livonia, ed. Brundage, p. 141; on St Louis, Joinville, ed. Evans, pp. 99, 101; ed. Corbett, p. 153: *Bernicles est le plus grief tourment que l'en puisse soufrir*, translates as 'barnacles'.

42 On Bohemond, Runciman, *Crusades*, iii, pp. 388–9; Villehardouin, ed. Shaw, p. 82; on 1453, Tedaldi in Jones, p. 5 and Barbaro, p. 56.

guard to the palace where terms were discussed. Similarly Ibn al-Ferat was an ambassador to Acre, and described how he was told by the sultan not to humble himself before the Christians, not to sit down unless the bench was as good as that on which the Christian king and his generals sat; he was told to hand his document directly to the king and not to one of his advisers. It was often important that the negotiator be a man of standing, and at Xativa, the ambassador for the Moslems was Sexi, said to be a very powerful man in the town, and a member of the kaid's council. During this siege, James I offered a guarantee to representatives of the Moslems: 'no one who comes to me shall be arrested, be his offence what it may', and negotiations continued. On many occasions, a negotiator needed to be a linguist, and, for example, on various occasions James I employed Arabic-speakers, as at Peniscola he found an Arabic-speaking Christian.[43]

The most interesting and authoritative medieval account of negotiations comes from the pen of a king, James I of Aragon. Balbi, at Malta, rightly said that it was hard to write about the intentions of princes, 'for these are not common knowledge'.[44] But for once, with James, we have direct comment from a royal commander. He was closely involved in negotiation, and expected to be kept informed, though he sometimes kept the cards close to his chest. He gives us a good deal of insight into the bargaining process, including moves which none but the commander could know.

At Licana, James described how Berenguer de Viller came to his tent one night and asked if he were asleep, since the enemy had just offered terms. Such an intimate view of negotiation is not elsewhere easy to find. When Xativa offered secret terms to James, he did not tell his own man, Don Rodrigo, because James himself did not wish to accept. James conducted his own negotiations with the kaid of the city, without consulting his men, though it is true they broke down. At Valencia, the citizens conducted secret negotiations with James himself, who says that the only person he confided in over this was his wife, the queen, who also attended the meetings. It was one of those occasions when the king wanted to accept a surrender, but the majority of the army: 'wished for the sack of the town'. In the end James got his agreement, granting a wait of five days, their lives and the right to take away belongings without being searched. He was sufficiently concerned to explain his own reasons: that it was better to settle rather than take the risk of something going wrong, such as himself becoming ill. When his own lords were informed of the settlement, they 'lost colour, as if someone had stabbed them to the heart'; but others were pleased, including the archbishop of Narbonne, who saw it as: 'the work of God'. James himself was filled with emotion at what he saw as his

43 On Constantinople, Villehardouin ed. Shaw, p. 74; on Acre, Ibn al-Farat in Gabrieli, p. 314. On Xativa and Peniscola, James I, ed. Forster, ii, pp. 438, 449; i, p. 287.
44 Balbi, p. 181.

great triumph, the climax of much effort: 'I dismounted, turned myself towards the East, and wept with my eyes, kissing the ground'.[45]

James explained how at Cellas the citizens asked for fifteen days before they surrendered, but when offered eight they accepted. Similarly at Burriana, James offered three days, the town asked for fifteen, and in the end they settled for five, with all the goods they could carry, and an escort. He wrote of Tamarit, that: 'if I promised not to harm them, they would give it up'. He was concerned to make clear his honourable conduct; and, although his own army was short of meat, once an agreement had been reached, he would not seize provisions from the town. On various occasions James chose agents whom he obviously hoped might achieve more than himself; thus, at Balaguer he got the countess to parley for him, with a knight speaking on her behalf, because the rebels had been her father's men, and it worked. On this occasion, a student also acted as a go-between for the king. James was proud of his own ability in subtle negotiation, and as he said: 'skill, in most cases, is better than strength'. He gave a nice example of his subtlety at Valencia: during a parley, he saved a heron from his falcons, then turned to his opponents and said that, as with the bird so with the siege, it was in his power to kill, but it was not his wish to do so.[46]

There were occasions when James did not get his own way, and several times he makes it clear that he bowed to his own advisers; as in Majorca, when he received the terms, and was prepared to accept them, but yielded to the majority view, and kept on fighting. There were other times when it was James who did not want to accept the terms, as later in Majorca, when he felt victory was near: 'they are at the last gasp, the wretches are done for'. He was always concerned about his reputation, and at Burriana claimed that he hoped to be wounded, so that if he had to retire, it would seem to be for honourable reasons: 'I could say that it was my wound that made me raise the siege'. At Peniscola, he was concerned that his men did not start cutting down trees after an agreement, in case the Saracens were offended, and should think he had not kept his word.[47]

The safety of ambassadors or representatives during negotiations was expected to be sacrosanct, and normally it was. The use of clerics and heralds for such talks underlined the special status of negotiators. Clerics were generally understood to be safe from attack in war, and had sufficient learning to comprehend the situation and debate the terms. One of the numerous examples of clerics negotiating was at Calais, where two cardinals acted on behalf of Philip VI. Heralds similarly became a privileged group during negotiations, generally dressed in distinguishing costume,

45 James I, ed. Forster, ii, pp. 582, 435–6: i, pp. 392, 396, 397.

46 James I, ed. Forster, i, pp. 60, 281, 82, 89–90, 92, 360. On Balaguer and the heron; ed. Casacuberta, i, I, p. 112: *mes val giny que forca*; i, V, p. 34: *e no lexam oceir la grua, ans la tolguem als falcons*.

47 James I, ed. Forster, i, pp. 161, 192, 279, 289.

respected for their knowledge of arms. They also played a rôle in judgement upon offenders against the knightly code. Even so, at Nesle, the besieged killed one of Burgundy's heralds, to which the duke responded with considerable anger.[48]

Throughout the middle ages, negotiators had found themselves at risk. In the Merovingian age, Murderic, though given a safe-conduct at Vitry-le-Brulé, was killed. Another negotiator who suffered, was the cleric who carried terms to the bishop of Bayeux in 1346; the message was torn into shreds, and the messenger thrown into prison, but the daring action escaped penalty, since Edward III could not spare the time to take revenge, and by-passed the town. Negotiators were often in danger from angry reactions. For example, when Henry V offered terms to Bonneville, the town sought the usual arrangement to surrender if no aid arrived within six days; the unfortunate messenger, who carried the terms to the dauphin, was hanged for his troubles. An unusual response, of another kind, was made by Sir John Cornwall at Sens, when he insisted that the bedraggled negotiator, who had been suffering with the others under siege, should go and have his beard trimmed before he was fit to be seen; but then terms were agreed. The two knights, negotiating for the crusaders in the last siege of Acre, were dismayed when, during negotiations, the stone from a Christian engine landed close to al-Ashraf, and in his anger he drew his sword on them, since he clearly expected hostilities to be halted during negotiation. In this case the knights were fortunate that one of al-Ashraf's caliphs persuaded him to put away his sword, on the grounds that the pigs were not worth the trouble of killing. Peter of Sevrey, the Marshal of the Temple, was less fortunate at Acre. He went out to parley with the Moslems, after the main town had been taken, only to be arrested and beheaded. At Beirut too, the negotiators were taken and, in this case, imprisoned. When two Greek ambassadors from Constantinople went to try and prevent the Turkish build up, they were made captive and beheaded, which was taken as a virtual declaration of war.[49]

James I of Aragon believed that negotiation was his own prerogative. Ambassadors were clearly seen as representatives of a ruler, which was their best protection. At Xativa James I proclaimed that anyone who dealt with the Moslems without his permission would be arrested. He was obviously fearful of treachery. A man from Cuenca was accused of parleying with the enemy, under pretext of making a tent, probably on behalf of Alfonso the Learned; he confessed, and was hanged on a tree as an example to others. Leaders, such as James, often themselves conducted negotiations, and such meetings were usually carried on with the greatest civility. The exchanges

[48] On Calais, Longman, i, p. 283; on Nesle, Commines, ed. Jones, p. 204.
[49] On Murderic, Gregory of Tours, ed. Thorpe, pp. 174–5; on 1346, Burne, *Crecy*, p. 144. On Bonneville and Sens, Wylie & Waugh, iii, pp. 53–4, 197. On Acre, and Beirut, Runciman, *Crusades*, iii, pp. 417, 420, 422. On Constantinople, Barbaro, p. 9.

between Richard the Lionheart and Saladin's brother are well known. At Rhodes in 1522, Suleiman met de Lisle-Adam three times, and presents were exchanged between them; each seems to have felt respect for his opponent.[50]

Spies and traitors could, of course, expect little mercy; they were considered as fair game, and were often tortured and killed. At Antioch there was a considerable problem for the Christians, with the enemy able to masquerade as, or indeed actually to be, Greek, Syrian or Armenian. Bohemond, probably rather for propaganda purposes and as a deterrent than from barbarity, ordered that spies should be strangled and then roasted for food, at which, according to William of Tyre, the spy problem vanished. Within the same city, there were fears about spies acting on the Christian behalf, and there was a plan to kill those suspected on the eve of the actual betrayal by Firuz. Saladin seems to have treated the military orders as a special case, exempt from mercy; he has generally had a reputation for fairness and tolerance, but after Hattin, when many Christians were spared, he ordered the execution of all the Templars and Hospitallers.[51]

When the crusaders besieged Nicopolis, in 1396, Boucicaut punished some of his own men who had apparently simply declared that the Turks were good enemies; he ordered them to have their ears cut off. When Master George came over to the Christians at Rhodes in 1480, and advised them on the placing of their guns, there was much suspicion when those particular spots were immediately selected as targets by the Moslems; he was accused of treachery and hanged. At Rhodes in 1522 the Jew, Apella Renata, was caught shooting out a message to the Turks by crossbow, and was summarily hanged and quartered. In the same siege the Portuguese, Blasco Diaz, was also found sending a message by crossbow written by the prior of Castile. After torture on the rack he was unable to walk, and was carried in a chair to his execution. One Italian at the siege of Malta, in 1565, favoured the acceptance of Turkish terms, and was hanged for his views: 'for saying publicly that we had no chance at all'.[52]

Successful Storm

Storm gave the attackers complete control over the lives and fate of the defeated, almost any atrocity was given the cloak of legality: rape, enslavement, killing, in addition to the seizure of homes and property. No mercy

[50] James I, ed. Forster, pp. 451, 455; on Rhodes, Brockman, p. 153.

[51] On Antioch, William of Tyre, ed. Babcock & Krey, i, p. 222. On Firuz and Saladin, Runciman, *Crusades*, i, pp. 231–4; ii, p. 460.

[52] On Nicopolis, Runciman, *Crusades*, iii, p. 459. On Rhodes, Brockman, pp. 82, 133, 139. On Malta, Balbi, p. 189

need be given, and none could be expected. The description of the situation, after the taking of Cherbourg, must have been only too common: of refugees streaming out along the roads, with infants in cradles, on heads, or round necks. Villehardouin described the refugees from Serres, during the making of the Latin Empire, leaving 'naked, unshod, and on foot'. At Cordoba, when it fell, the citizens departed in tears. And these were the lucky ones who had been granted their lives and their freedom.[53]

It is true that in the late medieval period, not only did chroniclers praise mercy, they also began, occasionally, to question the carrying out of the full rights of the victor; and modern historians, with modern susceptibilities, have followed them. But the normal medieval view was that the defeated had brought their fate upon themselves, and it was common practice throughout that time to enforce punitive rights, so that to criticise individual commanders, out of the thousands who exacted their due price, is a rather pointless exercise. An example would be the sack of Limoges in 1370; modern disapproval of the Black Prince rests upon the contemporary criticism, made by Froissart, about the 'fearful slaughter', but this was Froissart in his pro-French vein. He wrote: 'all who could be found were put to the sword, including many who were in no way to blame', over 3,000 had their throats cut. But a more usual contemporary opinion, seen from the besiegers' point of view, as, for example, in the words of Walsingham, saw no fault in the Prince's just actions. There had been no surrender, no agreement; the defeated asked to be treated 'according to the law of arms', and they were, as Lancaster said: 'we would not do anything else'. But our modern attitudes accord more with the comments of Froissart, who wrote: 'I do not know how they could be so pitiless towards poor folk, who were in no position to perform acts of treason'.[54]

It is probably hardly necessary to retail details of the full terms being exacted after a storm, but it would be wrong to ignore the fact that this was very common, and it needs to be emphasised that Limoges was not an exceptional atrocity. For example, though James I of Aragon is rightly seen as a reasonable commander, who often granted quarter, when he took Licana, he refused to make terms: 'I hanged from the castle wall those whom it was fitting to hang', and beheaded the nobles. The Christian crusaders who took Jerusalem, slaughtered until the streets ran with blood. When Zangi stormed Edessa, and recovered it from the Franks: 'neither age, condition, nor sex was spared'. At Damascus, where in 1192 Turks

53 On Cherbourg, Griffiths, p. 521; on Serres, Villehardouin, ed. Shaw, p. 130; on Cordoba, Lomax, p. 146.

54 On Limoges, e.g. Longman, ii, p. 176; 'indelible disgrace'. Froissart, ed. Brereton, p. 178; ed. Thompson in *Chronicles of the Hundred Years War*, pp. 139–40; ed. Lucke, vii, p. 250: *mes tout mis a l'espee, quanqus on trouvoit et controit, cil et celles qui point coupable n'i estoient; ne je ne scai comment il n'avoient pit des povres gens qui n'estoient mies tailliet de faire nulle trahison.* For Walsingham, see Barnie, pp. 77–8.

were thrown from the battlements, and those who yielded had their hands bound with thongs till they roared with pain, and were then sold into slavery, there had been no agreement, Richard the Lionheart refusing terms. In such cases, granting lives was a mercy, and not obligatory. The infamous atrocity committed by Richard at Acre, when the Moslem captives were taken out of the city and slaughtered, appears to be a case where an agreement was made, but not kept; it seems that Saladin failed to pay the ransom for the lives of the citizens within the agreed time. At Ghent 1,200 were either raped or killed. When the French took Winchelsea, the women in the church were raped and killed. At Caen 2,000 were killed in the Market, though the castle was able to surrender on terms; while at Rougemont, in 1420, the garrison of sixty was drowned in the Yonne. At Roche-Darrien, Philip VI allowed the massacre of the citizens, though the garrison was given a safe-conduct. When du Guesclin took Montmorillon in 1372, the whole garrison was killed; and, at Joan of Arc's capture of the Bastille at Orléans, all those not wounded or captured were killed; when Poix was taken, all the citizens were killed 'without mercy', and the town was burned 'as it deserved'.[55]

In all areas, massacres were equally common. For example, during the advance of Jenghiz Khan, at Bamian all were killed when it was taken, after the great khan's grandson had been killed there; and later there were massacres at Riajan in 1237, Vlad in 1238 after a six day siege, and at Kiev in 1240, though on that occasion the captain of the garrison was spared because of the courage he had shown. When the Mongols took Alamut, they seem to have carried out a census of the population, as if for taxation purposes, but then put all to death.[56] The prevalence of the conventions of storm are well demonstrated by the taking of Béziers, during the Albigensian Crusade. There were orthodox catholics in the city, as well as the heretics who were the target of the crusade; but the city had resisted and been taken by storm, and all within were slaughtered, regardless of their beliefs. Some of the last captures made by Moslems of Christian strongholds were touched with a degree of malice and revenge. At the recapture of Antioch, crosses were smashed in the churches, women were sold four for a dinar, pages of holy books were scattered, tombs overturned, and priests and monks had their throats slit. It was proclaimed: 'the God

[55] On Licana, James I, ed. Forster, ii, p. 584; on Jerusalem, *Gesta Francorum*, p. 91. For Edessa see William of Tyre, ed. Babcock & Krey, p. 143; ed. Huygens, ii, p. 720: *et quos de civibus habent obviam gladiis perimunt, conditioni, etati aut sexui non parcentes*. On Darum, Archer, pp. 238–9; on Acre, Baha ad-Din in Gabrieli, p. 223; on Ghent, Froissart, ed. Brereton, p. 240; on Caen and Rougemont, Seward, *Henry V*, pp. 105, 183. On Roche-Derrien, Burne, *Crecy*, p. 95; on Montmorillon, Longman, ii, p. 203; on Orléans, Burne, *Agincourt*, p. 252; on Poix, John le Bel, in *Chronicles of the Hundred Years War*, pp. 63–4; ed. Viard & Deprez, ii, p. 91: *et furent tous ceulx de la ville tuez sans mercy, et la ville arse, et fut fait selonc raison*.

[56] Runciman, *Crusades*, iii, pp. 245, 251, 300.

who gave you Antioch, has taken it away again'. When Tripoli was taken, not all were killed, some were sent into slavery, a common fate at this stage of the conflict; but when the island of St Thomas was captured, the Moslems rode through the shallow waters to slaughter anyone who moved, so that one of their number, approaching the place immediately afterwards, was shocked at the sight. He went by boat, and reported that he: 'found it heaped with putrefying corpses; it was impossible to land there because of the stench'.[57] Timur the Great, at the capture of Sebastea, assembled all the captured nobles and had great pits dug. The captives were then bound with their heads between their legs, nose to rear, and thrown in; they were then covered with planks and earth, so that they suffocated. The captives at Smyrna were also killed, and a tower was built of alternate layers of stones and skulls, looking outwards: 'it was indeed a strange sight to behold'. When Constantinople was taken, in 1453, all were cut down with scimitars: 'women and men, old and young', looted houses were marked with flags, and 'the blood flowed in the city like rain water in the gutters after a sudden storm'; bodies floated in the Dardanelles: 'like melons along a canal'. Still at Malta, in 1565, when the fort of St Elmo was stormed, the Turks refused quarter to anyone, though the corsairs from Africa held on to a few prisoners in the hope of ransom. Some Christians sought refuge in the church, 'hoping for some spark of humanity', but all within were killed. What to the modern mind are 'atrocities', were a normal part of medieval war.[58]

Just as with people, so with buildings and property, the successful attackers by storm could take or destroy. Perhaps because of the poverty of the pagans, there were some unusual demands made of the defeated during the northern crusades, including the handing over of clothes. On one occasion, in Spain, surrender terms included the making of clothes by the victors for the garrison and the citizens, presumably as a sort of compensation. At Casava, during the crusades, the victors received an unexpected bonus in the distribution of spoils: each soldier was given two pounds of pepper.[59] The sequel to many of our great sieges through this period was wide destruction of great cities, from Jerusalem to Constantinople. When the Franks captured Constantinople, much booty was taken, including holy objects and relics. One crusader thought it was 'unworthy to commit sacrilege, except in a holy cause'! This man was an abbot, and having forced a local priest to show him where the best relics were, opened an iron

[57] On Béziers, Sumption, pp. 92–4; on Antioch, Ibn 'abd al-Zahirn Gabrieli, p. 311; on Tripoli, Abu l-Fida in Gabrieli, p. 342.

[58] On Sebastea and Smyrna, Doukas, pp. 89, 98. On 1453, Barbaro, pp. 66–7; on Malta, Balbi, p. 90.

[59] On the North, Henry of Livonia, ed. Arbusow & Bauer, pp. 198–9: *mittentes eis tributa et waypas*. For Spain, James I, ed. Forster, i, p. 363; for Casava, William of Tyre, ed. Babcock & Krey, i, p. 438, ed. Huygens, i, p. 471.

Looting

chest, and plunged in both his hands, seizing what he could to hide in the folds of his robe. The city itself was stripped. Many objects were removed as trophies to Venice, including the four bronze horses now adorning the facade of St Mark's. At Constantinople in 1453, Mehmet claimed that the city was his, and tried to prevent damage, but nevertheless in Santa Sophia itself, altars were destroyed, eyes gouged from portrayals of saints, relics broken, and holy objects hacked to pieces with axes; wine was drunk from holy chalices, and ikons were used to light fires for cooking. One writer claimed that the great church saw 'every kind of vileness within it, making of it a public brothel and a stable'. The sack lasted for the three days normally allowed by Islamic law.[60]

Although commanders were given *carte blanche* by the conventions of siege warfare, after capture by storming, the conduct of some victors seems more open to criticism than others. For example, whatever the provocation given in insults about his birth, the decision of William the Conqueror to mutilate the unfortunate citizens of Alençon, by chopping off their hands and feet is beyond the normal savagery. The end of the siege of Granson might perhaps, even in medieval terms, be considered as an atrocity, since, although it surrendered, the whole garrison was put to death. This was certainly unusual, but the surrender had been unconditional, and this, in effect, rendered the circumstances virtually the same as a defeat by storm. A similar example was at Montcontour, where, although

60 On Constantinople in 1204, Riley-Smith, *Idea*, pp. 172–73; on 1453, Leonard of Chios and Riccherio in Jones, pp. 38, 123.

the place surrendered, all were put to death except for two leaders and six other men.[61]

Victors might prefer to indulge other pleasures than those of slaughter. Rape was a constant factor in the sequel to capture by storm, and was perpetrated by all nations; it was, of course, also the kind of lurid atrocity that a writer would make much of. The Turks were often accused of seeking sexual satisfaction from their captives. At the capture of Thessalonika by Murad: 'chaste virgins fell into the embraces of profligates, and noble women into the arms of the ignoble'. Mehmet himself was said to have paid the ransom for the minister Notaras at Constantinople, and for his family. But when Notaras refused to give up his son for the sultan's pleasure, the execution of Notaras and his sons followed. Lesser men fought over the pretty girls, while people 'of every class' were chained together. Women were grabbed by the hair and dragged weeping from the churches, to be taken into slavery. Sphrantzes says that the Turks forced themselves sexually upon captives of both sexes in Santa Sophia. Time and again in the accounts, the Greeks seem as horrified by the class humiliation as by the rapes and killings. Doukas wrote: 'the commonest Turk sought the most tender maiden'. He described also the rape of nuns, youths and virgins being dragged about, women having their breasts exposed, and being bound with their own veils. Some nuns preferred to throw themselves down wells rather than meet the fate worse than death offered by their Turkish captors.[62]

Slavery was a common consequence of storm, and seen as a lenient alternative to massacre. Moslems frequently took their prisoners into slavery during the late stages of the conflict in the Latin Kingdom. And, after the fall of that kingdom, Christians often inflicted the same fate upon their victims, as did Peter of Aragon, when he took Alexandria in 1365; many of the citizens were slaughtered, but some 5,000 were sold into slavery. On the Crusade of Nicopolis, in 1396, the Christians took Rahora by storm, most were killed, but 1,000 were made slaves, some of whom were Bulgar Christians. It was reported after the fall of the Latin Kingdom, that Christian slaves were being employed to do manual work, such as digging ditches, fed on only three bread rolls a day; some preferred to become Moslems, others managed to escape and become pirates. After the final fall of Constantinople, it was said that those slaves who had not so far been sold, were flogged in public in the hope of arousing pity so that someone would buy them. The son of George Sphrantzes was killed when he refused sex to a Turkish victor, while his sister was put into Mehmet's seraglio, where she died. But some slaves might be lucky: Cardinal Isidore

[61] On Alençon, William of Jumièges, p. 126; for Granson, Commines, ed. Jones, p. 279; and Montcontour, Longman, ii, p. 189.

[62] On Murad, Notaras, and the veils, see Doukas, pp. 172, 234, 227. On every class, Riccherio in Jones, p. 123; Sphrantzes, pp. 80–1.

Captives

escaped from Constantinople after exchanging his robes with those of a beggar; the beggar was executed, the cardinal was sold as a slave, but later recognised in Pera, where he was bought and released. The great hero of Malta, Jean Parisot de la Valette, though head of the Order of the Knights of St John of Jerusalem, had earlier been captured by the Turks, and served a period as a galley slave.[63]

The division of spoil was a matter to be settled by the victors. Surrender terms sometimes resulted in the winning of spoil, but one reason that armies often preferred victory by storm, if it could be achieved, was that it gave the right of spoil. There was a greater tendency in the East to include cash in the demands made, and to treat the whole of a city's population as liable to ransom. It also made possible considerable gains in siege warfare. The same style of settlements transferred to Spain, and the Cid, for example, saved himself from wandering poverty by success in siege war. In this warfare, booty was distributed in recognised fractions to the main commanders. William of Tyre, writing of the crusaders after the taking of Antioch, wrote: 'even those who had been hungry beggars, became suddenly rich'. A number of Englishmen, such as Sir John Fastolf, made fortunes out of the Hundred Years War, and this was one reason why the making of peace was often unpopular.[64]

Moslems had a convention of three days for sack, and Christians followed similar practice. The restoration of order was a vital matter for the

63 On Alexandria, Runciman, *Crusades*, iii, p. 446; on Acre, Richard, p. 457; on flogging, Doukas, p. 71. On Sphrantzes and Isidore, Runciman, *Fall*, pp. 152, 150. On Valette, Bradford, p. 29.

64 William of Tyre, ed. Babcock & Krey, i, p. 260. For Fastolf, see McFarlane, *England in the Fifteenth Century*, ch. 9, pp. 175–97.

victorious commander; it was usually important to satisfy his own nobles and men. This often meant that fair shares must be given, and rules frequently are found for proportions to be received by commanders, nobles and men. At Constantinople in 1204, the Franks and the Venetians agreed to an even division between the two groups. The Greeks claimed that two-thirds of the world's wealth was in the city. The spoils from the great city were tremendous; gold, silver, gems, furs, and silks: 'so much booty had never been gained in any city since the creation of the world'. Robert de Clari said that among the treasures was a cloth which Christ had put to his face: 'so that his features were imprinted on it'.[65] An agreement was made to collect all the booty in one place and share it out. After the election of the new Latin emperor, he was to have a quarter of the booty together with the palaces, while the rest would be shared equally between the Franks and the Venetians. Twelve Frenchmen and twelve Venetians would form a committee to allot fiefs and offices. Anyone who broke this agreement was to suffer excommunication. The shares for lesser men were also proportioned: a foot sergeant would receive one share, a mounted sergeant two shares, and a knight four. The count of St Pol hanged one knight, with his shield round his neck, for not putting his gains into the common collection. Sometimes spoils included something beyond gold and valuables. In the conquests from Byzantium, after the Fourth Crusade, land also had to be distributed, and according to the *Morea Chronicle*, there was a 'book in which was written the share of each man'. At Salonika the knights and young bachelors protested because they had been left out of the division of fiefs; treating all fairly, and in a way acceptable to all, was a far from easy business. James I of Aragon had faced a similar problem, after the surrender of Valencia. He appointed his own officials to distribute the spoil, as he had done in Majorca; this time, though, there were complaints, so he let two bishops and two barons take over the task. They found it so difficult, indeed impossible, to satisfy everyone, that finally they handed the job back to James and his officials.[66]

Having seen the normal consequences of being stormed: death, slavery, exile, loss of property, rape, torture and almost any horror one could envisage, it is hardly surprising to find that far more medieval sieges were settled by agreement than allowed to go on to the bitter end.

[65] On booty, the shares, and St Pol, see Villehardouin, ed. Shaw, pp. 92, 101, 94; ed. Faral, ii, p. 52: *et toz les chiers avoirs qui onques furent trove in terre*. On the cloth, Clari, ed. McNeal, p. 104; ed. Lauer, p. 83: *chele toaile . . . et Nostre Sires en envolepa seu visage, si que se forme i fu emprientee*.

[66] *Morea Chronicle*, p. 125; on Salonika, Clari, ed. McNeal, p. 121. On Valencia, James I, ed. Forster, i, p. 399; ii, pp. 401–2.

Surrender Terms

The settlement of a siege by surrender, thus avoiding the worst consequences of an attack by storm, was an old and honourable arrangement, recognised by virtually everybody throughout the middle ages. In 775, for example, Ubbecke surrendered on terms to the Saxons; similarly Moorish Barcelona yielded by agreement to Louis, the son of Charlemagne; at the end of the middle ages, in 1480, Rhodes surrendered on terms to the Turks. In fact more sieges ended in a surrender on terms, than by a storm attack. Sometimes, as in the viking siege of Paris, an agreement on terms could be made, without a surrender; the vikings were paid to go on elsewhere.[67]

There is little new in the later middle ages about the arrangements made for surrenders. Storm could still mean that any treatment might be meted out at the victor's will, but perhaps, more often now in the public gaze, a prince might choose to show mercy where there was no cause for any to be expected. This occurred to a point where anyone exacting full penalties was often accused of cruelty. Frederick II, at Faenza, gave every reason for his enemies to expect heavy punishment: fighting on bitterly, refusing terms on the grounds that he wanted vengeance for the earlier treatment of his mother, and for the killing of a man thought to be Frederick himself; but then, having taken the place, he showed mercy, at least to the extent of allowing lives, declaring that: 'there is nothing lighter than the yoke of empire'. James I of Aragon, like many conquerors, wished to keep the respect of the conquered, and often allowed the retention of their religion and customs: 'I granted them the free exercise of their law'. In order to make sure the terms were clear to his Moslem enemies, he often had charters of the surrender terms drawn up; and, for example, at Xativa, letters were sent to the Saracens in Arabic. Another way of demonstrating mercy was, in the case of pagans, to allow surrender in return for baptism as, for example, at Selburg during the Baltic Crusade. Christians were sometimes offered the opportunity of converting to Islam to save their lives, as at Rhodes in 1480, when they refused, declaring: 'we shall fight and meet death before we ally ourselves with Mohammed'.[68]

Alfred the Great's laws attempted to delay conflict without royal approval, by calling for a seven day cooling off period, before a place was attacked. A related idea, was to give a place a period to make up its mind about surrender before an attack began; this was done in the great viking siege of Paris, before the siege began in earnest. The agreement to

67 On 775, *Carolingian Chronicles*, p. 53; on 801, Ermold, p. 45; on Rhodes, Brockman, p. 151; on Paris, *St Vaast*, ed. Simson, pp. 67–8.

68 On Faenza, Masson, p. 309. James I, ed. Forster, i, pp. 365–6; ii, p. 483. On Selburg, Henry of Livonia, ed. Brundage, p. 74. For Rhodes, Brockman, p. 81.

surrender, after a period allowed for relief by an allied force, often in the medieval period by the feudal overlord of the threatened place, was extremely common.[69] The period of military service seems often to have influenced chosen periods, and the conduct of sieges. Both sides knew when attacking armies contained feudal forces, committed to come for a set period, often of forty days. A forty day delay might well mean that the attacking force would melt away; commanders of such forces, had to bear this in mind, and often chose to make their last major attempt at storm, on the eve of the likely departure of their forces. One notes the common practice of demanding surrender after a period of forty days, for example, at Kenilworth in 1266; at Hertford, against Prince Louis, a truce was allowed for twenty days, and then extended by an additional twenty days. In 1226 Theobald, count of Champagne, departed from Louis VIII's siege of Bourges because his forty days' service was up, though Louis still managed to press the siege to a successful conclusion after three months. The period of service was a perennial problem for Simon de Montfort in the Albigensian crusade, every winter leaving him with a manpower difficulty after most of his troops had returned home. His sieges often took on a desperate race for time because of this as, for instance, at Termes.[70]

The making of surrender agreements could be a very complicated and uncertain business. Sometimes it was done simply through negotiation, and the terms might be straightforward, for example, surrender on the understanding that all lives would be spared. But at times there would be haggling over terms, for example, over how much ransom must be paid, or over individuals to be excepted from the general agreement. And terms were not always made in the calm atmosphere of a peace conference. At Jerusalem, in 1187, Saladin at first refused terms to the Christians, demanding vengeance for the massacre of Moslems when Jerusalem had been taken on the First Crusade. The Christian garrison said that in that case they would kill all the Moslems within the city, destroy all the valuables, and then kill themselves; at this Saladin decided to relent, and terms were made. The final fall of Acre gives a good instance of how terms might be offered in a tight situation. After the town was taken, the Templars continued to resist; they agreed a surrender and began to allow the Moslems to enter their tower. The latter then abused some women and boys, and the Templar Knights decided that the agreement was not being kept, so took up arms again. Al-Ashraf then repeated his offer of terms. Marshal Peter of Sevrey went out to parley, only to find himself seized and beheaded. As a result the Templars took to arms yet again, until their tower was brought down by mining. In Spain, at Santisteban, the defeated were given quite

69 *Alfred*, ed. Keynes & Lapidge, p. 169. On Paris, Abbo, p. 17.

70 On Kenilworth, *Chronicle of Bury St Edmunds*, p. 35. On Hertford, from 'Guillaume le Maréchal' in *EHD*, ii, p. 85. For Bourges, Perry, p. 18; and Simon de Montfort, Sumption, p. 124.

good terms, which allowed them to go with cash, horses and mules; while at Cordoba, having agreed to surrender, the garrison decided that their attackers were short of provisions, so changed their minds and fought on. Lenient terms, indeed surrender terms of any kind, were not always popular with besieging armies, who stood to lose all they might gain by loot from a storm attack. At Calatrava, in Spain, the French deserted because they thought the surrender terms offered to the Moslems were too generous. Leaders on both sides had to bear in mind the possible political consequences of any agreement made, it had therefore to be broadly acceptable to their own people.[71]

In general, when surrender terms were agreed, the defeated could expect that they would be carried out. Even without reference to a particular agreement, in Anglo-Saxon England, the laws of Alfred the Great required that men who had surrendered should be looked after, unharmed, for thirty days, during which their kin and friends must be informed of their situation. Commanders, such as James I of Aragon, or Saladin at Ascalon, were concerned that their word given to the enemy of another religion, should nevertheless be kept. But even with agreed terms, the plight of the defeated must often have been pitiful, sometimes it seemed so, even to medieval chroniclers: William of Poitiers thought William the Conqueror was merciful at Arques, but still expresses pity over the sight of the defeated garrison emerging to exile, heads bowed, some with starving horses, others carrying saddles. The defeated garrison at Tortona are similarly described, as they came out: deathly pale, like corpses rising from their tombs. We should not believe that the fate of those who accepted defeat through surrender was a happy one. They may have escaped the most severe penalties meted out on those whose town was taken by storm, but they could suffer many deprivations, from loss of home and property, to demands for ransom, imprisonment or slavery. As Ibn Sa'id wrote, of his departure from Seville, after its capture in 1248, when terms were agreed that the population could sell their moveables and go with what they could carry, which after all was a fairly lenient arrangement: 'when I think of the happy life in Seville, the rest of my life seems only pain'.[72]

Surrender for lives was about the lowest agreement, and the least that the defeated would expect. This might mean banishment without goods, banishment with goods, or permission to stay on in the city. It could often be simply life as a slave, and in the crusades, this was certainly a common outcome as, for example, at Antioch in its final surrender, and similarly at Beaufort. Sometimes, no doubt because of the fear of broken agreements, a

71 On Jerusalem, Ibn al-Athir in Gabrieli, pp. 141–2; on Acre, Runciman, *Crusades*, iii, p. 420. On Santisteban and Cordoba, Lomax, pp. 145, 146; on Calatrava, Riley-Smith, *Crusades*, p. 139.

72 *Alfred*, ed. Keynes & Lapidge, p. 169. William of Poitiers, ed. Foreville, p. 63. On Tortosa, Otto of Freising, ed. Mierow, p. 142; on Seville, Lomax, p. 154.

Release of Frankish prisoners from Moslem captivity

more formal settlement was made, not only for the right to leave, but for the protection of a safe-conduct, and possibly an escort, to a safe refuge. The surrender of Krak, in the Holy Land, was only made with the agreement of a safe-conduct to get to Tripoli.[73] James I of Aragon incorporated many of his settlements into formal charters.

Ransom, or payment in return for lives, was a common feature of agreements, and a good deal of haggling over amounts occurred. At Jaffa, Saladin agreed to pay ten bezants for each man released, five for each woman, and three for each child. At Bani a lump sum of 50,000 dinar was agreed, and one of 200,000 at Acre; and in the vast majority of such agreements, the terms were kept. At Jerusalem, Saladin charged ten dinar for a man, five for a woman, and two for a child, to be paid within forty days on pain of enslavement. He was then offered a lump sum of 30,000 dinar for the poor, which was accepted, but apparently not considered sufficient for the whole population. Soldiers collected cash at the gates, and counted out those who could go free. The Franks were allowed to try and sell possessions to raise their own ransom, but it was hard to get a price in the circumstances. In the end, there remained 16,000 unfortunates, including 7,000 men, who were not covered and could not pay, and they became slaves. According to a Moslem source, some of these were ill-used; women who were usually guarded were profaned, red lips were kissed, they were seized as concubines. But those who paid up were allowed to remain

[73] Runciman, *Crusades*, iii, pp. 324, 325, 334.

in the city if they chose, though they were permitted to take up only menial positions, and had to pay tribute as non-believers.[74]

Ironically, although in some ways the ideas of just war and the influence of the church moved in the direction of mercy, the later centuries of the middle ages also saw an increase in atrocities and cruel behaviour. On the one side we seem at times to witness an improvement in the way sieges were settled; at Lille, in 1304, an agreement was reached by setting up a council of eight, consisting of four Frenchmen and four Flemings to represent each side, in order to settle the amount of compensation that should be paid to the French king.[75] On the other hand, there are many examples where treatment seems barbarous in its severity. Sometimes this came simply from the continuation of old practices, the right to treat at will after a place had been stormed, the change being less in the activities of the conquerors, than in the attitude of the chroniclers. Remote peoples were of course often seen as barbarous, as one may note, for example, with western ideas about the Tartars. They were seen as being beyond the pale, and it was perhaps not surprising that their siege terms should be monstrous. Matthew Paris affects horror at their demand on one occasion for gold, silver and three thousand virgins. They were also accused, on occasion, of offering mild terms which they would naturally fail to keep.[76]

Harshness also came from one of those perennial and unfortunate aspects of warfare, atrocities which increased with the degree of hatred felt towards the enemy. The Albigensian crusade, for example, was fought over two fundamental issues: a local homeland, and religious belief; it raised tremendous hostility between the combatants, and led to atrocities on both sides. The Cathars could be as cruel as the crusaders, cutting off ears, noses, feet or hands. They had little interest in the normal gains of war, no desire to ransom their captives, and it was indeed a fight to the death.

Time and again, the normal code of war was broken in this war. Terms were discussed at Carcassonne, but when Raymond-Roger learned that only he himself and eleven of the garrison would be allowed to depart, negotiations broke down; it was said to be as likely for the terms to be agreed, as that donkeys would fly. In the end easier terms were agreed, that the besieged could depart, though only in shirts and breeches. But although Raymond-Roger had been given a safe-conduct, it was ignored; he was captured and chained up, and left to die in prison, possibly murdered. At Montlaur the citizens were hanged after surrender, and at Bram all captives were blinded except one who was left to lead his fellows to Cabaret. At Termes the defeated prisoners had their eyes pierced, their lips and noses slit, while at Lavaur ninety knights were executed. Aimery de

74 On Jaffa, Archer, p. 287. On Ba'rin, Acre and Jerusalem: Ibn al-Athir in Gabrieli, pp. 43, 142; Baha ad-Din in Gabrieli, p. 222; Imad ad-Din in Gabrieli, p. 163.

75 *Annales Gandenses*, p. 79.

76 Oman, ii, p. 321; Matthew Paris, ed. Giles, ii, p. 31.

Montréal was taken out first, but the gallows collapsed, and so they were all put to the sword. Aimery's sister, Giraude, was pushed screaming down a well, and then stoned to death. Religions generally enjoin tolerance and mercy; but how often do religious believers carry out the worst acts of atrocity and hatred?[77]

Cathars were frequently executed in the wake of successful crusading sieges: 140 were burned on a pyre at Minerve, 300 at Lavaur killed by crusaders: 'with joy in our hearts', sixty at Les Cassès burned in a tower, 210 at Moissac, where the nephew of the archbishop of Rheims had been hacked to pieces after capture by the besieged, and the pieces shot out by mangonel. On one occasion, an aged Cathar was dragged from bed to be burned. At Montségur, all those who would not recant were chained and driven outside the fortress, taken to a great pyre of wood within a stockade, where over two hundred of them were burned alive, including the last Cathar bishop of Toulouse.[78]

The Mongol advance also seems to have seen a large number of surrenders, after which normal treatment was not given. When Baghdad was taken, the caliph surrendered, but all except the ruler himself were executed; the caliph was persuaded to show where his treasure was hidden, then he too was killed. It was said that a Mongol soldier, finding forty orphaned children in the street, killed them too, on the grounds that they would be unable to live without their mothers. But there is little doubt that accounts were often exaggerated, and we discover that even here there was not a complete massacre, and that Christian citizens, taking refuge in churches, were allowed to live. At Mayyafaraqin, in 1260, again the Christians were allowed to survive, but the Moslems were killed, and al-Kamil made to eat his own flesh till he killed himself.[79]

The breaking of agreements, or at least accusations regarding this, was probably more common in wars over religion than in other warfare. At Ma'arrat, one Christian leader offered protection to those Moslems who sheltered in the palace near the gate, but other Christians attacked them, took their goods, and killed or enslaved them.[80] Rather than seeing such incidents as typical of the lack of faith in keeping agreements, one should probably often see them as partial agreements made with only some of the defenders, or by individuals, which did not have the sanction of the whole army. Such restricted or private agreements, the latter almost always made in the expectation of personal benefit in cash or power, cannot be treated in the same way as fully agreed terms between two sides.

Even so, it is true that some agreed terms were not kept. A truce was made at Lisbon, where hostages were given; here it was stipulated that the

77 Sumption, pp. 99, 111, 122, 131.

78 Sumption, pp. 118, 132, 133, 151, 230, 240 and pp. 227–8.

79 Runciman, *Crusades*, iii, pp. 303, 305.

80 *Gesta Francorum*, pp. 79–80.

Moslem defenders should not put obstacles in the way of the engines, or make repairs to their defences while the truce operated. As so often proved to be the case, there was a dispute between Christian allies over the truce, in this case over which group should hold the hostages, including an attempt by force to decide the matter. One source says the German and Flemish contingents ignored the terms of the agreement, pillaging, attacking virgins and cutting throats; but the account of entry to the town suggests this is an exaggeration. Part of the agreement was that any individual who was found to have looted valuables in his possession should be beheaded.[81]

When Fellin was taken, during the Baltic Crusade, the Christians taking refuge in the church were promised their lives, but the first to come out were killed, and some bodies were thrown to dogs in the fields. When Jerusalem was retaken in 1244 by the Khwarismian Turks, in the wake of Frederick II's agreement, many Christians were killed, despite a surrender for the lives of those within; a safe-conduct, which had been given, was not kept. James I of Aragon described the breaking of an agreement made between himself and the kaid of Xativa. He claimed that the kaid had broken the agreement by attacking Don Rodrigo; and pointed to the terms written down in a charter: 'you have one part, and I the other, and according to what is contained in them, you have broken the agreement you made with me'. When the sultan, Baibars, captured Safed in 1265, an agreement was made, but massacre followed, and the skulls of the dead were displayed all around the city. At the fall of Acre in 1291, the sultan: 'granted them permission to go where they liked, but when they came out, he killed more than 2,000 of them'. It was claimed that the reason for this was that when the Christians had taken it in the first place, they had 'promised to spare the lives of the Moslems, and then treacherously killed them'. Now: 'the sultan gave his word to the Franks, and then had them slaughtered as the Franks had done to the Moslems'. After the fall of Constantinople, its neighbour Pera, which had remained neutral through the siege, surrendered to the Turks, but the citizens were then enslaved, and Mehmet was accused of sacking the town: 'as an enemy, breaking the oath which he had publicly sworn'. The agreement had apparently been not to destroy the place, and to allow the citizens to come and go freely, keeping their own laws and customs, and their churches.[82]

Law and order within realms increased in this period, but those who offended against the authorities were more likely to suffer serious penalties. Punishments could always be justified against rebels and traitors, and, increasingly, anyone who fought against a monarch was labelled thus.

[81] *De Expugnatione Lyxbonensi*, pp. 164–72.

[82] On Fellin, Henry of Livonia, ed. Brundage, p. 208; on Jerusalem, Runciman, *Crusades*, iii, pp. 224–5; on Xativa, James I, ed. Forster, ii, pp. 435, 447, 448; on Safed, Richard, ii, p. 394; on Acre, Abu l'Mahasin in Gabrieli, p. 348; on Pera, Riccherio in Jones, p. 124.

Medieval society was prepared to accept such harsh treatment; war was seen as divine punishment, soldiers as 'the flail of God'. Rebels within the realm and without, since opposing lands were often treated as owing allegiance to the crown concerned, were again often treated harshly. At Bedford in 1224, practically everyone who had fought within the walls of the castle was hanged, including the garrison's commander, William de Bréauté. It was said, after Edward I took Berwick, that thousands were killed, some thrown down wells or into the sea. It is also reported that this ruler of a civilised nation had a hundred heads taken in Wales, which was also treated as being in a state of rebellion. When Edward II took Leeds castle, the whole garrison was hanged on the spot. We have quoted an example earlier of Frederick II's deliberate, propagandist mercy at Faenza, but there were other occasions when his vengefulness was not stayed. At Carpaccio in 1246, the defenders so feared his anticipated rage that they threw themselves on their swords, or jumped from a high rock to the sea; Frederick blinded captive leaders, and some he branded with an impression of a papal bull on their foreheads, 'to give public notice of their treachery'. Edward III, again at the unfortunate Berwick, had the hostage, Thomas Seton, hanged before the eyes of his parents, and ordered that two hostages be hanged every day until the place surrendered. It is noticeable how often the worst atrocities of this period, as in others, occurred when in some way the war involved nationality.[83]

There is little doubt that apparent harshness was often the result of a partial surrender. It was common for the town to be taken while the garrison in the castle or citadel continued to resist; the garrison might then obtain surrender terms and be spared, while the citizens suffered the full rigours of the penalties which followed after capture by storm. At Tripoli, in 1109, it was agreed to release the governor and his troops, but the unfortunate citizens were excluded from the agreement, and were tortured and treated harshly as a result. There were many occasions when only the great were allowed to go, and in most cases they were prepared to sacrifice others for their own safety. After Hattin, Saladin permitted the countess and her family a safe-conduct from Tiberias; and when he took Jaffa, he was accused of taking money, and then beheading the citizens, but almost certainly this was another case of a deal made only with the garrison, which had continued to resist after the city had been stormed. At Jaffa again, during the last stages of the crusade, when taken by the Moslems, the garrison was allowed to leave. At Marqab the agreement seems to have been made with an even more precise division by rank; the garrison was

[83] For the flail, Contamine, p. 281; from Bonet. Compare Bonet, p. 125: 'war is not an evil thing, it is good and virtuous', or 'war comes from God'. On Bedford, *Chronicle of Bury St Edmunds*, p. 5; on Berwick, Prestwich, *Edward I*, p. 471. On Leeds, Fryde, p. 51; on Carpaccio, Matthew Paris, ed. Giles, ii, p. 187; on Seton, Nicholson, pp. 126–7.

allowed to go, but only the officers were allowed to take possessions. Obviously such conditions were often compromises made after a process of negotiation and bargaining. Even after the decisive victory of the Turks at Constantinople, one group who continued to resist from a tower, the Cretan sailors, were able to make a separate deal for surrender, and were allowed to sail away with their property. After the same siege, it seems that certain separate districts within the city were able to make bargains for themselves, and avoided the worst of the sack.[84]

Another aspect of harshness, was the symbolism of punishment. Humiliation of an offender was often an important ingredient, as when Peter of Brittany was allowed to keep the duchy, but was taken first to Paris in a halter.[85] The frequent agreements which allowed lives, but which insisted on the garrison going, for example, in shirts and breeches, or without arms, or without mounts, was all to demonstrate their humiliation. It might be said, finally, that even the apparently merciful settlements, were not necessarily light punishments. Citizens were often being banished from their homes, losing their property and everything they had lived for, to go into a risky and difficult exile; leaving their belongings behind might mean that they were heading for deprivation and possibly starvation. At Zierikzee, near Ghent, the citizens were allowed to go, but had to live without even tents for protection, and had to survive a week with virtually no food, the locals being forbidden on pain of death to give them assistance. The fate of those defeated in a siege should not be treated lightly.[86]

Conclusion

We have followed the history of siege warfare, however sketchily, from the fall of the Roman Empire to the Reformation. The most notable conclusion, is to find how similar are the methods and conventions which applied at the start, and still at the end. The symbolism of siege warfare, such as the handing over of keys or the use of white flags, is typical of the staying power of conventions. The loss of rights by those who suffered a storm attack, continued right through the period, though expectations of mercy probably increased gradually. The making of surrender terms, and the kind of terms enforced, do not alter greatly either through the period chronologically, or across the area we have covered geographically. There were some developments in the weaponry of siege warfare, and therefore necessarily in fortification, but such changes were all but universal in application,

84 On Tripoli and Tiberias, Ibn al-Qalanisi and Ibn al-Athir, in Gabrieli, pp. 25, 124. On Jaffa, Ambroise, ed. Hubert & La Monte, p. 407; on Jaffa and Marqab, Runciman, *Crusades*, iii, pp. 324, 395. On the Cretans, Runciman, *Fall*, pp. 140, 143.

85 Perry, p. 68.

86 On shirts and breeches, Sumption, p. 99; on Zierikzee, *Annales Gandenses*, p. 61.

and did not alter the tactics of siege warfare greatly. Perhaps the most significant weapon developments throughout our period were the introductions of Greek Fire in the early middle ages, the trebuchet in the central middle ages, and cannons in the late period. They were all of great significance, but they mainly improved existing methods of setting fire to fortifications, or battering them down, and were perhaps less dramatic in their impact on siege warfare than is often imagined, or than their impact on field warfare. Perhaps what we have learned above all, and what will remain longest in the mind, is the tremendous pain and deprivation which man can inflict upon his fellow, and yet which can be overcome; and the great courage under duress which the human race is able to display.

Bibliography

Primary Sources

Aachen, Albert of, *Historia Hierosolymitana*, RHC Occ., iv, pp. 265–713.
Abbo, *Le Siège de Paris par les Normands*, ed. H. Waquet, Paris, 1942.
Aethelweard, *Chronicle*, ed. A. Campbell, Edinburgh, 1962. Aguilers, Raymond of, *Historia Francorum Qui Ceperunt Iherusalem*, RHC Occ., iii, Paris, 1866.
Aguilers, Raymond of, *Historia Francorum Qui Ceperunt Iherusalem*, ed. J.J. & L.L. Hill, Philadelphia, 1968. (Translation).
Aguilers, Raymond of, *Liber*, ed. J.J. & L.L. Hill, Paris, 1969. (Latin).
Alfred the Great, Asser's Life of King Alfred and other Contemporary Sources, ed. S. Keynes & M. Lapidge, Harmondsworth, 1983.
Ambroise, *L'Estoire de la Guerre Sainte*, ed. G. Paris, Paris, 1897.
Ambroise, *The Crusade of Richard the Lionheart*, ed. M.J. Hubert, & J.L. La Monte, New York, 1976.
Anglo-Saxon Chronicle, The, ed. D. Whitelock, D.C. Douglas, S.I. Tucker, London, 1961.
Annales Bertiniani, ed. G. Waitz, MGH SRG no. 5, Hannover, 1883.
Annales Bertiniani, ed. F. Grat, J. Vielliard, S. Clemencet, Paris, 1964.
Annales Fuldenses, ed. G.H. Pertz & F. Kurze, MGH SRG, no. 7, reprint, Hannover, 1978.
Annales Gandenses, ed. H. Johnstone, Edinburgh, 1951.
Annales Marbacenses, ed. H. Bloch, MGH SRG, no. 9, Hannover & Leipzig, 1907.
Annales Placentini Gibellini, ed. G.H. Pertz, MGH SS, xviii, Hannover & Leipzig, 1925.
Annales Regni Francorum, ed. G.H. Pertz & F. Kurze, MGH SRG, no. 6, Hannover, 1895.
Annales Xantenses et Annales Vedastini, ed. B. de Simson, MGH SRG no. 12, Hannover & Leipzig, 1909.
Archer, T.A., *The Crusade of Richard the Lionheart, 1189–92*, London, 1888.
Archives d'Anjou, ed. P. Marchegay, Angers, 1843.
Asser, *Vita Alfredi*, ed. W. Stevenson, revised edn, Oxford, 1959.
Astronomer, The, *Vita Hludowici Imperatoris*, MGH SRG, no. 2, Hannover, 1829.
Avesbury, Robert of, *Historia de Mirabilis Gestis Edwardi Tertii*, ed. T. Hearne, Oxford, 1720.
Baker, Geoffrey le, *Chronicon*, ed. E.M. Thompson, Oxford, 1889.
Balbi di Correggio, Francisco, *The Siege of Malta, 1565*, ed. E. Bradford, London, 1965.
Barbaro, Nicolo, *Diary of the Siege of Constantinople, 1453*, ed. J.R. Jones, New York, 1969.

Barnwell Annals, in Walter of Coventry, Memorial, ed. W. Stubbs, 2 vols., RS no. 58, London, 1872–73, ii, pp. 196–279.
Basin, Thomas, *Histoire des Règnes de Charles VII et de Louis XI*, ed. J.E.J. Quicherat, 4 vols., SHF, Paris, 1855–59.
Basin, Thomas, *Histoire de Charles VII*, ed. C. Samaran, 2 vols., Paris, 1933–44; reissued edn, Paris, 1964.
Basin, Thomas, *Histoire de Louis XI*, ed. C. Samaran & M.C. Garand, 3 vols., Paris, 1963–72.
Bel, Jean le, *Chronique*, ed. J. Viard & E. Déprez, 2 vols., Paris, 1904–05.
Bonet, Honoré, *The Tree of Battles*, ed. G.W. Coopland, Liverpool, 1949.
Bouard, M. de, *Documents de l'Histoire de la Normandie*, Toulouse, 1972.
Bouchel, L., *Gregori Turonensis*, Paris, 1610.
Boucicaut, *Le Livre des Faicts*, ed. J.F. Michaud & J.J.F. Poujoulat, Paris, 1836.
Brut Y Tywysogion, ed. T. Jones, Cardiff, 1955.
Brut, The, ed. F.W.D. Brie, EETS. 2 vols., London, 1906, 1908.
Caen, Ralph of, *Gesta Tancredi*, RHC Occ., iii, Paris, 1866, pp. 587–716.
Cahen, C., 'Un Traité d'Armurie Composé pour Saladin', *Bulletin d'Etudes Orientales*, xi, 1945–6, pp. 16–18; xii, 1947–8, pp. 103–63.
Calendar of Documents of Scotland, ed. J. Bain, 4 vols., Edinburgh, 1881–88.
Calendar of Signet Letters of Henry IV and Henry V, 1399–1422, ed. J.L. Kirby, London, 1978.
Cantar de Mio Cid, ed. R.M. Pidal, 3 vols., Madrid, 1908–11.
Capitularia Regum Francorum, ed. A. Boretius & V. Krause, MGH Capitularia, I and II, Hannover, 1883, 1897.
Carolingian Chronicles, ed. W.W. Scholz & B. Rogers, Michigan, 1970.
Cartulaire de l'Abbaye Cardinale de la Trinité de Vendôme, ed. C. Métais, 2 vols., Paris, 1893.
Cartularium Saxonicum, ed. W.G. Birch, 3 vols., London, 1885–93.
Chanson de la Croisade Albigeoise, ed. E. Martin-Chabot, CHF, 3 vols., Paris, 1931–61. (Books 1 to 12 are by William of Tudela, the rest is anonymous).
Chartres, Fulcher of, *Chronicle of the First Crusade*, ed. M.E. McGinty, Philadelphia, 1941.
Chaucer, G., *The Canterbury Tales*, ed. N. Coghill, London, 1974.
Chaucer, G., *The Riverside Chaucer*, ed. L.D. Benson, Oxford, 1988.
Chronica Regio Coloniensis, ed. G. Waitz, MGH SRG, no. 18, Hannover, 1880.
Chronicle of Bury St Edmunds, 1212–1301, ed. A. Gransden, Edinburgh, 1964.
Chronicle of the Morea, Crusaders as Conquerors, ed. H.E. Lurier, New York, 1964.
Chronicles of the Reigns of Stephen, Henry II and Richard I, ed. R. Howlett, 4 vols., RS no. 82, London, 1889.
Chronique de Nantes, ed. R. Merlet, Paris, 1896.
Chronique du Religieux de St Denys, ed. M.L. Bellaguet, 6 vols., Paris, 1839–52.
Chroniques des Comtes d'Anjou et des Seigneurs d'Amboise, ed. L. Halphen & R. Poupardin, Paris, 1913.
Chroniques des Eglises d'Anjou, ed. P. Marchegay & E. Mabille, Paris, 1869.
Clari, Robert de, *La Conquête de Constantinople*, ed. P. Lauer, Paris, 1924.
Clari, Robert de, *The Conquest of Constantinople*, ed. E.H. McNeal, New York, 1936.
Coggeshall, Ralph of, *Chronicon Anglicanum*, ed. J. Stevenson, RS no. 66, London, 1875.

Commines, Philip de, *Mémoires*, ed. J. Calmette & G. Durville, CHF, 3 vols., Paris, 1924–25.

Commines, Philip de, *Memoirs, The Reign of Louis XI, 1461–53*, ed. M. Jones, Harmondsworth, 1972.

Comnena, Anna, *The Alexiad*, ed. E.R.A. Sewter, Harmondsworth, 1969.

Contemporary Chronicles of the Hundred Years War, ed. P.E. Thompson, London, 1966.

Coventry, Walter of, *Memorial*, ed. W. Stubbs, 2 vols., RS no. 58, London, 1873.

Cremona, Liudprand of, *Opera*, ed. J. Becker, MGH SRG, no. 41, reprint, Hannover & Leipzig, 1977.

Cremona, Liudprand of, *Works*, ed. F.A. Wright, London, 1930.

Crowland Chronicle Continuations, 1459–86, ed. N. Pronay & J. Cox, London, 1986.

De Expugnatione Lyxbonensi, ed. C.W. David, New York, 1976.

Deuil, Odo of, *De Profectione Ludovici in Orientem, the Journey of Louis VII to the East*, ed. V.G. Berry, New York, 1948.

Dialogue of the Exchequer, ed. D. Greenway, Oxford, 1984.

Dialogue of the Exchequer, ed. C. Johson, Edinburgh, 1950.

Die Kreuzzugsbriefe aus den Jahren 1088–1100, ed. H. Hagenmeyer, Innsbruck, 1901.

Doukas, *The Decline and Fall of Byzantium to the Ottoman Turks*, ed. H.J. Magoulias, Detroit, 1975.

Du Cange, *Glossarium mediae et infimae latinatis*, 5 vols., in 10 parts, Paris, 1883–87.

'Dunstable Annals', from *Annales Monastici*, ed. H.R. Luard, 5 vols., RS no. 36, London, 1866, iii.

Durham, Symeon of, *Historia Regum*, ed. T. Arnold, RS no. 75, 2 vols., 1882, 1885.

Eboli, Pietro da, *Carmen de rebus Siculis*, ed. G.B. Siragusa, FSI, Rome, 1905

Eboli, Pietro da, *De Rebus Siculis Carmen*, Codex Bernensis 120, Burgerbibliothek, Bern.

Eboli, Pietro da, *Liber ad Honorem Augusti*, ed. G.B. Siragusa, FSI, Rome, 1906.

Einhard, *The Life of Charlemagne*, ed. L. Thorpe, London, 1970.

Einhard, *Vita Karoli Magni*, ed. G.H. Pertz & G. Waitz, MGH SRG no. 25, Hannover & Leipzig, reprint, 1947.

Encomium Emmae Reginae, ed. A. Campbell, RHS, Camden, 3rd ser., lxxii, 1949.

English Chronicle of the Reigns of Richard II, Henry IV, Henry V and Henry VI, ed. J.S. Davies, London, 1856.

English Historical Documents, ed. D.C. Douglas; i, 2nd edn, 1979; ii, 2nd edn, 1981; ii, 1975; iv, 1969.

Ermold le Noir, *In Honorem Hludowici, Poème sur Louis le Pieux et Epîtres au Roi Pepin*, ed. E. Faral, Paris, 1932.

Fantosme, Jordan, *Chronicle*, ed. R.C. Johnston, Oxford, 1981.

Fauroux, M., *Receuil des Actes des Ducs de Normandie de 911 à 1066*, Caen, 1961.

Fragmentary Annals of Ireland, ed. J.N. Radner, Dublin, 1978.

Fredegar, *The Fourth Book of the Chronicle of*, ed. J.M. Wallace-Hadrill, Edinburgh, 1960.

Freising, Otto of, and Rahewin, *Gesta Friderici Primi Imperatoris*, ed. A. Waitz & B. de Simson, MGH SRG no. 12, Hannover & Leipzig, 1912.

Freising, Otto of and Rahewin, *The Deeds of Frederick Barbarossa*, ed. C.C. Mierow & R. Emery, New York, 1953.
Froissart, Jean, *Chronicles*, ed. G. Brereton, Harmondsworth, 1968.
Froissart, Jean, *Chronicles*, ed. J. Jolliffe, London, 1967.
Froissart, Jean, *Chroniques*, ed. S. Luce, 15 vols., Paris, 1869–1975.
Froissart, Jean, *Chroniques*, ed. T. Johnes, 2 vols., London, 1857.
Gabrieli, F., *Arab Historians of the Crusades*, London, 1969.
Geankoplos, D.J., *Byzantium, Church, Society and Civilization seen through Contemporary Eyes*, Chicago, 1984.
Gerhard, *Vita Sancti Oudalrici Episcopi*, MGH SS, iv, ed. G. Pertz, Hannover, 1841.
Gesta Francorum et Aliorum Hierosolimitanorum, ed. R. Hill, Oxford, 1972.
Gesta Fulconis Filii Warini, ed. J. Stevenson, RS no. 66, London, 1875.
Gesta Henrici Quinti, ed. F. Taylor & J.S. Roskell, Oxford, 1975.
Gesta Stephani, ed. K.R. Potter & R.H.C. Davis, Oxford, 1976.
Gildas, *The Ruin of Britain and Other Works*, ed. M. Winterbottom, London & Chichester, 1978.
Glastonbury, John of, *Chronicle*, ed. J.P. Carley & D. Townsend, Woodbridge, 1985.
Hahnloser, H.R., *Villard de Honnecourt*, 2nd edn, Graz, 1972.
Histoire des Ducs de Normandie et des Rois d'Angleterre, ed. F. Michel, Paris, 1840.
Historical Collections of a Citizen of London in the Fifteenth Century, ed. J. Gairdner, Camden Soc., NS 17, 1876; includes John Page, pp. 1–46; Lydgate, pp. 49–51; Gregory's Chronicle, pp. 52–239.
Howden, Roger of, *Chronicle*, ed. W. Stubbs, RS no. 51, 4 vols., London, 1868–71.
Howden, Roger of, *Gesta Regis Henri Secundi et Ricardi Primi*, ed. W. Stubbs, RS no. 49, 2 vols., 1867.
Howden, Roger of, *Chronicle*, ed. H.T. Riley, 2 vols., London, 1853.
Itinerarium Peregrinorum et Gesta Regis Ricardi, Chronicles and Memorials of the Reign of Richard I, ed. W. Stubbs, RS no. 38, London, 1864.
James I King of Aragon, *Chronicle*, ed. J. Forster, 2 vols., London, 1883.
James I King of Aragon (Jaume I), *Cronica*, ed. J.M. de Casacuberta, 2 vols., Barcelona, 1926 , 1962.
Joinville, Jean de, Life of St Louis, in *Chronicles of the Crusades*, ed. M.R.B. Shaw, Harmondsworth, 1963.
Joinville, Jean de, *History of St Louis*, ed. J. Evans & N. de Wailly, Oxford, 1938.
Joinville, Jean de, *La Vie de St Louis*, ed. N.L. Corbett, Quebec, 1977.
Jones, J.R.M., *The Siege of Constantinople, 1453, the Contemporary Accounts*, Amsterdam, 1972.
Journal d'un Bourgeois de Paris sous le Règne de Charles VII, ed J.F. Michaud & J.J.F. Poujoulat, iii, Paris, 1837.
Jumièges, William of, *Gesta Normannorum Ducum*, ed. J. Marx, Rouen & Paris, 1914.
Jumièges, William of, *Histoire des Normands*, ed. M. Guizot, Paris, 1826.
Juvaini, Ala ad-Din Ata-Malik, *The History of the World Conqueror*, ed. M.M. Qayvini & J.A. Boyle, 2 vols., Manchester, 1958.
Juvenal des Ursins, Jean, *Histoire de Charles VI Roy de France*, ed. J.F. Michaud & J.J.F. Poujoulat, Paris, 1836.

Knighton, Henry, *Chronicon*, ed. J.R. Lumby, 2 vols., RS no. 92, London, 1889, 1895.

Kyeser, Conrad, *Bellifortis*, ed. G. Quarg, 2 vols., Dusseldorf, 1967.

Lanercost Chronicle, ed. J. Stevenson, Edinburgh, 1839.

Langtoft, Peter, *Chronicle*, ed. T. Wright, 2 vols., RS no. 47, London, 1868.

Lewis, B., *Islam, from the Prophet Muhammed to the Capture of Constantinople, i, Politics and War*, New York, 1974.

Liber Historiae Francorum, ed. B.S. Bachrach, Laurence Kansas, 1973.

Livonia, Henry of, *Chronicle*, ed. J.A. Brundage, New York, 1961.

Livonia, Henry of, *Chronicon Livoniae*, ed. L. Arbusow & A. Bauer, MGH SRG no. 31, Hannover, 1955.

Lombard, Paul the, *Historia Langobardorum*, ed. G. Waitz, MGH SRG no. 48, Hannover, 1978.

Magni Rotuli Scaccarii Normanniae sub Regibus Angliae, ed. T. Stapleton, 2 vols., London, 1840, 1844.

Malmesbury, William of, *Chronicle of the Kings of England*, ed. J.A. Giles, London, 1895.

Malmesbury, William of, *De Gestis Regum Anglorum*, ed. W. Stubbs, RS no. 90, 2 vols., London, 1887, 1889.

Malmesbury, William of, *Historia Novella*, ed. K.R. Potter, Edinburgh, 1955.

Marcellinus, Ammianus, *Rerum Gestarum Libri Qui Supersunt*, ed. J.C. Rolfe, 3 vols., London, 1935–63.

Marcellinus, Ammianus, *The Later Roman Empire, 354–378*, ed. W. Hamilton & A. Wallace-Hadrill, Harmondsworth, 1986.

Maréchal, Guillaume le, ed. P. Meyer, 3 vols., Paris, 1891–1901.

Milemete, Walter de, *De Nobilitatibus, Sapientiis et Prudentiis Regum*, ed. M.R. James, Roxburghe Club, 1913.

Mommsen, T.E. & K.F. Morrison, *Imperial Lives and Letters of the Eleventh Century*, New York & London, 1962.

Monstrelet, Enguerrand de, *Chronicles*, ed. T. Johnes, 13 vols., London, 1810.

Monstrelet, Enguerrand de, *Chronique*, ed. L. Douët-D'Arcq, SHF, 6 vols., Paris, 1857–62.

Mortet, V., *Receuil des Textes Relatifs à l'Histoire de l'Architecture*, i, Paris, 1911.

Nithard, *De Dissensionibus Filiorum Ludowici Pii*, ed. P. Lauer, Paris, 1926.

Notker Babulus, *Gesta Karoli Magni Imperatoris*, ed. H.F. Haefele, MGH SRG no. 12, Berlin, 1959.

Novara, Philip de, *Mémoires*, ed. C. Köhler, Paris, 1913

Novara, Philip de, *The Wars of Frederick II against the Ibelins in Syria and Cyprus*, ed. J.L. La Monte & M.J. Hubert, New York, 1936.

Paderborn, Oliver of, *Historia Damiatana*, ed. J.J. Gavigan, 1948.

Paris, Matthew, *Chronica Majora*, ed. H.R. Luard, 7 vols., RS no. 57, London, 1872–83.

Paris, Matthew, *Chronicles*, ed. R. Vaughan, Gloucester, 1986.

Paris, Matthew, *English History*, ed. J.A. Giles, 3 vols., London, 1852.

Paris, Matthew, *Historia Anglorum*, ed. F. Madden, 3 vols., RS no. 44, London, 1866–69.

Passiones Leudegarii, MGH Scriptores Rerum Merovingicarum, v, ed. B. Krusch & W. Levison, Hannover & Leipzig, 1910, pp. 249–362.

Paston Letters and Papers of the Fifteenth Century, ed. N. Davies, 2 vols., Oxford, 1971, 1976.
Photius, Patriarch of Constantinople, *Homilies*, ed. C. Mango, Cambridge Massachusetts, 1958.
Poem of the Cid, The, ed. L.B. Simpson, Berkeley & Los Angeles, 1957.
Poema de Mio Cid, ed. C. Smith, Oxford, 1972.
Poitiers, William of, *Histoire de Guillaume le Conquérant*, ed. R. Foreville, Paris, 1952.
Procopius, *The Secret History*, ed. G.A. Williamson, Harmondsworth, 1966.
Prüm, Regino of, *Chronicon*, ed. F. Kurze, MGH SRG no. 50, reprint, Hannover, 1978.
Receuil des Actes de Charles III le Simple, ed. P. Lauer, Paris, 1949.
Richer, *Histoire de France*, ed. R. Latouche, 2 vols., Paris, 1930, 1937.
Richer, *Historia*, ed. J. Guadet, 2 vols., Paris, 1865. Rigord and William the Breton, *Oevres*, ed. H.F. Delaborde, 2 vols., Paris, 1882,
Riley-Smith, L.& J., *The Crusades, Idea and Reality, 1095–1274*, London, 1981.
Robertson, A.J., *Anglo-Saxon Charters*, Cambridge, 1939.
Rotuli Litterarum Clausarum, i, ed. T.D. Hardy, London, 1833.
Salisbury, John of, *Historia Pontificalis, Memoirs of the Papal Court*, ed. M.C. Chibnall, Edinburgh, 1956.
Siege of Caerlaverock, The, ed. N.H. Nicolas, London, 1828.
Sphrantzes, George, *Chronicle, as a Contemporary Greek Source for the Siege of Constantinople, 1453*, ed. M. Carroll, Amsterdam, 1985.
St Pathus, William de, *Vie de St Louis*, ed. H.F. Delaborde, Paris, 1899.
St Quentin, Dudo of, *De Moribus et Actis Primorum Normanniae Ducum*, ed. J. Lair, Caen, 1865.
Stearns, I., *The Greater Medieval Historians*, Washington DC, 1982.
Stenton, F.M., ed. , *The Bayeux Tapestry*, London, 1957.
Stevenson, J., *The Church Historians of England*, 5 vols., London, 1853–58.
Suger, *Oevres Complètes*, ed. A. Leroy de la Marche, Paris, 1867.
Theophanes, *The Chronicle of*, ed. H. Turtledove, Philadelphia, 1982.
Theophylact Simocatta, *The History of*, ed. M. & M. Whitby, Oxford, 1986.
Three Chronicles of the Reign of Edward IV, intro. K. Dockray, Gloucester, 1988.
Tours, Gregory of, *Histoire des Francs*, 2 vols., CHF, Paris, 1975, 1979.
Tours, Gregory of, *The History of the Franks*, ed. L. Thorpe, Harmondsworth, 1974.
Tours, Gregory of, *Historiae*, ed. B. Krusch & W. Levison, MGH Scriptores Rerum Merovingicarum, I, i, Hannover, 1951.
Tudebod, Peter, *Historia de Hierosolymitano Itinere*, ed. J.H. & L.L. Hill, Philadelphia, 1974. (English).
Tudebod, Peter, *Historia de Hierosolymitano Itinere*, ed. J.H. & L.L. Hill, Paris, 1977. (Latin).
Two of the Saxon Chronicles Parallel, ed. C. Plummer & J. Earle, Oxford, 1892.
Tyre, William of, *Chronicon*, ed. R.B.C. Huygens, 2 vols., Brepols, 1986.
Tyre, William of, *A History of Deeds Done Beyond the Sea*, ed. E.A. Babcock & A.C. Krey, 2 vols., New York, 1943.
Usamah, *Memoirs of an Arab-Syrian Gentleman*, ed. P.K. Hitti, Beirut, 1964.
Vaux-de-Cernay, Peter of, *Hystoria Albigensis*, ed. P. Guébin, Paris, 1951. (French translation).

Vaux-de-Cernay, Peter of, *Hystoria Albigensis*, ed. P. Guébin & E. Lyon, 3 vols., Paris, 1926–39.
Venette, Jean de, *Chronicle*, ed. R.A. Newhall & J. Birdsall, New York, 1953.
Vigeois, Geoffrey de, *Chronicle*, ed. P. Labbe, Paris, 1657.
Villani, *Cronica*, ed. G. Antonelli, 4 vols., Florence, 1823.
Villehardouin, Geoffrey de, 'The Conquest of Constantinople', in *Chronicles of the Crusades*, ed. M.R.B. Shaw, Harmondsworth, 1963.
Villehardouin, Geoffrey de, *La Conquête de Constantinople*, ed. E. Faral, 2 vols., Paris, 1938–39.
Vita Edwardi Secundi, ed N. Denholm-Young, Edinburgh, 1957.
Vitalis, Orderic, *The Ecclesiastical History*, ed. M. Chibnall, 6 vols., Oxford, 1969–81.
Vitruvius, *On Architecture*, ed. F. Granger, 2 vols., London, 1931, 1934.
Vitry, Jacques de, *Lettres*, ed. R.B.C. Huygens, Leiden, 1960.
Waurin, Jean de, *Receuil des Chroniques*, ed. W. & E.L.C.P. Hardy, 8 vols., RS nos. 39, 40, London, 1864–91.
Wendover, Roger, *Flores Historiarum*, ed. H.J. Hewlett, 3 vols., RS no. 84, London, 1886–89.
Widukind, *Rerum Gestarum Saxonicarum*, ed. G. Waitz & K.A. Kehr, MGH Scriptores, lx, Hannover, 1904.
Wilson, D.M., *The Bayeux Tapestry*, London, 1985.
Worcester, Florence of, *Chronicon ex Chronicis*, ed. B. Thorpe, 2 vols., EHS, London, 1848–49.
Worcester, John of, *Chronicle, Anecdota Oxoniensis*, ed. J.R. Weaver, Oxford, 1908.
Wrottesley, G., *Crecy and Calais from the Public Records*, London, 1898.
Wylie, J.H. & W.T. Waugh, *The Reign of Henry V*, 3 vols., Cambridge, 1914–29.

Secondary Sources

Abels, R.P., *Lordship and Military Obligation in Anglo-Saxon England*, London, 1988.
Abulafia, D., *Frederick II, a Medieval Emperor*, London, 1988.
Allmand, C.T., *Society at War, the Experience of England and France during the Hundred Years War*, Edinburgh, 1973.
Allmand, C.T., *The Hundred Years War, England and France at War, c.1300–c.1450*, Cambridge, 1988.
Anderson, W., *Castles of Europe*, London, 1980.
Appleby, J.T., *England Without Richard, 1189–1199*, London, 1967.
Atiya, A.S., *The Crusade in the Later Middle Ages*, London, 1938.
Atiya, A.S., *The Crusade of Nicopolis*, London, 1934.
Bachrach, B.S., *Merovingian Military Organization, 481–751*, Minneapolis, 1972.
Baldwin, J.W., *The Government of Philip Augustus*, Berkeley, 1986.
Barber, M., 'Catharism and the Occitan Nobility: the Lordships of Cabaret, Minerve and Termes', *IPMK*, iii, 1988, Woodbridge, 1990, pp. 1–19.
Barber, R.W., *The Life and Campaigns of the Black Prince*, London, 1979.
Barber, R.W., *The Reign of Chivalry*, New York, 1980.

Barnie, J., *War in Medieval Society, Social Values and the Hundred Years War, 1337–99*, London, 1974.
Bartlett, R.J., 'Technique Militaire et Pouvoir Politique, 900–1300', *Annales Economies, Sociétes, Civilisations*, xl, no. 5, 1986, pp. 1135–59.
Bates, D., *Normandy Before 1066*, Harlow, 1982.
Bates, D., *William the Conqueror*, London, 1989.
Beeler, J., *Warfare in England, 1066–1189*, New York, 1966.
Benecke, G., *Maximilian I, 1459–1519*, London, 1982.
Bennett, M., *Agincourt 1415*, London, 1991.
Beresford, G., 'Goltho Manor, Lincolnshire: the Buildings and their Surrounding Defences, c.850–1150', *ANS*, iv, 1981, pp. 13–36.
Berthelot, H., 'Histoire des Machines de Guerre et des Arts Mécaniques au Moyen Age', *Annales de Chimie et de Physique*, 7th ser., xix, 1900, pp. 289–420.
Billings, M., *The Cross and the Crescent*, London, 1987.
Bisson, T.N., *The Medieval Crown of Aragon*, Oxford, 1986.
Blair, J., 'William FitzAnsculf and the Abinger Motte', *AJ*, cxxxviii, 1981, pp. 146–48.
Boase, T.S.R., *Kingdoms and Strongholds of the Crusaders*, London, 1971.
Bradbury, J., 'Battles in England and Normandy, 1066–1154', *ANS*, vi, 1983, pp. 1–14.
Bradbury, J., 'Fulk le Réchin and the Origin of the Plantagenets', *RAB*, pp. 27–41.
Bradbury, J., 'Greek Fire in the West', *HT*, xxix, 1979, pp. 326–31, 344.
Bradford, E., *The Great Siege, Malta, 1565*, London, 1961.
Brockman, E., *The Two Sieges of Rhodes, 1480–1522*, London, 1969.
Brooke, C., *The Twelfth-Century Renaissance*, London, 1969.
Brown, E.A.R., 'The Tyranny of a Construct: Feudalism and Historians', *AmHR*, lxxix, 1974, pp. 1063–88.
Brown, R.A., *English Castles*, 3rd edn, London, 1976.
Brown, R.A., *Rochester Castle*, HMSO, London, 1969.
Brown, R.A., *The Normans and the Norman Conquest*, 2nd edn, Woodbridge, 1985.
Brown, R.A., ed., *Castles: A History and Guide*, Poole, 1980.
Browning, R., *The Byzantine Empire*, London, 1980.
Brundage, J.A., *The Crusades*, Boston, 1964.
Burne, A.H., *The Agincourt War*, London, 1956.
Burne, A.H., *The Battlefields of England*, 2nd edn, London, 1951.
Burne, A.H., *The Crecy War*, London, 1955.
Burns, R.I., *The Worlds of Alfonso the Learned and James the Conqueror*, Princeton, 1985.
Cahen, C., 'Un Traité d'Armurie Composé pour Saladin', *Bulletin d'Etudes Orientales*, xi, 1945–46, pp. 103–63.
Campbell, J., ed., *The Anglo-Saxons*, London, 1982. Campbell, J., *The Viking Age*, London, 1981.
Carpenter, D.A., *The Minority of Henry III*, London, 1990.
Cartellieri, A., *Philipp II. August, König von Frankreich*, 4 vols., Leipzig, 1899–1922.
Chambers, J., *The Devil's Horsemen*, 2nd edn, London, 1988.
Chaytor, H.J., *Savaric de Mauléon, Baron and Troubadour*, Cambridge, 1939.

Chibnall, M., 'Military Service in Normandy Before 1066', *ANS*, v, 1982, pp. 65–77.
Christiansen, E., *The Northern Crusades: the Baltic and the Catholic Frontier, 1100–1525*, London, 1980.
Clark, K., *Civilisation, a Personal View*, London, 1969.
Clephan, R.C., 'Notes on Roman and Medieval Engines of War', *Archaeologia Aeliana*, xxiv, 1903, pp. 69–114.
Cleve, T.C. Van, *The Emperor Frederick II of Hohenstaufen, Immutator Mundi*, Oxford, 1972.
Collins, A., *The Peerage of England*, 5th edn, 8 vols., London, 1779.
Constable, G., 'The Second Crusade as Seen by Contemporaries', *Traditio*, ix, 1953, pp. 213–79.
Contamine, P., *La Noblesse au Moyen Age*, Paris, 1976.
Contamine, P., *War in the Middle Ages*, Oxford, 1984.
Cook, D.R., *Lancastrians and Yorkists: the Wars of the Roses*, Harlow, 1984.
Coulson, C., 'Fortress Policy in Capetian Tradition and Angevin Practice', *ANS*, vi, 1983, pp. 13–38.
Coutil, L., *Le Château-Gaillard*, Paris, 1906.
Davidson, H.R.E., 'The Secret Weapon of Byzantium', *Byzantinische Zeitschrift*, lxvi, 1973, pp. 61–74.
Davis, R.H.C., *King Stephen*, 3rd edn, Harlow, 1990.
Davison, B.K., 'Early Earthwork Castles: a New Model', CG, iii, 1966, Chichester, 1969.
Deiss, J.J., *Captains of Fortune, Profiles of Six Italian Condottieri*, London, 1966.
Delbruck, H., *A History of the Art of War*, London, 1975.
Deville, A., *Histoire du Château-Gaillard*, Rouen, 1829.
Douglas, D.C., *The Norman Achievement*, London, 1969.
Du Boulay, F.R.H., *An Age of Ambition*, London, 1970.
Du Boulay, F.R.H., *Germany in the Later Middle Ages*, London, 1983.
Du Cange, C., *Glossarium mediae et infimae latinatis*, 5 vols., in 10 parts, Paris, 1883–87.
Duby, G., *La Société au XIe et XIIe Siècles de la Région Maconnaise*, Paris, 1953.
Duby, G., *The Chivalrous Society*, London, 1977.
Duffy, C., *Siege Warfare*, London, 1979.
Dunbabin, J., *France in the Making, 843–1180*, Oxford, 1985.
Erdmann, C., *The Origin of the Idea of Crusade*, Princeton, 1977.
Fawtier, R., *The Capetian Kings of France*, London, 1960.
Ferreiro, A., 'The Siege of Barbastro, 1064–65, a Reassessment', *JMH*, ix, 1983, pp. 129–44.
Finó, J-F., 'Machines de Jet Médiévales', *Gladius*, x, 1972, pp. 25–43.
Finó, J-F., *Forteresses de la France Médiévale*, Paris, 1967.
Finucane, R., *Soldiers of the Faith*, London, 1983.
Fleckenstein, J., *Early Medieval Germany*, Amsterdam, 1978.
Foote, P. & D.M. Wilson, *The Viking Achievement*, London, 1970.
Fourquin, G., *Lordship and Feudalism in the Middle Ages*, London, 1976.
Fowler, G.H., 'Munitions in 1224', *Publications of the Bedfordshire Historical Record Soc.*, v, 1920, pp. 117–32.
Fowler, K., *The Age of Plantagenet and Valois*, London, 1967.

France, J., 'The Departure of Tatikios from the Crusader Army', *BIHR*, xliv, 1971, pp. 137–47.
Fryde, N., *The Tyranny and Fall of Edward II*, Cambridge, 1979.
Fügedi, E., *Castle and Society in Medieval Hungary, 1000–1437*, Budapest, 1986.
Geanakoplos, D.J.G., *Byzantium, Church, Society and Civilization seen through Contemporary Eyes*, Chicago, 1984.
Gebelin, F., *The Châteaux of France*, London, 1964.
Gebelin, F., *The Châteaux of the Loire*, Paris, 1950.
Gibbon, E., *The History of the Decline and Fall of the Roman Empire*, ed. B. Radice, 8 vols., London, 1983–90.
Gies, J. & F., *Life in a Medieval Castle*, London, 1974.
Gille, B., *The Renaissance Engineers*, London, 1966.
Gillingham, J.B., *Richard the Lionheart*, 2nd edn, London, 1989.
Gillingham, J.B., *The Angevin Empire*, London, 1984.
Gillingham, J.B., *The Wars of the Roses*, London, 1981.
Gillmor, C.M., 'The Introduction of the Traction Trebuchet into the Latin West', *Viator*, xii, 1981, pp. 1–8.
Gimpel, J., *The Medieval Machine, the Industrial Revolution of the Middle Ages*, 2nd edn, Aldershot, 1988.
Godfrey, J., *1204, The Unholy Crusade*, Oxford, 1980.
Goodman, A., *The Wars of the Roses, Military Activity and English Society, 1452–97*, London, 1981.
Gottfried, R.S., *The Black Death*, London, 1983.
Gravett, C., *Medieval Siege Warfare*, London, 1990.
Green, J.A., *The Government of England under Henry I*, Cambridge, 1986.
Griffiths, R.A., *The Reign of King Henry VI, the Exercise of Royal Authority, 1422–61*, Tonbridge, 1981.
Guillot, O., *Le Comte d'Anjou et son Entourage au XIe Siècle*, 2 vols., Paris, 1972.
Hallam, E.M., *Capetian France, 987–1328*, Harlow, 1980.
Hallam, E.M., *Plantagenet Chronicles*, London, 1986.
Halphen, L., *Le Comté d'Anjou au XIe Siècle*, Paris, 1906.
Hamilton, B., *The Albigensian Crusade*, HA, London, 1974.
Hansen, P. V., 'Reconstructing a Medieval Trebuchet', *Military Illustrated Past and Present*, no. 27, 1990, pp. 9–11, 14–16.
Harper-Bill, C., C. Holdsworth and J. Nelson, eds., *Studies in Medieval History Presented to R. Allen Brown*, Woodbridge, 1989.
Harriss, G.L., ed., *Henry V, The Practice of Kingship*, Oxford, 1985.
Haskins, C.H., *The Renaissance of the Twelfth Century*, Cambridge Massachussetts, 1927.
Havighurst, A.F., *The Pirenne Thesis*, 3rd edn, Lexington Massachussetts, 1927.
Hay, D., *The Italian Renaissance in its Historical Background*, 2nd edn, Cambridge, 1977.
Hayward, H.W., 'Moslem North Africa', Setton, iii, pp. 457–512.
Héliot. P., 'Le Château-Gaillard et les Forteresses des XIIe et XIIIe Siècles en Europe Occidentale', CG, i, 1964, pp. 53–75.
Henderson, P., *Richard Coeur de Lion*, New York, 1958.
Herrnbrodt, A., 'Der Husterknupp', CG, i, 1962, Caen, 1964.
Heymann, F.G., 'The Crusades against the Hussites', Setton, iii, pp. 647–66.

Hill, B.H., *The Rise of the First Reich, Germany in the Tenth Century*, New York, 1969.
Hill, D. & J. Hassall, 'Viking Warfare, the Siege of Paris, 885–86', *Ago*, ix, 1971, pp. 16–23.
Hill, D.R., 'Trebuchets', *Viator*, iv, 1973, pp. 99–114.
Hodges, R. & D. Whitehouse, *Mohammed, Charlemagne and the Origins of Europe*, London, 1983.
Hogg, O.F.G., *English Artillery, 1326–1716*, London, 1963.
Hollister, C.W., *The Twelfth-Century Renaissance*, New York, 1969.
Holt, P.M., *The Age of the Crusades*, Harlow, 1986.
Hooper, N., 'Anglo-Saxon Warfare on the Eve of the Conquest: a Brief Survey', *ANS*, i, pp. 84–93.
Hope-Taylor, B., 'The Excavation of a Motte at Abinger Castle in Surrey', *AJ*, cvii, 1950, pp. 15–43.
Huuri, K., 'Zur Geschichte des mittelalterlichen Geschützwesens aus orientalischen Quellen', Societas Orientalis Fennica, *Studia Orientalia*, ix, no. 3, Helsingfors (Helsinki), 1941.
James, E., *The Origins of France, from Clovis to the Capetians, 500–1000*, London, 1982.
Jarrett, B., *The Emperor Charles IV*, London, 1935.
Johnson, E.N., 'The German Crusade on the Baltic', Setton, iii, pp. 545–85.
Johson, S., *Late Roman Fortifications*, London, 1983.
Jones, M., 'The Defences of Medieval Brittany', *AJ*, cxxxviii, 1 1981, pp. 149–204.
Jones, T.M., *War of the Generations, the Revolution of 1173–4*, Michigan, 1980.
Jordan, K., *Henry the Lion*, Oxford, 1986.
Jordan, W.C., *Louis IX and the Challenge of the Crusade*, Princeton, 1979.
Kaeuper, R.W., *War, Justice and Public Order; England and France in the Later Middle Ages*, Oxford, 1988.
Kamen, H., *A Concise History of Spain*, London, 1973.
Kantorowicz, E., *Frederick the Second, 1194–1250*, London, 1931.
Keen, M.H., *Chivalry*, London, 1984.
Keen, M.H., *The Laws of War in the Late Middle Ages*, London, 1965.
Kendall, P.M., *Louis XI*, London, 1971.
King, M.H. & W.M. Stevens, *Saints, Scholars and Heroes, Studies in Medieval Culture in Honour of C.W. Jones*, 2 vols., Minnesota, 1979.
Köhler, G., *Die Entwickelung des Kriegswesens und der Kriegführung in der Ritterzeit von Mitte des 11 Jahrhunderts bis zu den Hussitenkriegen*, 3 vols., Breslau, 1886–90.
Kugler, B. von, *Studien zur Geschichte des zweiten Kreuzzuges*, Stuttgart, 1866.
Labarge, M.W., *Gascony, England's First Colony*, London, 1980.
Labarge, M.W., *St Louis, the Life of Louis IX of France*, London, 1968.
Ladurie, E.L.R., *Montaillou*, Harmondsworth, 1980.
Lambert, M.D., *Medieval Heresy*, London, 1977.
Laven, P., *Renaissance Italy, 1464–1534*, London, 1966.
Le Patourel, J., *The Norman Empire*, Oxford, 1976.
Lethbridge, T.C., 'Excavations at Burwell Castle', *Procs. Cambridgeshire Antiquarian Soc.*, xxxvi, 1936, pp. 121–33.
Lewis, P.N., *The Wars of Richard I in the West*, unpublished thesis, London, 1977.

Leyser, K.J., *Medieval Germany and its Neighbours, 900–1250*, London, 1982.
Logan, F.D., *The Vikings in History*, London, 1983.
Lomax, D.W., *The Reconquest of Spain*, London, 1983.
Longman, W., *The History of the Life and Times of Edward III*, 2 vols., London, 1869.
Luttrell, A., 'The Hospitallers at Rhodes, 1421–1523', Setton, iii, pp. 314–39.
Maalouf, A., *The Crusades through Arab Eyes*, London, 1984.
MacKay, A., *Spain in the Middle Ages, from Frontier to Empire, 1000–1500*, Houndmills, 1977.
Mango, C., 'Heraclius, the Threat from the East and Iconoclasm, 610–843', in P. Whitting, *Byzantium, an Introduction*, 2nd edn, New York, 1981.
Martindale, J., 'The French Aristocracy in the Early Middle Ages: a Reappraisal', *PP*, 75, 1977, pp. 5–45.
Masson, G., *Frederick II of Hohenstaufen, a Life*, London, 1957.
Mayer, H.E., *The Crusades*, Oxford, 1972.
McFarlane, K.B., *England in the Fifteenth Century*, London, 1981.
McKitterick, R., *The Frankish Kingdoms under the Carolingians, 751–987*, Harlow, 1983.
Mercier, M., *Le Feu Grégeois*, Paris, 1952.
Morgan, D., *The Mongols*, Oxford, 1986.
Morgan, D., 'The Mongols and the Eastern Mediterranean', *Mediterranean Historical Review*, iv, 1989, pp. 198–211.
Morris, J., *The Age of Arthur*, London, 1973.
Munz, P., *Frederick Barbarossa, a Study in Medieval Politics*, London, 1969.
Munz, P., *Life in the Age of Charlemagne*, London, 1969.
Nelson, J., 'Ninth-Century Knighthood: the Evidence of Nithard', *RAB*, pp. 255–66.
Newby, P.H., *Saladin in his Time*, London, 1983.
Newhall, R.A., *The English Conquest of Normandy, 1416–24*, New York, 1924.
Nicholson, R., *Edward III and the Scots, the Formative Years of a Military Career, 1327–35*, Oxford, 1965.
Nicol, D.M., *The End of the Byzantine Empire*, London, 1979.
Norgate, K., *England under the Angevin Kings*, 2 vols., London, 1887.
Norgate, K., *John Lackland*, London, 1902.
Norgate, K., *Richard the Lionheart*, London, 1924.
Oman, C., *A History of the Art of War in the Middle Ages*, 2nd edn, 2 vols., London, 1924, reprint 1991.
Ormrod, W.M., *The Reign of Edward III, Crown and Political Society in England, 1327–77*, New Haven and London, 1990.
Ostrogorsky, G., *History of the Byzantine State*, Oxford, 1968.
Pacaut, M., *Frederick Barbarossa*, London, 1970.
Packe, M., *King Edward III*, London, 1983.
Partington, J.R., *A History of Greek Fire and Gunpowder*, Cambridge, 1960.
Payne-Gallwey, Sir R., *The Crossbow*, London, 1903.
Pernoud, R., *Joan of Arc*, London, 1964.
Perroy, E., *The Hundred Years War*, London, 1951.
Perry, F., *St Louis, the Most Christian King*, London, 1902.
Philips, C.H., *The Fall of Constantinople, A Symposium, 1953*, SOAS, London, 1955.

Pirenne, H., *Medieval Cities: their Origins and the Revival of Trade*, Princeton, 1925.
Pirenne, H., *Mohammed and Charlemagne*, London, 1939.
Poly, J.-P. & E. Bournagel, *La Mutation Féodale Xe au XIIe Siècles*, Paris, 1980.
Powicke, F.M., *The Loss of Normandy, 1189–1204*, 2nd edn, Manchester, 1961.
Prawer, J., *The Latin Kingdom of Jerusalem*, London, 1972.
Prestwich, M., *Edward I*, London, 1988.
Prestwich, M., *The Three Edwards, War and State in England, 1327–77*, London, 1980.
Prestwich, M., *War, Politics and Finance under Edward I*, London, 1972.
Pryor, J.H., *Geography, Technology, and War, Studies in the Maritime History of the Mediterranean, 649–1571*, Cambridge, 1988.
Queller, D.E., *The Fourth Crusade, the Conquest of Constantinople, 1201–04*, Leicester, 1978.
Renn, D.F., *Norman Castles in England*, 2nd edn, London, 1973.
'Repton', *Current Archaeology*, c, 1986, pp. 140–41.
Richard, J., *The Latin Kingdom of Jerusalem*, 2 vols., Amsterdam, 1979.
Riché, P. , *Daily Life in the World of Charlemagne*, Liverpool, 1978.
Riley-Smith, J., *The Atlas of the Crusades*, London, 1991.
Riley-Smith, J., *The Crusades, a Short History*, London, 1987.
Riley-Smith, J., *The Feudal Nobility and the Kingdom of Jerusalem, 1174–1277*, London, 1973.
Riley-Smith, J., *The First Crusade and the Idea of Crusading*, London, 1986.
Riley-Smith, J., *What Were the Crusades*, London, 1977.
Roesdahl, E., *Viking Age Denmark*, London, 1982.
Rogers, R., *Latin Siege Warfare in the Twelfth Century*, unpublished thesis, Oxford, 1985.
Ross, C., *Edward IV*, London, 1974.
Ross, C., *The Wars of the Roses*, London, 1976.
Runciman, S., *A History of the Crusades*, 3 vols., Cambridge, 1951.
Runciman, S., *Byzantine Civilization*, London, 1933.
Runciman, S., *The Fall of Constantinople, 1453*, Cambridge, 1969.
Runciman, S., *The First Crusade*, Cambridge, 1980.
Russell, F.H., *The Just War in the Middle Ages*, Cambridge, 1975.
Salies, A. de, *Foulques-Nerra Comte d'Anjou*, 2 vols., Paris and Angers, 1874.
Salway, P., *Roman Britain*, Oxford, 1981.
Sawyer, P.H., *Kings and Vikings, Scandinavia and Europe, 700–1100*, London, 1982.
Sawyer, P.H., *The Age of the Vikings*, London, 1971.
Schneider, R., *Die Artillerie des Mittelalters nach den Angaben der Zeitgenosse dargestellt*, Berlin, 1910.
Setton, K.M., *A History of the Crusades*, 6 vols., Wisconsin, 1955–89.
Seward, D., *Henry V as Warlord*, London, 1987.
Seward, D., *The Hundred Years War, the English in France, 1337–1453*, London, 1978.
Smail, R.C., *Crusading Warfare, 1097–1193*, Cambridge, 1956.
Smail, R.C., *The Crusaders*, London, 1973.
Smith, L.M., ed., *The Making of Britain: the Middle Ages*, London, 1985.
Smith, L.M., ed., *The Making of Britain: the Dark Ages*, London, 1984.
Soedel, W. & V. Foley, 'Ancient Catapults', *Scientific American*, March 1979, pp. 120–28.

Stamper, P., *Excavations of a Mid Twelfth-Century Siege Castle at Bentley, Hants*, Winchester, 1979.
Strayer, J.R., *The Reign of Philip the Fair*, Princeton, 1980.
Stubbs, W., *Germany in the Early Middle Ages, 476–1250*, London, 1908.
Sumption, J., *The Albigensian Crusade*, London, 1978.
Taylor, A., 'Master Bertram, Ingeniator Regis', *RAB*, pp. 289–304.
Thompson, A.H., *Military Architecture in Medieval England*, Oxford, 1912.
Thompson, J.W., *Feudal Germany*, Chicago, 1928.
Trevelyan, R., *Shades of the Alhambra*, London, 1984.
Tsangadas, B.C.P., *The Fortifications and Defense of Constantinople*, New York, 1980.
Tuchman, B., *A Distant Mirror, the Calamitous Fourteenth Century*, London, 1979.
Urban, W., *The Baltic Crusade*, De Kalb, 1975.
Vale, M.G.A., *Charles VII*, London, 1974.
Vale, M.G.A., *War and Chivalry, Warfare and Aristocratic Culture in England, France and Burgundy at the End of the Middle Ages*, London, 1981.
Vasiliev, A.A., *The Russian Attack on Constantinople in 860*, Cambridge Massachussetts, 1958.
Vaughan, R., *Valois Burgundy*, London, 1975.
Verbruggen, J.F., *The Art of Warfare in Western Europe during the Middle Ages*, Amsterdam, 1976.
Viollet-le-Duc, E.E., *Military Architecture*, 3rd edn, reprint, London, 1990.
Wacher, J., *Roman Britain*, London, 1978.
Wallace-Hadrill, J.M., *The Vikings in Francia*, Reading, 1975.
Warner, M., *Joan of Arc, the Image of Female Heroism*, London, 1981.
Warner, P., *Sieges of the Middle Ages*, London, 1968.
Warner, P., *The Medieval Castle*, London, 1973.
Warren, W.L., *Henry II*, London, 1973.
Warren, W.L., *King John*, 2nd edn, London, 1978.
Watt, M.W., *A History of Islamic Spain*, Edinburgh, 1965.
White, L. Jr., *Medieval Technology and Social Change*, Oxford, 1962.
Wolffe, B., *Henry VI*, London, 1981.
Wood, M., *In Search of the Dark Ages*, London, 1981.
Zaky, A.R., 'A Preliminary Bibliography of Medieval Arabic Military Literature', *Gladius*, iv, 1961, pp. 107–12.
Zaky, A.R., 'Gunpowder and Arabic Firearms in the Middle Ages', *Gladius*, vi, 1967, pp. 45–58.
Ziegler, P., *The Black Death*, London, 1969.

Index

Bold numbers indicate illustrations